# User Interfaces in VB .NET: Windows Forms and Custom Controls

MATTHEW MACDONALD

User Interfaces in VB .NET: Windows Forms and Custom Controls
Copyright ©2002 by Matthew MacDonald

ISBN (pbk): 1-59059-044-9

Printed and bound in the United States of America 12345678910

Trademarked names may appear in this book. Rather than use a trademark symbol with every occurrence of a trademarked name, we use the names only in an editorial fashion and to the benefit of the trademark owner, with no intention of infringement of the trademark.

Technical Reviewer: Gordon Wilmot

Editorial Directors: Dan Appleman, Peter Blackburn, Gary Cornell, Jason Gilmore, Karen Watterson, John Zukowski

Managing Editor: Grace Wong

Project Manager: Sofia Marchant

Copy Editor: Anne Friedman

Production Editor: Kari Brooks

Compositor: Susan Glinert Stevens

Artist: Kurt Krames

Indexer: Nancy Guenther

Cover Designer: Kurt Krames

Manufacturing Manager: Tom Debolski

Marketing Manager: Stephanie Rodriguez

Distributed to the book trade in the United States by Springer-Verlag New York, Inc., 175 Fifth Avenue, New York, NY, 10010 and outside the United States by Springer-Verlag GmbH & Co. KG, Tiergartenstr. 17, 69112 Heidelberg, Germany.

In the United States, phone 1-800-SPRINGER, email orders@springer-ny.com, or visit http://www.springer-ny.com.

Outside the United States, fax +49 6221 345229, email orders@springer.de, or visit http://www.springer.de.

For information on translations, please contact Apress directly at 2560 9th Street, Suite 219, Berkeley, CA 94710. Phone 510-549-5930, fax: 510-549-5939, email info@apress.com, or visit http://www.apress.com.

The information in this book is distributed on an "as is" basis, without warranty. Although every precaution has been taken in the preparation of this work, neither the author nor Apress shall have any liability to any person or entity with respect to any loss or damage caused or alleged to be caused directly or indirectly by the information contained in this work.

The source code for this book is available to readers at http://www.apress.com in the Downloads section.

*For Nora and Paul*

# Contents at a Glance

# Contents

# Preface

IN THE PAST FEW MONTHS, a deluge of .NET books has hit store shelves, each one eager to explain the new programming philosophy of the .NET world. In the excitement, many of these books have left out the tricks and insights needed to really master .NET programming. Part of the problem is that no single work can cover the entire .NET platform—a sprawling, ambitious framework that revolutionizes everything from Internet applications to data access technology. Many .NET books provide a good overview of essential concepts, but they can't deal with the subtleties needed for all types of development.

This book represents the start of the second wave of .NET books: closely focused works that give you the insight of experienced developers about a single aspect of .NET programming. *User Interfaces in VB .NET: Windows Forms and Custom Controls* takes a close look at all the ingredients you can use to design state-of-the-art application interfaces. It also delves into entirely new topics like custom-control design and GDI+, the next-generation painting framework for Windows. You won't just learn about anchoring and docking, you'll work with examples that show document-view architecture, custom-control layout engines, dockable windows, and hit testing with owner-drawn controls. You also learn how to design irregularly shaped forms, unshackle data binding, and build an integrated help system.

In short, this is the sort of .NET book that I would want to read as a professional developer. It's a book that goes beyond the basics and combines user interface design principles with practical guidelines for creating the next generation of software applications. And seeing as you *are* reading this introduction, you've probably already realized that this next generation will be built using the .NET Framework.

# About the Author

MATTHEW MACDONALD is an author, educator, and MCSD developer. He's a regular contributor to programming journals such as *Inside Visual Basic* and *C# Today*, and the author of several books about .NET programming, including *The Book of VB .NET* (No Starch) and *ASP.NET: The Complete Reference* (Osborne/McGraw-Hill). In a dimly remembered past life, he studied English literature and theoretical physics.

# About the Technical Reviewer

GORDON WILMOT is a director of ICEnetware Ltd., a company specializing in Internet and network management and monitoring software. He has held positions ranging from software engineer to systems architect and has been developing software using Microsoft products and architectures for over 20 years. Over this time he has designed and developed many products and systems for various industries such as finance, manufacturing, and telecommunications. All his spare time is eaten up by making cakes (badly) for his three-year-old twins, Charlotte and Georgina, and being beaten continuously by his seven-year-old son, Andrew, on the PS2. When he grows up, he'd still like to be an astronaut.

# Acknowledgments

THIS BOOK HAS BEEN, comparatively speaking, a lot of fun to write. As a result, I have a long list of people to thank.

Gary Cornell never ceases to amaze me with his ability to respond to emails mere seconds after they've departed from my outbox. I'm indebted to him for quickly and painlessly signing me on for this project. I also owe a sincere thanks to a number of other individuals at Apress who helped everything move swiftly and smoothly. They include Sofia Marchant, Kari Brooks, Grace Wong, Stephanie Rodriguez, and doubtless many others I never interacted with directly.

Gordon Wilmot performed the technical review for this book. Besides being quicker than most, he offered helpful feedback, including an invaluable tip about sorting items in the ListView control. Anne Friedman performed the copy editing, and her unerring light touch helped guarantee the final polished product. I owe a heartfelt thanks to both.

Finally, I'd never write *any* book without the support of my loving wife, her parents, and my parents (who started this whole mess with two gametes at the right place and the right time). Thanks everyone!

# Introduction

THE .NET REVOLUTION is in full swing, and the confusion that has surrounded it for the last year is finally lifting. Developers are no longer wondering whether .NET is designed for web services, distributed applications, object-oriented development, cross-language interoperability, painless deployment, or a new way to access data. Instead, we now realize that .NET is built for all of that, and much more. With .NET, Microsoft has bundled almost a dozen miniature revolutions into one marketing term, along with a class library stocked with hundreds of pieces of prebuilt functionality.

Unfortunately, you can't come to terms with the amazing breadth of the .NET framework by reading a single book. To become an expert .NET programmer, you need an in-depth exploration of the areas of development that interest you the most. In other words, it's time to forget about the broadly sweeping goals of .NET for a moment and focus on the nuts and bolts of how to design the next-generation of software applications.

This book explains how to program user interfaces applying the tools and techniques of the .NET world. You may already be familiar with some of the concepts that carry over from traditional development (like multiple-document interfaces, and the standard Windows controls and conventions). Other features are entirely new and will be unlike anything you have ever worked with before. But no matter what aspect of user interface design you're exploring, it all works through the .NET class library, which provides a new set of capabilities, subtleties, and quirks that every .NET programmer needs to master.

## About This Book

User interface design deals with several aspects of programming. The tendency in a book about a topic like this is to pursue one of these themes exclusively. With .NET, however, the programming framework is entirely new. A reference that only explains controls and commands is dangerous, and without a proper discussion of best practices and design tips, programmers are likely to wind up in a great deal of trouble—with applications that are difficult to enhance, debug, or scale up. For that reason, I've made the decision in this book to focus on three distinct themes.

## What This Book Teaches You

This book fills three roles. It provides the following:

- **An overview of how to design elegant user interface the average user can understand.** This is addressed directly in the first chapter and indirectly in Tips and Notes throughout the book.

- **A comprehensive examination of the user interface controls and classes in .NET.** Although this book is not a reference, it contains an exhaustive tour of almost every user interface element you'll want to use, including providers, components, and custom controls.

- **A tutorial with best practices and design tips for coding user interface and integrating help.** As a developer, you need to know more than how to add a control to a window. You also need to know how to create an entire user interface framework that's scalable, flexible, and reusable.

## What This Book Doesn't Teach You

Of course, it's just as important to point out what this book *doesn't* contain:

- A description of core .NET concepts like namespaces, assemblies, exception handling and types. These fundamentals are an important basis for .NET design, and they are already explained well in several works, including a number of excellent C# and VB .NET books from Apress.

- A primer on object-oriented design. No .NET programmer can progress very far without a solid understanding of classes, interfaces, and other .NET types. In this book, many examples rely on these basics, using objects to encapsulate, organize, and transfer information.

- A reference for Visual Studio .NET. The new integrated design environment provides powerful customization, automation, and productivity features that deserve a book of their own. Though this book describes a few control designers, for the most part it assumes that you already know how to use IDE to create controls and set properties.

- A comparison between .NET and its predecessors (including Visual Basic, C++, and even Java). Examining the evolution of the .NET language is largely a historical interest and while fascinating, it won't help you master modern .NET development any faster. The best approach is to leave your past language allegiances behind.

If you haven't learned the .NET fundamentals, you will probably still be able to work through this book. You will probably need to do so at a slower pace, and you may also need to refer to the MSDN help files to clear up a few issues along the way. On the other hand, if you have already read another, more general .NET book, you will benefit the most.

> **NOTE** *This book targets experienced developers. If you have never programmed with a language like Visual Basic, C++/C#, or Java before, this isn't the place to start. Instead, start with an introductory book on object-oriented design or programming fundamentals.*

## Code Samples

It's a good idea to check the online site to download the most recent, up-to-date code samples. You'll need to do this to test most of the more sophisticated code examples described in this book, because the full code listing is often left out. Instead, I focus on the most important conceptual sections so that you don't need to wade through needless extra pages to understand an important concept.

You can download the code directly from Apress at http://www.apress.com or from my own site at http://www.prosetech.com.

## Variable Naming

It seems that variable naming is about to become another religious issue where there is no clear standard, but developers take heated, uncompromising attitudes. Hungarian notation, which was the preferred standard for C++ and Visual Basic (in a slightly modified form), is showing its age. In the world of .NET, where memory management is handled automatically, it seems a little backward to refer to a variable by its data type, especially when the data type may change without any serious consequences, and the majority of variables are storing references to full-fledged objects.

To complicate matters, Microsoft recommends that objects use simple names for properties and methods, like COM components and controls. This system makes a good deal of sense, as data type considerations are becoming more and more transparent. Visual Studio .NET now takes care of some of the work of spotting the invalid use of data types, and its built-in IntelliSense automatically displays information about the data types used by a method.

In this book, data-type prefixes are not used for variables. The only significant exception is with control variables, where it is still a useful trick to distinguish between types of controls (like txtUserName and lstUserCountry), and with some data objects. Of course, when you create your programs you are free to follow whatever variable naming convention you prefer, provided you make the effort to adopt complete consistency across all your projects (and ideally across all the projects in your organization).

## Feedback

This book has the ambitious goal of being the best tutorial and reference for .NET user interface design. Toward that end, your comments and suggestions are extremely helpful. You can send complaints, adulation, and everything in between directly to apress@prosetech.com. I can't solve your .NET problems or critique your code, but I will benefit from information about what this book did right and wrong (and what it may have done in an utterly confusing way). You can also send comments about the web site support for this book.

## Chapter Overview

The following overview describes what each chapter covers. If you have some .NET experience, feel free to skip from chapter to chapter and read everything in the order you prefer. If, however, you're relatively new to .NET development it's probably easiest to read through the book sequentially, to make sure you learn the basics before encountering more advanced topics.

### Chapter 1: Creating Usable Interfaces

User interface design is about more than just knowing how to program the latest trendy interface element—it's also about conventions, consistency, and the best way to guide a user into unfamiliar territory. In this chapter, you learn the basics of interface design theory, and the principles that support every good design.

### Chapter 2: Designing with Classes and Tiers

For several years, programming books and articles have advocated a three-layered approach to application design that rigorously separates user interface from application code. Despite this emphasis, real-world applications rarely follow these best practices, and programmers usually discover and rediscover that they are far more time-consuming and awkward than most computer writers promise. In this chapter, you learn how a modern layered design becomes dramatically easier with .NET— and how it might work for you.

## Chapter 3: Control Class Basics

This chapter delves into the details of one of .NET's most feature-rich classes: the Control. In this chapter, you learn how the Control class defines the basic features for responding to key presses and mouse movements, defining control relations, and handling Windows messages. You also learn about some of the basic System.Drawing ingredients for points, rectangles, colors, and fonts.

## Chapter 4: Classic Controls

The classic controls include basic tools for input, selection, and display that have been used since the ancient days of 16-bit Windows programming. This chapter also includes a few .NET twists, like the owner-drawn menus, date controls, and the hyperlink label. It rounds up with demonstrations of control validation and drag-and-drop techniques.

## Chapter 5: Forms

The Form class is the basis for every application window in a .NET program. To use forms effectively, you need to understand how forms interact, scroll, and take ownership of each other. This chapter explains the basics, and considers exciting new techniques like visual inheritance, Windows XP styles, and irregularly shaped forms. It also explains how to make multi-paned, resizable windows that work.

## Chapter 6: Modern Controls

This chapter dissects everyone's favorite Windows controls, including TreeView, ListView, ToolBar and StatusBar. As these controls are introduced, you see some innovative ways to extend them with custom classes that provide useful higher-level features or are tailored for a specific type of data.

## Chapter 7: Custom Controls

Custom control development is one of the key themes of this book, and a remarkable feature of the .NET platform. This chapter considers the basic types of controls you can create, and introduces examples like a bitmap thumbnail viewer, a progress user control, and a directory tree. It also considers advanced topics like asynchronous control programming, and custom extender providers, which allow you to develop enhancements that can be latched onto any .NET control.

## Chapter 8: Design-Time Support for Custom Controls

Creating a custom control is easy, but making it behave well in the design-time environment often takes a little extra wizardry. In this chapter, you see how custom control designers, UITypeEditors, and context-menu verbs can equip your controls for Visual Studio .NET. You also tackle different models of custom control licensing.

## Chapter 9: Data Controls

Most applications need to deal with data at some point. This chapter considers how you can integrate data into your user interfaces without creating an interface that's tightly coupled to a specific data access strategy or data source. In other words, you learn how you can create user interface code that doesn't directly refer to field names or assume that data is retrieved all at once. The solutions lead you through an exhaustive look at .NET data binding—and how to extend it—and show how you can create data-aware custom controls.

## Chapter 10: MDI Interfaces and Workspaces

MDI interfaces are a hallmark of modern application design. .NET makes MDI as easy as setting a few simple Form properties. This chapter explores some of the best design practices behind MDI development, including synchronization and document-view architecture. It also looks at how you can create floating toolbars and design dockable windows.

## Chapter 11: Dynamic User Interface

Dynamic user interface—creating controls at runtime rather than at design-time—isn't a philosophy that can help you break free of some of Visual Studio .NET's most significant limitations. In this chapter you consider ways to implement dynamic content, show an example of dynamic control creation with a vector-based drawing framework, and consider how to create a custom layout engine.

## Chapter 12: GDI+ Basics

GDI+ is .NET's next-generation painting framework. In this chapter, you explore GDI+ from the ground up. You learn how you can draw inside and outside paint event handlers, how to handle form resizing, and how to use basic ingredients like brushes and pens. You also take a look at more advanced topics, including double-buffering to eliminate flicker, hit testing with rectangles and paths, and drawing standard UI elements like focus cues and disabled images.

## Chapter 13: GDI+ Controls

This chapter puts the GDI+ platform to work with examples that show a gradient label, marquee text, and a button control from scratch. You develop a bar-graphing control, and take another look at the vector based drawing example from Chapter 11 with GDI+ owner-drawn controls.

## Chapter 14: Help and Application-Embedded Support

The final chapter of this book examines how you can weave help into your user interfaces. You'll learn basic techniques for context-sensitive help, techniques to provide task-based help, and tricks that allow you to integrate help windows into your applications. You'll also learn about one of Microsoft's best-kept secrets: the free Microsoft Agent control, which provides an animated character that can guide the user.

# CHAPTER 1

# Creating Usable Interfaces

SOMETIMES IT SEEMS THAT no one can agree what user interface design really is. Is it the painstaking process an artist goes through to create shaded icons that light up when the mouse approaches? Is it the hours spent in a usability lab subjecting users to a complicated new application? Is it the series of decisions that determine how to model information using common controls and metaphors?

In fact, user interface design is really a collection of several different tasks:

- **User interface modeling.** This is the process where you look at the tasks a program needs to accomplish, and decide how to break these tasks into windows and controls. To emerge with an elegant design, you need to combine instinct, convention, a dash of psychology, and painstaking usability testing.

- **User interface architecture.** This is the overall design you use to arrange objects and code in your application. Creating a consistent, well-planned design makes it easy to extend, alter, and reuse portions of the user interface framework.

- **User interface coding.** This is the process where you write the code for managing the user interface with the appropriate classes and objects. Ideally, you follow the first two steps to lay out a specific user interface model and architecture before you begin this stage.

This book concentrates on the third, and most time-consuming step, where user interfaces designs are translated into code using the tools and techniques of .NET. However, it's impossible to separate good coding from good code design, and discussion about user interface architecture, the second item on the list, recurs throughout this book (and is the focus of the next chapter).

This chapter, however, focuses on the first task: user interface design. Here you'll examine the essential guidelines that no programmer can afford to ignore. You'll learn basic tips for organizing information, handling complexity, and entering into the mind of that often-feared final judge: the end-user.

You could skip ahead at this point, and dive right into .NET code. However, the greatest programming framework in the world won't solve some common, critical user interface mistakes. Learning how to design an interface is no less important that learning how to work with it in code.

## Why Worry About the Interface?

User interface is the thin outer shell that wraps a program's logic and provides a way for ordinary users to interact with it. Usually, user interfaces have three responsibilities:

- Interpreting what a user wants and translating it into the corresponding operations.

- Retrieving information and displaying it in different ways.

- Guiding users through a task (and steering them away from common mistakes).

User interfaces bear the weight of a program, because they are the only part the user interacts with. It doesn't matter what your program can do if it's trapped behind a limited, frustrating interface—it's a little like locking a concert pianist in a small, dark prison cell. As with anything else, people judge and identify programs based on what they can see from the outside. Friendly, enjoyable interfaces are able to attract users just because of the way of they look. Ugly and confusing interfaces, on the other hand, lead to a legacy of headaches for developers and end users.

In programming circles, user interfaces are often the subject of heated debate. Some developers resent the whole topic of user interface design because they feel it detracts from "real" programming. They dread the vaguely defined requirements, the hard-to-please end users, and the perception that they have to simplify the product of their perfectly natural first instincts. Another group is made of developers who love to experiment with the latest user interface fad. They aim to discover the newest and most avant-garde user interface controls before they have been adopted as standards, even when they lead to somewhat bizarre applications.

Ultimately, both approaches are bad news for end users, who just want a simple, unobtrusive interface that works exactly the way they expect. To create a good user interface—one that satisfies the average user—you need to know the unwritten rules of user interface design.

> **TIP** *It's sometimes suggested that there is no such as thing as bad interfaces— just interfaces that are suited for different types of users. Allow me to put this myth to rest. There are definitely bad (and even atrocious) interfaces. While it's certainly true that you need to tailor the interface to the audience, user confusion is usually the result of violating conventions.*

# A Brief History of User Interfaces

You might think that user interface design is a history of continuous innovation. In fact, user interface design is actually marked by a series of distinct eras. Typically, in each era one predominant approach develops. Then, at some unpredictable time, a lone programmer or innovative programming team creates a truly new user interface model that dazzles the world. In the following months, hundreds of developers rush to create similar but mutually incompatible versions. This process of false imitation continues for a while, until the next revolution.

So what are these eras of user interface development? It all began very simply.

## The Command-Line Era

Almost everyone who has any experience with computers has at least glimpsed the fabled command-line. Today's novice users instinctively think of it as some "back door" way of accessing features that are forbidden and hidden from most people. Even advanced computer users are sometimes bound by the superstition that a command-line lurks behind the scenes in the latest Windows operating system, secretly controlling things.

A command-line interface is the power user's dream. Of course, even power users have to learn somewhere, and most forget that the command line was not an easy tool to master.

The command-line is, in many respects, the original way of doing things, and it's arguable that it's not so much an interface design as a lack of any user interface, at least in the sense we use the term today. Command lines began as the basis for operating systems like DOS (see Figure 1-1) and UNIX, were the basis for early database applications like dBase, and continue to proliferate in unusual places. For example, the Visual Studio .NET interface provides a Command window that lets you interact with the IDE or execute simple lines of code against the currently running application. Besides a few rudimentary enhancements (like auto complete), it's still a basic command-line interface (see Figure 1-2).

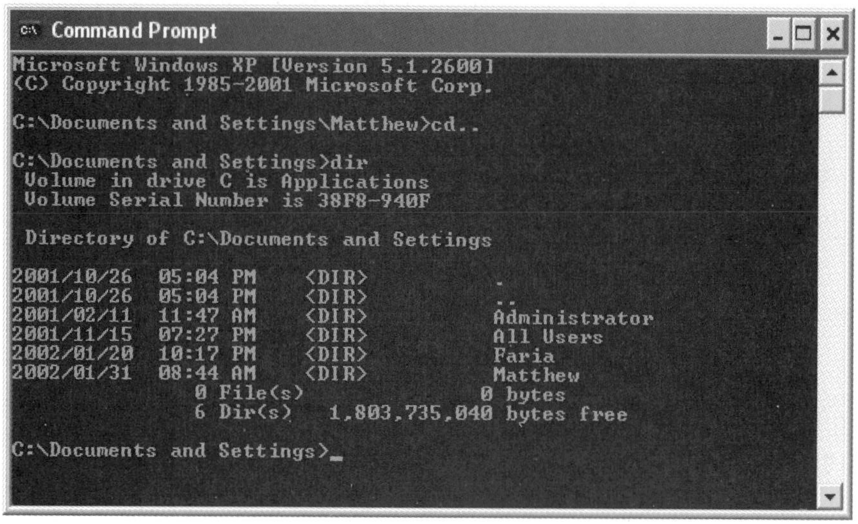

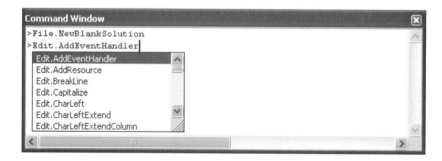

Figure 1-1. The archetypal command-line interface

Figure 1-2. The command line in Visual Studio .NET

Command-line interfaces are characterized by the following traits:

- **Ultimate control.** Users can do anything in any order, so long as they remember the "secret codes."

- **Ultimate lack of structure.** Users not only have to remember what to do, but what order to do it in. In DOS, just moving a file to a new directory can be an agonizing multistep operation. By default, the command-line assumes that each operation is atomic, and it doesn't associate one task with another.

- **A "hands off" treatment of user.** With a few minor exceptions, there's no helpful prompting, tips, or guidance.

- **No metaphors.** This makes it easy to grasp the basic process (type in words, press Enter), which never changes. However, it makes it impossible to guess how to do a related task based on a previous one. (For example, if you know how to copy a file in UNIX, you still don't know how to delete it.)

Today, a command-line model could still turn up in one of your user interfaces, but it's unlikely.

## The Question-Answer Model

The question answer model is one of the oldest user interface models, and it's still alive and well in the modern world. Its principles are the polar opposite of a command-line interface:

- **You are prompted at every step of the way.** Thus, you don't need to remember what the program requires. However, you are also immediately stuck if you are missing a piece of information, as question and answer programs are usually unidirectional—if you can't move forward, you can't go anywhere.

- **You have no control.** This can be either a blessing or a curse. If the program has an accurate idea of your needs, you are in a "benevolent dictator" scenario, which makes your life considerably less complicated. But if the program makes the wrong assumptions, you have no way to fight it.

- **You have ultimate guidance.** Some kind of instruction is provided at each step in the process.

- **You still have no metaphors.** Well, that's not exactly true—sometimes a superficial metaphor is used where the program invites you to imagine that a friendly guide is asking you a series of questions, and trying to do what you need.

The question-answer programming model has a valuable place in the world today, and it's seen commonly in Windows program with *wizards*. Wizards lead you through a set of questions, and then perform a complicated task for you.

As you've no doubt discovered, there are useful wizards (like those that set up hardware on your computer). There are also less useful wizards that seem to be more complicated, demanding, and restrictive than the program itself (like those that create documents for you in some popular graphics programs). Figure 1-3 shows the wizard Windows uses for adding new hardware.

*Figure 1-3. A genuinely useful wizard*

Question-answer programs are double-edged swords that can frustrate as much as they please. The next few sections outline a few key principles that can help you use this model.

### Ask what the user can tell you

It makes sense to ask a user to tell you what company made his or her printer. However, it doesn't make sense to ask a user whether you should convert tabs to spaces for DOS print operations. Instead, just pick a suitable default. Remember, no one likes to be asked a question they can't answer. When it comes to novice computer users, they might just give up altogether, or stop reading other prompts.

### Restrict it to a single task

A wizard works well for a single task that can only be accomplished in one way (like adding a printer driver). As soon as you start adding an element of variety or creativity, the wizard can't keep up. Don't think that you should be proud of a complex wizard that branches out conditionally to use different windows depending on previous user selections. All you've done is created a traditional single-screen DOS program, where tasks must be completed in separate windows and in a set order.

## Beware of forcing your preferences

Every wizard has its own hard-coded patterns. The user never has a choice about what order to answer questions or supply information, and that lack of control can frustrate anyone who wants to approach the task differently. Be forewarned, especially if you are using a wizard for a complex task: you are enforcing a single way of working according to your own assumptions and biases. If it doesn't match the way the majority of users want to work, it will only make them miserable.

## The Menu-Driven Model

The menu-driven model is the most easily recognizable user interface model. It came to popularity with document-based programs like DOS word processors, and then took over nearly every application with the Windows operating system. It's easy to see why: menus represent an attractive compromise, allowing you to prompt users without restricting the way they work.

- **Commands can be performed in any order.** You have the same freedom you have with the command-line interface.

- **Information is on the screen to prompt you.** You are never left on your own, and the very grouping of elements can sometimes help you remember what you want to do. For example, if you want to change spacing in Microsoft Word you might not know it has anything to do with paragraphs, but you would be able to decide that the Format menu is probably the best place to start your exploration.

Menus are one of the dominant interface elements in Windows programming, and they allow absolutely no room for experimentation or innovation. To create a menu, you copy Microsoft Office as closely as possible, even adding a vestigial File menu when your program has nothing to do with files or documents. Similarly, you would do best to emulate basic options like Edit, View, Window, and even Tools before you start adding menus organized around program-specific concepts. You'll learn more about Microsoft's role in your user interface design a little later in this chapter.

## The GUI Era

Shortly after the menu excitement subsided, everyone fell in love with pictures, buttons, and the worlds of the Macintosh and Microsoft Windows. The GUI era introduced an avalanche of concepts and user interface elements, several of which are often summarized with the acronym WIMP (windows, icons, mouse, and pointers). One key innovation in the GUI era was the introduction of the mouse, which provides more *points of entry* for interacting with an application (as in, "I want to click *here*"). Another change was the shift to realistic representation— for example, word processors that show a close approximation of how a printed document will look. A central idea in the GUI era was to base user interfaces on real-world metaphors. For example, if you want to delete a file, drag it to an icon that looks like a trash can, because that's what you use to dispose of rubbish in the real world.

Of course, some things are much harder to convey with pictures than others (for example, no application provides an icon that accurately suggests "synchronize my email"). At the same time that the GUI era arrived, user interface design started to be treated as a genuine science.

Some of the hallmarks of GUI era include

- **Visual clues.** A button with a gray border seems to pop off the window—it just looks pushable.

- **Real-world analogies.** A tabbed dialog box looks like a set of tabbed pages in a binder, Sticky-notes in Microsoft Outlook look like sticky-notes. Most contact management software tries to look like a wall calendar and an address book (see Figure 1-4 for an example). The idea is that the user already knows how to use these things in the real world.

- **Learning can be transferrable.** For example, if you learned how to delete a file, a program can provide a trash can that lets you delete a product record, and you might be able to guess how to use it instinctually based on the similarity. (Of course, metaphors enforce their own biases. Knowing how to format a paragraph won't help you format a floppy disk.)

All these points are essentially an effort to make a program so logical it's almost instinctual. The goal is for a user to require no special training, and just be able to apply assumptions garnered from other programs and the real world when learning a new application. Of course, because the focus is on the user, you need to know quite a bit about how an average user thinks before you can create the interface. This philosophy still holds today.

The GUI model provides a great deal of freedom for the developer (some might say too much freedom). In the Windows world, designing a first-rate user interface has less to do with inventing metaphors, and more to do with following established conventions.

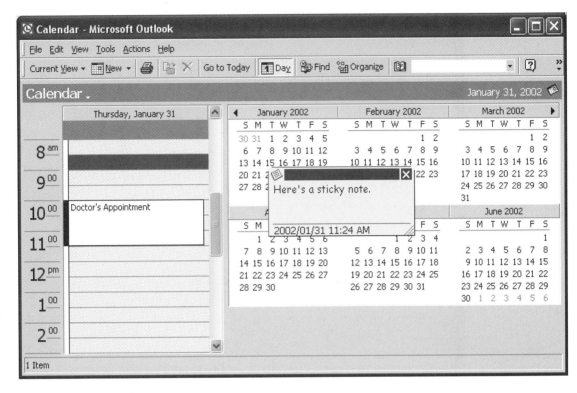

*Figure 1-4. A metaphor-based calendar and organizer*

## Creativity vs. Convention

Many user interface projects are sidetracked when they meet up with the developer's need for creativity. Unfortunately, an application's user interface doesn't just determine how a program looks, it also determines how it acts (or from the user's point of view, how it works).

Ask yourself this question: would car manufacturers allow the same degree of creativity that some developers take in application design? The world's reliance on vehicles (and the seriousness of any mistake) makes it almost impossible to imagine a car manufacturer taking the same kind of liberties. Every year, new car models appear that have been tweaked by entire design teams of engineers, with bold promises that they are entirely new and modern. It doesn't take much inspection to see that the air conditioners and radios always work almost exactly the same as before, down to the last button; the steering wheel looks and works exactly the same way; the seat configuration is generally unchanged; and the controls for starting, stopping, and slowing the car down are indistinguishable. The average driver could close his or her eyes and still locate the ignition in most cars.

Even in the better applications of today, this consistency is rare. If you install a new program on your computer, are you confident that Ctrl+S is the save document command? Will File ? Print send your document straight to the printer or give you a chance to tweak some setting first? And exactly where do you find the menu command for that all-important Preferences or Options window…under Tools, Edit, or File?

> **NOTE** *On the good side, some conventions are well followed (like using Esc to exit a dialog box). Other conventions have taken over just because Microsoft enforces them, like the editing commands built in to standard controls like the text box, and the way you resize or move a window.*

To make a long story short, convention is the way that users learn to work with a variety of software. Violating convention because convention is somehow inferior to your highly idiosyncratic vision is doomed to fail. It just multiplies the amount of information a user needs to know to use computer software.

## Consistency in .NET

Microsoft has made no secret that one of its goals with the .NET platform is to make the programming model more consistent for different programmers. You can see this in the different .NET languages, which share a consistent set of data types and functionality drawn from a shared class library. You can see this in the lavish use of interfaces and inheritance, which defines how specialized classes should work so they resemble other similar classes. You can even see this in the way Visual Studio .NET allows you to use its powerful debugging tools, regardless of whether you're working with code for a Windows project, ASP.NET page, or even a database stored procedure.

In short, if consistency is so prized by cutting-edge software developers, why would anyone assume it's not just as important for the beginning computer user?

## The "Act-Like-Microsoft" Principle

Windows developers have it rather easy. The secret to making a program that the average user can understand, and even enjoy, is usually just to copy Microsoft as closely as possible. That isn't to say that Microsoft has made the best choices in their applications—but for the most part, that isn't important. If the users of your application have ever used another application, chances are that it's been Microsoft Windows, Microsoft Office, or Internet Explorer. In fact, if your users are regular computer users, they probably spend the majority of their computing time with Word and Excel.

There's rarely a good reason for deviating from Microsoft standards. If average users have learned anything, it's the common keystrokes and menu organizations in an Office application. Not only that, but Microsoft is also known to pour ridiculous amounts of money into extensive usability tests, suggesting that their designs might not only be more recognizable than yours . . . they could very well be better.

If you aren't creating an office productivity or document-based application, you should still pay careful attention to Microsoft's designs. In almost every field, they have a well-worn example (including playing music, browsing the Internet, and reading email). In some cases, you might need to investigate another application (like Adobe Photoshop in the graphics arena), but Microsoft is generally the standard.

> **TIP**  *Remember, when you follow expected conventions, you don't just make it easier for users to learn your application. You also help train those users for the next programmer's software.*

## Administrative Utilities

One good example of a Windows convention is found in Microsoft's design of system and management utilities. These utilities almost always use a paired TreeView and ListView control, loosely resembling Windows Explorer. In Windows 2000 and later operating systems, Microsoft uses this design everywhere it can, even stretching the convention to apply it to computer hardware configuration and user management (see Figure 1-5).

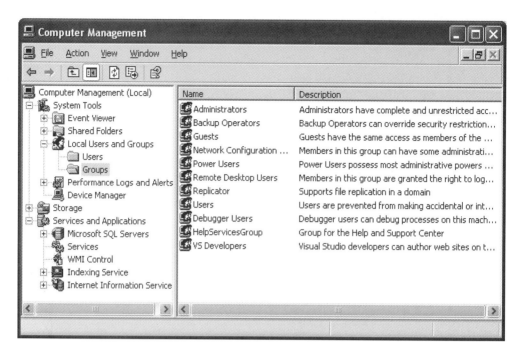

*Figure 1-5. Explorer-like user interface*

This type of design has significant merits. First of all, it's easy to see how items are related. The TreeView suggests the basic levels of grouping and subgrouping. You can often add multiple TreeView levels to combine features that would be scattered across several different windows. You can also gather a great deal of information without leaving the window. The ListView pane can be adapted to show a variety of different types of data, without obscuring the navigational controls (the TreeView), allowing the users to be at ease. Finally, it doesn't enforce any required order for performing tasks. It also makes use of graphical icons to help break up the monotony of what can be a great deal of information displayed at once.

This design also has some idiosyncrasies. For example, the menu conventions favor a streamlined Action menu instead of File and Tools menus. Sometimes records are edited in a special window that appears in place of the ListView, while in other cases a separate window pops up to allow the changes. It's also extremely ambitious. It could quickly confuse more basic users, who tend to have trouble understanding the relationship between the TreeView and the ListView control. Thus, the use of this interface style depends on your target audience.

In an impressive attempt to achieve standardization, this design is found in almost all of Microsoft's current programs, from SQL Server to Visual Studio .NET. It's an example of a lesser known, yet keenly important Microsoft standard: the Microsoft Management Console (MMC) framework. Currently, you can't create MMC applications in .NET, but you can (and should) follow the organization and conventions for common utility and management tasks like configuring users or browsing a database. You'll see examples of this style in the later chapters of this book.

Ultimately, you need to know both your application type and your audience. For example, while the MMC design is ideal for advanced tasks, Microsoft Office provides the canonical rules for document-based applications geared to less experienced users.

## Know Your Application Type

If you can't identify the type of application you are creating, you are in for a rough time. Here are some common types (which you'll examine in this book):

- **The configuration utility.** This may be based on a single control panel or organized into a more sophisticated wizard.

- **The workspace.** This is a pattern followed for sophisticated applications, particularly for proprietary software where it may be the only application used on certain workstations. The workspace is an "application desktop" that combines a set of features into a common environment that may add some kind of status display.

- **The document editor.** This is one of the most common Windows application types.

- **The monitor.** Generally, this is a system tray program that lurks in the background, automatically performing certain tasks when directed by the user or when it receives notification from the operating system. For example, it might wait for a file and automatically copy or import it. If you need to interact with this program, it's typically through a context menu for its system tray icon.

- **The data browser.** This is generally organized as an Explorer-type of application that lists records, and allows you to view and update them.

## Know Your User

Different audiences require different degrees of assistance. The user browsing quickly and effortlessly through the intricacies of the Windows registry with regedit.exe is not the same user who turns to Microsoft Agent for help creating a graph.

However, this fact is often used as a crutch to excuse complicated interfaces based on the imagined requirements of professional users. As a rule, it is possible to design an interface that combines power-user shortcuts and first-time-user guidance. In fact, it's essential. The users of your application will have different requirements when they first begin to use the software (or evaluate it for a potential purchase) than when they master it as part of their daily routine. A good interface recognizes these challenges, and helps guide users as much as necessary, without obstructing functionality. For example, consider Microsoft Word, where novice users find their way around using the menus for clues, intermediate users save clicks with the toolbar icons, and power users can work speedily with shortcut keys and drag and drop. Not only does this interface handle multiple user levels, it helps users *graduate* from one level to another, because toolbar buttons match menu commands, and menu text includes the relevant shortcut keys.

> **NOTE**   *Be careful not to overestimate the user. The typical programmer spends an incredible amount of time planning and working with an application, and can't really imagine what it would be like to see the application for the first time.*

The greatest art of user interface design is creating applications that can be used efficiently by different levels of users. To master this art, you need to know where to impose restrictions, and how to handle complexity.

## Handling Complexity

Some programmers (and many more management types) believe the myth that when users complain that an application is too complicated, it's because a specific feature is not prominently available. The immediate solution is often just to slap a new button somewhere that will supposedly make it quicker to access features and thus render the program easier to use. Unfortunately, life (and user interface programming) isn't that easy.

For example, consider the sample audio recorder and its "improved" version, both shown in Figure 1-6. It may be a little quicker to open and save files, but is the interface actually easier to use?

In reality, when a user complains that an interface is confusing, it's rarely because it lacks a few quick shortcut controls or time-saving features. Rather, it's almost always a sign that the user interface is not logically organized. Adding more buttons to the audio recorder doesn't just make the interface look ugly; it also makes it seem impossibly complicated.

*Figure 1-6. Two approaches to an audio recorder*

## Segmenting Information

Deciding how to divide a product's functionality into separate applications, windows, and controls is the most important user interface decision you will make. One common pattern is to group different types of information into similar management windows. For example, a database application might have an add/remove/configure window for configuring customer records or product records. Other applications use a task-based approach, with a wizard that steps through multiple steps leading to a single goal. Before beginning an application, you should identify the most obvious logical divisions, and build your application along those lines.

Some other principles are outlined here:

- Use the common Windows analogies. These are "obvious" metaphors (for example, document icons represent files) and shouldn't require any imaginative power.

- Don't let metaphors take over your program. For example, you shouldn't find a cute way to reuse a metaphor when it will just make a program more confusing. (An example of this problem is the Macintosh's use of a trash can to delete files *and* eject floppy disks.)

- Use the right controls to offload the work. Controls like the TreeView, ListView, and DataGrid can handle the basic user interface infrastructure.

- Hide unnecessary information.

- Appearing complex is being complex. A program appears logical when it does what the user expects. Keep this in mind, and you can create the illusion of an intuitive program.

## Inductive User Interface

Microsoft has a new methodology designed to make user interfaces simpler by breaking features into individual self-explanatory windows. Each window is used for one task, rather than the common combined window that incorporates a set of tasks related to a single type of information. This type of interface, geared for the lowest (and most common) level of computer user, often combines web-style forms and requires more windows than usual. A current example of inductive user interface (IUI) design is Microsoft Money 2000.

IUI is in its infancy. No clear conventions exist, and it's fairly labor extensive to design. For most programmers it makes sense to ignore IUI until it is a better established and more conventionalized model (and one with more .NET support). You can read the initial IUI guidelines in the MSDN (online at http://msdn.microsoft.com/library/en-us/dnwindev/html/iuiguidelines.asp).

## Helpful Restrictions

Most programmers fall into the category of "power users" of computer systems. It's for that reason that it sometimes comes as a bit of a surprise when programmers learn that one of the kindest things they can do for a user is to impose restrictions. To a developer, restrictions often seem to run contrary to the goal of application programming, because they make a program "less able" to do things. However, when you use intelligent restrictions you may curb the overall abilities of your program, but you increase the efficiency and confidence of the average user.

## Restricting the User's Ability to Make a Mistake

If you aren't careful, a great deal of code can be wasted attempting to detect and deal with errors. The problem is that once a user error has occurred, there is no elegant way to report it to the user and help the user continue. No matter how carefully worded or helpful the error message attempts to be, it's likely to make the user feel foolish, guilty, and frustrated. (In fact, usability studies show us that users will probably just click OK or Cancel as soon as the message appears to clear it from the screen, and then try the same thing over again.)

It doesn't matter whether you display this message after the user clicks the OK button or (worse yet) as soon as a field loses focus. Mentally, the user has moved on to the next task, and the error message is an interruption.

A better approach is to spend your energy preventing errors from happening in the first place. For example:

- Limit the number of characters a text box can accept, and use the key press event to make sure invalid characters are ignored.

- Use drop-down lists when the user is selecting one of several predefined choices.

- Disable (or "grey out") invalid options. In the case of a complex application with many menu options and toolbars, you may need to centralize this task in some sort of state function or link different user interface elements. You'll see examples of both techniques in later chapters.

## Restricting the User's Choices

Another common myth in user interface programming is that the more advanced an application is, the more options it should provide. Some developers even believe that if you can't decide between two different ways to provide a feature, you should do both, and allow the user to choose. Unfortunately, this type of logic (deciding not to decide) is shirking your duty as a user interface designer. The end user will not have the same in-depth understanding of the application, and may not even know that a configuration option is available or how it works. Adding more options dramatically raises the number of possible problems, and guarantees a lack of consistency across different installations.

The basic rule is that if something appears more complicated, it *is* more complicated. Adding gratuitous options can make simple operations complicated. Think of the incredible complexity of nonconfigurable devices like a car or a microwave. If microwave users had to navigate through a series of menus that gave options about the pitch of the "food ready" beep, the intensity of the interior light, and the time display mode, the common household appliance would suddenly become much more intimidating. Even more practical enhancements, like allowing the user to fine-tune power levels, preset cooking time a day in advance, or set the platter rotation speed probably aren't worth the added complexity.

Heavily customizable applications also bury genuinely useful options in a slew of miscellaneous, less important properties. Few users dig through the whole list to find the important options—you actually reduce the usable features of an application as you add extraneous elements. Most options can either be eliminated and handled by a reasonable default, or should graduate to a prominent place where the average user can configure them. Remember that every time you give a user an option you are forcing the user to make a decision. Many users become increasingly unsettled and less confident as they pass by options that they don't understand.

## Restricting the User's Imagination

If you've ever worked at a Help desk, you probably understand that the human mind thinks in terms of cause and effect. The human bias to identify underlying reasons for events is so strong that users actually invent explanations for mysterious problems or unexpected behavior with their applications, even if these explanations seem wildly fantastical to a more experienced user.

When designing a program, you need to restrict this natural tendency. Some ways you can do this include

- Give feedback for long tasks. Some possibilities include a continuously updating dialog box message, progress bar, or status bar text. When feedback isn't arriving, most users assume the program isn't working.

- Show; don't tell. The average user generally views long-winded dialog boxes that explain what will happen next with mistrust. It's far better to avoid written explanations, and find another way to convey the information (or just direct the user to an important area of the screen). For example, many drawing programs now use thumbnail previews that allow users to see the result of an action before it is started.

- Avoid the super-intelligent interface. People love to see the demon in the machine. Even in a painstakingly designed application like Microsoft Word, automatic features for capitalizing text and applying formatting often confound users of all levels. Don't assume your application can determine what the user intends to do. Automatic fixes and modifications are not only likely to frustrate the user by removing control, they can also insult users.

- Always include a print preview. Just about every user wants to see what the finished product will look like, even when all the information is already on-screen. With .NET, it's easier than ever to create a preview that matches the pagination and formatting of the final copy.

These tips can't redeem a terrible interface. However, if used when needed, they can bridge the gap between an attractive application, and one that's truly *usable*.

## Programming User Interface for the Web

.NET provides web controls that resemble their common Windows counterparts, even maintaining their state automatically and raising server-side events. The programming models are so similar that user interface code can sometimes be transferred from one environment to the other. With new features like discon- nected data access, you can even create a common back end of business objects that can be used in desktop and web applications.

There are still some restrictions inherent to the world of HTML. Most significant, HTML is not a windowing system. There's no practical way to create equivalents for secondary windows, message boxes, or floating tool windows. Because of these limitations, it's extremely difficult to create some application types that are easy for desktop applications, like document editors. There are also no rich menu controls. It's very likely that third-party component developers will start to create custom .NET menu controls that can render themselves as client-side DHTML, but for now you need to use button navigation panes or other controls.

The part of the .NET framework that allows you to create web applications is ASP.NET. ASP.NET elegantly solves some long-standing problems with Internet applications, but it also introduces a few of its own wrinkles. For example, to react to an ASP.NET control event, you need to trigger a postback, which sends the page back to the server. This takes a short, but noticeable amount of time. It makes it impractical to update a display based on control changes, and impossible to use capture events like mouse movements or key presses. For reasons like this, you can't perform some types of automatic validations or restrictions. Instead, you need to validate all the controls after all the information is entered and the page is submitted. ASP.NET also introduces data binding as a key technique. It works quite a bit differently than data binding in a desktop application, however, and requires special considerations. Finally, you should also be aware that there is little standardization in the Internet world. Most users can agree about attractive and ugly sites, but the web developer who adopts the visual style of another web site is accused of copying, not praised for following convention.

## The Last Word

User interface is really a blend of common sense, bitter experience, and a little luck. Many other books treat the subject in more detail, and can provide some fascinating reading. (One interesting resource is *User Interface Design for Programmers*, a short and insightful book from Apress.) There are also seminal works from Microsoft on Windows conventions, although the most well known, *Microsoft Windows User Experience*, is starting to show its age and no longer reflects modern controls and Microsoft's latest trends. Parts of

*Microsoft Windows User Experience* can be read online on MSDN at
`http://msdn.microsoft.com/library/en-us/dnwue/html/welcome.asp`.

A large part of this chapter has focused on a back-to-basics approach that stresses organization and logic instead of graphic artistry. However, sometimes it's OK to be cool. For example, the next generation game wouldn't get anywhere it if looked like Microsoft Excel. The dividing line is usually drawn between productivity applications and entertainment. For example, WinAmp can get away with a highly proprietary interface, but you might find that the market for skinnable word processors isn't nearly as large.

Now that you have a basic understanding of what makes an interface truly usable, it's time to shift your focus to the underlying architecture that makes it all possible. In the next chapter, you learn about what objects, classes, and tiers have to do with user interface programming, and how .NET lets you work with them.

# CHAPTER 2

# Designing with Classes and Tiers

SOME DEVELOPERS RESENT user interface programming because they believe it's all about painting icons, rewording text, and endlessly tweaking dialog boxes until an entire company agrees that an application looks attractive. Certainly, making a program usable, elegant, and even impressive (or cool) is no trivial task. It can even make the difference between indifferent customers and an enthusiastic audience that's willing to promote your product tirelessly. This kind of excitement about a program's look and feel has driven obscure products like Kai's Power Tools and even Microsoft Windows to great success, and it can't be overlooked. However, developers who are involved in creating and maintaining sophisticated enterprise-level applications realize that there is another set of design considerations for user interface programming. These are considerations about application architecture.

Application architecture determines how a user interface "plugs in" to the rest of an application. Today's development software (like MFC, Visual Basic, and .NET) makes this interaction relatively straightforward and, as a result, developers usually spend little or no time thinking about it. User interface code is usually inserted wherever is most immediately convenient at the time the program is written. This almost always leads to interface code that's tightly bound to a particular problem, scenario, or data source, and heavily interwoven with the rest of the application logic. The interface code might look good on the outside, but it's almost impossible to enhance, reuse, or alter with anything more than trivial changes. To make the jump from this type of scattered user interface coding to a more modern style you have to stop thinking in terms of windows and controls, and start looking at user interface as an entire interrelated framework.

This chapter explains how the principles of object-oriented programming and three-tier architecture apply to user interface design. It identifies the overall concepts that you'll return to again and again throughout the book, including:

- How controls and windows use objects.

- Why inheritance is more important for user interface design than for business logic.

- How the .NET framework approaches user interface design, and how it affects your coding practices.

- What makes an interface data-driven and well encapsulated.

- What the dream of three-tier design promises, why it's so hard to achieve, and whether other solutions are possible.

The emphasis in this chapter is on general concepts. You'll see some code, but you won't learn about the intricate details like the properties and methods that controls provide. All these details are explored as we delve deeper into controls and user interface coding in the chapters that follow.

## Classes and Objects

Today, it's generally accepted that the best way to design applications is by using discrete, reusable components called *objects*.

A typical .NET program is little more than a large collection of class definitions. When you start the program, your code creates the objects it needs using these class definitions. Your code can also make use of the classes that are defined in other referenced assemblies and in the .NET class library (which is itself just a collection of useful assemblies).

## *The Roles of Classes*

It's important to remember that although all classes are created in the same way in your code, they can serve different logical roles:

- **Classes can model real-world entities.** For example, many introductory books teach object-oriented programming using a Customer object or an Invoice object. These objects allow you to manipulate data, and they directly correspond to an actual *thing* in the real world.

- **Classes can serve as useful programming abstractions.** For example, you might use a Rectangle class to store width and height information, a FileBuffer class to represent a line of binary information from a file, or a WinMessage class to hold information about a Windows message. These classes don't need to correspond to tangible objects; they are just a useful way to shuffle around related bits of information and functionality in your code. Arguably, this is the most common type of class.

- **Classes can collect related functions.** Some classes are just a collection of shared (static) methods that you can use without needing to create an object instance. These helper classes are the equivalent of a library of related functions, and might have names like GraphicsManipulator or FileManagement. In some cases, a helper class is just a sloppy way to organize code and represents a problem that should really be broken down into related objects. In other cases it's a useful way to create a repository of simple routines that can be used in a variety of ways.

Understanding the different roles of classes is crucial to being able to master object-oriented development. When you create a class, you should decide how it fits into your grand development plan, and make sure that you aren't giving it more than one type of role. The more vague a class is, the more it resembles a traditional block of code from a non–object-oriented program.

## Classes and Types

The discussion so far has reviewed object-oriented development using two words: classes and objects. Classes are the definitions, or object templates. Objects are "live" classes in action. The basic principle of object-oriented design is that you can put any class to work, and use it to create as many objects as you need.

In the .NET world, however, these terms are a little blurred. The .NET class library is really built out of *types*, and classes are just one kind of type. To get the most out of this book, you should already know the basics about .NET types and how they can be used. If you need to refresh your memory and get reacquainted with .NET's object family, use the following sections.

### Structures

Structures are like classes, but are generally simpler. They tend to have only a few properties (and even fewer important methods). A more important distinction is that structures are value types, while classes are reference types. This means that structures act differently in comparison and assignment operations. If you assign one structure variable to another, .NET copies the contents of the entire structure, not just the reference. Similarly, when you compare structures, you are comparing their contents, not the reference.

```
StructureA = StructureB  ' StructureA has a copy of the contents of StructureB.
                         ' There are two duplicate structures in memory.

If StructureA = StructureB Then
    ' This is True as long as the structures have the same content.
    ' Using full binary comparisons like this can slow down performance.
End If
```

Some of the structures in the class library include Int32, DateTime, and graphics ingredients like Point, Size, and Rectangle.

## Classes

This is the most common type in the class library. All the Windows and Internet controls are full-fledged classes. The word "classes" is sometimes used interchangeably with "types" (or even "objects") because classes are the central ingredients of any object-oriented framework like .NET. Many traditional programming constructs (like collections and arrays) are classes in .NET.

Unlike structures, classes use reference-equality:

```
ObjectA = ObjectB    ' ObjectA and ObjectB now both point to the same thing.
                     ' There is one object, and two ways to access it.

If ObjectA Is ObjectB Then
    ' This is True if both ObjectA and ObjectB point to the same thing.
    ' This is False if they are separate, yet identical objects.
End If
```

Occasionally, a class can override this behavior. For example, the String class is a full-featured class in every way, but it overrides equality and assignment operations to work like a simple value type. This tends to be more useful (and intuitive). For example, if a string acted like a reference type it would be harder to validate a password. You would need a special method to iterate through all the characters in the user-supplied text, and compare each one separately. Arrays, on the other hand, behave like traditional objects. If you want to perform a sophisticated comparison or copy operation on an array, you need to iterate through every item in the array and copy or compare it manually.

## Delegates

Delegates define the signature of a method. For example, they might indicate that a function has a string return value, and accepts two integer parameters. Using a delegate, you can create a variable that points to specific method and invoke the method through the delegate.

```
' To define a delegate, identify the method's parameters and return type.
Public Delegate Function StringProcessFunction(Input As String) As String
```

You can then create a delegate variable based on this definition:

```
Dim StringProcessor As StringProcessFunction
```

```
' This variable can hold a reference to any method with the right signature.
' It can be a shared method or an instance method. You can then invoke it later.
' (Here we assume that our code contains a function named CapitalizeString.)
StringProcessor = AdressOf CaptitalizeString
```

```
' This invokes the CaptializeString function.
Dim returnValue As String = StringProcessor("input text")
```

Besides being an interesting way to implement type-safe function pointers, delegates are also the foundation of .NET's event handling.

## Enumerations

Enumerations are simple, static types that allow developers to choose from a list of constants. Behind the scenes, an enumeration is just an ordinary integer where every value has a special meaning as a constant. However, because you can refer to enumerations by name, you don't need to worry about forgetting a hard-coded number, or using an invalid value.

```
' You define enumerations in a block.
Public Enum SqlQuery
        SelectAllOrders
        SelectAllCustomers
End Enum
```

You create them like any other variable:

```
Dim DBQuery As SqlQuery
```

```
' You assign and inspect enumerations using an object-like syntax.
DbQuery = SqlQuery.SelectAllOrders
```

Enumerations are particularly important in user interface programming, which often has specific constants and other information you need to use but shouldn't hard-code.

## Interfaces

Interfaces are special contracts that define properties and methods that a class must implement. Interfaces have two main purposes in life. First, they allow polymorphism, which means many different objects that use the same interface can all be treated the same way. For example, if you implement an interface called IFileAccess, a client program may not know the specific details about your class, but if it understands IFileAccess it knows enough to use a set of basic file access functionality.

```
' You can access a supported interface by casting.
Dim RecognizedObject As IFileAccess
RecognizedObject = CType(MysteryObject, IFileAccess)

' If IFileAccess supports a method, the object that implements it will too.
RecognizedObject.OpenFile()
```

Interfaces are also useful in versioning situations, because they allow you to enhance a component without breaking existing clients. You simply need to add a new interface.

## More About Objects

If you haven't had much experience with this type of object-oriented or interface-based programming, I encourage you to start with a book about .NET fundamentals, like *A Programmer's Introduction to C#* or *Programming VB.NET: A Guide for Experienced Programmers*, both from Apress. (Or, you can refer to my own *The Book of VB .NET*, from No Starch.) Classes and other types are the basic tools of the trade, and you need to become comfortable with them before you can start to weave them into full-fledged object models and architectures.

## User Interface Classes in .NET

The first step when considering class design is to examine what rules are hard-wired into the .NET framework. Your goal should be to understand how the assumptions and conventions of the .NET platform shape user interface programming. Once you understand the extent of these rules, you will have a better idea about where the rules begin and end and your object designs must take over.

> **TIP** *The next section wades through a number of examples, and it uses code with properties and classes you may not have seen before. Remember, all these details reappear and are expanded on in later chapters. The task at hand now is to understand how .NET thinks about control objects, and how these objects interact together.*

## Controls Are Classes

In the .NET framework, every control is a class. Windows controls are clustered in the System.Windows.Forms namespace. Web controls are divided into three core namespaces, including System.Web.UI, System.Web.UI.HtmlControls, and System.Web.UI.WebControls.

In your code, a control class acts the same as any other class. You can create it, set its properties, and use its methods. The difference is in the lineage. Every Windows control inherits from System.Windows.Forms.Control, and acquires some basic functionality that allows it to paint itself on a window. In fact, even the containing window inherits from the Control base class.

On its own, a control object doesn't do much. The magic happens when it interacts with the Windows Forms engine. The Windows Forms engine handles the Windows operating system messages that change focus or activate a window, and tells controls to paint themselves by calling methods and setting properties. The interesting thing is that although these tasks are performed automatically, they aren't really hidden from you. If you want, you can override methods and fiddle with the low-level details of the controls. You can even tell them to output entirely different content.

So it's clear how you create a control—you just create an instance of a control class, as you would do with any other object. Here's an example that defines a text box:

```
Dim txtUserName As New System.Windows.Forms.TextBox()
```

You can then set various properties for your control:

```
txtUserName.Name = "txtUserName"
txtUserName.Location = New System.Drawing.Point(64, 88)
txtUserName.Size = New System.Drawing.Size(200, 20)
txtUserName.TabIndex = 0
txtUserName.Text = "Enter text here!"
```

These properties configure some important information, like the size and position of the text box. But none of this actually creates a visible control in a window. How does the Common Language Runtime know whether you are just creating a control to use internally (perhaps to pass to another method) or if you want it to be painted on a specific form and able to receive input from the user?

The answer is in class relations.

## Controls Contain Other Controls

The System.Windows.Forms.Control class provides a property called Controls, which exposes a collection of child controls. For example, a Windows Form has a Controls property that contains the first level of contained controls that appear in the window. If you have other container controls on the form, like group boxes, they may have their own child controls.

In other words, controls are linked together by class relations using the Controls collection. Because every control is a special class that derives from System.Windows.Forms.Control, every control supports the ability to contain other controls. (In fact, in Chapter 10 you'll see an example of docking windows that works by placing a form control *inside* a panel control.)

> **TIP** *To be technically accurate, this collection is actually the special .NET type System.Windows.Forms.Control.ControlCollection. This collection is customized to make sure that it can only contain controls, not other types of objects. However, you don't really need to know that to use the collection successfully.*

Figure 2-1 shows a sample window, and Figure 2-2 diagrams the relationship of the controls it contains.

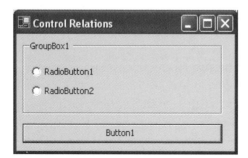

*Figure 2-1. A sample form*

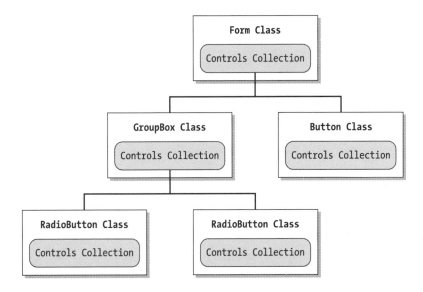

*Figure 2-2. Control containment for a sample form*

To associate a control with a window, you just need to add it to the form's Controls collection. Like most collection classes, the Controls collection provides some standard methods like Add() and Remove().

For example, the following line of code takes the text box control object and registers it with the form. The text box immediately appears in the window:

```
frmMain.Controls.Add(txtUserName)
```

Or, if it you want the text box to be located inside a group box or panel:

```
' Add the panel to the form.
frmMain.Controls.Add(pnlUserInfo)

' Add the textbox to the panel.
pnlUserInfo.Controls.Add(txtUserName)
```

The control's location property is automatically interpreted in terms of the parent control. For example, (0, 0) is the top left corner of the container, and (100, 100) is 100 pixels from both the top and left edges.

If you add a control to a form window that already exists, it appears immediately. If, however, the form hasn't been displayed yet, you'll need to use the form's Show() or ShowDialog() method. Forms are the only controls that know how to display themselves, and they automatically handle the responsibility of coordinating the display of all their contained controls.

```
frmMain.Show()
```

A control can be removed from a window by using the Remove() method of the Controls collection. In this case, you need to supply a variable that references the control you want to remove.

```
' Remove the textbox control.
frmMain.pnlUserInfo.Controls.Remove(txtUserName)
```

All controls, whether they are text boxes, buttons, labels, or something more sophisticated, are added to (and removed from) container controls in the same way. In the next section, you'll see how you use this to your advantage by defining and displaying your custom controls.

> **NOTE**  *With Web Forms, the process is similar, but there is never a need to explicitly show a page. HTML isn't a genuine windowing system, and the user is always restricted to seeing one page at a time. You can add a Web control to the current page using the Controls collection of the System.Web.UI.Page class, which is analogous to that of the System.Windows.Forms.Form class. If you want to show another page, however, you need to redirect the user, and let the destination page take over the processing. I won't talk about web interfaces any further in this book, because they have dramatically different needs than Windows applications.*

## Controls Derive from Other Controls

In *Moving to VB .NET,* Dan Appleman suggests that inheritance is an over-hyped feature with a few specific uses, but a host of potential problems and considerations. In his words, inheritance is the "coolest feature you'll never use," and many object-oriented gurus would be quick to agree. While inheritance can be useful when creating your business and data objects, it's generally not the best approach, and never the only one.

In the world of controls, however, inheritance just might be the single most useful feature you'll discover. Essentially, inheritance allows you to acquire a set of specific functionality for free. You don't need to worry about how to handle the messy infrastructure code for what you want to do. Instead, you simply inherit from a class in the .NET library, add a few business-specific features, and throw it into your program.

This approach can be used to create customized controls quickly and easily. Below is the definition for a custom text box. It has all the powerful features of a text box, manages its appearance automatically, provides sophisticated user editing capability, and takes care of basic details like painting itself and managing focus. In addition, the custom text box adds two new features. It has a property that returns the total number of letters in the text string (NumberOfLetters), and a method that quickly trims off extra dashes (TrimDashes). To provide this functionality, it uses some standard .NET tricks to iterate through a string, and it makes use of the Trim() method that's built into the string object.

```
Public Class CustomTextBox
    Inherits Windows.Forms.TextBox

    Public ReadOnly Property NumberOfLetters() As String
        Get
            Dim Letters As Integer = 0
            Enumerator = Text.GetEnumerator()

            Do While Enumerator.MoveNext()
                If Char.IsLetter(Enumerator.Current) Then
                    Letters += 1
                End If
            Loop
            Return Letters
        End Get
    End Property

    Public Sub TrimDashes()
        Me.Text.Trim("-")
    End Sub

End Class
```

You can use this class in exactly the same way that you would use a class from the .NET library:

```
Dim txtUserName As New CustomControlProject.CustomTextBox()
txtUserName.Name = "txtUserName"
txtUserName.Location = New System.Drawing.Point(64, 88)
txtUserName.Size = New System.Drawing.Size(200, 20)
txtUserName.TabIndex = 0
txtUserName.Text = "Enter text in the custom textbox here!"
frmMain.Controls.Add(txtUserName)
```

The interesting part of this example is not what's in the code, but what is left out. Clearly, there are a lot of Windows-specific details that you don't need to worry about when using inheritance to create a custom control. You also don't need to create separate ActiveX components (and countless versioning headaches). Custom controls in .NET are painless and powerful.

Chapters 7 and 8 examine a variety of custom control programming techniques, and show you how to license, distribute, and manage them in the development environment. Custom control examples also reappear throughout the book. You'll use them to:

- Solve control synchronization problems

- Automate control validation

- Rigorously organize code

- Preinitialize complex controls

- Tailor controls to specific types of data, even replacing basic members with more useful higher-level events and properties

Creating custom controls is a key way of playing with .NET, and one of the most important themes of this book.

## Inheritance and the Form Class

Inheritance isn't just used when you want to extend an existing class with additional features. It's also used to gain access to important parts of functionality in .NET. One of the best examples is the System.Windows.Form class.

In a Windows application, you could create an instance of a System.Windows.Form and manually go about adding controls and attaching events. However, if you are creating your project in Visual Studio .NET, it defaults to a more structured approach.

When you start designing a new window in the IDE, Visual Studio .NET automatically creates a customized class that inherits from the Form class. This class encapsulates all the logic for adding child controls, setting their properties, and responding to their events in one neat package. It also provides you with an easy way to create identical copies of a form, which is particularly useful in document-based applications.

Below is a simplified example of a custom form class that contains a simple constructor method. When the form is instantiated in a program, it automatically creates and configures a text box, and then adds it to the form.

```
Public Class MainForm
    Inherits System.Windows.Forms.Form

    Friend WithEvents txtUserName As New System.Windows.Forms.TextBox()

    Public Sub New()
        MyBase.New()
        txtUserName.Name = "txtUserName"
        txtUserName.Location = New System.Drawing.Point(64, 88)
        txtUserName.Size = New System.Drawing.Size(200, 20)
        txtUserName.TabIndex = 0
        txtUserName.Text = "Enter text here!"
        Me.Controls.Add(txtUserName)
    End Sub

End Class
```

**NOTE** *Note that the keyword Me (or this in C#) is used to access the current form instance. This allows you to write generic code that can be applied to any instance directly inside the form class.*

The custom form class automatically gains all the features of a standard Windows.Forms.Form object, including the ability to display itself with the Show() and ShowDialog() methods.

```
' Create the form (at this point, its constructor code will run and add
' the textbox control).
Dim frmCustomForm As New MainForm()

' Show the form.
frmCustomForm.Show()
```

Notice how the only control MainForm contains (a text box) is referenced with a member variable, so that it can be easily accessed in your code. This means that once the form has been created, there are really two different ways to access the text box. The simplest way is to use the form-level member variable:

```
frmCustomForm.txtUserName.Text = "John"
```

It's up to you whether you want to make the member variable accessible to other classes in your program. By default, all control variables in C# are private, so they aren't available to other classes. In Visual Basic .NET projects, all controls are declared with the Friend keyword, and any other class can access them as long as it exists in the current project. This is similar to the way that previous versions of VB worked. Either way, the difference is minor. Generally, Visual Studio .NET tries to discourage you from breaking encapsulation and fiddling with the user interface of a form from another class. However, there is *always* one open back door. No matter what the language, you can always access controls directly through the form's Controls collection.

## The Controls Collection

Generally, the member variables allow flat access to the controls on a form. All the controls on the form have corresponding member variables. On the other hand, only the first level of controls appears in the Controls collection. Controls that are inside container controls like group boxes, tab controls, or panels, will appear in the Controls collection of the control that contains them (as diagrammed in Figure 2-2).

Unfortunately, controls are only indexed by number in the Controls collection. That means the best way to find a control that you need is to iterate through the entire collection and examine each control one by one, until you find a match. You can look for a specific type of control, or a specifically-named control. For example, when a control is created in Visual Studio .NET, it is automatically given a Name property that matches the name used for the member variable.

```
txtUserName.Name = "txtUserName"
```

This is just a convenience—you are not forced to set the name property. However, it allows you to easily look up the control by iterating through the Control collection:

```
' Search for and remove a control with a specific name.
Dim ctrl As Control
For Each ctrl in frmCustomForm.Controls
    If ctrl.Name = "txtUserName" Then
        frmCustomForm.Controls.Remove(ctrl)
    End If
Next
```

**NOTE** *The Controls collection is always accessible to other forms. However, you shouldn't use this as a back door to allow one form to modify another. For one thing, using a string to identify the name of a control is extremely fragile—if the original form is changed, the code may stop working, but it won't raise a helpful design-time or compile-time error. If forms need to interact, they should do so indirectly. For example, one form should call a method in an application class that then calls the appropriate method or sets the appropriate property in another form. You'll see some of these issues in Chapter 10.*

## Generating Code with Visual Studio .NET

So far you've looked at the code to create control objects dynamically (a topic explored in much more detail in Chapter 11). When you use Visual Studio .NET to create code at design-time, the story is a little different—or is it?

When you create a Windows application in Visual Studio .NET, the IDE creates a customized form class. As you add, position, and configure controls in the design-time environment, Visual Studio .NET adds the corresponding code to a special region of the Form class, inside a method called InitializeComponent(). The form's constructor calls the InitializeComponent() method—meaning that the generated code is automatically executed every time you create an instance of your Form class (even before the form is displayed). A sample (commented and slightly shortened) Form class with an InitializeComponent() method is shown below. It configures the window shown in Figure 2-1.

```
Public Class TestForm
    Inherits System.Windows.Forms.Form

    ' Form level control variables.
    ' They provide the easiest way to access a control on the window.
    Friend WithEvents GroupBox1 As New System.Windows.Forms.GroupBox()
    Friend WithEvents Button1 As New System.Windows.Forms.Button()
    Friend WithEvents RadioButton1 As New System.Windows.Forms.RadioButton()
    Friend WithEvents RadioButton2 As New System.Windows.Forms.RadioButton()

    Public Sub New()
        MyBase.New()

        ' Add and configure the controls.
        InitializeComponent()
    End Sub
```

```
Private Sub InitializeComponent()
    ' This is our way of telling the controls not to update their layout
    ' because a batch of changes are being made at once.
    Me.GroupBox1.SuspendLayout()
    Me.SuspendLayout()

    ' (Set all the properties for all our controls here.)
    ' (Configure the form properties here.)

    ' Add the radio buttons to the GroupBox.
    Me.GroupBox1.Controls.Add(Me.RadioButton1)
    Me.GroupBox1.Controls.Add(Me.RadioButton2)

    ' Add the button and group box controls to the form.
    Me.Controls.Add(Me.Button1)
    Me.Controls.Add(Me.GroupBox1)

    ' Now it's back to life as usual.
    Me.GroupBox1.ResumeLayout(False)
    Me.ResumeLayout(False)
End Sub

End Class
```

The upshot is that a form and its controls are always created and configured through code, even when you design it with the IDE. The only difference between the theoretical code examples in this chapter and designed code is that the latter uses a dedicated InitializeComponent() method for better organization.

> **TIP** *If you look at this code in a form you've created in Visual Studio .NET, you'll notice a couple of changes from the code listing I've shown. First, controls are defined and then created in two separate steps (and the creation takes place in the InitializeComponent() method). Second, controls are added all at once using the Controls.AddRange() method, which accepts an array of control objects, and saves a few lines of code at the expense of readability. Finally, the InitializeComponent() method has a special <System.Diagnostics.DebuggerStepThrough> attribute preceding it, which indicates that this code will be ignored for the purposes of debugging.*

# Interacting with a Control

One interesting and little-known fact about .NET controls is that they provide two different forms of interaction. The first, and less common one, is by creating custom classes and overriding methods.

For example, imagine you have a text box that's designed for numeric entry, and you want to examine every key press to make sure that it corresponds to a number, and not a letter. To perform this type of task, you can create a customized text box, and override the OnKeyPress() method to add this extra verification logic.

```
Public Class NumericTextBox
    Inherits System.Windows.Forms.TextBox

    Protected Overrides Sub OnKeyPress(ByVal e As KeyPressEventArgs)
        MyBase.OnKeyPress(e)
        If Char.IsControl(e.KeyChar) = False And _
          Char.IsDigit(e.KeyChar) = False Then
            e.Handled = True
        End If
    End Sub

End Class
```

The OnKeyPress() method is invoked automatically by the Windows Forms engine when a key is pressed in a TextBox control. The overridden method in the example above checks to see if the entered character is a number. If it isn't, the Handled flag is set to True, which cancels all further processing, effectively making sure that the character will never end up in the text box.

This design pattern is useful if you use a number of controls with extremely similar behavior. If, on the other hand, you need to fine-tune behavior for distinct, even unique tasks, this approach is extremely poor. For example, consider a button control. You could react to a button click by creating a special class for every button on your application, and giving each button its own overridden OnClick() method. While your program would still be well encapsulated, it would quickly become completely disorganized, swamped by layers of button classes that have little to do with one another.

## The View-Mediator Pattern

The approach that .NET encourages circumvents this problems by using events. When you create a form in Visual Studio .NET, a custom class is derived for the form, but all the contained classes are used as is. The event handling logic is inserted as a series of special methods, which are added to the custom form class.

In other words, every form acts as a giant switchboard for all the controls it contains. This type of design pattern, which is so natural to .NET and most Windows development that you might not have even noticed it, is called the View-Mediator pattern. It dictates that one central class organizes each individual window.

Here's the same text box example you saw earlier, rewritten as form-level event handler:

```
Public Class MainForm
    Inherits System.Windows.Forms.Form

    Friend WithEvents txtUserName As New System.Windows.Forms.TextBox()

    Public Sub New()
        MyBase.New()
        txtUserName.Name = "txtUserName"
        txtUserName.Location = New System.Drawing.Point(64, 88)
        txtUserName.Size = New System.Drawing.Size(200, 20)
        txtUserName.TabIndex = 1
        txtUserName.Text = "Enter text here!"
        Me.Controls.Add(txtUserName)
    End Sub

    Private Sub KeyPress(ByVal sender As Object, ByVal e As KeyPressEventArgs) _
      Handles txtUserName.KeyPress
        If Char.IsControl(e.KeyChar) = False And _
         Char.IsDigit(e.KeyChar) = False Then
            e.Handled = True
        End If
    End Sub

End Class
```

You'll notice that the actual logic for processing the key press is identical, but the way it's integrated into the application is completely different. The form is now responsible for the validation, *not* the control itself. This is an ideal approach if the form needs to handle the complex validation of multiple different controls. It's a less suitable approach if you need to perform the same type of validation for the same control in different windows, because you'll probably need to copy the code into multiple form-level event handlers.

You should also remember that the point of a switchboard is to route calls to a new destination. In other words, when you create the event handler for a button's Click event, this event handler usually has two purposes:

- Forward the command to another object that can handle the task.

- Update the display.

Depending on the button, only one of these tasks may be necessary. But the important concept you should realize is that an event handler is generally part of a user interface object—the form switchboard. It's meant to handle user interface tasks, and delegate more complicated operations to other objects.

## Smart Controls

So far you have seen two distinct ways to use controls from the .NET class library:

- Create an instance of a generic control class "as is." Then, configure its properties (approach 1)..

- Define a new class that inherits from a generic control class, and customize this class for your needs. Then, create an object based on this specialized class (approach 2)..

The difference is shown in Figure 2-3.

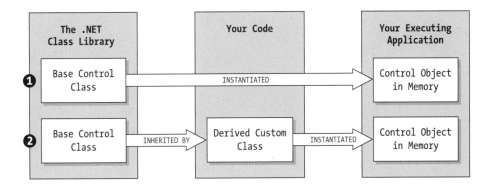

*Figure 2-3. Two ways to interact with controls*

Visual Studio .NET uses inheritance (the first method) when you create forms. When you configure controls, however, it inserts them as is, and adds the appropriate logic for modifying their properties (the second method). This is the default approach in .NET, but it is not the only approach.

When Visual Studio .NET adds controls and derives a custom form class, it is making a design decision for you. This decision helps clear out the clutter that would result from creating dozens of custom control classes. However, like all design decisions, it's not always right for all people and in all situations. For example, if you use numerous similar controls (like text boxes that refuse numeric input), you may find yourself duplicating the same code in event handlers all over your program. In this case, you might be better off to step beyond Visual Studio .NET's default behavior, and create customized controls with some additional intelligence.

When you are creating a new application and planning how to program its user interface, one of the most important tasks is deciding where to draw the line between smart controls (custom control classes) and smart switchboards (custom forms with event handling logic). A good decision can save a lot of repetitive work. Chapters 6 and 9 consider some examples that show how you can add a bit of sense to important controls like the TreeView and ListView. Hopefully, you'll realize that custom controls are not just for redistributing neat user interface elements, but also for building intelligence into parts of a large application, and helping to reduce repetition and enforce consistency across different modules.

> **NOTE** *This book includes a special chapter about custom controls, which describes how to package them for redistribution, and covers some advanced options. However, unlike most .NET books, I also explore custom control classes throughout. Creating these smart controls is a crucial ingredient in designing a user interface framework, not just an additional topic.*

## Smart Forms

As explained earlier, every form class in your application is a custom class that derives from System.Windows.Forms. However, you can use multiple layers of form inheritance to centralize and reuse important form functionality. This topic is commonly referred to as visual inheritance (although it's no different than any other type of control class inheritance), and it's described in detail in Chapter 5. Figure 2-4 diagrams this relationship. Ordinary form use is numbered as approach 1, while visual inheritance is approach.

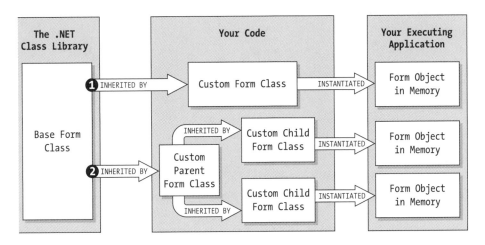

*Figure 2-4. Ordinary forms and visual inheritance*

So far, you've explored the basic object-oriented foundation of .NET user interface programming. The remainder of the chapter considers some higher-level architectural topics like encapsulation and three-tier design. These are the best practices you'll want to keep in mind when planning your user interface classes.

## Encapsulation

Encapsulation is the principle that suggests objects should have separate, carefully outlined responsibilities. Everything they need to fulfill these responsibilities should be wrapped up, hidden from view, and accomplished automatically, where possible. Encapsulation is often identified as a pillar of object-oriented programming, but it has played a part in program design since the invention of software. A properly encapsulated function, for example, performs a discrete well-identified task independently, and has a much better chance of being reused in another application (or even the same program).

The best way to start separating your user interface code is to think more consciously about encapsulation. The custom form class, with its "switchboard" design, is an excellent example of encapsulation at work. However, it also presents a danger. It potentially encourages you to mix in a great amount of additional material through the form's event handlers. A large part of good user interface programming is simply a matter of resisting this urge.

Of course, there are finer points to perfecting encapsulation. Custom controls, which handle some basic user interface operations on their own, are another good example. The following sections present guidelines that can help you keep encapsulation in mind. These techniques are not all immediately obvious. In this book,

I'll return to the principle of encapsulation often, and show specific examples with common controls.

## Use Enumerations and Resource Classes

User interface controls often require sets of constants, and trying to hard-code them is a tempting trap. Instead, you should create enumerations with meaningful names, and place them in dedicated resource classes. For example, you can define enumerations that help you manage and identify different levels of nodes in a TreeView control (see Chapter 6), distinguish different types of items in a ListView, or just pass information to other methods in your program. Extraneous details like SQL statements should also be strictly confined to distinct resource classes.

## Use Collections

Objects are only as good as the way you can access them. On it's own, a data object is a group of related information. By using a collection or other classes that contain collections, you can represent the underlying structure of an entire set of complex data, making it easier to share with other parts of your program.

## Restrain from Sharing Control References

It's easy to pass control references to helper methods. For example, you can create utility classes that automatically fill common list controls. However, this type of design, where you rely on extraneous classes to perform user interface tasks, can make it extremely difficult to make even simple modifications to the user interface. As a rule of thumb, business code should never rely on the existence of a specific type of user interface control.

## Define a Data Transfer Plan

The single greatest challenge when creating a reusable object framework is deciding how to retrieve data and insert it into the corresponding controls, without mingling the business and the presentation logic. In order to succeed, you may need to tolerate slightly long-winded code. You also need to create a clearly defined plan for transferring data that can be shared by all your forms and controls. In .NET, life just became a lot easier—the DataSet object makes a perfect, nearly universal solution for transferring information.

## Use a Central Switchboard

The form acts as a switchboard for all the controls it contains. However, you shouldn't rely on forms for anything more. Instead, you should be able to remove a form, add a new one, or even combine forms without having to rewrite much logic. To accomplish this, forms should always hand off their work to another central switchboard, like an application class. For example, it may be easy to update a record in accordance with a user's selections by creating a new object in the form code and calling a single method. However, if you add another layer of indirection by forcing the form to call a more generic update method in a central application switchboard, your user interface gains a little more independence and gets closer to the ideal of three-tier design. Figure 2-5 shows how this process might work when updating a customer record. The update is triggered in response to a control event. The event handler calls a DoCustomerUpdate() form method, which then calls the required methods in the CustomerDB business object (and creates it if necessary).

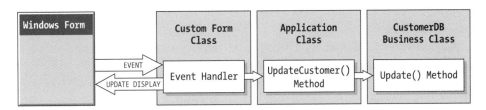

*Figure 2-5. Using form and application switchboards*

## Create Data-Driven User Interfaces

As you prepare for a three-tier architecture, it's a good idea to start designing your user interface around the data it manages. This may sound like a slightly old-fashioned concept in today's object-oriented way, but it's actually a good habit to prevent yourself from subconsciously combining user interface and business processing logic.

Think of your user interface as having one "in" and one "out" connection. All the information that flows into your user interface needs to use a single consistent standard. All forms should be able to recognize and process this data. To achieve this, you might want to use data objects that rely on a common interface for providing data. Or, you might want to standardize on .NET's new DataSet object, which can convert information into XML and back seamlessly. The second part of Chapter 9 explores the ways you can tame data in a user interface.

> **TIP** *When is a data-driven interface just another bit of jargon? Probably when you aren't creating an application based on processing, displaying, and managing data. In the business world, the majority of applications deal with databases, and the majority of their work is processing and formatting complex information. For that reason, a great deal of emphasis is placed on how this information is managed and transferred. If, on the other hand, you plan to create the next three-dimensional action game, the rules may change.*

## Developing in Tiers

The basic principle of three-tier design is simple. An application is divided into three distinct subsystems. Every class belongs to only one of these three partitions, and performs just one kind of task. The three tiers are usually identified as:

- A presentation layer, which converts a user's actions into tasks and outputs data using the appropriate controls.

- A business layer, where all the calculations and processing specific to the individual business are carried.

- An underlying data layer, which shuttles information back and forth from the database to the business objects.

An object in one tier can only interact with the adjacent tiers, as shown in Figure 2-6.

Almost everyone agrees that this sort of structure is the best way to organize an application, but it's not always easy to implement this design. Though the schematic looks simple, modern user interfaces are usually quite complicated, and sometimes make assumptions or have expectations about the way they will receive information. The result is that everyone recommends this model, but very few developers successfully follow it.

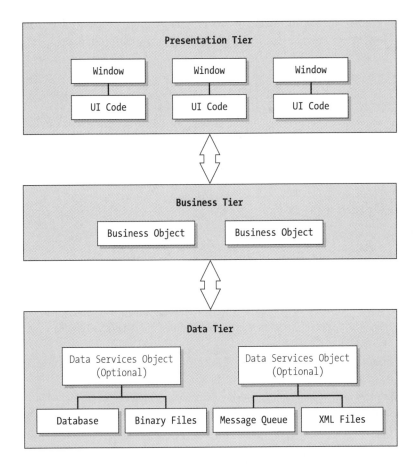

*Figure 2-6. Three-tier design*

## Problems with Three-Tier Design

Before you can solve the problems of three-tier design, you have to understand what these problems are. The problems, although not insurmountable, are found in every tier.

### Presentation tier

Though it doesn't explicitly state it, three-tier design really requires a fair degree of consistency among user interface controls. In the real world, this consistency doesn't exist. For example, making what is conceptually a minor change—like substituting a ListView control for a DataGrid—requires a totally different access model. DataGrids are filled exclusively by data binding. ListViews, on the other hand, act like a collection of items. To get information into other ListView columns, you have to add a collection of fields to each individual item. These quirks are easy enough to master (and you will sort through them in Chapter 6), but they don't make it possible to create business objects that can quickly and efficiently fill common controls.

## Business tier

In three-tier design, it's assumed that the user interface is isolated from the underlying data source. Information for a control is requested through a layer of business objects. This can be a problem if you create business objects that try to model real-world entities. For example, if you need to retrieve a list of customers and some summary information based on all customer orders, you would be crazy to try and work with individual Customer and Order objects. Consider the process:

1. The user interface layer requests some information from the business layer.

2. The business layer creates hundreds of Customer and Order objects by retrieving information from the data layer. These objects are organized into large collections. Each property for each object is set according to the corresponding field in the corresponding row.

3. The user interface layer iterates through all these objects, withdrawing and calculating the relatively simple information it needs to actually display the required rows. Each field is extracted separately as an individual property, which requires a separate line of code. The code is very readable, but far from elegant or efficient.

Some three-tier designs get around this by creating a very thin business layer that might just consist of a pile of utility functions for retrieving rows as arrays. But is this really a good object-oriented design?

## Data tier

Keeping the data tier separate from the business tier is another battle. To optimize performance, databases in enterprise applications usually rely on stored procedures, views, and other optimized ways to retrieve and update data. However, the user interface tier can't be built in a database-friendly way, because it is designed to be completely generic. It also can't rely on tricks that programmers' love, like dynamically generated SQL statements, because it is supposed to be completely isolated from the data tier. The result is a tradeoff, where you can favor any one of the following approaches:

- Create a "thin" business layer that uses methods that correspond very closely to stored procedures and other database-specific parameters. In fact, some programs use business objects that are just thin wrappers on top of a live cursor-based database connection (like an ADO recordset). Unfortunately, this business layer requires significant rework if the database changes.

- Create an average business layer that lets the user interface retrieve whatever data it wants. The business tier relies on accessing the database using generic SQL statements. It's very expandable and generic, but database performance will be terrible.

- Create a "thick" business layer that tries to match requests from the user interface with an optimized execution path for a specific database. With a little luck and careful coding, performance could be as good as the first option, and the layer could be nearly as generic as the second. However, writing this tier is a major programming undertaking that takes exponentially more time.

## Three-Tier Design Consistency

There's nothing explicitly wrong with three-tier design, but it isn't a magic solution. For one thing, it's a rather vague recommendation that has more guidelines than requirements. Developers can interpret it any way they want.

For example, consider an application that reads customer information from a database and displays it in an attractive list control. At first glance, it seems like a straightforward task. But consider the number of different ways it could be modeled with objects:

- A CustomerData class fetches information from the database, and returns it as a DataSet. Your code then manually reads the DataSet and adds the information to a list control.

- A CustomerData class fetches information from the database. You also create a customized CustomerList control class that knows how to fill itself using the DataSet it receives from CustomerData.

- A CustomerData class fetches information from the database. However, the CustomerData class also receives a reference to the list control that needs to be filled. The CustomerData class has the built-in smarts to know how to fill the list control's collection of items.

- A CustomerData class fetches information from the database. A special helper class, FillListFromDataSet handles the conversion of the information in the DataSet to information in the generic list control.

Which approach is the best one? It's difficult to say. The third option is somewhat suspicious, because it seems that the CustomerData class is being given additional responsibilities beyond the scope it was designed for. Some of the other scenarios make assumptions about the appropriate way to exchange data. But the greatest problem with all of these examples is that there is no guarantee that the other classes in the application will follow this pattern.

**TIP** *An object-oriented framework sets out rules that determine how objects will interact and communicate. When creating a user interface, you have to develop your framework at the same time that you plan your individual objects.*

## Fixing Three-Tier Design

By now you have probably realized that the most important decision you can make is to define how your user interface objects should interact. This is the simplest way to improve your designs without adopting a single specific solution.

To get a better idea about how you might apply three-tier design in the .NET world, consider the simple application below. It uses a TreeView that displays a list of product categories drawn from a database. When you expand a category node, you see all the relevant products. When a record is selected, the corresponding information appears on a list on the left (see Figure 2-7).

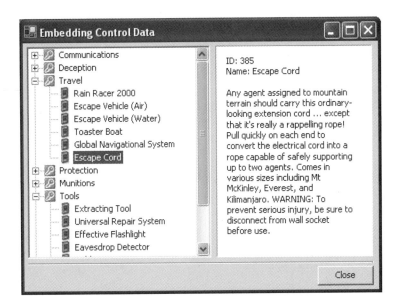

*Figure 2-7. An intelligent TreeView database browser*

There are several important considerations:

- The whole tree can't necessarily be filled at once. (Whether it actually should depends on the size of the database.) The solution needs the flexibility to be able to fill parts of the trees "just in time," and potentially make multiple trips to the database. An even better solution might make use of threading to asynchronously fetch and add results, or create some kind of paged list.

- The component that returns the data can't assume that the information is destined for a TreeView—the design may change, or the same information may be reused in multiple locations.

- The TreeView needs to be able to accept the data in an easily interpretable format. It shouldn't need to recognize specific database tables and fields by their "real" names.

Obviously, there are different ways this application can retrieve information from the database. It could use custom data objects, but that would require category and product objects that use multiple property procedures. The user interface code would then have to retrieve these properties specifically by name, and decide on an appropriate order. For some applications, this approach would work, but in this case it would choke a relatively simple browser with extra classes and code.

## The DataSet to the Rescue

Instead, information in our example is sent in a neat package called the DataSet. The DataSet is found in the System.Data class, and is often referred to as a part of Microsoft's ADO.NET technology. Unlike the objects in earlier ADO, the DataSet is an ideal solution for information transfer in an application.

- It's much more generic. All .NET languages support the DataSet.

- It's inherently portable across language and platform boundaries, because it allows you to quickly swap information into XML (which is another great way to shuffle information around in a program).

- It's inherently disconnected. Unlike some business objects created in ADO, that are really just Rowset objects with hidden cursors, the DataSet is a discrete copy of information, which makes it easy to transfer and even hold for as long as you want.

- The DataSet loosely mirrors a database. Your business layer can easily add column mapping and perform other tricks, making sure the user interface layer gets exactly what it expects, regardless of the underlying data source.

- The DataSet can contain several tables at once. It can contain data relationships, which makes it easy to navigate through the data, but these relationships are independent of whatever relationships exist in the actual data source.

- It has update possibilities. If you want to hold onto the DataSet, you can make use of built-in methods to withdraw the changed rows and resubmit them to the appropriate business object.

In other words, the DataSet might just save three-tier design. It allows a way to transfer information that's much more lightweight than dedicated classes, but not necessarily tied to a specific database. You can browse through its rows and fields as collections, which makes it easy to add information to list-like controls without needing to look for specific field names. Of course, when you want to start formatting column widths and setting column orders, your user interface may need to know a fair amount of information about the data. As long as you place this information in a central repository (generally a resource class with shared members), your user interface will be extensible and easy to change.

> **NOTE** *Where's the code? In this chapter, the emphasis is on concepts. If you really need to see the specific implementation details—which use a combination of data embedding, a dedicated data class, and the ADO.NET data objects—skip ahead to Chapter 9, which shows this code and several other data-enabled user interface controls.*

## Validation and Business Objects

Before continuing, allow me to debunk one myth about business objects. It's sometimes argued that business objects are an ideal way to store and transfer data because they can provide integrated error checking. In all honesty, the value of this error checking is limited. First, it's duplicating information in the database, which adds extra overhead for writing the code. More important, the error checking happens when the value is assigned, which is too late for it to be useful in the actual user interface. As you learned in the last chapter, the best thing you can do for users is to restrict their ability to make mistakes. That means you have to act on an error as soon as it happens, or better yet, forbid it entirely.

No matter what, your user interface has to be designed with some business rules built-in (for example, forbidding letters in a text box that represents an invoice amount). Your data source performs the final error checking. There's not much use in adding new layers of error checking between these two (except to verify that your client code is behaving correctly). Even the best three-tier design can't escape the need to import business rules into the interface.

## Other Types of Application

The TreeView DataSet example above is a viable solution for many traditional database applications, which allow information to be reviewed, analyzed, and modified. Other types of applications may need other allowances.

- For example, a three-dimensional action game breaks down the barrier between the user interface and the "business" layer. Every object in the game is tightly bound to its on-screen appearance, and also makes use of a slew of programming algorithms to calculate how it moves and what it does. Object communication for this type of application is completely different.

- As another example, consider a live running tutorial. This kind of application might lend itself most easily to three-tier design. The information in a file is completely processed and delivered in a business object. The user interface is consistent, probably using a single window with several custom classes and a main controller. The controller retrieves information from the business objects, and delivers it to the appropriate user interface class, which handles the display.

- Or consider document-based applications. These applications are also easier to implement as three-tier designs, because they are based around a well-defined view that allows you to modify a single underlying data object. There just isn't the variety of information and ways of interacting with it that makes many database or hybrid applications more difficult to program and organize.

## The Last Word

Three-tier design is an abstraction. No successful application will implement it exactly. However, it's also a powerful guideline that helps you shape how classes interact in your application. It may seem strange to start talking about DataSets and business objects in a book on user interface design. (In fact, there are other excellent .NET books entirely on data access.) But as you'll see, when you set specific rules about how the user interface tier can communicate with other parts of your program, you start to make the transition from a simple collection of objects to a true user interface framework.

The following chapters of this book focus on mastering the tools of .NET user interfaces. Considerations for design and user interface architecture crop up periodically, but they take a back seat to the amazing new programming model of .NET. This chapter was designed to give you the background in application architecture that you need to understand this "other layer." If you keep the considerations of this chapter in mind as you continue reading, you'll discover an entirely new and richer way to program user interfaces.

This chapter also introduced you to the broad picture of user interface in the .NET world, and the basic design assumptions that Visual Studio .NET makes automatically. These decisions can be altered, and the .NET framework itself allows you a considerable amount of freedom to create the exact framework that you want. In later chapters you'll learn how to exploit this freedom to create all types of custom controls.

# CHAPTER 3

# Control Class Basics

THIS CHAPTER EXPLORES the Control class, which provides basic functionality for the family of Windows controls. You will learn about fundamental topics like mouse and keyboard handling, focus, and control relations. Along the way, I'll also introduce some important pieces of the System.Drawing namespace that allow you to create structures that represent colors, fonts, rectangles, and points.

## The Windows Forms Package

.NET provides two toolkits for user interface design: one for web applications, and one for Windows development. This chapter introduces the Windows Forms package, which allows you to create the traditional rich graphical interfaces found in everything from office productivity software to arcade games. The one detail that all these applications have in common is the fact that they are built out of windows—tiny pieces of screen real estate that can present information and receive user input.

It's easy to imagine that "Windows Forms" refers to a special part of the .NET class library, where fundamental classes like Form and Control are stored. This is true, but it isn't the whole story. More accurately, Windows Forms is the technology that allows the Common Language Runtime to interact with control objects and translate them into the low-level reality of the Windows operating system. In other words, you create objects that represent controls and windows, and the Common Language Runtime handles the details like routing messages, keeping track of window handles, and calling functions from the Windows API.

This idea isn't new. In the past, developers have used the MFC framework in C++, WFC in J++, and Visual Basic's own "Ruby" forms engine to insulate themselves from some of the low-level details of Windows programming. These frameworks all provide an object-oriented wrapper around the Windows API (which, on its own, is a disorganized collection holding hundreds of miscellaneous C routines). These frameworks were well intentioned, but they have all suffered from a few problems.

- **Lack of consistency.** If you learn how to use MFC, you still won't know anything about creating Visual Basic user interfaces. Even though every framework ultimately interacts with the Windows API, they have dramatically different object models and philosophies.

- **Thin layer/thick layer problems.** Frameworks tend to be either easy to use, or powerful, but not both. MFC is really only a couple of steps away from Windows messages and low-level grunt work. On the other hand, Visual Basic developers have the benefit of a simple framework, but face the lingering dread that they will need to delve into the raw Windows API for complex or unusual tasks that are beyond Visual Basic's bounds.

- **Subjugation to Windows API rules.** The Windows API dictates certain harsh realities. For example, once you create a fixed-border window, you can't make its border resizable. These limitations make sense based on how the Windows API is organized, but they often lead to confusing inconsistencies in a framework's object model.

The result of these limitations is that there are essentially two types of frameworks: those that are complicated to use for simple tasks (like MFC), and those that are easy to use for simple tasks, but difficult or impossible to use for complex tasks (like VB). These object models provide a modern way to code user interfaces, but many programmers wonder why they should abstract the Windows API when its restrictions remain.

## The .NET Solution

.NET addresses these problems by becoming more ambitious. The result is a user interface framework that uses some innovative sleight-of-hand to perform tasks that are difficult or impossible with the Windows API. Here are some examples—tasks that .NET can perform but the Windows API cannot:

- Change fixed style properties like the selection type of a list box or the border type of a window.

- Change a form's owner.

- Move an MDI child window from one MDI parent window to another.

- Transform an MDI child window into an MDI parent and vice versa.

- Move controls from one window to another.

Clearly this list includes a couple of tricks that a self-respecting application will probably never need to use. Still, they illustrate an important fact: .NET doesn't just provide an easier object model to access the Windows API; it also provides capabilities that extend it. The result is a framework that works the way you would intuitively expect it to work based on its objects.

**NOTE** *The samples for this chapter include a project called ImpossibleAPI, which shows one of these "broken rules"–a child window that can jump between different MDI parents whenever the user clicks a button.*

All of this raises an interesting question. How can a programming model built on the Windows API actually perform feats that the Windows API can't? Truthfully, there's nothing in the preceding list that couldn't be simulated with the Windows API with a fair bit of effort. For example, you could appear to change the border style of a window by destroying and recreating an identical window. To do so you would have to rigorously track and restore all the information from the previous window.

In fact, this is more or less what takes place in .NET. If you examine the control or window handle (the numeric value that identifies the window to the operating system), you'll see that it changes when you perform these unusual operations. This signifies that, on an operating system level, .NET actually provides you with a new window or control. The difference is that .NET handles this destruction and recreation automatically. The illusion is so perfect that it's hardly an illusion at all (any more than the illusion that .NET web controls can maintain state, or that television shows continuous movement, rather than just a series of still images).

The cost of this functionality is a runtime that requires a fair bit of intelligence. However, .NET programs already need an intelligent runtime to provide modern features like improved code access security and managed memory. The Windows Forms are just another part of the ambitious and sprawling .NET framework.

Some programmers may still feel they need to resort to the Windows API. You can still use API calls in your .NET applications without too much trouble. However, I encourage you to abandon those habits and start dealing with the new .NET abstractions. Not only is it easier, it also provides a short path to some remarkable features.

> **TIP** *One of the best pieces of advice for beginning Visual Basic programmers in traditional VB development was to master the Windows API. This low-level look at the system was often indispensable for solving problems that the built-in Ruby engine couldn't. However, in .NET the story changes. If you are a VB .NET developer (or a C# developer, or any other .NET developer), you'll get the most benefit by studying the low-level details of the .NET object libraries, not the API. Believe it or not, the operating system details will not be as important in the next generation of software development. Instead, you'll need to know the full range of properties, methods, and types that are at your fingertips to unlock the secrets of becoming a .NET guru.*

## The Control Class

Chapter 2 introduced .NET control classes, and examined their place in the overall architecture of an application. To summarize:

- You create and manipulate controls and forms using .NET classes. The Common Language Runtime recognizes these classes, and handles the low-level Windows details for you.

- You use a control from the .NET class library by creating an instance of the appropriate class, and adding it to the Controls collection of a container control, like a panel or form. Whether you add the control at design-time or run-time, the task is the same.

- You configure controls by setting properties. In addition, you can react to control events in two ways: by creating an event handler (typically in the Form class), or by deriving a custom control and overriding the corresponding method.

Every .NET control derives from the base class System.Windows.Forms.Control. Depending on the complexity of the control, it may pass through a few more stages in its evolution. Figure 3-1 shows some the basic hierarchy of controls.

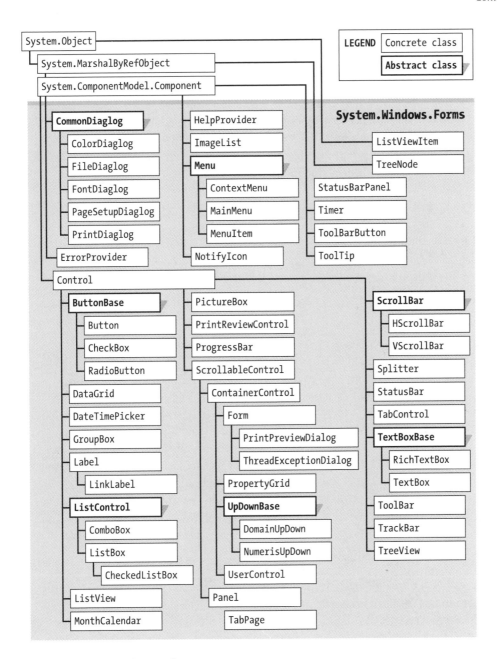

*Figure 3-1. Control hierarchy*

On its own the Control class has no real purpose. It's mainly interesting for the basic functionality that it defines. Sorting through the functionality is no easy task. The 200+ members include countless properties, events that fire to notify you when most common properties are changed (like VisibleChanged, TextChanged, SizeChanged, and so on), and methods that reset values to their defaults, along with some more useful and unusual members. The sections in this chapter sort through many of the properties under broad topic-specific headings like "color" and "focus." Before you begin your exploration, you may want to check out some of the basic and system-related members in Table 3-1.

*Table 3-1. Basic Control Members*

| Member | Description |
| --- | --- |
| Name | Provides a short string of descriptive text that identifies your control. Usually (and by default, if you are using Visual Studio .NET), this is the same as the name of the form-level member variable that refers to the control. However, there's no direct relation; the Name property is just provided to help you when iterating through a control collection looking for a specific item. |
| Tag | Provides a convenient place to store an object. The Tag property is not used by the .NET framework. Instead, you use it to store associated data (like a data object or a unique ID). It's particularly useful when dealing with list controls. Unlike the Tag property in previous versions of Visual Basic, it can store any type of information or even a full-fledged object. |
| Controls and ControlAdded and ControlRemoved events | The Controls collection stores references to all child controls. You can use the associated events to automate layout logic, as you'll see in Chapter 11. |
| DesignMode | Returns True if the control is in design mode. It's useful when you are deriving or creating a custom control, so you don't perform time-consuming or system-endangering operations when the program is not running (like an automatic refresh). |

*Table 3-1. Basic Control Members (Continued)*

| Member | Description |
|---|---|
| Invoke() and InvokeRequired | These members are used in multithreaded programming. InvokeRequired returns True if the control is hosted on a different thread than the current thread of execution. In this case, you should not attempt to use the control directly. Instead, place the code that manipulates the control in a separate method, and pass a delegate that points to this method to the Control.Invoke() method. This ensures that your code will be marshaled to the correct thread. |
| Dispose() | This method, which is called automatically by the .NET framework as part of the form infrastructure, releases the resources held by a control (like the operating system window handle). |

Because every control is derived from the Control class, you can always use it as a lowest common denominator for dealing with some basic Control properties in your application. For example, consider the form below, shown in Figure 3-2, which provides a text box, label, and button control. You'll find this example in the online samples as the ControlMedley project.

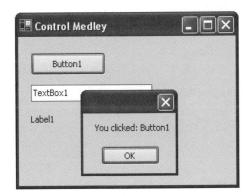

*Figure 3-2. A medley of different controls*

The Click event for all these controls (and the underlying form) is handled by one event handler. The event handler code is generic: it converts the object reference of the sender into the control type, and then displays a message with the name of the clicked control.

```
Private Sub ctrlClick(ByVal sender As System.Object, ByVal e As EventArgs) _
   Handles MyBase.Click, Button1.Click, Label1.Click, TextBox1.Click

    Dim ctrl As Control = CType(sender, Control)
    MessageBox.Show("You clicked: " & ctrl.Name)

End Sub
```

This is one of the ways that you can replace control arrays, which were a Visual Basic 6 standby. In fact, this technique is more powerful than control arrays because it allows you to handle similar events from any type of control, rather than limiting you to one type of control (e.g., a Button) and one type of event (e.g., Button.Click).

## Position and Size

A control's position is defined by the distance between its top-left corner and the top-left corner of its container. Often, the container is a form, but it could also be a container control like a panel or group box. Similarly, the size is measured as the width and height of the control from the top-left point. By convention, the position measurement is positive in the downward and rightward directions.

> **NOTE**  *In the later chapters on GDI+, you will discover that is possible to create specialized controls that have irregular boundaries by using the Region property. Chapter 5 previews this technique with irregularly shaped forms.*

All values are integers measured in pixels. They are provided through several properties (including Top, Left, Right, and Bottom for position, and Width and Height for size), as shown in Figure 3-3. Although you can manipulate any of these properties, the preferred way for setting position is by using the Location property with a Point structure. Similarly, the preferred way to define size is to use the Size property with a Size structure. These basic structures originate from the System.Drawing namespace.

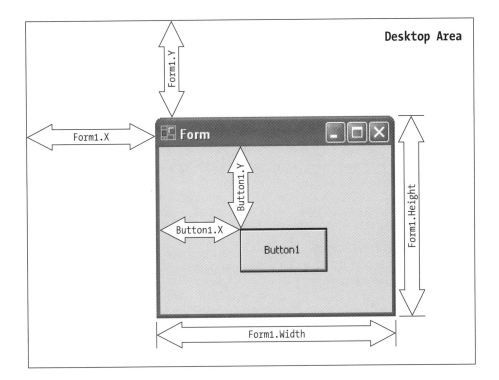

*Figure 3-3. Control measurements*

The following code shows how you can set the location and size of a control using the Point and Size structures.

```
Dim pt As New System.Drawing.Point()
pt.X = 300    ' The control will be 300 pixels from the left
pt.Y = 500    ' The control will be 500 pixels from the top.
ctrl.Location = pt

Dim sz As New System.Drawing.Size()
sz.Width = 500
sz.Height = 60
ctrl.Size = sz

' Just for fun, set another control to have the same size.
ctrl2.Size = ctrl.Size
```

By importing the System.Drawing namespace and using some handy constructors, you can simplify this code considerably.

```
ctrl.Location = New Point(300, 500)  ' Order is (X, Y)
ctrl.Size = New Size(500, 60)        ' Order is (Width, Height)
```

This latter approach is the one that Visual Studio .NET takes when it creates code for your controls at design-time. There are other size and position-related properties, such as those used for anchoring and docking when creating automatically resizable forms. These are described in detail in Chapter 5.

> **TIP** *The Visual Studio .NET designer provides a slew of tools that make it easier to lay out controls. Look under the Format menu for options that let you automatically align, space, and center controls. You can also right-click a control and choose to "lock" it in place, ensuring that it won't accidentally be moved while you create and manipulate other controls.*

## Color

Every control defines a ForeColor and BackColor property. For different controls, these properties have slightly different meanings. In a simple control like a label or text box, the foreground color is the color of the text, while the background color is the area behind it. These values default to the Windows system-configured settings.

Colors are specified as Color structures from the System.Drawing namespace. It's extremely easy to create a color object, because you have several different options. You can create a color using:

- An ARGB (alpha, red, green, blue) color value. You specify each value as integer.

- An environment setting from the current color scheme. You choose the correspondingly named property from the SystemColors class.

- A predefined .NET color name. You choose the correspondingly named property from the Color class.

- An HTML color name. You specify this value as a string using the ColorTranslator class.

- An OLE color code. You specify this value as an integer (representing a hexadecimal value) using the ColorTranslator class.

- A Win32 color code. You specify this value as an integer (representing a hexadecimal value) using the ColorTranslator class.

The code listing that follows shows several ways to specify a color using the Color, ColorTranslator, and SystemColors types. In order to use this code as written, you must import the System.Drawing namespace.

```
' Create a color from an ARGB value
Dim Alpha As Integer = 255, Red As Integer = 0
Dim Green As Integer = 255, Blue As Integer = 0
ctrl.ForeColor = Color.FromARGB(alpha, red, green, blue)

' Create a color from an environment setting
ctrl.ForeColor = SystemColors.HighlightText

' Create a color using a .NET name
ctrl.ForeColor = Color.Crimson

' Create a color from an HTML code
ctrl.ForeColor = ColorTranslator.FromHtml("Blue")

' Create a color from an OLE color code
ctrl.ForeColor = ColorTranslator.FromOle(&HFF00)

' Create a color from a Win32 color code
ctrl.ForeColor = ColorTranslator.FromWin32(&HA000)
```

The next code snippet shows how you can transform the KnownColors enumeration into an array of strings that represent color names. This can be useful if you need to display a list of valid colors (by name) in an application.

```
Dim ColorNames() As String
ColorNames = System.Enum.GetNames(GetType(KnownColor))
```

Changing a color name string back to the appropriate enumerated value is just as easy using the special shared Enum.Parse() method. This method compares the string against all the available values in an enumeration, and chooses the matching one.

```
Dim MyColor As KnownColor
MyColor = System.Enum.Parse(GetType(KnownColor), ColorName)

' For example, if ColorName is "Azure" then MyColor will be set
' to the enumerated value KnownColor.Azure (which is also the integer value 32).
```

Incidentally, you can use a few useful methods on any Color structure to retrieve color information. For example, you can use GetBrightness(), GetHue(), and GetSaturation().

Here's a complete program that puts all of these techniques to work. When it loads, it fills a list control with all the known colors. When the user selects an item, the background of the form is adjusted accordingly (see Figure 3-4).

```
Public Class ColorChange
    Inherits System.Windows.Forms.Form

    ' (Designer code omitted.)
    Friend WithEvents lstColors As System.Windows.Forms.ListBox

    Private Sub ColorChange_Load(ByVal sender As System.Object, _
     ByVal e As System.EventArgs) Handles MyBase.Load
        Dim ColorNames() As String
        ColorNames = System.Enum.GetNames(GetType(KnownColor))
        lstColors.Items.AddRange(ColorNames)
    End Sub

    Private Sub lstColors_SelectedIndexChanged(ByVal sender As System.Object, _
     ByVal e As System.EventArgs) Handles lstColors.SelectedIndexChanged

        ' Set color.
        Dim SelectedColor As KnownColor
        SelectedColor = System.Enum.Parse(GetType(KnownColor), lstColors.Text)
        Me.BackColor = System.Drawing.Color.FromKnownColor(SelectedColor)

        ' Display color information.
        lblBrightness.Text = "Brightness = " & _
                             Me.BackColor.GetBrightness.ToString()
        lblHue.Text = "Hue = " & Me.BackColor.GetHue.ToString()
        lblSaturation.Text = "Saturation = " & _
                             Me.BackColor.GetSaturation.ToString()
    End Sub

End Class
```

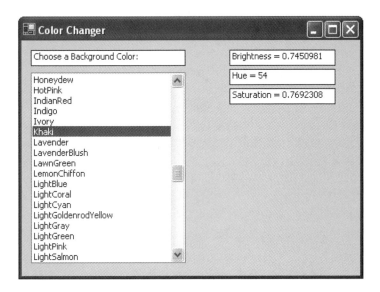

*Figure 3-4. A color changing form*

## Fonts and Text

The Control object defines a Text property that is used by derived controls for a variety of purposes. For a text box, the Text property corresponds to the information displayed in the text box, which can be modified by the user. For controls like labels, command buttons, or forms, the Text property refers to static descriptive text displayed as a title or caption.

The font of a control's text is defined by the Font property, which uses an instance of the System.Drawing.Font class. Note that a Font object does not just represent a typeface (like Tahoma). Instead, it encapsulates all details about the font family, point size, and styles (like bold and italic).

```
' You can create a font with one of the 13 constructors.
ctrl.Font = New Font("Tahoma", 8, FontStyle.Bold)
```

**TIP** *A traditional default font for Windows programs is often Microsoft Sans Serif. However, newer applications since Windows 98 consistently use the slightly more attractive Tahoma font (which is also better for input, as it distinguishes between characters like a lowercase "l" and uppercase "I"). You should use the Tahoma font in your applications.*

A Control.FontHeight property is also provided, which returns the height of your chosen font in pixels. This setting allows you to perform calculations when you are drawing special graphics or text on a control manually. For example, you could manually space lines the appropriate amount when drawing text directly onto a form background.

Note that font families are set using a string, rather than a type-safe enumerated property. If you try to create an object using a name that does not correspond to an installed font, .NET automatically (and unhelpfully) defaults to the Microsoft Sans Serif font. An error does not occur. You may want to explicitly check the Font.Name property to check if this automatic substitution has been made.

To determine what fonts are installed on the system, you can enumerate through them with the System.Drawing.Text.InstalledFontCollection class. The example below adds the name of every installed font to a list box.

```
Dim Family As FontFamily, Fonts As New InstalledFontCollection
For Each Family In Fonts.Families
    lstAvailableFonts.Add(Family.Name)
Next
```

The online samples for this chapter include a FontViewer utility that uses this technique to create a list of fonts. The user can choose a font from a drop-down list control, and a sample line of text will be painted directly on the window (see Figure 3-5). To perform the font painting, the application uses some of the GDI+ methods you'll see in Chapter 12.

> **NOTE**  *Note that the Font property does not always configure the appearance of the text in the control. For example, the font of all windows is defined by the system and is unchangeable. Instead, the Form.Font property defines the default font for all contained controls.*

## Access Keys

Some controls (namely buttons and menu items) allow a character in their caption to be highlighted and used as an access key. For example, button controls often underline one character in the caption. If the user presses the Ctrl key and that character, the button is "clicked" automatically. To configure these shortcuts keys just add an ampersand (&) before the special letter, as in "Sa&ve" to make "v" the access key. (If you actually want to use an ampersand, you'll need to include the text "&&".)

*Figure 3-5. A simple font viewer*

## Control Relations

Chapter 2 described how controls like forms, panels, and group boxes can contain other controls. To add or remove a child control, you use the collection provided in the Controls property. Control objects also provide other properties that help you manage and identify their relationships, as you see in Table 3-2.

*Table 3-2. Members for Control Relationships*

| Member | Description |
|---|---|
| HasChildren | Returns True if the Controls collection has at least one child control. |
| Controls | A special collection that allows you to add or examine child controls. |
| Parent | A reference to the parent control (the control that contains this control). This could be a form, or a container control like a group box. You can set this property to swap a control into a new container. |
| TopLevelControl and FindForm() | The TopLevelControl returns a reference to the control at the top of the hierarchy. Typically, this is the containing form. The FindForm() method is similar, but it returns null if the control is not situated on a form. |
| Contains() | This method accepts a control, and returns True if this control is a child of the current control. |

*Table 3-2. Members for Control Relationships (Continued)*

| Member | Description |
|--------|-------------|
| GetChildAtPoint() | This method accepts a Point structure that corresponds to a location inside the current control. If a child control is located at this point, it is returned. |
| ContextMenu and Menu | These properties return the associated context menu (for a basic control) or menu object (for a form). Note that context menus must be explicitly displayed by your code before the user can interact with them, while pull-down menus appear automatically. |

## Focus and the Tab Sequence

In the Windows operating system, a user can only work with one control at a time. The control that is currently receiving the user's key presses is the control that has focus. Sometimes this control is drawn slightly differently. For example, the button control uses a dotted line around its caption to show that it has the focus. Figure 3-6 shows focused and unfocused buttons with both the classic Windows look and Windows XP visual styles.

*Figure 3-6. Focused buttons*

To move the focus, the user can click the mouse or use the tab key. The developer has to take some care to make sure that the tab key moves focus in a logical manner (generally from left to right and then down the form). The developer also has to choose the control that should receive the focus when the window is first presented.

All controls that support focusing provide a Boolean TabStop property. When set to True, the control can receive focus. When set to False, the control is left out of the tab sequence and can only be reached using a mouse click.

> **TIP**  *You should set the TabStop property to False for controls that can accept key presses but are not directly accessed by the user in your application. For example, you might provide a DataGrid control, but use it to display static information. Of course, setting the TabStop to False also means the user will need to use the mouse to scroll the control, if its contents extend beyond the bounds of its display region.*

To set the tab order, you configure a control's TabIndex property. The control with a TabIndex of 0 gets the focus first. When the user presses the tab key, the focus moves to the next control in the tab order, as long as it can accept focus. Visual Studio .NET provides a special tool, shown in Figure 3-7, that allows you to quickly set tab order. Just select View ➤ Tab Order for the menu. You can then assign TabIndex values by clicking controls in the desired order.

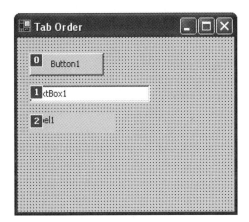

*Figure 3-7. The Visual Studio .NET tab order tool*

Label controls have a TabIndex setting even though they cannot receive focus. This allows you to use a label with an access key. When the user triggers the label's access key, the focus is automatically forwarded to the next control in the tab order. For that reason, you should give your labels an appropriate place in the tab order, especially if they use access keys. (You create an access key by placing an ampersand character before a letter in the label's text.)

Controls that are invisible or disabled (commonly known as "greyed out") are generally skipped in the tab order, and are not activated regardless of the TabIndex and TabStop settings. To hide or disable a control, you set the Visible and Enabled properties, respectively. Note that if you hide or disable a control at design time, the appearance is not modified. This is a deliberate idiosyncrasy designed to make it easier to work with controls at design time, and it is recommended that custom controls also follow this pattern. Some other properties and methods for managing the focus programmatically are described in Table 3-3.

*Table 3-3. Members for Dealing with Focus at Runtime*

| Member | Description |
| --- | --- |
| Focused | Returns True if the control currently has the focus. |
| ContainsFocus | Returns True if the control or one of its children currently has the focus. |
| Focus() | Sets the focus to the current control. |
| SelectNextControl() | Sets the focus to the next control in tab order. This is the programmatic equivalent of pressing the tab key. |
| GetNextControl() | Returns a reference to the next control in the tab order, without moving the focus. |
| LostFocus and GotFocus events | These events fire after the focus has moved. They do not give you the chance to stop the focus change, and are thus poor choices for validation routines. If you insist on programmatically resetting the focus in an event handler for one of these events, you may trigger a neverending loop of focus events. Instead, use the validation events or the ErrorProvider control, which are described in Chapter 4. |

**TIP** *The GetNextControl() and SelectNextControl() methods are particularly useful when you are combining some type of interactive wizard or application help, as it can direct the user to an important control or part of the screen.*

# Responding to the Mouse and Keyboard

Controls also provide some built-in intelligence for dealing with the keyboard and mouse. These include low-level events that react to key presses and mouse movement, and methods that return key and mouse button state information, as shown in Table 3-4.

*Table 3-4. Events for Reacting to the Keyboard*

| Event | Description |
|-------|-------------|
| KeyDown | Occurs when a key is pressed while the current control has focus. The event provides additional information (through KeyEventArgs) about the state of the Alt and Ctrl keys and the key code. |
| KeyPress | This is a higher-level event that occurs once the key press is complete (but before the character appears, if the control is an input control). The event provides a KeyPressEventArgs object with information about the key character. The KeyPressEventArgs object also provides a Handled property, which you can set to True to cancel further processing, effectively canceling the character and suppressing its display in an input control. |
| KeyUp | This occurs when a key is released, just after the KeyPress event. It provides information through a KeyEventArgs object. |

Generally you will react to the KeyDown and KeyUp events when you need to react to special characters like the arrow keys, which do not trigger KeyPress events. The KeyPress event is used when you need to restrict input and perform character validation.

If you want to update the display or react to a changed text value in an input control, you would probably not use any of these events. Instead, you should react to the higher-level Changed event, which fires when any modifications are made. The Changed event will fire if you modify the text programmatically or the user deletes the text with the right-click menu.

Forms provide a Boolean KeyPreview property. If you set this to True, your form receives key press events when any of its controls have focus, and it receives these events before the control does (Table 3-5). This technique is useful if you are programming a customized interface or a game where you need to take complete control of the keyboard. You'll also see in Chapter 14 that this technique is useful when you are handling the F1 key to create your own context-sensitive help system.

*Table 3-5. Events for Reacting to the Mouse*

| Event | Description |
|-------|-------------|
| MouseEnter | Occurs when the mouse moves into a control's region. |
| MouseMove* | Occurs when the mouse is moved over a control by a single pixel. Event handlers are provided with additional information about the current coordinates of the mouse pointer. Be warned that a typical mouse movement can generate dozens of MouseMove events. Event handlers that react to this event can be used to update the display, but not for more time-consuming tasks. |
| MouseHover | Occurs when the mouse lingers, without moving, over the control for a system-specified amount of time (typically a couple of seconds). Usually, you react to this event to highlight the control that is being hovered over, or update the display with some dynamic information. |
| MouseDown* | Occurs when a mouse button is clicked. |
| MouseUp* | Occurs when a mouse button is released. For many controls, this is where the logic for right-button mouse clicks is coded, although MouseDown is also sometimes used. |
| Click | Occurs when a control is clicked. Generally, this event occurs after the MouseDown event but before the MouseUp event. For basic controls, a Click event is triggered for left-button and right-button mouse clicks. Some controls have a special meaning for this event. One example is the button control. You can raise a Button Click event by tabbing to the button and pressing the Enter key, or clicking with the left mouse button. Right-button clicks on a button trigger MouseDown and MouseUp events, but not Click events. |
| DoubleClick | Occurs when a control is clicked twice in succession. A Click event is still generated for the first click, while the second click generates the DoubleClick event. |
| MouseWheel | Occurs when the mouse wheel moves while the control has focus. The mouse pointer is not necessarily positioned over the control. |
| MouseLeave | Occurs when the mouse leaves a control's region. |

* Indicates that the event handler uses the MouseEvent delegate, and provides additional information about the location of the mouse pointer (and X and Y properties), the mouse wheel movement (Delta), and the state of the mouse buttons (Button).

The MouseMove, MouseDown, and MouseUp events provide additional information about the state of the mouse buttons. Separate MouseDown and MouseUp events are triggered for every mouse button. In this case, the MouseEventArgs.Button property indicates the button the caused the event.

```
Private Sub lbl_MouseUp(ByVal sender As Object, _
  ByVal e As System.Windows.Forms.MouseEventArgs) Handles lbl.MouseUp

    If e.Button = MouseButtons.Right
        ' This event was caused by a right-click.
        ' Here is a good place to show a context menu.
    End If

End Sub
```

In the MouseMove event, however, the Button property indicates *all* the buttons that are currently depressed. That means that this property could take on more than one value from the MouseButtons enumeration. To test for a button, you need to use bitwise arithmetic.

```
Private Sub lbl_MouseMove(ByVal sender As Object, _
  ByVal e As System.Windows.Forms.MouseEventArgs) Handles lbl.MouseMove

    If (e.Button And MouseButtons.Right) = MouseButtons.Right
        ' The right mouse button is currently being held down.
        If (e.Button And MouseButtons.Left) = MouseButtons.Left
            ' You can only get here if both the left and the right mouse buttons
            ' are currently held down.
        End If
    End If

End Sub
```

Every control also provides a MousePosition, MouseButtons, and ModifierKeys property for information about the mouse and keyboard. These properties are less useful than the event data. For example, if you use them in an event handler they retrieve information about the *current* location of the mouse pointer, not the position where it was when the event was triggered. Additionally, the MousePosition property uses screen coordinates, not control coordinates. However, this information can still be useful when you are reacting to an event that doesn't provide mouse information. In Chapter 11 you'll see how it can be used with a dynamic drawing application.

## A Mouse/Keyboard Example

The mouse and keyboard events have some subtleties, and it's always best to get a solid and intuitive understanding by watching it in action. The sample code for this chapter provides an ideal example that creates a list of common mouse and keyboard events as they take place. Each entry also includes some event information, giving you an accurate idea of the order in which these events occur, and the information they provide.

MouseMove events are not included in the list (because they would quickly swamp it with entries), but a separate label control reports on the current position of the mouse (see Figure 3-8).

For example, here's the code that adds an entry in response to the pic.MouseLeave event:

```
Private Sub pic_MouseLeave(ByVal sender As Object, ByVal e As System.EventArgs) _
  Handles pic.MouseLeave
    Log("Mouse Leave")
End Sub
```

The private Log() function adds the string of information, and scrolls the list control to the bottom to ensure that it is visible.

```
Private Sub Log(ByVal data As String)
    lstLog.Items.Add(data)

    ' Scroll to the bottom of the list.
    Dim ItemsPerPage As Integer = lstLog.Height \ lstLog.ItemHeight
    lstLog.TopIndex = lstLog.Items.Count - ItemsPerPage
End Sub
```

## Mouse Cursors

One other useful mouse-related property is Cursor. It sets the type of mouse cursor that is displayed when the mouse is moved over a control, and it applies to all child controls. If your application is about to perform a potentially time-consuming operation, you might want to set the form's Cursor property to an hourglass. You can access standard system-defined cursors using the static properties of the Cursors class.

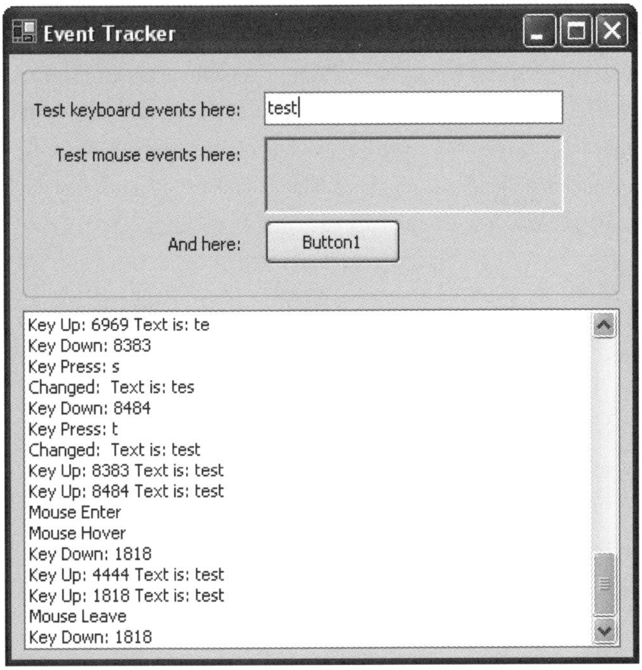

*Figure 3-8. An event tracker*

```
MyForm.Cursor = Cursors.WaitCursor
' (Perform long task.)
MyForm.Cursor = Cursors.Default
```

You can also create a custom cursor using the Cursor class, load a custom cursor graphic, and assign it to a control.

```
Dim MyCursor As New Cursor(Application.StartupPath & "mycursor.cur")
MyCustomControl.Cursor = MyCursor
```

Cursor files are similar to icons, but they are stored in a special .cur file format. Currently, animated cursors (.ani files) are not supported.

# Graphics and Painting

Controls provide a variety of events and properties related to painting. You'll find information about how to take control of these details (Table 3-6) and draw your own custom controls in the GDI+ chapters later in this book.

*Table 3-6. Graphics-Related Members*

| Member | Description |
| --- | --- |
| BackgroundImage | Allows you to show a picture in the background of a control. |
| Image (or ImageList and ImageIndex) | These properties aren't a part of the basic Control class, but they do appear in many common controls, including labels, buttons, checkboxes, and radio buttons. It allows you to insert a picture alongside or instead of text, as shown in Figure 3-8. You can set the image directly through the Image property, or by using a linked ImageList, as described in Chapter 6. |
| ImageAlign | Allows you to align a picture to any side or corner. It's not a part of the basic Control class, but it is found in many common controls. |
| ResizeRedraw | Indicates whether the control should automatically redraw itself when its size changes. The default is True. |
| CreateGraphics() | Creates a System.Drawing.Graphics object for the control (otherwise known as a device context). Used for custom drawing, as explained in Chapter 12. |
| Invalidate() and Refresh() | Triggers a repaint of the control. |
| Paint event | Occurs when the control is redrawn. Provides the device context, allowing you to perform some custom GDI+ drawing. |
| Resize event | Occurs when the control is resized, just before redrawing takes place. |

You can create an Image object using the shared Image.FromFile() method, which reads a standard bitmap format (like a BMP, GIF, JPEG, or PNG file).

```
Button1.Image = Image.FromFile(Application.StartupPath & "\mypic.bmp")
```

The Image class provides its own set of properties and methods. Some of the most interesting include RotateFlip(), which changes the picture orientation by rotating or inverting it, and GetThumbnailImage(), which returns an image object of the specified size that condenses the information from the original Image.

```
Dim MyImage, MyThumbnail As Image
MyImage = Image.FromFile(Application.StartupPath & "\mypic.bmp")

' Rotate by 270 degrees and flip about the Y-axis.
MyImage.RotateFlip(RotateFlipType.Rotate270FlipY)

' Create a 100 x 100 pixel thumbnail.
MyThumbnail = MyImage.GetThumbnailImage(100, 100, Nothing, Nothing)
```

Figure 3-9 shows common controls with embedded pictures. These can be added using the thoughtfully included Image and ImageAlign properties. However, if you place an image over a portion of the control text, the text will overwrite the image. No word wrapping is provided.

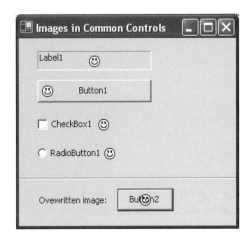

*Figure 3-9. Common control picture support*

## Low-Level Members

The .NET framework hides the low level ugliness of the Windows API, but it doesn't render it inaccessible. This is a major advantage of .NET over other frameworks like traditional VB: it adds features without removing any capabilities.

For example, if you want to use a DLL or Windows API function that requires a window handle, you can just retrieve the control's Handle property. The only special .NET consideration is that you should retrieve the handle immediately before you use it. Changing some properties can cause the control to be recreated, and receive a new handle.

You've probably also realized by now that low-level Windows messages are abstracted away in .NET controls, and replaced with more useful events that bundle additional information. If, however, you need to react to a message that doesn't have a corresponding event, you can handle it directly by overriding the PreProcessMessage() method. (You can also attach global message filters for your entire application by using the Application.AddMessageFilter() method).

This book focuses on pure .NET programming, and won't get into most of these tricks, which are really workarounds based on traditional Windows programming. If you do want to examine these features, try starting with the members described in Table 3-7.

*Table 3-7. Low-level Members*

| Member | Description |
| --- | --- |
| Handle | Provides an IntPtr structure (a 32-bit integer on 32-bit operating systems) that represents the current control's window handle. |
| RecreatingHandle | Set to True while the control is being recreated with a new handle. |
| GetStyle() and SetStyle() | Sets or gets a control style bit. Generally you will use higher-level properties to accomplish the same thing. |
| PreProcessMessage(), ProcessCmdKey(), ProcessKeyMessage(), ProcessKeyPreview(), and WndProc() | These methods are involved in processing a Windows message, which is represented as a Message structure. You can override these methods and use them to process special messages or block standard ones. |

## The Last Word

This chapter provided a lightning tour through the basics of .NET controls, including how they interact, receive messages, process keystrokes and mouse movements, and handle focus. It also detailed the basic ingredients from the System.Drawing namespace for creating and managing colors, fonts, images, and more. The next chapter puts this high-level theory to a more practical purpose by teaching you to master the basic set of windows controls.

# CHAPTER 4

# Classic Controls

THIS CHAPTER CONSIDERS some of the most common types of controls, like menus, text boxes, and buttons. Many of these controls have existed since the dawn of Windows programming and don't need much description. To keep things interesting I'll present some related .NET variants. For example, at the same time that you look at the label, list box, and domain controls, you will learn about the hyperlink label, checked list box, and rich date controls. I'll also describe menus in detail, and show you a few new tricks, including how you can add thumbnail images to owner-drawn menu items, and attach context menus to other controls.

The final part of this chapter demonstrates two advanced .NET features. First, you learn how you can add support for drag-and-drop operations to your .NET applications, and allow the user to move controls and transfer information. Then you examine different ways to implement validation to gracefully handle invalid input before it becomes a problem.

## Types of Controls

Not all controls are created equal. .NET uses specialized controls that don't appear on forms, enhance other controls, and provide backward compatibility with legacy ActiveX controls. The next few sections provide a whirlwind tour of these specialized control types, and how they fit into the .NET class library.

### Invisible Controls

Invisible controls don't require a portion of form real estate. These include controls that never have a visual appearance, like the Timer and the ErrorProvider. They also include others that appear in special circumstances or in windows of their own, like the ContextMenu and the common dialog controls (OpenFileDialog, SaveFileDialog, ColorDialog, and so on).

When you drag an invisible control onto the form surface, a special icon appears for it in the component tray (see Figure 4-1). You configure its properties through this icon. If you look at the automatically generated code for the form, you'll see that the code for creating the invisible control is added as it would be for a normal control. However, the invisible control is not added to the form's Controls collection.

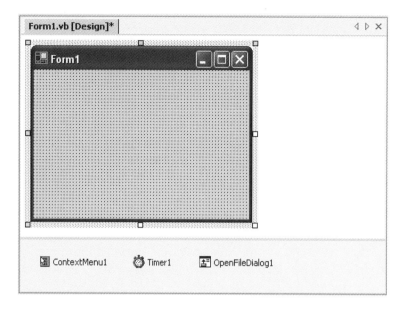

*Figure 4-1. The component tray*

In some cases, it's worth asking whether invisible controls are really controls at all. For example, the Timer is just a special way to automate user interface changes. In some respects, it's simpler than true multithreaded programming because it uses safe task switching and automatically performs its work on the user interface thread, ensuring that you don't need to marshal calls when interacting with a control. (In other words, there is no need to use the Control.Invoke() method, because the controls in the form are always on the same thread as the timer.) However, it's a far stretch to call the Timer a true control in the sense that the text box and label are.

> **NOTE** *Invisible controls don't derive from the Control class. Instead, they derive from System.ComponentModel.Component (the Control class also derives from this class). The Component class adds the basic features needed for an item to be hosted in a container and provides a Dispose() method that causes it to release its resources immediately.*

Often, invisible controls can be created more flexibly at runtime in your own code. In some cases (like when you want to share one invisible control between forms), it's a necessity. For the most part, it's a matter of preference. One example is the common dialog controls, which are described in the following chapter. Menus are another example of invisible controls, and are described later in this chapter.

## Provider Controls

Providers are a special type of invisible control. They extend the properties of other controls on the current form. For example, the ToolTipProvider allows any control to display a tooltip when the mouse hovers over it. To use the ToolTipProvider, drag an instance of it onto the form.

You can then set a tooltip in one of two ways:

- At design-time, select the appropriate control and look in the Properties window for the property "ToolTip on tipProvider" (where tipProvider is the name of the ToolTipProvider control).

- At runtime, use the ToolTipProvider.SetToolTip() method. You can also use the GetToolTip() method to retrieve a control's tooltip.

```
tips.SetToolTip(txtName, "Enter Your Name Here")
```

> **TIP**  *There really isn't any difference between using the SetToolTip() method and the extended ToolTip property provided by the designer. With providers, Visual Studio .NET simply translates what you type in the Properties window into the appropriate method call, and adds the code to the form class. So when you set the ToolTip property, you are still in fact using the SetToolTip() method.*

You can also configure some generic tooltip settings by adjusting the properties of the ToolTipProvider control, as detailed in Table 4-1.

*Table 4-1. ToolTipProvider Members*

| Member | Purpose |
| --- | --- |
| Active | The same as Enabled for most controls. When set to False, no tooltips are shown. |
| AutomaticDelay, AutoPopDelay, InitialDelay, ReshowDelay | These settings specify the number of milliseconds before the tooltip appears, the time that it remains visible if the mouse is stationary, and the time required to make it reappear. Generally, you should use the default values. |
| ShowAlways | If set to True, tooltips appear when the mouse hovers over a control even if the window containing the control does not currently have focus. |
| SetToolTip(), GetToolTip(), and RemoveAll() | These methods allow you to attach a descriptive string to a control and retrieve it. To remove a tooltip, you can either attach an empty string, or use RemoveAll() to clear all tooltips at once. |

.NET does not provide many provider controls, as they are generally used for specialized features. Toward the end of this chapter, you'll see an example that uses the ErrorProvider with control validation. Later, in Chapter 13, you see how the HelpProvider can be used to enable context-sensitive help. But perhaps the most interesting information about providers appears in Chapter 7, where you see how you can create custom provider controls.

## ActiveX Controls

.NET includes excellent interoperability features that allow you to continue using COM components and ActiveX controls in your current applications. If you are using Visual Studio .NET, the process is even automated for you.

To add an ActiveX control to one of your projects in Visual Studio .NET, right-click the toolbox and select Customize Toolbox. Select the COM Components tab, and find the appropriate control on the list, and put a check mark next to it (see Figure 4-2).

Nothing happens until you add an instance of this control to a form. The first time you do this, Visual Studio .NET automatically creates a special interop assembly for you. For example, if you add the MSChart control, which has no direct .NET equivalent, it creates a file with a name like AxInterop.MSChart20Lib_2_0.dll.

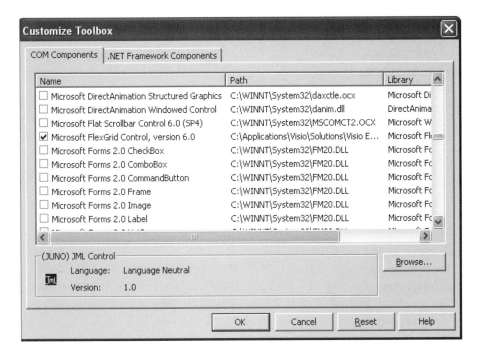

*Figure 4-2. Adding a COM reference*

The "Ax" at the beginning of the name identifies the fact that this interop assembly derives from System.Windows.Forms.AxHost. This class is used to create any .NET wrapper for an ActiveX control. It works "in between" your .NET code and the ActiveX component, as shown in Figure 4-3.

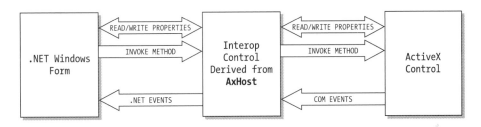

*Figure 4-3. AxHost interaction*

The control on your form is a legitimate .NET control, as you can see by examining the automatically generated designer code that defines and instantiates it. For example, here's the code for an interop class that supports the MSChart control:

```
Me.AxMSChart1.Location = New System.Drawing.Point(36, 24)
Me.AxMSChart1.Name = "AxMSChart1"
Me.AxMSChart1.OcxState = CType(resources.GetObject("AxMSChart1.OcxState"), _
 System.Windows.Forms.AxHost.State)
Me.AxMSChart1.Size = New System.Drawing.Size(216, 72)
Me.AxMSChart1.TabIndex = 4
```

You can see that this control supports basic .NET properties like Size and Location. It also uses a special OcxState property (inherited from the AxHost class) that retrieves the persisted state of an ActiveX control. From your program's point of view, you can communicate with a normal .NET control that supports .NET event handling and the basic set of features in the Control class. The AxHost-based control quietly communicates with the original ActiveX control, and mimics its behavior on the form. You can even dynamically resize the control and modify its properties using the built-in property pages, and it will respond exactly as it should.

In some cases, the new class may introduce changes. For example, when the MSFlexGrid control is imported, it changes the syntax used to set some properties into method calls:

```
grid.set_ColWidth(1, 3000)        ' This was grid.ColWidth(1) = 3000
grid.set_ColAlignment(0, 1)       ' This was grid.ColAlightment(0) = 1
```

Fortunately, you can always use the Object Browser to get to the bottom of any new changes.

If you are a war-hardened COM veteran, you can create interop controls by hand. However, this process is time-consuming and error-prone, and generally won't produce a better result than Visual Studio .NET's automatic support. Instead, you might want to subclass the interop control that Visual Studio .NET creates. In other words, you could create a custom control that inherits from the interop control. This extra layer gives you the chance to add additional .NET features, and won't hamper performance.

## Should You Import ActiveX Controls?

Importing controls is easy, and it most cases it works without a hitch. Right now, it might be required to convert existing programs without rewriting large pieces of functionality. And while it is possible to recreate .NET controls for the MSChart or Internet Explorer Web Browser components, it can be time consuming.

You should also be aware of some of the potential problems:

- **ActiveX licensing issues are back.** .NET controls demonstrate the amazing xcopy installation capability of the .NET platform. ActiveX controls, however, need to be registered and reregistered whenever a change occurs. This isn't a new problem, but the return of on an ugly one.

- **Security issues appear.** The .NET framework uses a special fine-grain approach to security, which allows controls to be used in semi-trusted environments with most of their functionality intact. ActiveX controls require full unmanaged code permission, which makes them more difficult to use in some scenarios.

- **Performance could be affected.** Generally, this is the least likely concern. ActiveX emulation is extremely fast in .NET. In some cases, certain controls may exhibit problems, but that will be the exception.

.NET controls will always be the best solution, and in the coming months there will be a proliferation of new third-party options that surpass most of the ActiveX controls used today. Until that time, you may want to use the built-in ActiveX interop, particularly if you have custom controls and don't have the time or budget to redesign them for .NET.

Some of ActiveX controls that you still need to use in the .NET world (at least for the time being) include:

- Microsoft's Web Browser control for displaying HTML content.

- Any ActiveX control related to help, including Microsoft's new MS Help 2.0 components, which you explore in Chapter 14.

- Special grid or charting controls (some of which were included with previous Visual Studio releases) like Microsoft's FlexGrid, DataRepeater, and Charting controls. The .NET framework provides some basic tools, and there are sure to be a host of third party .NET controls in this area, but not all the existing controls have been brought over.

- Microsoft controls for animation or hosting media player.

- Microsoft Office-based components (including charting and spreadsheet components).

- Specialty Microsoft controls like the masked edit text box and the drop-down image list (although these can be manually recreated with .NET code without too much difficulty).

# The Classic Control Gallery

Now that you've learned about control fundamentals, it's time to look at some of the familiar controls every programmer knows and loves.

## *Labels*

Label controls are used to place static text on a form. The text is contained in Text property, and aligned according the TextAlign property. Some other label properties are listed in Table 4-2.

*Table 4-2. Label Properties*

| Property | Description |
|---|---|
| RenderTransparent | When set to True, makes the label's background transparent, allowing you to superimpose text on other controls like picture boxes. Of course, you can't control it if text displayed in a label is anti-aliased, often making it insufficient for splash screens and other situations where you need professional graphics. (In these cases, GDI+ features or prerendered bitmaps are the ticket.) |
| AutoSize, PreferredHeight, and PreferredWidth | .NET labels support automatic resizing, which dynamically adjusts size to fit the text string and font you apply. To use these features, set the AutoSize property to true, and specify the ideal size in the PreferredHeight and PreferredWidth properties. |
| Image and ImageAlign | Label controls can also contain a picture (reference in the Image property), although they will not wrap around it. You will have finer-grained control by using separate label and picture controls. |
| UseMnemonic | When set to True, ampersands in the label's Text will be automatically interpreted as Ctrl access keys. The user can press this access key, and the focus is forwarded to the next control in the tab order (for example, a labeled text box). |

## LinkLabel

This specialty label inherits from the Label class, but adds some properties that make it particularly well suited to represent links. For example, many applications provide a clickable link to a company web site in an About window.

The LinkLabel handles the details of displaying a portion of its text as a hyperlink. This portion is identified in the LinkArea property using a special structure that identifies the first character or the link and the number of characters in the link. Depending on the LinkBehavior property, this linked text may be always underlined, displayed as normal, or it may become underlined when the mouse hovers over it.

Here's the basic code that creates a link on the web site address:

```
lnkWebSite.Text = "See www.prosetech.com for more information."

' Starts at position 4, and 17 characters long.
lnkWebSite.LinkArea = New LinkArea(4, 17)
lnkWebSite.LinkBehavior = LinkBehavior.HoverUnderline
```

You need to handle the actual LinkClicked event to make the link functional. In this event handler, you should set the LinkVisited property to true so that the color is updated properly, and perform the required action. For example, you might start Internet Explorer with the following code:

```
Private Sub lnkWebSite_LinkClicked(sender As Object, _
  e As LinkLabelLinkClickedEventArgs) Handles lnkWebSite.LinkClicked

    ' Change the color if needed.
    lnkWebSite.LinkVisited = True
    ' Use the Process.Start method to open the default browser with a URL.
    System.Diagnostics.Process.Start("http://www.prosetech.com")

End Sub
```

If you need to have more than one link, you can use the Links property, which exposes a special collection of Link objects. Each Link object stores its own Enabled and Visited properties, as well as information about the start and length of the link (Start and Length). You can also use the LinkData object property to associate some additional data with a link. This is useful if the link text does not identify the URL (for example a "click here" link).

```
lnkBuy.Text = "Buy it at Amazon.com or Barnes and Noble."
lnkBuy.Links.Add(10, 10, "http://www.amazon.com")
lnkBuy.Links.Add(24, 16, "http://www.bn.com")
```

The LinkClicked event provides you with a reference to the Link object that was clicked. You can then retrieve the LinkData, and use it to decide what web page should be shown.

```
Private Sub lnkBuy_LinkClicked(sender As Object, _
  e As LinkLabelLinkClickedEventArgs) Handles lnkBuy.LinkClicked, _
  lnkWebSite.LinkClicked

    e.Link.Visited = True
    System.Diagnostics.Process.Start(CType(e.Link.LinkData, String))

End Sub
```

Figure 4-4 shows both of these LinkLabel examples. Additional information about the LinkLabel and LinkLabel.Link classes is provided in Tables 4-3 and 4-4.

*Table 4-3. LinkLabel Properties*

| Property | Description |
| --- | --- |
| ActiveLinkColor, DisabledLinkColor, LinkColor, and VisitedLinkColor | Sets colors for the links in the LinkLabel (the rest of the text has its color determined by the standard ForeColor property). Links can be visited, disabled, enabled (normal), or active (while they are in the process of being clicked). |
| LinkArea and Links | LinkArea specifies the position of the link in the text. If you have more than one link, you can use the Links property instead, which is a special LinkCollection class. |
| LinkBehavior | Specifies the underlining behavior of the link using the LinkBehavior enumeration. |
| LinkVisited | When set to True, the link appears with the visited link color. |

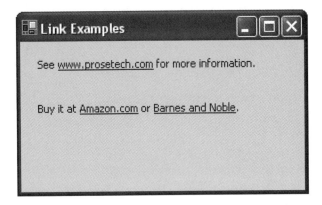

*Figure 4-4. Two LinkLabel examples*

*Table 4-4. LinkLabel.Link Properties*

| Property | Description |
|---|---|
| Enabled | Allows you enable or disable a link. Disabled links do not fire the LinkClicked event when clicked. |
| Length and Start | Identifies the position of the link in the LinkLabel. |
| LinkData | Provides an object property that can hold additional data, like the corresponding URL. You can retrieve this data in the LinkClicked event handler. |
| Visited | When set to True, the link appears with the visited link color. |

## Button

Quite simply, buttons are used to "make things happen." The most important thing to remember about buttons is that their Click event has a special meaning: it occurs when you trigger the button in any way, including with the keyboard, and it is not triggered by right-button mouse clicks. Buttons are old hat to most developers, but Table 4-5 lists a couple of interesting members that may have escaped your attention.

*Table 4-5. Special Button Members*

| Member | Description |
|---|---|
| PerformClick() | "Clicks" the button programmatically. Useful for wizards and other feature where code "drives" the program. |
| DialogResult | If set, indicates that this button will close the form automatically, and return the indicated result to the calling code, provided the window is shown modally. This technique explained in Chapter 5, in the section about dialog forms. |

## TextBox

Another staple of Windows development, the text box allows the user to enter textual information. The previous chapter explained how you can react to and modify key presses in the text box. Interestingly, text boxes provide a basic set of built-in functionality that the user can access through a context menu (see Figure 4-5).

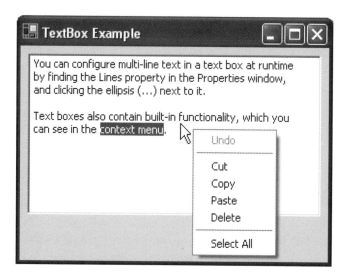

*Figure 4-5. The built-in TextBox menu*

Much of this functionality is also exposed through TextBox class members. See Table 4-6 for a complete rundown.

*Table 4-6. TextBox Members*

| Property | Description |
| --- | --- |
| AcceptsReturn and Multiline | If you set Multiline to True, the text box can wrap text over the number of available lines (depending on the size of the control). You can also set AcceptsReturn to True, so that a new line is inserted in the text box whenever the user hits the Enter key (otherwise, pressing the Enter key will probably trigger the form's default button). |
| AcceptsTab | If True, when the user presses the Tab key it inserts a hard tab in the text box (rather than causing the focus to move to the next control in the tab order). |
| AutoSize | When set to True, a single line text box's height is adjusted to match the corresponding font size. |
| CanUndo | Determines whether the text box can undo the last action. An Undo operation can be triggered using the Undo() method, or when the user right-clicks on the control and choose Undo from the context menu. |
| Cut(), Copy(), Paste(), Clear(), Undo(), Select(), SelectAll() | These methods allow you to select text and trigger operations like copy and cut, which work with the clipboard. The user can also access this built-in functionality through the context menu for the text box. |
| CharacterCasing | Forces all entered characters to become lowercase or uppercase, depending on the value you use from the CharacterCasing enumeration. |
| MaxLength | The maximum number of characters or spaces that can be entered in the text box. |
| PasswordChar | If this property is set to a character, that character appears in place of the text box value, hiding its information. For example, if you set this to an asterisk, the password "sesame" will appear as a series of asterisks (*****). |

*Table 4-6. TextBox Members (Continued)*

| Property | Description |
|---|---|
| SelectedText, SelectionLength, and SelectionStart | The SelectionStart and SelectionLength properties allow you to set the text that is currently selected in the text box. |
| ReadOnly | If True, the contents of a read-only text box can be modified in your code, but not by the user. Making a text box read-only instead of disabling it allows the text to remain clearly visible (instead of "greyed out") and it allows the user to scroll through if it does not fit in the display area. |

## CheckBox and RadioButton

The CheckBox and RadioButton controls provide a Checked property that indicates whether the control is checked or "filled in." After the state is changed, a Checked event occurs.

A special three-state check box can be created by setting the ThreeState property to True. You need to check the CheckState property to examine whether it is Checked, Unchecked, or Indeterminate (shaded but not checked).

By default, the control is checked and unchecked automatically when the user clicks it. You can prevent this by setting AutoCheck to False, and handling the Click event. This allows you to programmatically prevent a check box or radio button from being checked (without trying to "switch it back" after the user has made a change).

## PictureBox

A picture box is one of the simplest controls .NET offers. You can set a valid image using the Image property, and configure a SizeMode from the PictureBoxSizeMode enumeration. For example, you can set the picture to automatically stretch to fit the picture box.

```
pic.Image = System.Drawing.Image.FromFile("mypic.bmp")
pic.SizeMode = PictureBoxSizeMode.StretchImage
```

## List Controls

.NET provides three basic list controls: ListBox, CheckedListBox, and ComboBox. They all inherit from the abstract ListControl class, which defines basic functionality that allows you to use a list control with data binding. Controls can be bound to objects like the DataSet, arrays, and ArrayList collections, regardless of the underlying data source (as you'll see in Chapter 8).

```
' Bind a list control to an array of city names.
Dim CityChoices() As String = {"Seattle", "New York", "Signapore", "Montreal"}
lstCity.DataSource = CityChoices
```

You can access the currently selected item in several ways. You can use the SelectedIndex property to retrieve the zero-based index number identifying the item, or the Text property to retrieve the displayed text. You can also set both of these properties to change the selection:

```
' Search for the item with "New York" as its text, and select it.
lstCity.Text = "New York"

' Select the first item in the list.
lstCity.SelectedIndex = 0
```

If you are using a multiselect ListBox, you can also use the SelectedIndices or SelectedItems collections. Multiselect listboxes are set based on the SelectionMode property. You have two multiselect choices: SelectionMode.MultiExtended, which requires the user to hold down Ctrl or Shift while clicking the list to select additional items, and SelectionMode.MultiSimple, which selects and deselects items with a simple mouse click or press of the Space key. The CheckedListBox provides similar CheckedIndices and CheckedItems properties that provide collections of checked items.

Here's an example that iterates through all the checked items in a list, and displays a message box identifying each one:

```
Dim Item As String
For Each Item In chkList.CheckedItems
    ' Do something with checked item here.
    MessageBox.Show("You checked " & Item)
Next
```

You can also access all the items in a list control through the Items collection. This collection allows you to count, add, and remove items. Note that this collection is read-only if you are using a data-bound list.

```
lstFood.Items.Add("Macaroni")        ' Added to bottom of list.
lstFood.Items.Add("Baguette")        ' Added to bottom of list.

lstFood.Items.Remove("Macaroni")     ' The list is searched for this entry.
lstFood.Items.RemoveAt(0)            ' The first item is removed.
```

Table 4-7 dissects the properties offered by all list controls.

*Table 4-7. List Control Properties*

| Property | Description |
| --- | --- |
| CheckOnClick | If set to True, the checkbox for an item is toggled with every click. Otherwise, a double-click is required. |
| IntegralHeight | If set to True, the height is automatically adjusted to the nearest row-multiple height, ensuring no half-visible rows are shown in the list. |
| ItemHeight | The height of a row with the current font, in pixels. |
| Items | The full collection of items in the list control. |
| MultiColumn and HorizontalScrollbar | A multicolumn list control automatically divides the list into columns, with no column longer than the available screen area. Vertical scrolling is thus never required, but you may need to enable the horizontal scroll bar to see all the columns easily. |
| SelectedIndex, SelectedIndices, SelectedItem, SelectedItems, and Text | Provide different ways to access the currently selected item (an Object type, which is typically a string), its zero-based index number, or its text. The CheckedListBox uses CheckedItems and CheckedIndices properties instead of SelectedItems and SelectedIndices. |
| SelectionMode | Allows you to configure a multiselect list control using one of the SelectionMode values. Multiple selection is not supported for CheckListBox controls. |
| Sorted | If set to True, items are automatically sorted alphabetically. This generally means you should not use index-based methods, as item indices change as items are added and removed. |

*Table 4-7. List Control Properties (Continued)*

| Property | Description |
|----------|-------------|
| TopIndex | The index number representing the topmost visible item. You can set this property to scroll the list. |
| ThreeDCheckBoxes | Configures the appearance of check boxes for a CheckedListBox. |
| UseTabStops | If set to true, embedded tab characters are expanded into spaces. |

The ComboBox control provides a few different properties (detailed in Table 4-8). It also supports the same selection properties and Items collection. In addition, it can work in one of three modes, as specified by the DropDownStyle property. In ComBoxStyle.DropDown mode, the combo box acts as a nonlimiting list where the user can type custom information. In ComboBoxStyle.DropDownList, pressing a key selects the first matching entry. The user cannot enter items that are not in the list.

> **TIP** *You should always make sure to choose the right kind of combo. DropDown style is ideal for a list of selected choices that is not comprehensive (like a field where users can type the name of their operating system). The available list items aren't mandatory, but they will encourage consistency. The DropDownList style is ideal for a database application where a user is specifying a piece of search criteria by using the values in another table. In this case, if the value doesn't exist in the database, it's not valid, and can't be entered by the user.*

*Table 4-8. Special ComboBox Properties*

| Property | Description |
|----------|-------------|
| DropDownStyle | Sets the type of drop-down list box. It can be a restrictive or nonrestrictive list. |
| DropDownWidth | This specifies the width of the drop-down portion of the list. |
| DroppedDown | This Boolean property indicates if the list is currently dropped down. You can also set it programmatically. |
| MaxDropDownItems | This specifies how many items will be shown in the drop-down portion of the list. |
| MaxLength | For an unrestricted list, this limits the amount of text that can be entered by the user. |

## List controls with objects

In the preceding examples, the Items property was treated like a collection of strings. In reality, it's a collection of objects. To display an item in the list, the list control automatically calls the object's ToString() method. In other words, you could create a custom data object, and add instances to a list control. Just make sure to override the ToString() method, or you will end up with a series of identical items that show the fully-qualified class name.

For example, consider the following Customer class:

```
Public Class Customer
    Public FirstName As String
    Public LastName As String
    Public BirthDate As Date

    Public Sub New()
    End Sub

    Public Sub New(ByVal firstName As String, ByVal lastName As String, _
      ByVal birthDate As Date)
        Me.FirstName = firstName
        Me.LastName = lastName
        Me.BirthDate = birthDate
    End Sub

    ' This provides the text that will be used in the list control.
    Public Overrides Function ToString() As String
        Return FirstName & " " & LastName
    End Function
End Class
```

You can add customer objects to the list control natively. Figure 4-6 shows how these Customer objects appear in the list.

```
lstCustomers.Items.Add(New Customer("Maurice", "Respighi", DateTime.Now))
lstCustomers.Items.Add(New Customer("Sam", "Digweed", DateTime.Now))
lstCustomers.Items.Add(New Customer("Faria", "Khan", DateTime.Now))
```

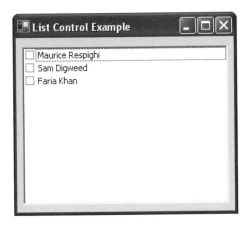

*Figure 4-6. Filling a list box with objects*

## Other Domain Controls

Domain controls are controls that restrict user input to a finite set of valid values. The standard ListBox is an example of a domain control, because a user can only choose one of the items in the list. Figure 4-7 shows an overview of the other domain controls provided in .NET.

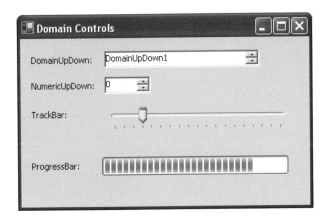

*Figure 4-7. The domain controls*

### DomainUpDown

This control is similar to a list control in that it provides a list of options. The difference is that the user can only navigate through this list using the up/down arrow buttons, and moving to either the previous or following item. List controls are generally more useful, because they allow multiple items to be shown at once.

To use the DomainUpDown control, add a string for each option to the Items collection. The Text or SelectedIndex property returns the user's choice.

```
' Add Items.
udCity.Items.Add("Tokyo")
udCity.Items.Add("Montreal")
udCity.Items.Add("New York")

' Select the first one.
udCity.SelectedIndex = 0
```

### NumericUpDown

The NumericUpDown list allows a user to choose a number value by using up/down arrow buttons (or typing it in directly). You can set the allowed range using the Maximum, Minimum, and DecimalPlaces properties. The current number in the control is set or returned through the Value property.

```
' Configure a NumericUpDown control.
udAge.Maximum = 120
udAge.Minimum = 18
udAge.Vale = 21
```

### TrackBar

The track bar allows the user to choose a value graphically by moving a tab across a vertical or horizontal strip (use the Orientation property to specify). The range of values is set through the Maximum and Minimum properties, and the Value property returns the current number. However, the user sees a series of "ticks" and not the exact number. This makes the track bar suitable for a setting that doesn't have an obvious numeric significance or where the units may be arbitrary, such as when setting volume levels or pitch in an audio program.

```
' Configure a TrackBar.
barVolume.Minimum = 0
barVolume.Maximum = 100
barVolume.Value = 50

' Show a tick every 5 units.
barVolume.TickFrequency = 5

' The SmallChange is the amount incremented if the user clicks an arrow button
' (or presses an arrow key).
' The LargeChange is the amount incremented if the user clicks the barVolume
' (or presses PageDown or PageUp).
tackbar.SmallChange = 5

barVolume.LargeChange = 25
```

## ProgressBar

The progress bar is quite different than the other domain controls because it doesn't allow any user selection. Instead, you can use it to provide feedback about the progress of a long running task. As with all the number-based domain controls, the current position of the progress bar is identified by the Value property, which is only significant as it compares to the Maximum and Minimum properties that set the bounds of the progress bar. You can also set a number for the Step property. Calling the Step() method then increments the value of the progress bar by that number.

```
' Configure the progress bar.
' In this case we hard-code a maximum, but it would be more likely that this
' would correspond to something else (like the number of files in a directory).
progress.Maximum = 100
progress.Minimum = 0
progress.Value = 0
progress.Step = 5

' Start a task.
Dim i As Integer
For i = progress.Minimum To progress.Maximum Step progress.Step
    ' (Do work here.)

    ' Increment the progress bar.
    progress.Step()
Next
```

## *Organizational Controls*

The GroupBox and Panel are two container controls that are used to group related controls. Radio buttons, for example, must be grouped into a container in order to be associated together as a unit.

The Panel control is similar to the GroupBox control; however, only the Panel control can have scroll bars, and only the GroupBox control displays a caption (set in the Text property). Also, the Panel control supports DockPadding, which makes it a necessary ingredient in complex resizable forms, as you'll see in the next chapter. The GroupBox control does not provide this ability.

## The Date Controls

Retrieving date information is a common task. For example, requiring a date range is a good way to limit database searches. In the past, programmers have used a variety of different controls to retrieve date information, including text boxes that required a specific format of month, date, and year values.

The modern date controls make life much easier. For one thing, they allow dates to be chosen from a graphical calendar view that's easy to use and prevents users from choosing invalid dates (like the 31$^{st}$ day in February, for example). They also allow dates to be displayed in a range of formats.

There are two date controls: DateTimePicker and MonthCalendar. DateTimePicker is ideal for choosing a single date value, and requires the same amount of space as an ordinary drop-down list box. When the user clicks the drop-down button, a full month calendar page is shown. The user can page from month to month (and even year to year) looking for a specific date with the built-in navigational controls. The control handles these details automatically.

The MonthCalendar shows a similar expanded display, with a single month at a time. Unlike the DateTimePicker, it allows the user to choose a range of dates. Both controls are shown in Figure 4-8.

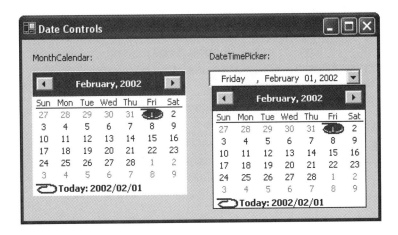

*Figure 4-8. The date controls*

## The DateTimePicker

The DateTimePicker allows a user to choose a single date. One nice thing about the DateTimePicker is that it automatically takes the computer's regional settings into consideration. That means you can specify Short for the DateTimePicker.Format property, and the date might be rendered as yyyy/mm/dd format or dd/mm/yyyy depending on the date settings. Alternatively, you can specify a custom format by assigning a format string to the CustomFormat property, and make sure the date is always presented in the same way on all computers. Figure 4-9 shows the different date formats.

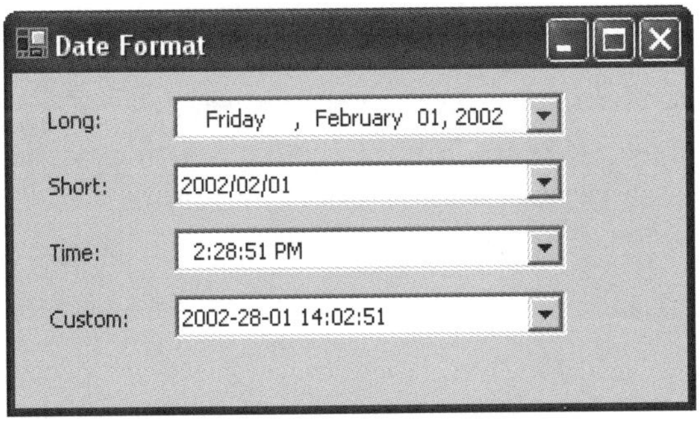

*Figure 4-9. Common date formats*

The selected date is provided in the Value property. One important detail about date controls is that they always use the System.DateTime date type, which represents a date *and* time. Depending on your needs, you might configure a date control to show only the day or time portion. In this case, you may need to be careful to retrieve just the appropriate part.

For example, imagine you are using a DateTimePicker control, which allows the user to choose the start date for a database search. The date control is configured to show dates in the long format, which doesn't include time information.

When the form loads, you configure the date control:

```
dtStart.Value = DateTime.Now    ' Sets dtStart to the current date and time.
```

The user might then click on a different date. However, choosing a different date only updates the month, year, and day components of the date. The time component remains, even though it is not displayed!

```
' The next line performs a search based on date and the original time.
' This articifically limits the returned results.
Dim SQLSelect = "SELECT * FROM Orders WHERE Date >'" & _
  dtStart.Value.ToString() & "'"
```

If you initialized the DateTimePicker at lunchtime, you could lose the first half day from your search.

There are a number of ways to avoid this problem. For example, you can use the DateTime.Date property, which returns another DateTime object that has its time portion set to 0 (midnight).

```
' This gets the full day.
Dim SQLSelect = "SELECT * FROM Orders WHERE Date >'" & _
  dtStart.Value.Date.ToString() & "'"
```

You could also use the DateTime.Today property to set the initial value instead of DateTime.Now. This is a good technique for the MonthCalendar control as well. The MonthCalendar automatically sets the time component for the currentValue to 0 when the user selects a date, but if the user leaves the default date unchanged, and you've assigned a date with information, the time portion remains.

You can also use a DateTimePicker to represent a time value with no date component. To do so, set the Format property to Time. You also need to set the UseUpDown property to true. This prevents the drop-down month display from being shown, and you can use up/down scroll button instead to increment the highlighted time component (hours, minutes, or seconds).

Table 4-9 lists the important properties of the DateTimePicker control.

*Table 4-9. DateTimePicker Properties*

| Properties | Description |
|---|---|
| CalendarFont, CalendarForeColor, CalendarMonthBackground, CalendarTitleBackColor, CalendarTitleForeColor, and CalendarTrailingForeColor | These properties configure the calendar's font and the color used for parts of its interface. The default colors are provided as static read-only fields for this class (like DefaultTitleForeColor). Note that the CalendarTrailingForeColor changes the color of the "trailing" dates. These are the dates that appear on a month page from the previous month (at the beginning) or from the next month (at the end). They are used to fill in the grid. |
| ShowCheckBox and Checked | ShowCheckBox displays a small check box inside the drop-down listbox. Unless it is checked, the date cannot be modified. |
| Format and CustomFormat | The Format property specifies a value from the DateTimePickerFormat enumeration. Alternatively, you can manually specify an exact form by assigning a format string to the CustomFormat property (like "yyyy/MM/DD hh:mm:ss"). |
| DropDownAlign | Determines whether the drop-down month page lines up with the left or right of the listbox. |
| MaxDate and MinDate | Sets a maximum and minimum date, beyond which the user cannot select. This is a great tool for preventing error messages by making invalid selections impossible. |
| ShowUpDown | When set to True, disables the drop-down month pages and uses up/down scroll buttons for incrementing part of the date. This is ideal for time-only values. |
| Text and Value | Text returns the formatted date as a string, according to how it is currently displayed. Value returns the represented DateTime object. |

## MonthCalendar

The MonthCalendar control looks like the DateTimePicker, except that it always shows the month page display, and it doesn't allow the user to enter a date by typing it into a list box. That makes the MonthCalendar slightly less useful, except for situations when you need to let the user select a range of contiguous dates.

You set the maximum number of dates that the user can select in the MaxSelectionCount property. The user selects a group of dates by dragging and clicking. Selected dates must always be next to each other. The first and last selected dates are returned as DateTime objects in the SelectionStart and SelectionEnd properties. Figure 4-10 shows a range of four days.

```
' Set a range of four days.
dt.SelectionStart = New DateTime(2003, 01, 17)
dt.SelectionEnd = New DateTime(2003, 01, 20)
```

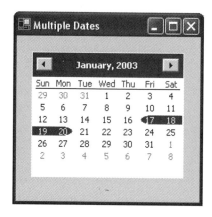

*Figure 4-10. Selecting multiple dates*

Depending on your needs, you may still need to perform a significant amount of validation with selected dates to make sure they fit your business rules. Unfortunately, you can't easily use the DateChanged and DateSelected events for this purpose. They only fire after an invalid date has been selected, and you have no way to remove the selection unless you choose a different date range. Information about the original (valid) date range is already lost.

Though the MonthCalendar control looks similar to the DateTimePicker, it provides a different set of properties, adding some features while omitting others. Table 4-10 lists the most important properties.

*Table 4-10. MonthCalendar Properties*

| Property | Description |
| --- | --- |
| AnnuallyBoldedDates, MonthlyBoldedDates, and BoldedDates | These properties accept arrays of DateTime objects, which are then shown in bold in the calendar. MonthlyBoldedDates can be set for one month and are repeated for every month, while AnuallyBoldedDates are set for one year and repeated for every year. |
| FirstDayOfWeek | Sets the day that will be shown in the leftmost column of the calendar. |
| MaxDate, MinDate, and MaxSelectionCount | Sets the maximum and minimum selectable date in the calendar, and the maximum number of contiguous dates that can be selected at once. |
| ScrollChange | The number of months that the calendar "scrolls through" every time the user clicks a scroll button. |
| SelectionEnd, SelectionStart, and SelectionRange | Identifies the selected dates. The SelectionRange property returns a special structure that contains a SelectionEnd and SelectionStart date. |
| ShowToday and ShowTodayCircle | These properties, when True, show the current day in a special line at the bottom of the control and highlight it in the calendar with a circle, respectively. |
| ShowWeekNumbers | If True, displays a number next to each week in the year from 1 to 52. |
| TodayDate and TodayDateSet | TodayDate indicates what date is shown as "today" in the MonthCalendar. If you set this value manually in code, TodayDateSet is True. |
| TitleBackColor, TitleForeColor, and TrailingForeColor | Sets colors associated with the MonthCalendar. Note that the TrailingForeColor changes the color of the "trailing" dates. These are the dates that appear on a month page from the previous month (at the beginning) or from the next month (at the end). They are used to fill in the grid. |

WARNING   *The MonthCalendar control doesn't properly support Windows XP styles. If you try to use this control with a project that uses Windows XP styles, the display does not appear correctly when the user selects more than one date at a time.*

## Menus

Applications use two kinds of menus: main and context. Main menus provide a comprehensive set of options just below a window's title bar, and use standard headings like File, Edit, and Help. Context menus are floating or "pop up" menus that provide additional options. Typically, context menus appear when the user right-clicks a user interface element (like an object, or a system tray icon). Like main menus, context menus can contain nested layers of menus, but they tend to be much simpler.

Consider the partial menu shown in Figure 4-11. In .NET, this menu is modeled as a collection of objects, as shown in Figure 4-12. MenuItem objects make up every part of a menu except the top-level container.

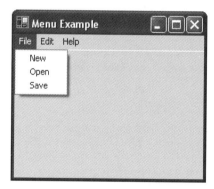

*Figure 4-11. A sample menu*

The next code snippet shows how to create the first part of this menu (all the entries contained under the File heading). Generally, you use the Visual Studio .NET IDE to create menu and configure items automatically through the custom menu designer.

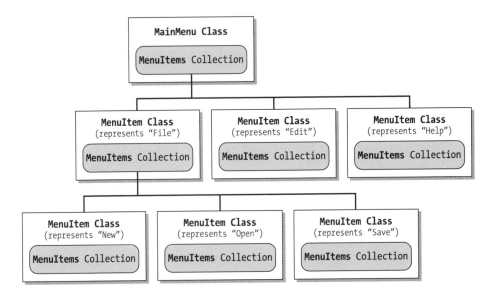

*Figure 4-12. Menu objects in .NET*

```
' Build the menu starting with the deepest nested level
' (in this case, New, Open, and Save).

Dim mnuNew As New MenuItem()
mnuNew.Text = "New"

Dim mnuOpen As New MenuItem()
mnuOpen.Text = "Open"

Dim mnuSave As New MenuItem()
mnuSave.Text = "Save"

' Create the top-level File menu.
Dim mnuFile As New MenuItem()
mnuFile.Text = "File"

' Add the contained menu items to the File menu.
mnuFile.MenuItems.Add(mnuNew)
mnuFile.MenuItems.Add(mnuOpen)
mnuFile.MenuItems.Add(mnuSave)

' Create the main menu container.
Dim mnuMain As New MainMenu()
```

```
' Add the File menu to the main menu.
mnuMain.Add(mnuFile)

' Attach the main menu to the form.
Me.Menu = mnuMain
```

The next few sections dissect the .NET menu objects.

## The Menu Class

In .NET, main menus, context menus, and menu items are all treated slightly differently. All of them inherit from the abstract Menu class (see Figure 4-13).

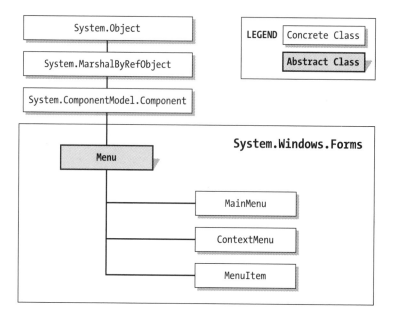

*Figure 4-13. The menu object hierarchy*

The Menu class contains a collection of MenuItem objects that corresponds to a single menu level, and provides functionality that lets you clone or merge these items into another menu, and find the top-level menu container.

*Table 4-11. Members of the Abstract Menu Class*

| Member | Purpose |
|--------|---------|
| Handle | The internal operating system "handle" (number) that identifies this menu. It could be required for a low-level API call. |
| IsParent | Returns True if this menu contains other menu items. |
| MenuItems | The collection of MenuItem objects that represent the next level of the menu. |
| CloneMenu() | Allows you to copy an array of MenuItem objects into the current menu. This method can be used to transfer items between a MainMenu and a ContextMenu, or vice versa. |
| GetContextMenu() and GetMainMenu() | Returns the ContextMenu or MainMenu object that contains this menu, even if this menu is nested several layers deep in the hierarchy. |

## The MainMenu and ContextMenu Classes

At the top level, menu items are always contained in a MainMenu or ContextMenu class. These classes, which inherit from Menu, add a few additional frills. For example, the MainMenu class allows you to determine the form that owns the menu, while the ContextMenu class allows you to find the associated control and react to the Popup event when the menu is displayed (Tables 4-12 and 4-13). As you'll see, MainMenu and ContextMenu can't be treated equivalently in your code. This means that you can't display part of a main menu as a context menu, as you would in a Visual Basic 6 application.

*Table 4-12. ContextMenu Members*

| Member | Purpose |
|--------|---------|
| SourceControl | Indicates the control that "owns" this context menu (or null). |
| Popup event | Allows you to customize the menu when the menu is about to appear but has not yet been displayed. You can use this event to configure the context menu appropriately by hiding, adding, or disabling some items depending on the current state of your application. |
| Show() | Displays the context menu on the screen, at the indicated position. |

*Table 4-13. MainMenu Members*

| Member | Purpose |
| --- | --- |
| CloneMenu() | This new (alternative) CloneMenu() method can be called without arguments to create a duplicate copy of the MainMenu object. |
| GetForm() | Returns the Form object that contains the menu. |

> **WARNING**   *Watch out—the MainMenu class adds a new CloneMenu() method for duplicating the menu. If you're transferring a few menu items from one menu to another, you'll want to use the CloneMenu() method inherited from the Menu class instead.*

## The MenuItem Class

Each command and submenu in a menu is represented by a MenuItem object. The MenuItem class is the most full-featured menu object, with several properties for configuring appearance and reacting to menu events, as described in Table 4-14.

*Table 4-14. MenuItem Members*

| Member | Purpose |
| --- | --- |
| BarBreak and Break | These properties allow you to create the unusual menus shown in Figure 4-14. Break, when set to True, instructs .NET to place the menu item in a separate column For example, if you create an entire submenu of menu items with Break set to True, they appear as a horizontal menu arranged from left to right. BarBreak works identically, except it displays a vertical line as a column separator between menu items. These properties must be set in code—they aren't available in the Properties window. |
| Checked and RadioCheck | If set to True, a check mark is displayed next to the highlighted menu item. If RadioCheck is set to True, the menu item displays a bullet instead of a check mark when its Checked property is True. Typically the check mark style is used for a value that can be toggled on and off, while the radio button style is used when you provide a mutually exclusive list of menu selections, from which the user can choose only one. |

*Table 4-14. MenuItem Members (Continued)*

| Member | Purpose |
|---|---|
| DefaultItem | The default menu item for a menu is displayed in bold type. If the user double-clicks a submenu that contains a default item, the default item is selected automatically, and the submenu is closed. DefaultItem is usually provided as a guide for the user, and indicates the most common choice. |
| Enabled | Sets whether the menu should be selectable or disabled and displayed in "greyed out" text. |
| Index | The numeric index of a menu item in its parent's MenuItems collection. You can modify this index to reposition the menu item. |
| MergeOrder and MergeType | This specifies the behavior for this menu when being merged with another menu, either programmatically through the MergeMenu() method, or automatically with MDI forms. The MergeOrder is a number representing relative position (0, the default, is first in the menu). MergeType defines the merge behavior using one of the values from the MenuMerge enumeration. |
| OwnerDraw and the DrawItem and MeasureItem events | When OwnerDrawn is set to True, the default menu user interface is not provided for you. Instead, you need to handle the DrawItem and MeasureItem events. |
| Shortcut and ShowShortcut | Shortcut sets a hotkey from the Shortcut enumeration (like Ctrl+N or F8). ShowShortcut determines whether the shortcut is displayed with the text for the menu item. |
| Text | Sets the text for menu item. Use the ampersand character to precede the access key (as in E&xit to make "x" the access key). |
| Visible | If set to False, the menu item is not be shown at all. |
| CloneMenu() | Duplicates a menu. This method keeps all event handlers intact, and is useful when you need to reuse the same entries in a context menu as in a main menu. |

*Table 4-14. MenuItem Members (Continued)*

| Member | Purpose |
| --- | --- |
| MergeMenu() | Combines the children of two menus into a single list. You could use this technique to create a context menu that contains the entries from two different submenus in the main menu. Just remember to use CloneMenu() first, and then merge the duplicate copy of the menus. |
| PerformClick() and PerformSelect() | Triggers the appropriate Click or Select event for the MenuItem. These methods are rarely used, except if you are creating wizards or other tools that drive an application by "remote control." |
| Popup event | Occurs when the menu item's submenu is just about to be displayed. You can use this to dynamically tailor a menu just in time when it is selected. The Popup event is not raised for menus that do not contain submenu items. |
| Select event | Occurs when a menu item is highlighted, but not selected. This can occur when the menu item is scrolled over by using the keyboard controls, or hovered over with the mouse. |
| Click event | Occurs when the menu item is clicked with the mouse or triggered with the keyboard. |

## The Visual Studio .NET Menu Designer

Visual Studio.NET includes built-in support for creating any type of menus. To start, drag a main menu or context menu onto your form. It will appear in the component tray. To design a menu, click once to select it, and then type text in the onscreen "type here" areas (see Figure 4-15).

Every time you add a new menu item, a "type here" area appears for a submenu and a new menu item. You can also drag and drop menu items in any order you want, and configure each menu item's name and properties in the Properties window when it is selected. Right-click a menu item and select Insert Separator to add a horizontal dividing line between menu entries.

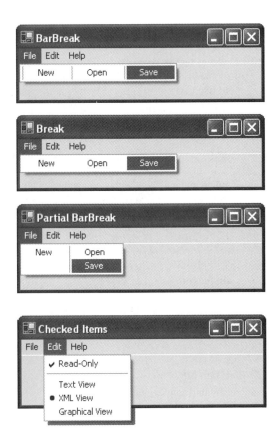

Figure 4-14. *Menu variations*

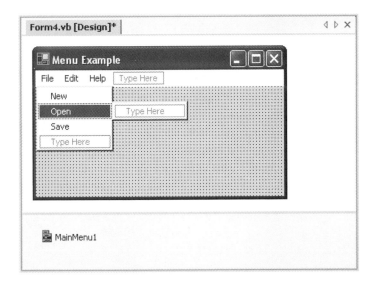

Figure 4-15. *The Visual Studio .NET menu designer*

## Attaching a Menu

Unlike other controls, main menus are not added to the Controls collection of the hosting form. Instead, they are specifically set using the Menu property of the form. Once this link is set, the menu automatically appears at the top of the form.

```
Me.Menu = mnuMain                    ' Attach the mnuMain MainMenu object.
```

Context menus use a similar technique with the ContextMenu property.

```
ctrl.ContextMenu = mnuContext  ' Attach the mnuContext ContextMenu object.
```

Context menus, however, are not automatically shown. Instead, you need to show them manually using the ContextMenu.Show() method. Typically, you perform this task in the MouseUp event for the linked control.

The example that follows displays the control's context menu. It uses the sender parameter, making it completely generic. You could use this event handler for every control with a context menu in your application.

```
Private Sub lbl_MouseUp(ByVal sender As Object, _
 ByVal e As System.Windows.Forms.MouseEventArgs) Handles lbl.MouseUp

    ' Convert the sender parameter into a valid control reference.
    Dim ctrl As Control = CType(sender, Control)

    ' If the right mouse button was pressed, show the menu.
    If e.Button = MouseButtons.Right Then
       ctrl.ContextMenu.Show(ctrl, New Point(e.X, e.Y))
    End If

End Sub
```

Using a control's ContextMenu property is really just a convenience. You can display a context menu at any time, in response to any event, even if you haven't set the ContextMenu property of a nearby control. However, using the ContextMenu property allows you to write a generic method that can handle the MouseUp event for multiple controls. Your code simply needs to retrieve the ContextMenu property of the control that fired the event.

## Menu Events

There are two ways you can handle menu selection events. You can write an individual event handler for the Click event of every MenuItem. This is ideal if you are writing all the menu code inside the current form.

```
Private Sub mnuOpen_Click(ByVal sender As System.Object, _
  ByVal e As System.EventArgs) Handles mnuOpen.Click
    ' (Do something here.)
End Sub

Private Sub mnuNew_Click(ByVal sender As System.Object, _
  ByVal e As System.EventArgs) Handles mnuNew.Click
    ' (Do something here.)
End Sub

Private Sub mnuSave_Click(ByVal sender As System.Object, _
  ByVal e As System.EventArgs) Handles mnuSave.Click
    ' (Do something here.)
End Sub
```

However, if your menu just hands the task off to another class, it probably makes sense to handle all menu events in the same event handler. (In this case, your event handler acts as a generic switchboard). You can then determine which MenuItem fired the event by converting the sender parameter into a MenuItem object and examining its Text, or just by comparing object references (which is preferred, because the compiler alerts you if you refer to a nonexisting MenuItem, but it doesn't alert you if you enter incorrect menu text). The following code snippet handles the Click event of three MenuItem objects, and compares the event sender to the appropriate form-level variables to determine which item was clicked.

```
Private Sub mnu_Click(ByVal sender As System.Object, _
  ByVal e As System.EventArgs) Handles mnuOpen.Click, mnuNew.Click, mnuSave.CLick

    If sender Is mnuOpen Then
        MyApp.DoOpen()
    ElseIf sender Is mnuNew Then
        MyApp.DoNew()
    ElseIf sender Is mnuSave Then
        MyApp.DoSave()
    End If

End Sub
```

This approach of handling all menu clicks in one method also provides an easy way to implement the standard MFC logic, where a help string is displayed in another control (typically a status bar) whenever a menu item is highlighted.

## Copying and Cloning a Menu

.NET imposes some restrictions on menus. Items cannot belong to more than one menu, and they cannot be shared between types of menus. In many applications, a context menu is actually a subset of a main menu. To set this up with .NET, you need to copy the appropriate branch of the menu.

You might attempt this with the logical-appearing code shown below:

```
' A flawed approach.
Dim mnuContext As New ContextMenu()
Dim mnuItem As MenuItem


' Attempt to copy the menu items from the File menu.
For Each mnuItem In mnuFile.MenuItems
    mnuContext.MenuItems.Add(mnuItem.Text)
Next
```

Unfortunately, this will copy the items but lose the event handlers. To preserve the event handling logic, you need to use the CloneMenu() method, as shown here:

```
' A copy operation that preserves event handlers.
Dim mnuContext As New ContextMenu()
Dim mnuItem As MenuItem


' Copy the menu items from the File menu into a context menu.
For Each mnuItem In mnuFile.MenuItems
    mnuContext.MenuItems.Add(mnuItem.CloneMenu())
Next
```

## Merging a Menu

In some cases, you might want to create a context menu that contains the entries from two different submenus. While you could do this by duplicating and manipulating the individual MenuItem objects, the easiest way is by using the built-in MenuItem.MergeMenu() method.

The example below combines the menu items in the top-level File and Edit menus.

```
' Create a copy of the menus you want to merge.
Dim mnuMergeFile, mnuMergeEdit As MenuItem
mnuMergeFile = mnuFile.CloneMenu()
mnuMergeEdit = mnuEdit.CloneMenu()

' Merge the duplicate copy of the menus.
mnuMergeFile.MergeMenu(mnuMergeEdit)

' Now add the merged menu to the appropriate control.
Me.ContextMenu = mnuMergeFile
```

## Owner-Drawn Menus

If this is your first look at .NET menus, you may be disappointed to see that they don't support the common Windows convention of using embedded thumbnail bitmaps to help distinguish common items. To solve this problem, you could purchase a third-party control, but luckily the logic is easy to implement on your own. All it requires is a dash of GDI+.

The steps for creating an owner-drawn menu are as follows.

1. Set the OwnerDraw property for the menu items to True. Note that even when you do this, you can still see the menu item in the design environment and configure its Text property.

2. Handle the MeasureItem event. This is where you tell .NET how much space you need to display the menu item.

3. Handle the DrawItem event. This is where you actually write the output for the item to the screen. In our case, this output consists of text and a small thumbnail image.

The first step is easy enough. The second step requires a little bit more work. To specify the required size, you need to set the ItemHeight and ItemWidth properties of the MeasureItemEventArgs class with a value in pixels. However, the size required depends a great deal on the font and text you use. Fortunately, the MeasureItemEventArgs class also provides a reference to the graphics context for the menu, which provides a useful MeasureString() method. This method returns a Size structure that indicates the space required.

To keep your code manageable, you should use a single event handler to measure all the menu items. In our example, this includes a "New," "Open," and "Save" menu entry.

```
Private Sub mnu_MeasureItem(ByVal sender As System.Object, _
  ByVal e As System.Windows.Forms.MeasureItemEventArgs) _
  Handles mnuNew.MeasureItem, mnuOpen.MeasureItem, mnuSave.MeasureItem

    ' Retrieve current item.
    Dim mnuItem As MenuItem = CType(sender, MenuItem)

    ' Assume that Tahoma 8pt is being used for the menu.
    Dim MenuFont As New Font("Tahoma", 8)

    ' Measure size needed to display text.
    ' We add 30 pixels to the width to allow a generous spacing for the image.
    e.ItemHeight = e.Graphics.MeasureString(mnuItem.Text, MenuFont).Height + 5
    e.ItemWidth = e.Graphics.MeasureString(mnuItem.Text, MenuFont).Width + 30

End Sub
```

When displaying a drop-down menu, Windows automatically measures the size of each item, and uses the greatest required width for all menu items.

The final step of displaying the menu item is similarly straightforward. You must find the appropriate picture, and write both the text and image to the screen using the graphics context provided by the DrawItem event handler and the DrawString() and DrawImage() methods. A little additional code is required to perform the correct highlighting for selected items. The result is shown in Figure 4-16.

```
Private Sub mnu_DrawItem(ByVal sender As Object, _
  ByVal e As System.Windows.Forms.DrawItemEventArgs) _
  Handles mnuNew.DrawItem, mnuOpen.DrawItem, mnuSave.DrawItem

    ' Retrieve current item.
    Dim mnuItem As MenuItem = CType(sender, MenuItem)

    ' Determine whether a highlighted background is needed.
    ' Note that bitwise comparison is required to evaluate the state,
    '  as several state flags may be set in conjunction.
    If e.State And DrawItemState.Selected = DrawItemState.Selected Then
        e.DrawBackground()
    End If

    ' Retrieve the image from an ImageList control.
    Dim MenuImage As Image = imgMenu.Images(mnuItem.Index)
```

```
' Draw the image.
e.Graphics.DrawImage(MenuImage, e.Bounds.Left + 3, e.Bounds.Top + 2)


' Draw the text with the supplied colors and in the set region.
e.Graphics.DrawString(mnuItem.Text, e.Font, New SolidBrush(e.ForeColor), _
  e.Bounds.Left + 25, e.Bounds.Top + 3)


End Sub
```

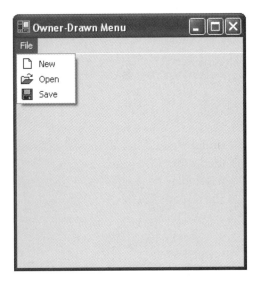

*Figure 4-16. An owner-drawn menu*

Note that this code uses the Windows standard font and colors, which are provided in properties like e.Font and e.ForeColor. Alternatively, you could create your own Color or Font objects and use them. The next example shows more flexible custom formatting.

> **TIP** *You don't need to worry about invisible menu items. If the Visible property is set to False, .NET will not fire the MeasureItem and DrawItem events. You would, however, have to add the drawing logic if you wanted to let your custom menu draw separator items (when the menu text is set to "-"), checkmarks, or greyed out text and images (when the menu item is disabled).*

## An Owner-Drawn Menu Control

Writing the correct code in the MeasureItem and DrawItem event handlers requires some tweaking of pixel offsets and sizes. Unfortunately, in our current implementation there is no easy way to reuse this logic for different windows (not to mention different applications). A far better approach is to perfect your menu as a custom control, and then allow this control to be reused in a variety of projects and scenarios.

The following example adopts this philosophy, and shows a menu control that provides an Image, Font, and ForeColor property. This custom menu item handles its own drawing logic. All the client code needs to do is set the appropriate properties. The code also extends the previous example by correctly drawing disabled menu items.

```
Public Class ImageMenuItem
    Inherits MenuItem

    Private _Font As Font
    Private _ForeColor As Color
    Private _Image As Image

    Public Property Font() As Font
        Get
            Return _Font
        End Get
        Set(ByVal Value As Font)
            _Font = Value
        End Set
    End Property

    Public Property Image() As Image
        Get
            Return _Image
        End Get
        Set(ByVal Value As Image)
            _Image = Value
        End Set
    End Property
```

```
Public Property ForeColor() As Color
    Get
        Return _ForeColor
    End Get
    Set(ByVal Value As Color)
        _ForeColor = Value
    End Set
End Property


Public Sub New(ByVal Text As String, ByVal Font As Font, _
  ByVal Image As Image, ByVal ForeColor As Color)
    MyBase.New(Text)
    Me.Font = Font
    Me.Image = Image
    Me.ForeColor = ForeColor
    Me.OwnerDraw = True
End Sub


Public Sub New(ByVal Text As String, ByVal Image As Image)
    MyBase.New(Text)
    Me.Font = New Font("Tahoma", 8)
    Me.Image = Image
    Me.ForeColor = SystemColors.MenuText
    Me.OwnerDraw = True
End Sub


Protected Overrides Sub OnMeasureItem(ByVal e As _
  System.Windows.Forms.MeasureItemEventArgs)

    MyBase.OnMeasureItem(e)
    ' Measure size needed to display text.
    e.ItemHeight = e.Graphics.MeasureString(Me.Text, Me.Font).Height + 5
    e.ItemWidth = e.Graphics.MeasureString(Me.Text, Me.Font).Width + 30

End Sub


Protected Overrides Sub OnDrawItem(ByVal e As _
  System.Windows.Forms.DrawItemEventArgs)
```

```
            MyBase.OnDrawItem(e)
            ' Determine whether a highlighted background is needed.
            Dim TextColor As Color
            If Me.Enabled = False Then
                TextColor = SystemColors.GrayText
            If e.State And DrawItemState.Selected = DrawItemState.Selected Then
                e.DrawBackground()
                TextColor = e.ForeColor
            Else
                TextColor = Me.ForeColor
            End If


            ' Draw the image.
            If Not Image Is Nothing Then
                If Me.Enabled = False Then
                    ControlPaint.DrawImageDisabled(e.Graphics, Image, _
                        e.Bounds.Left + 3, e.Bounds.Top + 2, SystemColors.Menu)
                Else
                    e.Graphics.DrawImage(Image, e.Bounds.Left + 3, e.Bounds.Top + 2)
                End If
            End If


            ' Draw the text with the supplied colors and in the set region.
            e.Graphics.DrawString(Me.Text, Me.Font, New SolidBrush(TextColor), _
                e.Bounds.Left + 25, e.Bounds.Top + 3)

        End Sub

    End Class
```

Because this class inherits from MenuItem, you can add instances of it to any MenuItems collection. Here's an example that creates the same menu you considered in your previous example by using the ImageMenuItem control:

```
mnuFile.MenuItems.Add(New ImageMenuItem("New", imgMenu.Images(0)))
mnuFile.MenuItems.Add(New ImageMenuItem("Open", imgMenu.Images(1)))
mnuFile.MenuItems.Add(New ImageMenuItem("Save", imgMenu.Images(2)))
```

Alternatively, you can use the other supplied constructor to configure an unusual font and color combination. For example, the code that follows creates a submenu that lists every font, with each name displayed in its own typeface (see Figure 4-17).

```
Dim Family As FontFamily, Fonts As New InstalledFontCollection()

For Each Family In Fonts.Families
    Try
        mnuFonts.MenuItems.Add(New ImageMenuItem(Family.Name, _
            New Font(Family, 10), Nothing, Color.CornflowerBlue))
    Catch
        ' Catch invalid fonts/styles and ignore them.
    End Try
Next
```

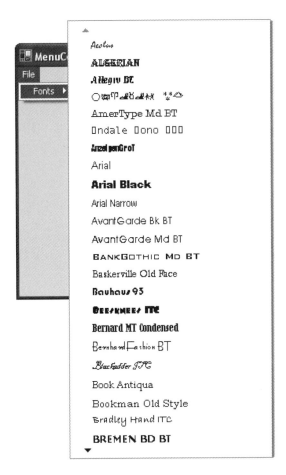

*Figure 4-17. Displaying a list of installed fonts*

Unfortunately, there is no easy way to insert an ImageMenu object into a menu using the integrated Visual Studio .NET menu designer. If you want to bridge this gap, you would have to create a custom MainMenu and ContextMenu objects, and then develop custom designers for them that would allow ImageMenu objects to be inserted. Chapter 8 introduces custom designers.

**TIP** *You can mix owner-drawn ImageMenu objects and ordinary MenuItem objects in the same menu without any complications.*

Now that you have a grip on the basic suite of .NET controls, the remainder of the chapter dives into two more interesting topics: adding drag-and-drop ability, and creating advanced validation code.

## Drag-and-Drop

Drag-and-drop operations aren't quite as common today as they were a few years ago, because programmers have gradually settled on other methods of copying information that don't require holding down the mouse button (a technique that many users find difficult to master). For example, a drawing program is likely to use a two-step operation (select an object, and then draw it on) rather than a single drag-and-drop operation. Programs that do support drag-and-drop often use it as a shortcut for advanced users, rather than a standard way of working.

Drag-and-drop is also sometimes confused with the ability to "drag" a picture or piece of user interface around a window. This "fake" drag-and-drop is useful in drawing and diagramming applications (including the drawing application developed in Chapters 11 and 13), but it needs to be coded manually. In this section, you will learn about both types of dragging operations.

### "Fake" Drag-and-Drop

True drag-and-drop is a user-initiated way to exchange information between two controls. You don't need to use drag-and-drop events to create objects that the user can move around the form (Figure 4-18). For example, consider the following program that allows a user to click on a picture box, drag it around, and release it somewhere else on the form.

*Figure 4-18. Dragging a control around*

Conceptually, a control is being dragged and dropped, but all the logic takes place in the appropriate mouse handling events. A Form level IsDragging variable keeps track of when fake drag-and-drop mode is currently switched on.

```
' Keep track of when fake "drag and drop" mode is enabled.
Private IsDragging As Boolean = False

' Store the location where the user clicked the control.
Private ClickOffsetX, ClickOffsetY As Integer

' Start dragging.
Private Sub lblDragger_MouseDown(ByVal sender As System.Object, _
  ByVal e As System.Windows.Forms.MouseEventArgs) Handles lblDragger.MouseDown
    IsDragging = True
    ClickOffsetX = e.X
    ClickOffsetY = e.Y
End Sub

' End dragging.
Private Sub lblDragger_MouseUp(ByVal sender As System.Object, _
  ByVal e As System.Windows.Forms.MouseEventArgs) Handles lblDragger.MouseUp
    IsDragging = False
End Sub

' Move the control (during dragging).
Private Sub lblDragger_MouseMove(ByVal sender As Object, _
  ByVal e As System.Windows.Forms.MouseEventArgs) Handles lblDragger.MouseMove
```

```
If IsDragging = True Then
    ' The control coordinates are converted into form coordinates
    ' by adding the label position offset.
    ' The offset where the user clicked in the control is also
    ' accounted for. Otherwise, it looks like the top-left corner
    ' of the label is attached to the mouse.
    lblDragger.Left = e.X + lblDragger.Left - ClickOffsetX
    lblDragger.Top = e.Y + lblDragger.Top - ClickOffsetY
End If

End Sub
```

There are three components that factor into the position calculation:

- The e.X and e.Y parameters provide the position of the mouse over the control, where (0,0) is the top-left corner of the control.

- The lblDragger.Left and lblDragger.Top properties give the position between the top-left corner of the control, and the top-left corner of the form.

- The ClickOffsetX and ClickOffsetY variables give the position between the control's top-left corner and where the user actually clicked to start dragging. By taking this into account, the label acts as though it is "glued" to the mouse at that point.

## Authentic Drag-and-Drop

Real drag-and-drop operations are quite a bit different. Essentially, they work like this:

1. The user clicks a control and holds the mouse button down. At this point, some information is set aside and a drag-and-drop operation begins.

2. The user moves the mouse over another control. If this control can accept the current type of content (for example, a picture or text) the mouse cursor changes to a special drag-and-drop icon. Otherwise, the mouse cursor becomes a circle with a line drawn through it.

3. When the user releases the mouse button, the control receives the information, and decides what to do with it.

Unlike our fake drag-and-drop example, a real drag-and-drop operation can easily take place between controls, or even two different applications, as long as the drag-and-drop contract is followed.

The example program below uses drag-and-drop to take a picture from a label control and draw it onto a picture box control. The actual drawing operation uses GDI+ methods that you examine in more detail later in this book. All other details are generic parts of any drag-and-drop application (Figure 4-19). You'll find the complete code with the samples for this chapter under the project name AuthenticDragAndDrop.

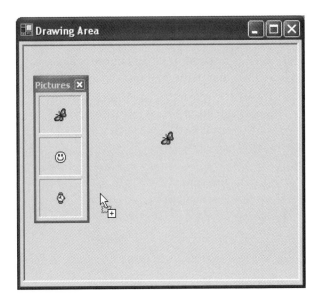

*Figure 4-19. A sample drag-and-drop application*

The first step is to configure the picture box control to accept dropped information.

```
picDrawingArea.AllowDrop = True
```

To start the drag-and-drop, you can use the DoDragDrop() method of the source control. In this case, it is one of three labels. Dragging is initiated in the MouseDown event for the label.

```
Private Sub lblPicture_MouseDown(ByVal sender As Object, _
  ByVal e As MouseEventArgs) Handles lblPictureOne.MouseDown, _
  lblPictureTwo.MouseDown, lblPictureThree.MouseDown

    Dim lbl As Label = CType(sender, Label)
    lbl.DoDragDrop(lbl.Image, DragDropEffects.Copy)

End Sub
```

The same event handler handles the MouseDown event for each label. In the event handler, the generic sender reference (which points to the object that sent the event) is converted into a label. Then, a drag-and-drop copy operation is started. The information associated with this operation is the image from the label control.

To allow the picture box to receive information, you need to verify that the information is the correct type in the DragEnter event, and then set a special event argument (e.Effect). DragEnter occurs once when the mouse moves into the bounds of the control.

```
Private Sub picDrawingArea_DragEnter(ByVal sender As Object, _
  ByVal e As System.Windows.Forms.DragEventArgs) Handles picDrawingArea.DragEnter

    If (e.Data.GetDataPresent(DataFormats.Bitmap)) Then
        e.Effect = DragDropEffects.Copy
    Else
        e.Effect = DragDropEffects.None
    End If

End Sub
```

The last step is to respond to the information once it is dropped, by handling the DragDrop event. You can do anything you want with the dropped information. In the current example, a GDI+ drawing operation is started (although it could make just as much sense to create a new object in that location and set its Image property).

```
Private Sub picDrawingArea_DragDrop(ByVal sender As Object, _
  ByVal e As System.Windows.Forms.DragEventArgs) Handles picDrawingArea.DragDrop

    Dim g As Graphics = picDrawingArea.CreateGraphics
    g.DrawImage(e.Data.GetData(DataFormats.Bitmap), _
      New Point(e.X - Me.Left, e.Y - Me.Top))

End Sub
```

Note that the event handler provides screen coordinates, which must be converted into the appropriate coordinates for the picture box.

Practically, you can exchange any type of object through a drag-and-drop operation. However, while this free-spirited approach is perfect for your applications, it isn't wise if you need to communicate with other applications. If you want to drag-and-drop into other applications, you should use data from a managed base class (like String or Image), or an object that implements ISerializable or IDataObject (which allows .NET to transfer your object into a stream of bytes, and reconstruct the object in another application domain).

## Validation

The best possible way to prevent invalid input is to make it impossible for users to enter it. You accomplish this by forcing users to choose from lists, and creating custom controls that automatically format data and ignore invalid key presses. Of course, sometimes this task is too daunting and you need to settle on the next best thing, which is checking for errors after the fact. If you take this approach, it's important that you report the error as soon as possible, preferably before the user continues to enter more information. The easiest way is to react to validation events.

Validation events were designed to let you check information as soon as it is entered, rather than waiting for the whole form to be submitted. This kind of instantaneous error checking is very useful:

- Without it, users might be afraid to submit a form because they know there is a possible error.

- Users might enter several pieces of invalid data at the same time. If you don't check the data until the form is submitted, your program then has to find some way to report about all the mistakes at once.

- By the time users submit a form, they might have already forgotten about the particular field they entered incorrectly.

Validation solves this information by checking the field as soon as the user is finished entering it and changes focus to another control (either to enter new information, like choosing a text box, or to perform an action, like clicking a button).

In the past, developers have tried to create "do-it-yourself" validation by responding to a control's LostFocus event. The problem with this event is that it occurs *after* the focus has already moved on. If you reset the focus because of invalid input, another control then receives its own LostFocus event. If both controls have invalid data, they may fight endlessly between each other, trying to move the focus somewhere else.

.NET handles this problem with the Validating and Validated events. These events occur after the user has chosen to move to another control (for example, by pressing the Tab key), but before the focus has been changed, in the following order:

1. Leave

2. Validating

3. Validated

4. LostFocus

The Validated event allows you to respond to correctly entered data. The Validating event is more useful. It allows you to verify the data and, if it fails the test, stop the focus from moving to the new control.

Validation only takes place if the source control (the control to be validated) has the CausesValidaton property set to True. In addition, the validation won't take place until the focus changes to a control that also has its CausesValidation property set to True. Table 4-15 shows some examples of what can happen when tabbing from one control to another.

*Table 4-15. .NET Validation*

| Source Control | Destination Control | Result |
|---|---|---|
| CausesValidation is False | Doesn't matter | Validation code is ignored |
| CausesValidation is True | CausesValidation is True | Validation is performed for the source control. |
| CausesValidation is True | CausesValidation is False | Validation is postponed until the focus changes to a CausesValidation control. A this point, all the controls that need to be validated are validated in order, until one is found with invalid input and the process is canceled. |

# A Validation Example

The program shown in Figure 4-20 uses validation to verify that neither text box is left blank. If the user tries to change focus without entering any information, a message box appears, and the focus is reset to the empty text box.

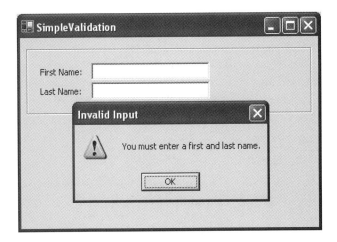

*Figure 4-20. A validation example*

The validation code for this application is shown here:

```
Private Sub txtName_Validating(ByVal sender As Object, _
  ByVal e As System.ComponentModel.CancelEventArgs) _
  Handles txtFirstName.Validating, txtLastName.Validating

    If CType(sender, TextBox).Text = "" Then
        MessageBox.Show("You must enter a first and last name.", _
        "Invalid Input", MessageBoxButtons.OK, MessageBoxIcon.Warning)
        e.Cancel = True
    End If

End Sub
```

Note that buttons handle validation differently than other controls. They don't validate on a focus change except when they are clicked. If the user tries to click a button and validation fails, the focus is reset, and the Click event is ignored.

Attempting to close with the top-right close button (displayed as an "X") also triggers validation. (This creates a problem if you need to let users escape from a form without completing the operation. The solution is to create a Cancel button that closes the form, and has its CausesValidation property set to False.)

## Validating with the ErrorProvider

Interrupting users with a message box is a relatively crude way of alerting them to an error. It's better to provide some kind of onscreen indication about the problem, like an explanatory error message next to the incorrect input.

The .NET framework provides an elegant way to accomplish this with its new error provider control. The ErrorProvider displays a special error icon next to an invalid control. If the user hovers the mouse above the control, a detailed message appears (see Figure 4-21).

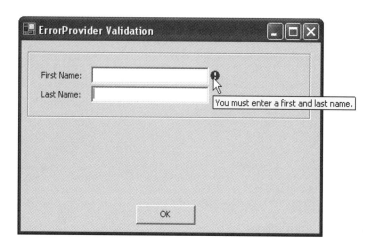

*Figure 4-21. The ErrorProvider*

The ErrorProvider is a special provider control. You add it once to your form, and you can use it to display an error icon next to any control. To add the ErrorProvider, drag it into the component tray, or create it manually in code. In the latter case, make sure you keep a form-level reference to use later.

You show the error icon next to a control using the ErrorProvider.SetError() method. The following code segment shows the same text box validating code, but is rewritten to indicate the error using the ErrorProvider control instead of a message box.

```
Private Sub txtName_Validating(ByVal sender As Object, _
  ByVal e As System.ComponentModel.CancelEventArgs) _
  Handles txtFirstName.Validating, txtLastName.Validating

    If CType(sender, TextBox).Text = "" Then
        errProvider.SetError(sender, "You must enter a first and last name.")
    Else
        errProvider.SetError(sender, "")
    End If

End Sub
```

> **NOTE** *The ErrorProvider control can serve any number of input controls on the same form, and display as many simultaneous error icons and warning messages as needed. Every warning icon automatically appears to the immediate right of the input control; there is no way to place it explicitly.*

Note that you must explicitly clear the error message after validation succeeds. In this example, the validation event doesn't cancel the action; it just displays the error icon. This is a more user-friendly alternative, but it means that you need to explicitly check if the form has any errors before allowing users to continue if they have clicked on the OK button.

```
Private Sub cdmOK_Click(ByVal sender As System.Object, _
  ByVal e As System.EventArgs) Handles cmdOK.Click

    If errProvider.GetError(txtFirstName) = "" And _
      errProvider.GetError(txtLastName) = "" Then
        Me.Close()
    Else
        MessageBox.Show("You still have invalid input.", "Invalid Input", _
        MessageBoxButtons.OK, MessageBoxIcon.Warning)
    End If

End Sub
```

If you have a lot of controls, it makes more sense to iterate through the whole collection, rather than writing code checking each control individually:

```
Private Sub cmdOK_Click(ByVal sender As System.Object, _
  ByVal e As System.EventArgs) Handles cmdOK.Click

    Dim InvalidInput As Boolean = False
    Dim ctrl As Control
    For Each ctrl In Me.Controls
        If errProvider.GetError(ctrl) <> "" Then
            InvalidInput = True
            Exit For
        End If
    Next

    If InvalidInput = True Then
        MessageBox.Show("You still have invalid input.", "Invalid Input", _
          MessageBoxButtons.OK, MessageBoxIcon.Warning)
    Else
        Me.Close()
    End If

End Sub
```

## Validating with Regular Expressions

The ErrorProvider control is an ideal way to weave error feedback into your application. However, writing the actual validation code can still be painful and time consuming. One way to streamline your work is to use the .NET regular expression classes, which allow you to search text strings for specific patterns.

Here's an example that validates an email address, by verifying that it contains an at sign (@) and period (.) and doesn't include spaces or special characters. Unlike our previous example, this code is performed in the KeyPress event handler, which ensures that the error provider icon is updated immediately after any change.

```
Private Sub txtEmail_KeyPress(ByVal sender As Object, _
  ByVal e As System.Windows.Forms.KeyPressEventArgs) Handles txtEmail.KeyPress

    Dim Expression As New System.Text.RegularExpressions.Regex("\S+@\S+\.\S+")
    If Expression.IsMatch(CType(sender, TextBox).Text) Then
        errProvider.SetError(sender, "")
    Else
        errProvider.SetError(sender, "Not a valid email.")
    End If

End Sub
```

Regular expressions almost constitute an entire language of their own, with special characters and metacharacters. Most programmers and organizations create their own regular expression classes that provide commonly used expressions. One possible example is shown below.

```
Public Class RegularExpressions
    Public Const Email As String = "\S+@\S+\.\S+"

    ' 4-10 character password that starts with a letter.
    Public Const Password As String = "[a-zA-Z]\w{3,9}"

    ' A sequence of 3-2-4 digits, with each group separated by a dash.
    Public Const SSN As String = "\d{3}-\d{2}-\d{4}"
End Class
```

Once you have created this type of resource class, you can use it easily to create a RegEx object:

```
Dim Expression As New Regex(RegularExpressions.Email)
```

A brief list of some common regular expression metacharacters is shown in Table 4-16. You can use these characters to create your own regular expressions. However, it's often easier to look up a pre-made regular expression that suits your data using the Internet or a dedicated book on the subject.

*Table 4-16. Regular Expression Metacharacters*

| Character | Matches |
| --- | --- |
| * | Zero or more occurrences of the previous character or subexpression. For example, a*b matches aab or just a. |
| + | One or more occurrences of the previous character or subexpression. For example, a+b matches aab but not a. |
| ( ) | Groups a subexpression that is treated as a single element. For example, (ab)+ matches ab and ababab. |
| \| | Either of two matches. For example, a\|b matches a or b. |
| [ ] | Matches one character in a range of valid characters. For example, [A-C] matches A, B, or C. |
| [^ ] | Matches a character that is not in the given range. For example, [^A-C] matches any character except A, B, and C. |
| . | Any character except newline. |

*Table 4-16. Regular Expression Metacharacters (Continued)*

| Character | Matches |
|-----------|---------|
| \s | Any whitespace character (like a tab or space). |
| \S | Any non-whitespace character (like a tab or space). |
| \d | Any digit character. |
| \D | Any character that is not a digit. |
| \w | Any word character (letter, number, or underscore). |

## The Last Word

This chapter has toured through the most common Windows controls, and demonstrated a few .NET twists like owner-drawn menus and the ErrorProvider control. You've also learned about the basic types of controls, the techniques you can use for drag-and-drop support, and the best ways to integrate validation code into your forms. The next chapter continues with the last core topic for Windows user interface programming: forms.

# CHAPTER 5

# Forms

WINDOWS ARE THE BASIC ingredients in any desktop application—so basic that the operating system itself is named after them. However, there's a fair deal of subtlety in exactly how you use a window, not to mention how you resize its content. This subtlety is what makes windows (or *forms*, to use .NET terminology) one of the most intriguing user interface topics.

This chapter explores how forms interact and take ownership of one other, and how forms are used to manage events. It also examines the basic classes involved, and considers the far from trivial problem of resizable windows. You learn how to design split-window interfaces, use the dazzling Windows XP control styles, and create irregularly shaped windows that will amaze your programming colleagues. Finally, the end of this chapter considers the advantages and limitations of visual inheritance, which offers an elegant way to create form templates.

## The Form Class

The Form class is a special type of control that represents a complete window. It almost always contains other controls. The Form class does not derive directly from Control; instead, it acquires additional functionality through two extra layers, as shown in Figure 5-1.

The Form class provides a number of basic properties that determine appearance and window style. Many of these properties (listed in Table 5-1) will be familiar if you are a seasoned Windows programmer because they map to styles defined by the Windows API.

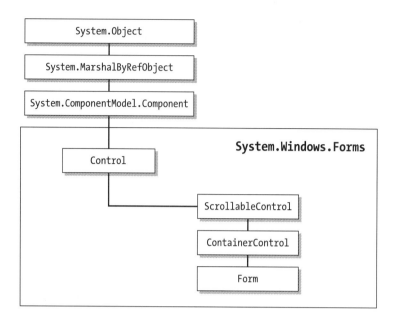

*Figure 5-1. The Form class lineage*

*Table 5-1. Basic Style Properties*

| Member | Description |
| --- | --- |
| FormBorderStyle | Specifies a value from the FormBorderStyle enumeration that identifies the type of window border, including its appearance and whether or not it can be resized. |
| ControlBox | Boolean property that determines whether the window has the system menu box at the top left corner. |
| MaximizeBox | Boolean property that determines if the window has the maximize box at the top right corner. |
| MinimizeBox | Boolean property that determines if the window has the minimize box at the top right corner. |
| HelpButton | Boolean property that determines if the window has the Help question mark icon at the top right corner. This button, previously used to trigger context-sensitive Help, has fallen into disuse in recent years. |
| Icon | References the System.Drawing.Icon object that is used to draw the window icon in the top left corner. |

*Table 5-1. Basic Style Properties (Continued)*

| Member | Description |
|--------|-------------|
| ShowInTaskBar | Boolean property that determines whether the window has an associated box that appears in the Windows task bar. This is generally used for main forms, but is not required for secondary windows like configuration forms, About boxes, and modal dialogs. |
| SizeGripStyle | Determines whether the sizing grip is shown on the bottom right corner of the window. |
| WindowState | Identifies (and allows you to configure) the current state of a resizable window. Possible values are Normal, Maximized, and Minimized. |
| TopMost | When set to True, this window is always be displayed on top of every other window in your application, regardless of form ownership. This can be a useful setting for tool windows. |
| Opacity | A percentage value that makes a form partially transparent if set to a value less than 100 percent. For example, if you set this to 10 percent, the form and all its controls are almost completely invisible, and the background window clearly shows through. This feature is only supported on Windows 2000 and later operating system. While interesting, this feature should not be used by the application programmer. |
| TransparencyKey | Identifies a color that becomes transparent. Any occurrence of this color becomes invisible whether it is in the form background, another control, or even a picture contained inside a control. These transparent settings act like "holes" in your window. You can even click to activate another window if you see it through a transparent region. This feature is only supported on Windows 2000 or later. Generally, if you need this type of functionality you are better off creating an irregularly shaped form, as described later in this chapter. |

The Form class defines references to two special buttons, as shown in Table 5-2. These properties add automatic support for the Enter and Escape keys.

*Table 5-2. Special Form Buttons*

| Member | Description |
| --- | --- |
| AcceptButton | The button referenced by this property is automatically "clicked" when the user presses the Enter key. This is also sometimes known as the default button. It should always be the least threatening button. Typically, this is form's OK or Close button, unless that button could accidentally commit irreversible changes. |
| CancelButton | The button referenced by this property is automatically "clicked" when the user presses the Esc key. This is usually a Cancel button. |

As you saw in Chapter 2, the preferred way to use .NET forms is to derive a custom class from the Form class. .NET forms also serve as switchboards that contain the event handling code for all their child controls. Technically, any method in any class can be used to listen for a control event. However, designing an application without using form "switchboards" is sure to mingle user interface and business code in a hopeless muddle. Instead, you should use the view-mediator pattern and handle control events with methods in your custom form class. This is the Visual Studio .NET default.

The Form class also defines some events of its own. These events (shown in Table 5-3) allow you to react when the form acquires focus, is about to be closed, or is first loaded into memory.

*Table 5-3. Form Events*

| Event | Description |
| --- | --- |
| Activated and Deactivated | These events are the form equivalent of the LostFocus and GotFocus events for a control. Deactivated occurs when the user clicks a different form in the application, or moves to another application. Activated occurs when the user switches to the window. You can also programmatically set the active form with the Activate() method, and you can retrieve the active form by inspecting the static ActiveForm property. |

*Table 5-3. Form Events (Continued)*

| Event | Description |
|-------|-------------|
| Load | Occurs when the form first loads. It gives you the chance to perform additional control initialization (like accessing a database and filling a list control). |
| Closing | Occurs when the form is about to close, as a result of the user clicking the close button or the programmatic use of the Close() method. The CancelEventArgs object provides a Cancel property that you can set to True to force the form to remain open. Event handlers for this event often provide a message box prompting the user to save the document. This message box typically provides Yes, No, and Cancel buttons. If Cancel is selected, the operation should be cancelled and the form should remain open. |
| Closed | Occurs when the form has closed. |

Finally, every form has a special designer region, which contains the constructor and an InitializeComponent() method that is executed immediately when the form object is created. The code in the designer region creates all the controls and sets all the properties that you have configured at design time. Even for a simple window, this code is quite lengthy, and shouldn't be modified directly (as Visual Studio .NET may become confused, or simply overwrite your changes). However, the hidden designer region is a great place to learn how to dynamically create and configure a control. For example, you can create a control at design time, set all its properties, and then simply copy the relevant code, almost unchanged, into another part of your code to create the control dynamically at runtime.

The previous chapters have presented the skeleton structure of a custom Form class, which is detailed here:

```
Public Class MyForm
    Inherits System.Windows.Forms.Form

    ' (Your custom form-level variables go here)

#Region " Windows Form Designer generated code "
    Public Sub New()
        MyBase.New()
        InitializeComponent()
    End Sub
```

```
    ' (Control member variable declarations go here.)

    Private Sub InitializeComponent()
        ' (Control and form initialization code goes here.)
    End Sub
#End Region

    ' (Your control event handling code goes here.)

End Class
```

In the next few sections, you examine more advanced properties of the Form class and the classes it inherits from. You also learn the basic approaches for showing and interacting with forms.

## Form Size and Position

The Form class provides the same Location and Size properties that every control does, but with a twist. The Location property determines the distance of the top left corner of the window from the top left corner of the screen (or desktop area). Furthermore, the Location property is ignored unless the StartPosition property is set to Manual. The possible values from the FormStartPosition enumeration are shown in Table 5-4.

*Table 5-4. StartPosition Values*

| Value (from the `FormStartPosition` enumeration) | Description |
| --- | --- |
| CenterParent | If the form is displayed modally, the form is centered relative to the form that displayed it. If this form doesn't have a parent form (for example, if it's displayed modelessly), this setting is the same as WindowsDefaultLocation. |
| CenterScreen | The form is centered in the middle of the screen. |
| Manual | The form is displayed in the location specified by the Location property, relative to the top left corner of the desktop area. |

*Table 5-4. StartPosition Values (Continued)*

| Value (from the FormStartPosition enumeration) | Description |
|---|---|
| WindowsDefaultLocation | The form is displayed in the Windows default location. In other words, there's no way to be sure exactly where it will end up. |
| WindowsDefaultBound | The form is displayed in the Windows default location, and with a default size (the Size property is ignored). This setting is rarely used, because you usually want exact control over a form's size. |

Sometimes you need to take a little care in choosing an appropriate location and size for your form. For example, you could accidentally create a window that is too large to be accommodated on a low-resolution display. If you are working with a single-form application, the best solution is to create a resizable form. If you are using an application with several floating windows the answer is not as simple.

You could just restrict your window positions to locations that are supported on even the smallest monitors, but that's likely to frustrate higher-end users (who have purchased better monitors for the express purpose of fitting more information on their screen at a time). In this case, you usually want to make a runtime decision about the best window location. In order to do this, you need to retrieve some basic information about the available screen real estate using the Screen class.

Consider the following example that manually centers the form when it first loads using the Screen class. It retrieves information about the resolution of the screen using the Screen.PrimaryScreen property.

```
Private Sub DynamicSizeForm_Load(ByVal sender As System.Object, _
  ByVal e As System.EventArgs) Handles MyBase.Load

    Dim scr As Screen = Screen.PrimaryScreen
    Me.Left = (scr.WorkingArea.Width - Me.Width) \ 2
    Me.Top = (scr.WorkingArea.Height - Me.Height) \ 2

End Sub
```

The members of the Screen class are listed in Table 5-5.

*Table 5-5. Screen Members*

| Member | Description |
| --- | --- |
| AllScreens (static) | Returns an array of Screen objects, with one for each display on the system. This method is useful for systems that use multiple monitors to provide more that one desktop (otherwise, it returns an array with one Screen object). |
| Primary (static) | Returns the Screen object that represents the primary display on the system. |
| Bounds | Returns a Rectangle structure that represents the bounds of the display area for the current screen. |
| GetBounds() (static) | Accepts a reference to a control, and returns a Rectangle representing the size of the screen that contains the control (or the largest portion of the control, if it is split over more than one screen). |
| WorkingArea | Returns a Rectangle structure that represents the bounds of the display area for the current screen, minus the space taken for the taskbar and any other docked windows. |
| GetWorkingArea() (static) | Accepts a reference to a control, and returns a Rectangle representing the working area of the screen that contains the control (or the largest portion of the control, if it is split over more than one screen). |
| DeviceName | Returns the device name associated with a screen as a string. |

A common requirement for a form is to remember its last location. Usually, this information is stored in the registry. The code that follows shows a helper class that automatically stores information about a form's size and position using a key based on the name of a form.

```
Public Class RegistryForm

    Public Shared RegPath As String = "Software\App\"

    Public Shared Sub SaveSize(ByVal frm As System.Windows.Forms.Form)
        ' Create or retrieve a reference to a key where the settings
        ' will be stored.
        Dim Key As RegistryKey
        Key = Registry.LocalMachine.CreateSubKey(RegPath & frm.Name)

        Key.SetValue("Height", frm.Height)
        Key.SetValue("Width", frm.Width)
        Key.SetValue("Left", frm.Left)
        Key.SetValue("Top", frm.Top)
    End Sub

    Public Shared Sub SetSize(ByVal frm As System.Windows.Forms.Form)
        Dim Key As RegistryKey
        Key = Registry.LocalMachine.OpenSubKey(RegPath & frm.Name)

        ' If the value isn't found the value from the passed in form object is
        ' used instead, which effectively leaves the size and location unchanged.
        frm.Height = CType(Key.GetValue("Height", frm.Height), Integer)
        frm.Width = CType(Key.GetValue("Width", frm.Width), Integer)
        frm.Left = CType(Key.GetValue("Left", frm.Left), Integer)
        frm.Top = CType(Key.GetValue("Top", frm.Top), Integer)
    End Sub

End Class
```

To use this class in a form, you call the SaveSize() method when the form is closing (for example, in a Form.Closing event handler):

```
RegistryForm.SaveSize(Me)
```

and call the SetSize() method when the form is first opened (for example, in a Form.Load event handler):

```
RegistryForm.SetSize(Me)
```

In each case, you pass a reference to the form you want the helper class to inspect.

## Scrollable Forms

The Form class inherits some built-in scrolling support from the ScrollableControl class. Generally, forms do not use these features directly. Instead, you will probably use scrollable controls like rich text boxes to display scrollable document windows. However, these features are still available, rather interesting, and effortless to use.

Figure 5-2 shows a form that has its AutoScroll property set to True. This means that as soon as a control is added to the form that does not fit in its visible area, the required scrollbars will be displayed. The scrolling process takes place automatically.

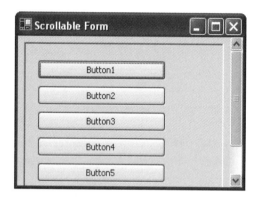

*Figure 5-2. A scrollable form*

**NOTE** *To get a scrollable form to display correctly, you may need to call the form's Refresh() method to update the window. In some tests, problems occurred when this method was not used.*

If Figure 5-2 looks a little strange, that's because it is. Scrollable forms make a few appearances in Windows applications (Microsoft Access is one example) but are relatively rare. They should be discouraged as unconventional. Instead, it probably makes more sense to use another class that derives from ScrollableControl, like Panel (see Figure 5-3).

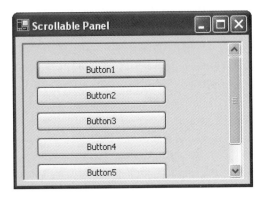

*Figure 5-3. A scrollable panel*

By default, scrollbars aren't shown unless a control is off the edge of the form, or you explicitly set the Boolean HScroll and VScroll properties. However, you can configure an AutoScrollMinSize, which specifies the required space, in pixels, between each control and the window border. If this minimum space is not provided, scroll bars are shown.

The form class doesn't derive directly from ScrollableControl. Instead, it derives from the ContainerControl (which, in turn, derives from ScrollableControl). Like the ScrollablControl class, the ContainerControl class doesn't provide many members that you are likely use. It includes a ProcessTabKey() method that the .NET framework uses transparently to manage focus, a ParentForm property that identifies the form that contains this control, and an ActiveControl property, that identifies or sets the control that currently has focus.

## Showing a Form

To display a form, you need to create an instance of the Form class and use the Show() or ShowDialog() method.

```
Dim frmMain As New MainForm()
frmMain.Show()
```

The Show() method creates a modeless window, which doesn't stop code from executing in the rest of your application. That means you can create and show several modeless windows, and the user can interact with them all at once. When using modeless windows, synchronization code is sometimes required to make sure that changes in one window update the information in another window to prevent a user from working with invalid information.

The ShowDialog() method, on the other hand, interrupts your code. Nothing happens on the user interface thread of your application until the user closes the window (or the window closes in response to a user action). The controls for all other windows are "frozen," and attempting to click a button or interact with a control has no effect (other than an error chime, depending on Windows settings). This makes the window ideal for presenting the user with a choice that needs to be made before an operation can continue. For example, consider Microsoft Word which shows its Options and Print windows modally, forcing you to make a decision before continuing. On the other hand, the windows used to search for text or spellcheck a document are shown modelessly, allowing the user to edit text in the main document window while performing the task. You can also use a different version of the ShowDialog() method that accepts a reference to a form in your application. The code in that form will be halted until the modal window is closed, but the user can use other windows in your application, if they exist.

> **TIP** *If you are designing a multithreaded application, it is possible to show windows on more than one thread. In this case, a modal window only stops the code on its thread, and your application may show more than one modal window at once. However, it is strongly recommended that multithreaded applications use one thread for user interface code. This prevents synchronization problems that can occur if a thread tries to access a user interface control that it did not create (and therefore does not legitimately own).*

## Custom Dialog Windows

Often when you show a dialog window, you are offering the user a choice. The code that displays the window waits for the result of that choice, and then acts on it.

You can easily accommodate this design pattern by creating some sort of public variable on the dialog form. When the user makes a selection in the dialog window, this special variable is set, and the form is closed. Your calling code can then check for this variable and determine what to do next based on its value. (Remember, even when a form is closed, the form object and all its control information still exists until the variable referencing it goes out of scope.)

For example, consider the form shown in Figure 5-4, which provides two buttons: Cancel and OK.

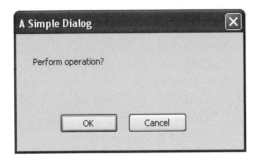

*Figure 5-4. A simple dialog form*

The form class provides a UserSelection property, which uses a custom enumeration to identify the action that was used to close the window:

```
Public Class DialogForm
    Inherits System.Windows.Form

    ' (Windows designer code omitted.)

    Enum SelectionTypes
        OK
        Cancel
    End Enum

    ' This property must be public so the caller can access it.
    Public UserSelection As SelectionTypes

    Private Sub cmdOK_Click(ByVal sender As Object, ByVal e As EventArgs) _
      Handles cmdOK.Click
        UserSelection = SelectionTypes.OK
        Me.Hide()
    End Sub

    Private Sub cmdCancel_Click(ByVal sender As Object, ByVal e As EventArgs) _
      Handles cmdCancel.Click
        UserSelection = SelectionTypes.Cancel
        Me.Hide()
    End Sub

End Class
```

The code that creates the form shows it modally. It then checks the UserSelection property after the window is closed to determine what action the user selected:

```
Dim frmDialog As New DialogForm()
frmDialog.ShowDialog()


' The code uses a custom enumeration to make the code readable and less
' error-prone.
Select Case frmDialog.UserSelection
    Case DialogForm.SelectionTypes.OK Then
        ' (Do something here.)
    Case DialogForm.SelectionTypes.Cancel Then
        ' (Do something else here.)
End Select


' Release the form and all its resources.
frmDialog.Dispose()
```

This is an effective, flexible design. In some cases, it gets even better: You can save code by using .NET's built-in support for dialog forms. This technique works best if your dialog only needs to return a simple value like Yes, No, OK, or Cancel. It works like this: In your dialog form, you set the DialogResult of the appropriate button control to one of the values from the DialogResult enumeration (found, like all user interface types, in the System.Windows.Forms namespace). For example, you can set the Cancel button's result to DialogResult.Cancel, and the OK button to DialogResult.OK. When the user clicks the appropriate button, the dialog form is immediately closed, and the corresponding DialogResult is returned to the calling code. Best of all, you don't need to write any event handling code to make it happen.

Your calling code would interact with a .NET dialog window like this:

```
Dim frmDialog As New DialogForm()
Dim Result As DialogResult
Result = frmDialog.ShowDialog()

Select Case Result
    Case DialogResult.OK
        ' The window was closed with the OK button.
    Case DialogResult.Cancel
        ' The window was closed with the Cancel button.
End Select
```

The code is cleaner and the result is more standardized. The only drawback is that you are limited to the DialogResult values shown in the list below (although you could supplement this technique with additional public form variables that would only be read if needed).

- OK

- Cancel

- Yes

- No

- Abort

- Retry

## *IgnoreForm Interaction*

Once you create a form, it continues to exist until you end your application or explicitly call the Close() method. As with all controls, even when the control variable goes out of scope and is destroyed, the actual control continues to exist. However, without the form variable, your code has no way to access the form.

This isn't a problem if you code your forms independently, and place all the code that uses the form inside the appropriate Form class. This code can simply use the Me reference to access the form (as Me always points to the current instance of a class). However, things become a little trickier if you need to allow interaction between forms. For example, if you want to configure a control on one form using the code inside another form, you need to make sure you create and retain the required form variable, so it's available when you need it.

All this raises at least one good question: where should you store the references to a form that you might need later? Once common choice is to create a special global class that does little more than provide a reference to the forms in your application. The following code presents one such example that retains shared references to two forms. Remember, shared members are always available, so you won't need to create an instance of the AppForms class.

```
Public Class AppForms
    Public Shared frmMain As Form
    Public Shared frmSecondary As Form
End Class
```

You can then refer to the forms you need to use in any code module with the following syntax:

```
AppForms.frmMain.Show()
```

Keep in mind that the AppForms class doesn't actually set the form references. You'll need to do that when you create and display the form. One easy way to automate this process is to insert a little code into the Form.Load event handler:

```
Private Sub MainForm_Load(ByVal sender As Object, _
  ByVal e As EventArgs) Handles MyBase.Load

    ' Register the newly created form instance.
    AppForms.frmMain = Me

End Sub
```

This approach works well if every Form class is only created once. If you want to track multiple instances of the same form, you probably want to use a collection object in your AppForms class. The example below uses a Hashtable, which means that every form can be indexed in the collection with a key. If you don't need this ability, you could use the ArrayList object, or even create a custom collection class. Both collection types are found in the System.Collections namespace.

```
Public Class AppForms
    Public Shared frmMain As Form
    Public Shared SecondaryForms As New Hashtable()
End Class
```

Forms can add themselves to this collection as needed:

```
Private Sub SecondaryForm_Load(ByVal sender As Object, _
  ByVal e As EventArgs) Handles MyBase.Load

    ' Register the newly created form instance.
    AppForms.SecondaryForms.Add(Me)

End Sub
```

When trying to read from variables like frmMain, you should also explicitly check if the value is Nothing (in other words, it hasn't yet been created) before attempting to access the form object.

Of course, you should minimize the need for form interactions, as they complicate code unnecessarily. If you do need to modify a control in one form based on an action in another form (a common requirement when designing wizard-like features), create a dedicated method in the target form. That makes sure that the dependency is well identified, and adds another layer of indirection, making it easier to accommodate changes to the form's interface. Figures 5-5 and 5-6 show two examples for implementing this pattern. Figure 5-5 shows a form that triggers a second form to refresh its data in response to a button click. This form does not directly attempt to modify the second form's user interface; instead, it relies on a custom intermediate method called DoUpdate(). The second example, Figure 5-6, shows a case where more than one form needs to be updated. In this case, the acting form relies on a higher-level application method, which calls the required form update methods (perhaps by iterating through a collection of forms).

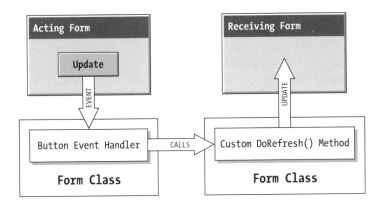

*Figure 5-5. A single form interaction*

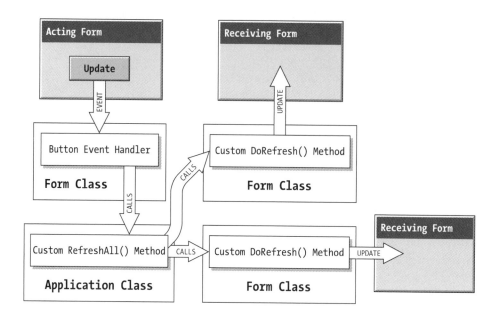

*Figure 5-6. A one-to-many form interaction*

> **NOTE** *These rules don't apply for MDI applications, which have built-in features that help you track child and parent windows. Chapter 10 presents a few detailed examples of how MDI forms should interact with one another.*

## Form Ownership

.NET allows a form to "own" other forms. Owned forms are useful for floating toolbox and command windows. One example of an owned form is the Find and Replace window in Microsoft Word. When an owner window is minimized, the owned forms are also minimized automatically. When an owned form overlaps its owner, it is always displayed on top. Table 5-6 lists the properties of the Form class that support owned forms.

*Table 5-6. Ownership Members of the Form Class*

| Member | Description |
| --- | --- |
| Owner | Identifies a form's owner. You can set this property to change a form's ownership, or release an owned form. |
| OwnedForms | Provides an array of all the forms owned by the current form. This array is read-only. |
| AddOwnedForm() and RemovedOwnedForm() | You can use these methods to add or release forms from an owner. It has the same result as setting the Owner property. |

The following example (shown in Figure 5-7) loads two forms, and provides buttons on the owner that acquire or release the owned form. You can try this sample (included in code download for this chapter with the project name FormOwnership) to observe the behavior of owned forms.

```
Public Class Owner
    Inherits System.Windows.Forms.Form

    ' (Windows designer code omitted.)

    Private frmOwner As New OwnedForm()

    Private Sub Owner_Load(ByVal sender As System.Object, _
     ByVal e As System.EventArgs) Handles MyBase.Load
        frmOwner.Show()
    End Sub

    Private Sub cmdAddOwnership_Click(ByVal sender As System.Object, _
     ByVal e As System.EventArgs) Handles cmdAddOwnership.Click
        Me.AddOwnedForm(frmOwner)
        frmOwner.lblState.Text = "I'm Owned"
    End Sub

    Private Sub cmdReleaseOwnership_Click(ByVal sender As System.Object, _
     ByVal e As System.EventArgs) Handles cmdReleaseOwnership.Click
        Me.RemoveOwnedForm(frmOwner)
        frmOwner.lblState.Text = "I'm Free!"
    End Sub

End Class
```

*Figure 5-7. An owned form tester*

## Windows XP Styles

If you are using the Windows XP visual styles on your computer, you have probably already noticed an anomaly with .NET. Any .NET application you create in Windows XP uses the Windows XP styles for the non-client area (such as the border and minimize/maximize buttons) but not for the actual form surface. Basic user interface elements, like buttons, check boxes, and radio buttons, still have the antiquated look that they've used since the early days of Windows 95.

Fortunately, you can enable Windows XP styles in your .NET applications. To do so, you need to create a special manifest file. This manifest file is an ordinary text file with the same name as your application, plus the extension .manifest (e.g., TheApp.exe would have the manifest file TheApp.exe.manifest—with what looks like two extensions). This file needs to go in the same directory as your program.

All the manifest file does is instruct Windows that your application should use the new version of the Comctl32.dll file, if available. This file is part of Windows XP and is used for the visual styles (it is also not redistributable to non-XP computers).

An example .manifest file is shown in the following, and is provided in the root directory of the code download for this book. You can copy this file exactly for your applications. Ideally, you should modify the name value (currently set to "TheApp"), but this change isn't necessary.

```
<?xml version="1.0" encoding="UTF-8" standalone="yes"?>
<assembly xmlns="urn:schemas-microsoft-com:asm.v1" manifestVersion="1.0">
<assemblyIdentity
    version="1.0.0.0"
    processorArchitecture="X86"
    name="TheApp"
    type="win32" />
```

```
<dependency>
<dependentAssembly>
<assemblyIdentity
    type="win32"
    name="Microsoft.Windows.Common-Controls"
    version="6.0.0.0"
    processorArchitecture="X86"
    publicKeyToken="6595b64144ccf1df"
    language="*" />

</dependentAssembly>
</dependency>
</assembly>
```

This gets you part of the way, but you also need to configure all your form's button-style controls, like Button, CheckBox, and RadioButton. These controls all have a FlatStyle property, which you must be set to System (not Standard) for Windows XP to supply its visual styles.

Once you are finished, run your application. The changes won't appear inside the development environment. Figure 5-8 shows the differences between the classic Windows look and Windows XP styles for some common controls.

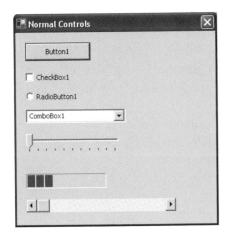 

*Figure 5-8. Windows XP visual styles*

**TIP**  *You can safely supply a manifest file for applications that run on older operating systems. If your application is executed on a non-Windows XP computer, the manifest file is harmlessly ignored, and the ordinary control appearance remains.*

## Prebuilt Dialogs

.NET provides some custom dialog types that you can use to show standard operating system windows. The most common of these is the MessageBox class, which exposes a shared Show() method. You can use this code to display a standard Windows message box (see Figure 5-9):

```
MessageBox.Show("You must enter a name.", "Name Entry Error", _
              MessageBoxButtons.OK, MessageBoxIcon.Exclamation)
```

*Figure 5-9. A simple message box*

The message box icon types are listed in Table 5-7. The button types you can use with a message box are:

- AbortRetryIgnore

- OK

- OKCancel

- RetryCancel

- YesNo

- YesNoCancel

*Table 5-7. MessageBoxIcon Values*

| MessageBoxIcon | Displays |
|---|---|
| Asterisk or Information | A lowercase letter i in a circle. |
| Error, Hand, or Stop | A white X in a circle with a red background. |
| Exclamation or Warning | An exclamation point in a triangle with a yellow background. |
| None | No icon. |
| Question | A question mark in a circle. |

In addition, .NET provides useful dialogs that allow you to show standard windows for opening and saving files, choosing a font or color, and configuring the printer. These classes all inherit from System.Windows.Forms.CommonDialog. For the most part, you show these dialogs like an ordinary window, and then inspect the appropriate property to find the user selection.

For example, the code for retrieving a color selection is as follows:

```
Dim MyDialog As New ColorDialog()

' Sets the initial color select to the current color,
' so that if the user cancels, the original color is restored.
MyDialog.Color = Shape.ForeColor

MyDialog.ShowDialog()

Shape.ForeColor = MyDialog.Color
```

The dialogs often provide a few other properties; for example, with a ColorDialog you can set AllowFullOpen to False to prevent users from choosing a custom color, and ShowHelp to True to allow them to invoke Help by pressing F1. (In this case, you need to handle the HelpRequest event.)

The OpenFileDialog provides its own set of properties, which allow you to validate the user's selection, allow multiple files to be selected, and set the filter string used for allowed file extensions:

```
Dim MyDialog As New OpenFileDialog()

MyDialog.Filter = "Image Files(*.BMP;*.JPG;*.GIF)|*.BMP;*.JPG;*.GIF" & _
                  "|All files (*.*)|*.*"
MyDialog.CheckFileExists = True
MyDialog.Multiselect = True

MyDialog.ShowDialog()

Dim File As String, SelectedFiles As String = ""
For Each File In MyDialog.FileNames
    SelectedFiles &= File & " "
Next

lblDisplay.Text = "You chose: " & SelectedFiles
```

The PageSetupDialog and PrintDialog behave slightly differently, because they allow the user to set multiple printing options at once. With .NET, you do not have to retrieve and apply these settings. Instead, you just set the PrintDocument object for the current document in the Document property, and all the appropriate settings are applied automatically when the user selects them.

```
Dim MyDialog As New PageSetupDialog()

MyDialog.Document = MyDocument
MyDialog.ShowDialog()
```

Also, with the PrintDialog, you need to make sure to examine the dialog result to decide whether the user has chosen to continue with the print operation.

```
Dim MyDialog As New PrintDialog()

MyDialog.Document = MyDocument
Dim Result As DialogResult = MyDialog.ShowDialog()

If Result = DialogResult.OK Then
    ' (Initiate printing here.)
End If
```

Table 5-8 provides an overview of the prebuilt dialog classes. Figure 5-10 shows a small image of each window type.

*Table 5-8. Common Dialog Classes*

| Class | Description |
|---|---|
| ColorDialog | Displays the system colors and controls that allow the user to define custom colors. The selected color can be found in the Color property. |
| OpenFileDialog | Allows the user to select a file, which is returned in the FileName property (or the FileNames collection, if you have enabled multiple file select). Additionally, you can use the Filter property to set the file format choices, and use CheckFileExists to enforce validation. |
| SaveFileDialog | Allows the user to select a file, which is returned in the FileName property. You can also use the Filter property to set the file format choices, and use set the CreatePrompt and OverwritePrompt Boolean properties to instruct .NET to display a confirmation if the user selects a new file or an existing file, respectively. |
| FontDialog | Allows the user to choose a font face and size, which is provided in the Font property (and its color through the Color property). You can limit the size selection with properties like MinSize and MaxSize, and you can set ShowColor and ShowEffects to configure whether the user changes the font color and uses special styles like underlining and strikeout. |
| PageSetupDialog | Allows the user to configure page layout, page format, margins, and the printer. To use this dialog, simply place the PrintDocument object for the document you want to print in the PageSetupDialog.Document property. Then, all settings are automatically set in your PrintDocument object when the user accepts them. Additionally, you can use properties like AllowMargins, AllowOrientation, AllowPaper, and AllowPrinter to choose the elements of this dialog that are shown to the user. |
| PrintDialog | Allows users to select a printer, choose which portions of the document to print, and invoke printing. To use this dialog, simply place the PrintDocument object for the document you want to print in the PrintDialog.Document property. |
| PrintPreviewDialog | This is the only dialog that is not a part of standard Windows architecture. It provides a painless way to show a print preview—just assign the PrintDocument to the Document property and display the form. The same logic you write for handling the actual printing is used automatically to construct the preview. Alternatively, you can use the PrintPreviewControl to show the same preview inside one of your custom windows. |

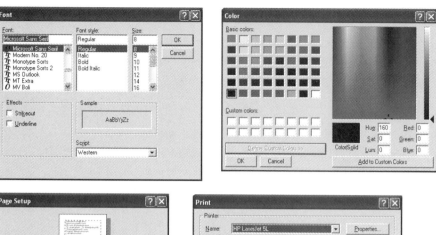

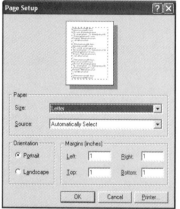

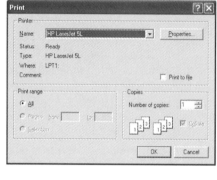

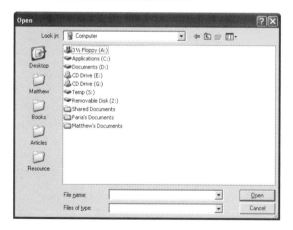

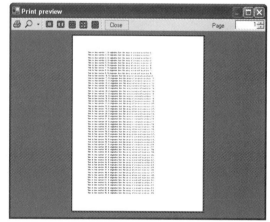

*Figure 5-10. Common dialogs*

# Resizable Forms

Every week, Windows developers from every programming language spend countless hours trying to solve the problem of resizable windows. Some purchase third-party ActiveX controls designed to transform static forms into resizable wonders automatically. These components are easy to use, but generally provide mediocre results that aren't suitable for professional applications. Other developers ignore the problem, and stubbornly lock interfaces into fixed-size dialog boxes, making them seem unmistakably primitive. Most developers eventually give in, and write lengthy code routines to resize their forms by hand.

In .NET the picture has finally improved. Two new features—anchoring and docking—provide built-in support for resizable forms. These features allow you to configure a few properties, and end up with intelligent controls that adjust themselves automatically. The catch? It's extremely easy to create the equivalent of the mediocre ActiveX resizing control. In other words, you can end up with a window that resizes its controls in an embarrassingly unprofessional way with far less effort than was needed before.

Matching a good resizing approach with a sophisticated interface is possible, but it requires a little more subtlety and a few tricks. This chapter describes these tricks, such as adding container controls and using the DockPadding property. Along the way, you learn how to create scrollable windows and controls, and see a full-fledged Explorer-style application that uses automatic resizing the right way.

## *The Problem of Size*

The resizable forms dilemma stems from the fact that the Windows operating system supports a variety of monitors at several different resolutions. A window that looks decently sized on one computer may shrink to a toy-like box on another, or even stretch beyond the bounds of the desktop, obscuring important controls.

For many simple applications, these types of problems are not serious because programmers usually design their applications for a set minimum standard resolution (such as 640 × 480 or, more commonly today, 800 × 600). It's also generally accepted that users with much larger viewable areas expect to run several programs at once, and purchased larger screens so that they can put different programs side-by-side. They don't expect to use up the extra viewable area with larger fonts or extra whitespace in a dialog box.

However, a document-based application can't afford to ignore these considerations. Users with more available space expect to be able to use it to see more information at a time. Programs that ignore this consideration (see for example Figure 5-11) are irredeemably frustrating.

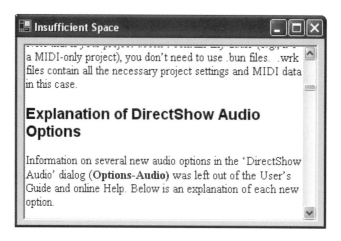

*Figure 5-11. A frustrating window*

> **TIP** *Generally, a form needs to be resizable as soon as it stores more content than it can show at once. For example, a configuration window with a few settings does not need to be resizable, because all the information is available. On the other hand, a window that shows a scrolled text view or a data grid can benefit from more space, and so should be resizable.*

Ever since the dawn of Windows 95 and 32-bit programming, developers have found it increasingly difficult to avoid writing manual code to resize windows (in the older days of Windows programming, they just didn't bother at all). The emphasis on MDI interfaces has also contributed to this change. In an MDI (Multiple Document Interface) application, users expect to be able to resize, maximize, minimize, tile, and otherwise arrange all the child windows.

## A Traditional Solution

The most common solution is to write procedures that dynamically resize the window, by responding to a resize event or message. The code for this type of dynamic resizing is generally not very complicated, particularly in Visual Basic. Unfortunately, if your window has more than a couple of controls, it is long, repetitive, and ugly. It's also hard to alter or debug when the form changes even slightly, and a nightmarish example of hard-coded values and cryptic lines of code. Consider the historical example shown below of a simple Visual Basic resize routine:

```vb
' This is unavoidably ugly VB6 code!

Private Sub Form_Resize()

    On Error Resume Next

    ' Check for reentrancy.
    Static FormResizeInProgress As Boolean
    If FormResizeInProgress = True Then Exit Sub

    FormResizeInProgress = True

    ' Check if form is smaller than minimum allowed size.
    If Me.WindowState = vbNormal Then
        If Me.Width < 5800 Then
            Me.Width = 5800
        End If
        If Me.Height < 5800 Then
            Me.Height = 5800
        End If
    End If

    ' Adjust frames.
    fraInfo.Width = Me.Width - 300
    fraItems.Width = Me.Width - 300
    fraItems.Height = Me.Height - 2700

    ' Adjust buttons.
    cmdAdd.Left = gridItems.Left + Me.Width - 2760 + 260
    cmdDel.Left = cmdAdd.Left
    cmdEdit.Left = cmdAdd.Left
    cmdComplete.Left = Me.Width - cmdComplete.Width - 230
    cmdComplete.Top = Me.Height - cmdComplete.Height - 550

    ' Adjust grid.
    gridItems.Height = Me.Height - 3400
    gridItems.Width = Me.Width - 2760

    FormResizeInProgress = False

End Sub
```

Believe it or not, this code is taken from a real VB application, and slightly simplified. It provides a typical example of resizing in the 20th century. The result is workable, although not that impressive (see Figure 5-12).

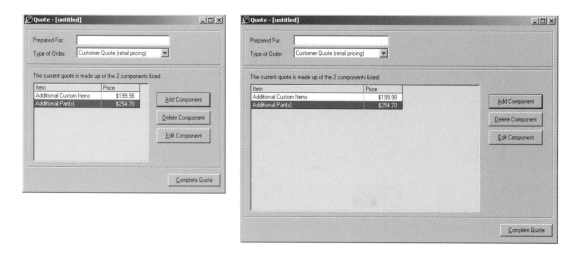

*Figure 5-12. A simple resizable form*

Besides the hard-coded values and general lack of readability, this example also suffers from a few quirks:

- This code springs into action *after* the form has been resized. That means it can't prevent a user from making the window too small (or too large), it can only quickly override the change. If the user has the Show window contents while dragging environment setting enabled, the result is a window that flickers back and forth between the user's attempted change and the stubbornly resistant VB code.

- You have to check the current state of the window, or perform some error handling. The resize event fires when a window is minimized or maximized, and trying to change its size is impossible.

- Resizing the form inside the form's resize event triggers another resize event. If the program doesn't carefully guard against reentrancy it can get trapped in an endless loop.

The Windows API can get around some of these limitations, but it can also generate cryptic bugs and crash the IDE. If you come to .NET from a Java or C#

background, you no doubt have your own resizable window horror stories. You'll also be grateful to find that .NET makes life quite a bit simpler. In fact, you can accomplish everything shown in our VB 6 example and more—without a single line of code.

## Minimum and Maximum Size

The first useful feature the form class introduces for managing size is the MaximumSize and MimimumSize properties. These properties stop users abruptly when they try to resize a form outside its set limits. For example, the Address Book program included with Windows 2000/XP won't let you shrink it any smaller than the size of the toolbar (see Figure 5-13).

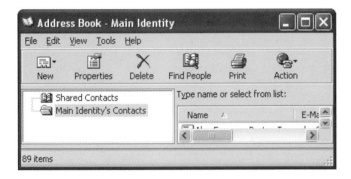

*Figure 5-13. The Address Book's minimum size*

If you have the Show window contents while dragging environment setting enabled, the border suddenly becomes fixed when you hit the minimum size, as though it's glued in place. Similarly, you can set a maximum size, although this is less conventional. In this case, even when you try to maximize a window, it won't go beyond the set size, which can confuse the user.

The Visual Studio .NET IDE also stops you from resizing your form to an invalid size at design time when you have these properties set. If you set the form size to an invalid value in code, no error will occur. Instead, your window just automatically shrinks or expands to a valid size if it's outside the bounds of the allowed MinimumSize or MaximumSize properties.

One final caveat: both of these settings are ignored if you make your window a MDI child inside another window. In that case, your window is freely resizable.

## Anchoring

Anchoring allows you to latch a control on to one of the form's corners. Anchored controls always stay a fixed distance from the point they are bound to. By default, every control is anchored to the top left corner. That means that when you move the window (and hence the top left corner), the controls follow. If you resize the form, however, the controls stay in place, because the position of the top left corner hasn't changed.

On the other hand, you can use .NET to anchor a control to a different corner. For example, if you chose the top right corner, the control moves as you expanded the window width-wise to stay within a fixed distance of the corner. If you expand the form height-wise, the control stays in place, because it's anchored to the top. It doesn't need to follow the bottom edge.

To anchor a button in .NET, you set the Anchor property using one of the values from the AnchorStyles enumeration. It's almost always easiest to set anchoring at design-time using the Properties window. A special designer lets you select the edges you are anchoring to by clicking them in a miniature picture, as shown in Figure 5-14. You don't need to run your program to test your anchoring settings; the Visual Studio .NET IDE provides the same behavior.

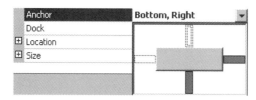

*Figure 5-14. Setting control anchoring at design-time*

### Resizing controls with anchoring

Anchoring to one corner works best with controls that don't need to change size, but should remain in a consistent position. This typically includes buttons (for example, OK and Cancel should always remain at the bottom of the window) and simple controls like labels and text boxes. If you use this type of anchoring on every control, you create a window that gradually spreads out as it enlarges, providing that dreaded "third-party component" effect.

Instead, you can anchor a control to more than one side at once. Then, as you expand the window, the control needs to expand to keep a fixed distance from all the anchored sides. Table 5-9 lists some of the ways that you can combine anchor settings for different effects, and Figure 5-15 shows a window that uses fixed-corner anchoring for a button, and side-to-side anchoring for a text box.

> **TIP**  *When using a resizable ListBox control, be sure to set the IntegralHeight property to False. This ensures that the ListBox can grow evenly. Otherwise, the ListBox is automatically resized to ensure that no list item is partially displayed. This causes it to "jump" awkwardly between valid sizes as its height grows or shrinks.*

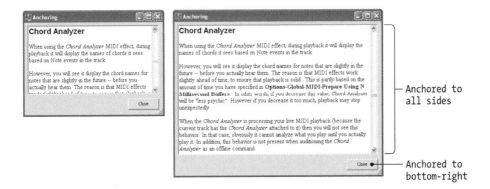

*Figure 5-15. Two ways to use anchoring*

*Table 5-9. Common Anchoring Choices*

| Anchoring | Description |
| --- | --- |
| Top + Left | Equivalent to no anchoring. Controls remain a fixed distance from the top left corner, but they don't move or expand as the form changes size. |
| Bottom + Right | The control moves to keep a fixed distance from the bottom right corner. |
| Bottom + Left | The control moves to stay at the bottom of the form, but it does not move to the side. |
| Top + Right | The control moves to stay at the right of the form, but it does not move down. |
| Top + Bottom | The control's height expands as the form lengthens. |
| Right + Left | The control's width expands as the form widens. |
| Top + Bottom + Right + Left | The control's width and height expand as the form is enlarged. |

The controls that benefit the most from anchoring to more than one side are those that contain more information than they can display at once. For example, a DataGrid, RichTextBox, or even ListBox control may present a scrolled view into a large amount of information. It makes sense for these controls to resize to use available screen area. On the other hand, a button should never be set to resize. Doing so impersonates the low-quality add-in controls that performed resizing automatically.

**NOTE** *The problems I keep mentioning with ActiveX controls for automatic resizing is that most tried to apply the same strategy to every window (there are a couple of rare exceptions). The result is that every control resized itself in pretty much the same way. In a real window, however, some controls are more important and need more space. Other controls don't need to change at all, and can look rather ridiculous if they are sized radically bigger than their contents. Ultimately, resizing is another area where you must follow user interface design conventions from established Windows applications.*

## Containers and anchoring

Rather than try to anchor every control in a window, you should use one or more container controls to save some work. Containers also make it easier to rearrange portions of user interface at once, or even transplant them from one form to another.

To use anchoring with container controls, you need to understand that anchoring is always relative to the container. That means that if you place a button inside a group box and you anchor it to the bottom right, it will be anchored to the bottom right corner of the group box. It won't move when the size of the form changes; it will move only when the size of the container changes. For example, consider the button shown in Figure 5-16. The form is resized, but the group box doesn't change, and so the button also remains in place.

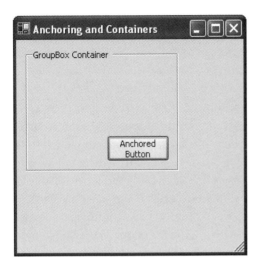

*Figure 5-16. Anchored controls follow a corner in the container.*

Nothing happens in the previous example, because there's no change in the container. To get around this, you could anchor the group box to all sides of the window. Then, as the group box grows, the button will move to keep a consistent distance from the bottom right corner. This version is shown in Figure 5-17.

*Figure 5-17. Anchoring the control and its container*

Container controls become particularly important when you start to add docking and split windows to your designs.

## Docking

Docking allows a control to bind itself to an edge in the form or container control. When you resize the container, the control resizes itself to fit the entire edge. A control can be bound to any one edge, or it can be set to fill the entire available area. The only limitation is that you can't dock and anchor the same control (if you think about it for a moment, you'll realize that it wouldn't make sense anyway).

For example, you can solve the problem you saw with the button in the container control by docking the group box to the right edge of our form. Now, when you resize the window, the group box expands to fit the edge. Because the button inside is anchored to the bottom right corner of the group box, it also moves to the right side as the form is enlarged. Similarly, you could set the group box docking to fill, so that it would automatically resize itself to occupy the entire available area. Figure 5-18 shows an example of this behavior.

*Figure 5-18. A docked group box*

To configure docking, you set the control's Dock property to one a value from the DockStyle enumeration. Typically, you use the Property window to choose a setting at design-time.

If you experiment with docking, your initial enthusiasm quickly drains away, as you quickly discover that:

- Docked controls insist on sitting flush against the docked edge. This results in excessive crowding, and doesn't leave a nice border where you need it.

- Docked controls always dock to the entire edge. There's no way to tell a docked control to bind to the first half (or 50 percent) of an edge. It automatically takes the full available width, which makes it difficult to design a real interface.

Every control that derives from the ScrollableControl class has an additional feature called dock padding. Dock padding allows you to insert a buffer of empty space between a container and its docked controls. The only important classes that derive from ScrollableControl are Panel, Form, and UserControl. The GroupBox control does not provide any padding.

Figure 5-19 shows another example with a group box and a contained button. Because the Form is the container for the group box, you need to modify the form's padding property by finding DockPadding in the properties window, expanding it, and setting All to 10 (pixels). Now the group box will still bind to all sides, but it will have some breathing room around it.

*Figure 5-19. A docked group box with padding*

At this point you may wonder why you need docking at all. It seems like a slightly more awkward way to accomplish what anchoring can achieve easily.

However, in many cases, anchoring alone is not enough. There are two common scenarios:

- You are using an advanced window design that hides and shows various window elements. In this scenario, docking forces other controls to resize and make room, while anchoring leads to overlapping controls.

- You want to create a window that the user can resize, like a split window design. In this case, you need to use docking, because it allows controls to resize to fit the available space.

You examine both of these designs in the next section.

> **TIP**  *The sample code for this chapter includes a program that lets you play with a number of different combinations of anchoring and docking, so you can see how they do or don't solve a problem.*

## Splitting Windows

One of the most recognizable user interface styles in applications today is the split window look (arguably popularized by Windows Explorer). In fact, split-window view applications are beginning to replace the former dominant paradigm of MDI, and Microsoft has led the change (although many developers, myself included, still favor MDI design for many large-scale applications).

In .NET, split-window designs are refreshingly easy to create, which is a dramatic departure from most other programming environments. To create a split window requires just three easy steps:

1. Start by docking a control to one side of the window.

2. Add the Splitter control, and dock it to the same side.

3. Add another control, and set its docking to Fill so it occupies the rest of the window.

The example in Figure 5-20 shows this technique with a TreeView and a ListView. By moving the position of the splitter bar at runtime, the user can change the relative size of these two controls.

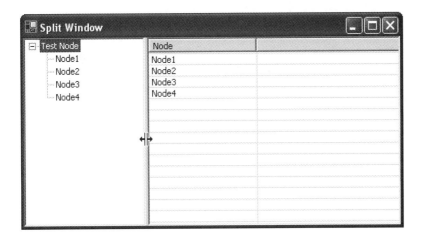

*Figure 5-20. A basic splitter bar*

In this case, the window is somewhat claustrophobic. To improve the spacing, you can set a buffer using the form's DockPadding property. However, this won't add any extra spacing between the controls and the splitter bar—to add that, you need to anchor the ListView and TreeView in separate docked Panels, as you consider in the next example.

You can also set the SplitterBar.MinSize property to configure the smallest size (in pixels) to which the first docked control can be resized. You can also set the SplitterBar.MinExtra property to configure the minimum size for the controls on the other side of the splitter.

## Docking with Panels

Rather than docking specific controls, as in the preceding example, it's more common to dock two Panel controls, one on each side of the splitter bar. That way, you can include several controls together in the Panel, and fine-tune their spacing. You can then use anchoring to cause the controls inside the Panel to resize themselves to fit its contents. This is where docking and container controls really begin to become useful.

Figure 5-21 shows an example taken from Chapter 9, which uses a customized TreeView/ListView explorer.

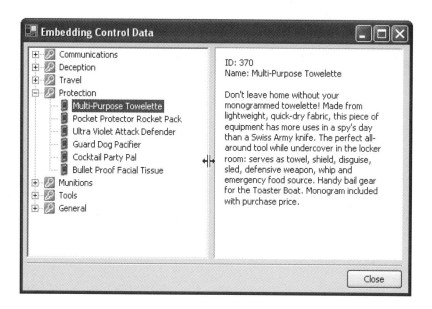

*Figure 5-21. Advanced docking*

The panel on the left includes a single TreeView, but the panel on the right includes two label controls spaced inside a panel, in order to give a pleasing border around the label text. (If the same window simply used a single label control with a border, the text in the label would sit flush against the border.) The horizontal rule and Close button at the bottom of the window aren't included in the resizable portion of the window. Instead, they are anchored in a separately docked panel, which is attached to the bottom of the form

To implement this design, a panel control is first docked to the bottom to hold the Close button. Then, the TreeView, SplitterBar, and ListView controls are docked to fill the upper portion of the window. The diagram in Figure 5-22 shows the docking.

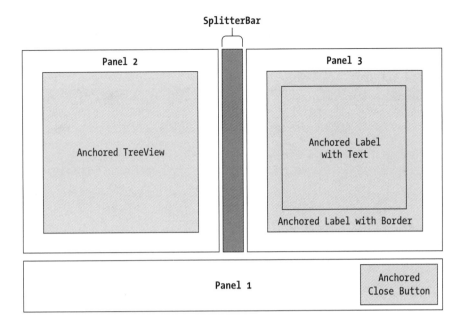

*Figure 5-22. A docking strategy*

When designing this user interface, you may find that Visual Studio .NET is a little inflexible. If you dock the panels in the wrong order, you won't achieve the desired effect, and you'll need to copy all the controls to another form, and add the panels back one at a time in the correct docking order. Of course, the professional finished result is worth this minor aggravation.

## Other Split Windows

Another reason to split a window is to provide two different views of the same data. Consider the example shown in Figure 5-23, which shows an HTML page using Microsoft's ActiveX web browser control and an ordinary text box. In this case, the splitter is docked to the top of the control, and becomes a horizontal bar.

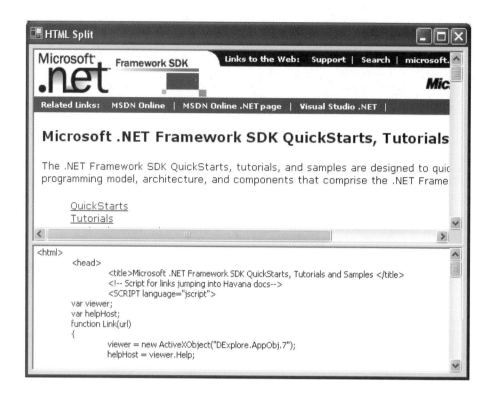

*Figure 5-23. A split view on a single document*

You could also add another vertical splitter to create a compound view. For example, consider Figure 5-24, which provides a list of HTML files the user can select from.

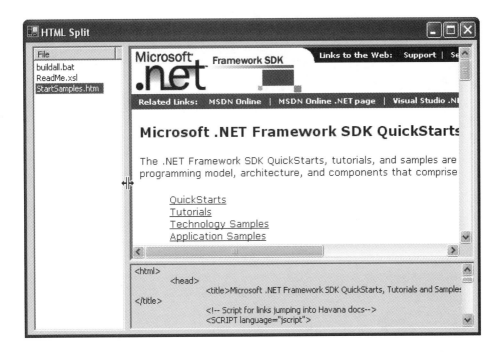

*Figure 5-24. Multiple splits*

One of the best characteristics of docked designs is that they easily accommodate hidden or modified controls. For example, Figure 5-25 shows an alternate design that allows the file selection panel to be collapsed and then restored to its original size with the click of the button. The contents of the window automatically resize themselves to accommodate the additional portion when it is displayed.

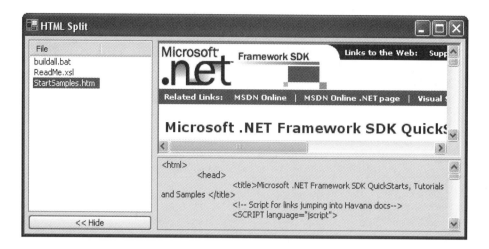

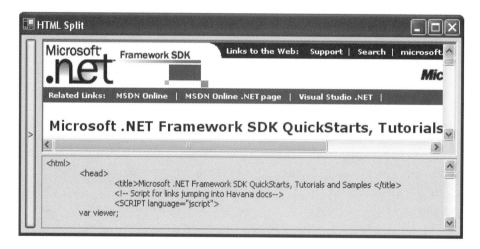

*Figure 5-25. A collapsible split window*

The code for this operation is trivial:

```
Private Sub cmdHide_Click(ByVal sender As System.Object, _
  ByVal e As System.EventArgs) Handles cmdHide.Click

        pnlFileList.Visible = False
        pnlShow.Visible = True

End Sub
```

```
Private Sub cmdShow_Click(ByVal sender As System.Object, _
   ByVal e As System.EventArgs) Handles cmdShow.Click

       pnlShow.Visible = False
       pnlFileList.Visible = True

End Sub
```

This sample is included in the code for this chapter, with the project name HTMLSplitWindow.

> **TIP** *When designing a split window, it is best to start by creating and docking panel controls. Otherwise, if you need to modify your design, you may need to start over. When using panels, you can always add any controls you require simply by dropping them inside the appropriate panel.*

## Irregularly Shaped Forms

Irregularly shaped forms are often the trademark of cutting-edge consumer applications like photo editors, movie makers, and MP3 players. In the past, creating them required a fair bit of API wizardry. Now with .NET, creating a shaped form is almost effortless, thanks to the new GDI+ model that's included as part of the .NET framework.

To create a simple shaped window in .NET, all you need to do is create a form, and assign a new shape to its Region property (this is the same process followed to create a custom shaped control). There is more than one way to create a Region, but the easiest is by using the GraphicsPath class, which allows you to build up a complex shape out of as many subshapes as you need.

First, begin by importing the required GDI+ namespace:

```
Imports System.Drawing.Drawing2D
```

You can then create and apply the GraphicsPath. The following example code defines an ellipse with the same bounds of the form. Once it's assigned to the Region property of the form, only the part of the form that fits inside the ellipse is displayed (see Figure 5-26).

```
Private Sub Form1_Load(ByVal sender As System.Object, _
    ByVal e As System.EventArgs) Handles MyBase.Load

    Dim Path As New GraphicsPath()
    Path.AddEllipse(0, 0, Me.Width, Me.Height)
    Me.Region = New Region(Path)

End Sub
```

*Figure 5-26. A shaped form*

You can see part of the original window border at the top and bottom of the shaped form, and the single contained button in the middle. However, the form acts completely like an ellipse. For example, if you click in the cutout portion that the original rectangular form occupied (for example, just above the left edge of the ellipse), you will not select the form. Instead, you select whatever application is currently underneath the form. This convenience is a great step forward—with ordinary GDI code, shaped controls looked like shapes but still behaved like the original rectangles in many ways.

You can also create a shaped form made up of a combination of shapes. In fact, these shapes don't even need to overlap! The following example illustrates a more unusual shaped form, shown in Figure 5-27:

```
Private Sub Form1_Load(ByVal sender As System.Object, _
    ByVal e As System.EventArgs) Handles MyBase.Load

    Dim Path As New GraphicsPath()
    Path.AddEllipse(0, 0, Me.Width \ 2, Me.Height \ 2)
    Path.AddRectangle(New Rectangle(Me.Width \ 2, Me.Top \ 2, _
                                    Me.Width \ 2, Me.Top \ 2))
```

```
Path.AddEllipse(Me.Width \ 2, Me.Height \ 2, Me.Width \ 2, Me.Height \ 2)

Me.Region = New Region(Path)

End Sub
```

*Figure 5-27. A noncontiguous shaped form*

## Shaped Form Content

There are two problems you will quickly notice with shaped forms:

- The Region defines a shape, but this shape does not provide any borders. Instead, a shaped form is just a geometric figure that reveals the underlying form.

- Ordinary controls (like standard windows buttons) aren't well suited for a shaped form—the styles seem to clash.

To handle these problems, you need to create your graphical content from scratch. You can accomplish this by using GDI+ to create owner-drawn controls, as you'll see in Chapter 12 and Chapter 13. An easier approach is just to design the appropriate images in a dedicated graphics program, and import them into your .NET controls.

For example, you can set the BackgroundImage property for the form to a picture that has the same shape you want to use, and includes a border. You can also substitute picture box controls for buttons. Figure 5-28 shows one such example.

*Figure 5-28. An irregular form with graphical content*

In order to make the images behave like buttons, some additional logic is required to offset the button when it is clicked.

```
Private Sub pic_MouseDown(ByVal sender As Object, _
  ByVal e As System.Windows.Forms.MouseEventArgs) Handles picOne.MouseDown, _
  picTwo.MouseDown, picThree.MouseDown, picFour.MouseDown

    Dim pic As PictureBox = CType(sender, PictureBox)
    pic.Top += 2
    pic.Left += 2

End Sub

Private Sub pic_MouseUp(ByVal sender As Object, _
  ByVal e As System.Windows.Forms.MouseEventArgs) Handles picOne.MouseUp, _
  picTwo.MouseUp, picThree.MouseUp, picFour.MouseUp

    Dim pic As PictureBox = CType(sender, PictureBox)
    pic.Top -= 2
    pic.Left -= 2

End Sub
```

Additionally, the images are enhanced to support hot tracking. Whenever the mouse pointer positions itself above a button, a different image is displayed. This image looks the same as the normal button image, but has its text highlighted in yellow. The code to implement this technique simply retrieves the required picture from a ListView control.

```
Private Sub pic_MouseEnter(ByVal sender As Object, ByVal e As System.EventArgs) _
    Handles picOne.MouseEnter, picTwo.MouseEnter, picThree.MouseEnter, _
    picFour.MouseEnter

    Dim pic As PictureBox = CType(sender, PictureBox)
    pic.Image = imgSelectedButtons.Images(CType(pic.Tag, Integer))

End Sub

Private Sub pic_MouseLeave(ByVal sender As Object, ByVal e As System.EventArgs) _
    Handles picOne.MouseLeave, picTwo.MouseLeave, picThree.MouseLeave, _
    picFour.MouseLeave

    Dim pic As PictureBox = CType(sender, PictureBox)
    pic.Image = imgNormalButtons.Images(CType(pic.Tag, Integer))

End Sub
```

You can try this code by running the IrregularlyShapedForms project included with the code download for this chapter.

## Moving Shaped Forms

Another limitation of shaped forms is that they often omit the nonclient title bar portion, which allows the user to easily drag the form around the desktop. To remedy this problem, you need to add a control that takes over the responsibility for the form's title bar.

For example, you could add a picture box or a label control. This control needs to handle the MouseDown, MouseUp, and MouseMove events, and reposition the form accordingly (Figure 5-29). The code is similar to that used in Chapter 4 for fake drag and drop operations.

```vb
Dim FormDragging As Boolean
Dim PointClicked As Point

Private Sub lblDrag_MouseDown(ByVal sender As Object, _
   ByVal e As System.Windows.Forms.MouseEventArgs) Handles lblDrag.MouseDown

    ' Set drag mode on.
    FormDragging = True

    ' Store the offset where the control was clicked.
    PointClicked = New Point(e.X, e.Y)

End Sub

Private Sub lblDrag_MouseMove(ByVal sender As Object, _
   ByVal e As System.Windows.Forms.MouseEventArgs) Handles lblDrag.MouseMove

    If FormDragging Then
        Dim PointMoveTo As Point

        ' Find the current mouse position in screen coordinates.
        PointMoveTo = Me.PointToScreen(New Point(e.X, e.Y))

        ' Compensate for the position the control was clicked.
        PointMoveTo.Offset(-PointClicked.X, -PointClicked.Y)

        ' Compensate for the non-client region (title bar).
        ' This code is not necessary if you explicitly hide the title bar
        ' by setting the form's BorderStyle to None.
        PointMoveTo.Offset(0, -25)

        ' Move the form.
        Me.Location = PointMoveTo
    End If

End Sub

Private Sub lblDrag_MouseUp(ByVal sender As Object, _
   ByVal e As System.Windows.Forms.MouseEventArgs) Handles lblDrag.MouseUp

    FormDragging = False

End Sub
```

*Figure 5-29. Moving a shaped form*

## Forms with Holes

There's also one other approach to creating irregularly shaped forms. You can define a special color for the form that will automatically be cut out by setting the form's TransparencyKey property. For example, if you choose dark blue, all occurrences of dark blue in your form become invisible. This includes occurrences of the color in an image, a control, or even the form's background. In fact, these holes aren't just invisible—you can even click through them to activate a program underneath!

Figure 5-30 shows an example from the online samples that contains several picture box controls that contain the TransparencyKey color as their background. At runtime, these picture boxes disappear.

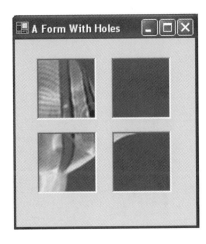

*Figure 5-30. A form (with the desktop showing through)*

# Visual Inheritance

Visual inheritance is a fancy name for form inheritance, which is similar to the custom control pattern you use to create specialized .NET controls. Depending on how you use visual inheritance, you can really accomplish two things:

- Use a common form template (visual appearance) for several different windows. This might be useful to create a wizard or standardized About window.

- Use form functionality in several different windows. This allows you to create a framework that you might use for different types of view windows in a MDI application. Every window will have its own look, but it might reuse some of the same buttons to close the window or open a file.

And, as with any type of inheritance, visual inheritance gives you many different ways to customize how the descendent class can use, extend, or override the inherited class.

To create a simple example of form inheritance, you might create a wizard form like the one shown in Figure 5-31. It uses a blank header area for title text, a large surface area for additional content, and a next and previous button at the bottom. In this example (found in the code for this chapter under the project name VisualInheritance), the base form is named Ancestor.

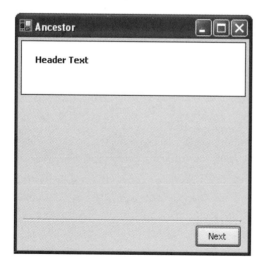

*Figure 5-31. An ancestor form for a wizard*

To create an inherited form that uses this form, you first need to compile the project (unless the form is already stored in a separate assembly from your project). Then, right-click the project item in the Solution Explorer and choose Add ➤ Inherited Form. You'll be prompted to choose a new form name, and select the form you want to derive from (see Figure 5-32).

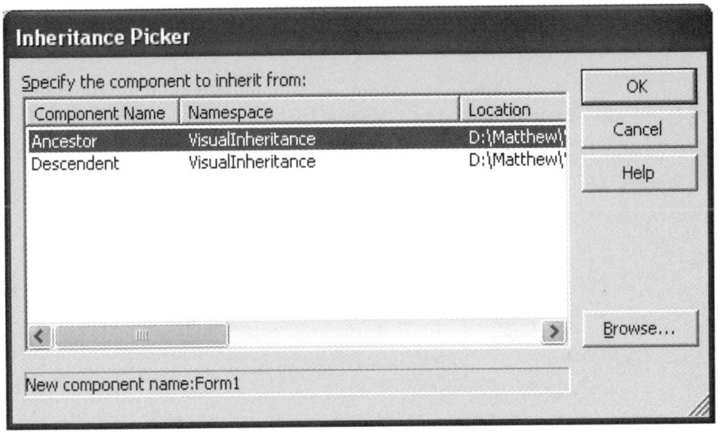

*Figure 5-32. Inheriting from a form*

Of course, you don't actually need to use the wizard to create an inherited form. All you really need to do is create a Form class, and change the standard class declaration (which inherits from the System.Windows.Forms class) to inherit from your custom class. Make sure you use a fully qualified name that includes both the project namespace (in this case, VisualInheritance) and the form name.

```
Public Class Descendent
    Inherits VisualInheritance.Ancestor
```

You'll notice that the inherited form contains all the controls that you defined in the original form, but it doesn't allow you to move them, change their properties, or add event handlers. You can, however, add new controls, write their event handlers, and change the size (or any other property) for your descendant form. In the basic example, this doesn't allow the flexibility you need. For example, the user needs to have some way to configure the label control in the title area and override the function of the next and previous buttons. Fortunately, this is all easy if you understand a few basics about inheritance.

> **TIP**  *Whenever you change an ancestor form, you must recompile the project before you see the appropriate changes in the descendant form. Just right-click the project in the Solution Explorer and choose Build to create the assembly without launching it.*

## Making an Ancestor Control Available

By default, every control on the original Ancestor form is declared with the Friend modifier. This keyword allows access to other forms in the same project, but it doesn't allow any access to your derived form. To change this state of affairs, simply modify the controls you want to configure to use the Protected modifier instead. You can change the declaration by looking through the form code, or you can use the Properties window, and look for the special Modifiers property.

Once you've made this change, you'll find that you can configure any aspect of the inherited controls, including their appearance and position. The values used in the base form become the default values in the derived form, but any changes you make are recorded in the derived form's designer code and applied automatically when the form is created.

## Adding an Ancestor Property

In our wizard example, creating protected-level controls may not be the best approach. Quite simply, it allows too much freedom to change the original layout. Take the header text, for example. The creator of the derived form should be able to enter custom text into the control, but other details (like its font, color, and position) shouldn't be modifiable, as they risk compromising the standardized layout you've established.

To code a better solution, you could create a special property in the base form. The client could then use this property to set the header text, without being allowed any greater degree of control.

```
Public Property HeaderText() As String
    Get
        Return lblHeader.Text
    End Get
    Set(ByVal Value As String)
        lblHeader.Text = Value
    End Set
End Property
```

In your Ancestor form, this property is available through code—and it also appears as value the user can set in the Properties window (see Figure 5-33). In fact, you can add other attributes to this property that configure the description it shows and the category it will appear in, but that topic is explored in Chapter 10.

*Figure 5-33. A custom property*

## Overriding an Event Handler

Your base form might also contain event-handling logic. If this logic is generic (for example, it simply closes the form) it is suitable for all descendants. In the case of your previous and next buttons, there clearly is no generic code that can be written. Instead, the descendant needs to override the event handling code.

To accomplish this, you need to declare that the event handler is overridable in your ancestor form:

```
Protected Overridable Sub cmdNext_Click(ByVal sender As System.Object, _
    ByVal e As System.EventArgs) Handles cmdNext.Click
        MessageBox.Show("Ancestor form event handler.")
End Sub
```

You can then override the routine in your descendant form:

```
' Do NOT include the Handles keyword!
Protected Overrides Sub cmdNext_Click(ByVal sender As System.Object, _
  ByVal e As System.EventArgs)
    MessageBox.Show("Descendant form event handler.")
End Sub
```

Note that this code does *not* include the Handles keyword. That's because the original routine (the one you are overriding) is already connected to the event. If you add the Handles keyword here, the same code would actually be invoked twice as the event is handled in the base form and the derived form. Another way to get around this situation is just to mark the control as Protected. In this case, you don't need to include an ancestor event handler; instead, the derived form can write event-handling code directly. The side effect is that you lose your protection, and any other aspect of the control can also be modified in the derived form.

In some cases, you might want to execute both the extra code in the descendant form, and the original code. You can accomplish this by using the MyBase reference. The code that follows, for example, results in the display of two message boxes, one from the Ancestor form, followed by one from the derived form.

```
Protected Overrides Sub cmdNext_Click(ByVal sender As System.Object, _
  ByVal e As System.EventArgs)
    ' Call the original version.
    MyBase.cmdNext_Click(sender, e)

    MessageBox.Show("Descendant form event handler.")
End Sub
```

Finally, in some cases you might want to *force* an event handler to be over-ridden. For example, in our example a wizard form can't be considered complete unless it has the necessary event handling logic behind added to its next button. However, it's impossible to code this logic at the ancestor level. To force the derived class to override this event handler (as a precautionary measure), you can declare the event handler with the MustOverride qualifier.

```
Protected MustOverride Sub cmdNext_Click(ByVal sender As System.Object, _
  ByVal e As System.EventArgs) Handles cmdNext.Click
```

In this case, the Ancestor form class must also be declared MustInherit.

```
Public MustInherit Class Ancestor
```

Be warned that this pattern can confuse the Visual Studio .NET IDE, and could even cause it to stop displaying your derived forms (although the code will work without a hitch).

As you master visual inheritance, you might want to expand the inheritance technique to include your custom controls. Chapter 7 is dedicated to this approach.

## The Last Word

In this chapter you've traveled from the basics of Windows forms—creating them, displaying them, and handling their interactions, to advanced techniques using shaped forms and visual inheritance. In many respects, these new developments hint at two of the themes I take up in the rest of the book. Shaped forms give just a taste of what you encounter in Chapters 12 and 13, which dive headfirst into GDI+. Visual inheritance provides a preview into some of custom control designs you explore with control inheritance throughout this book. Both techniques represent the step from ordinary user interface programming to the more advanced techniques of a UI guru.

# CHAPTER 6
# Modern Controls

MANY OF THE CONTROLS you've looked at so far (like buttons, menus, and text boxes) have been around since the early days of Windows 3.1 without much more than the occasional facelift. As development entered the 32-bit world, more sophisticated controls began to appear and gain popularity. Controls like the TabControl, ListView, and TreeView began to do wonders organizing complex information. At the same time, the ToolBar and StatusBar revamped the look of the standard Windows application with a more modern feel.

In this chapter, you learn about all these controls. More important, you learn the tricks and techniques you need to master them. Custom control classes, one of my favorite themes, returns in this chapter with a few remarkable examples. You see how to create subclassed controls that are fine-tuned for specific data, or can automatically communicate and synchronize themselves with other controls.

## The ImageList

The ImageList is a special type of collection that holds images of a preset size and color depth. Other controls access pictures in the ImageList using the appropriate index numbers. In this way, an ImageList acts as a resource for other controls, providing icons for controls like the ToolBar and TreeView.

> **NOTE**  *In some respects, the ImageList isn't really a control. It doesn't have a graphical representation, and the end user never interacts with it directly. On the other hand, ImageList objects are usually created and configured at design time when you are building the user interface. They are also closely linked to other modern controls like ListView, TreeView, and ToolBar controls.*

To create an ImageList at design time, drag it onto your form (it will appear in the component tray). The basic properties for the ImageList are described in Table 6-1.

*Table 6-1. ImageList Members*

| Member | Description |
|---|---|
| ColorDepth | A value from the ColorDepth enumeration that identifies the color resolution of the images in the control. Some common choices are 8-bit (256 color mode), 16-bit (high color), and 24-bit (true color). |
| Images | The collection of Image objects that are provided to other controls. |
| ImageSize | A Size structure that defines the size of the contained images. ImageList controls can only contain images that share the same size and color-depth. Images are converted to the specified format when they are added. |
| TransparentColor | Some image types, like icons and GIFs, define a transparent color that allows the background to show through. By setting the Transparent Color property, you can define a new transparent color that will be used when this image is displayed. This is useful for graphic formats that don't directly support transparency, like bitmaps. |
| Draw() | This method provides a quick and easy way to take an image and output it to a GDI+ drawing surface. |

**TIP** *Transparent regions are a must when mixing custom images and standard controls. If you simply use an icon with a gray background, your interface becomes garish and ugly on a computer where the default color scheme is not used, as a gray box appears around the image You also run into problems if the icon can be selected, at which point it is highlighted with a blue background.*

You can add, remove, and rearrange images using the ListView designer. Just click the ellipsis (...) next to the Images property in the Properties window. Images can be drawn from almost any common bitmap file, including bitmaps, GIFs, JPEGs, and icons. When you add a picture, some related read-only properties about its size and format appear in the window (see Figure 6-1).

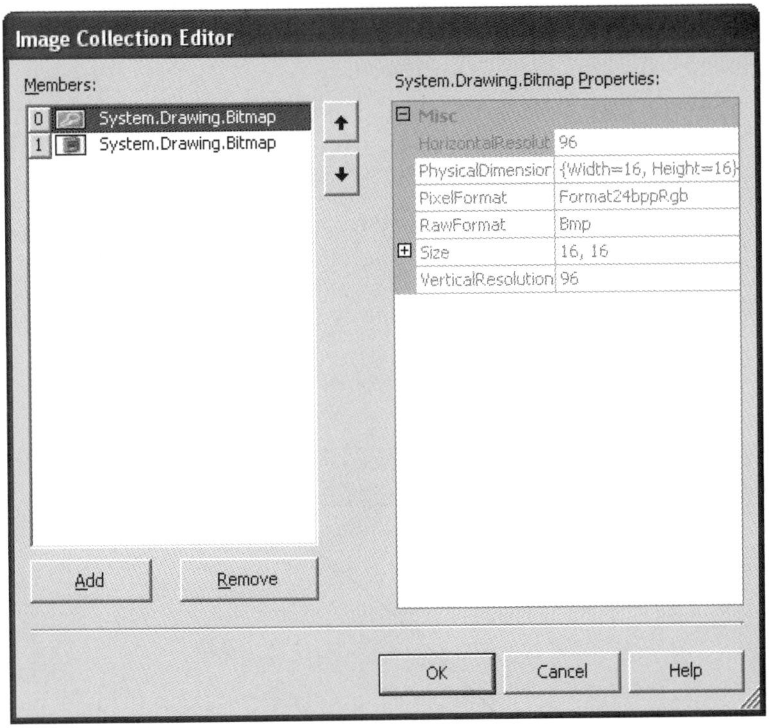

*Figure 6-1. The ImageList designer*

## Dealing with the ImageList in Code

If you look at the automatically generated code, you'll see that the image files you add are stored in a resource file in your project (as is any binary data added at design time). When the form is loaded, the images are deserialized into Image objects and placed in the collection. A special class, the ImageListStreamer, makes this process a simple one-line affair, regardless of how many images are in your ImageList. This code is inserted automatically by VS .NET, and doesn't need to be modified manually

```
Me.ImageList1.ImageStream = CType( _
    resources.GetObject("imagesLarge.ImageStream"),_
    System.Windows.Forms.ImageListStreamer)
```

If you want to have an ImageList object around for a longer period (for example, to use in different forms), you should create it directly in code. You might also want to create Image objects out of graphic files rather than use a project resource.

First, you need a variable to reference the ImageList.

```
Public IconImages As New ImageList()
```

Then, you can create a method that fills the ImageList.

```
' Configure the ImageList.
IconImages.ColorDepth = System.Windows.Forms.ColorDepth.Depth8Bit
IconImages.ImageSize = New System.Drawing.Size(16, 16)

' Get all the icon files in the current directory.
' (using the System.IO.Directory class)
Dim IconFile As String, IconFiles As String()
IconFiles = Directory.GetFiles(Application.StartupPath, "*.ico")

' Create an Image object for each file and add it to the ImageList.
' You can also use an Image subclass (like Icon).
For Each IconFile In IconFiles
    Dim NewIcon As New Icon(IconFile)
    IconImages.Images.Add(NewIcon)
Next
```

Once you have images in an ImageList control, you can use them to provide pictures to another control. Many modern controls provide an ImageList property, which stores a reference to an ImageList control. Individual items in the control (like tree nodes or list rows) then use an ImageIndex or similar property, which identifies a single picture in the ImageList by index number (starting at 0). You look at examples that use this technique later in this chapter.

In the meantime, you should also note that the ImageList can be a useful way to store images that you need to use in any scenario. The example below loops through an ImageList and draws its images directly onto the surface of a form. The result is shown in Figure 6-2.

```
' Get the graphics device context for the form.
Dim g As Graphics = Me.CreateGraphicse
Dim i As Integer

' Draw each image using the ImageList.Draw() method.
For i = 0 To IconImages.Images.Count - 1
    IconImages.Draw(g, 10, 10 + i * 30, i)
Next

' Release the graphics device context.
g.Dispose()
```

As with all manual drawing, these icons are erased as soon as the form is repainted (for example if you minimize and then maximize it). I tackle this issue in Chapter 12.

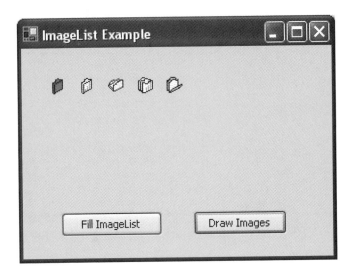

*Figure 6-2. Directly outputting an ImageList*

## ListView and TreeView

The ListView and TreeView are probably the most widespread and distinctive controls in modern application design. As far as controls go, they have it all: an attractive appearance, a flexible set of features, and an elegant ability to combine different types of functionality and information. Thanks to Windows Explorer, they are also widely recognized and understood by intermediate users.

These days, it's hard to find programs that *don't* use TreeView and ListView. The Windows operating system makes heavy use of them in configuration and administration windows. Other Microsoft software that uses the MMC snap-in model follows suit, like SQL Server and even configuration utilities for the .NET platform (see Figure 6-3).

| Assembly Name | Version | Locale | Public Key Token |
|---|---|---|---|
| CustomMarshalers | 1.0.3300.0 | neutral | b03f5f7f11d50a3a |
| Microsoft.VisualStudio | 1.0.3300.0 | neutral | b03f5f7f11d50a3a |
| Microsoft.VSDesigner | 7.0.3300.0 | neutral | b03f5f7f11d50a3a |
| mscorlib | 1.0.3300.0 | neutral | b77a5c561934e089 |
| System | 1.0.3300.0 | neutral | b77a5c561934e089 |
| System.Design | 1.0.3300.0 | neutral | b03f5f7f11d50a3a |
| System.Drawing | 1.0.3300.0 | neutral | b03f5f7f11d50a3a |
| System.Drawing.Design | 1.0.3300.0 | neutral | b03f5f7f11d50a3a |
| System.Windows.Forms | 1.0.3300.0 | neutral | b77a5c561934e089 |
| System.Xml | 1.0.3300.0 | neutral | b77a5c561934e089 |
| Accessibility | 1.0.3300.0 | neutral | b03f5f7f11d50a3a |
| ADODB | 2.7.0.0 | neutral | b03f5f7f11d50a3a |
| ADODB | 7.0.3300.0 | neutral | b03f5f7f11d50a3a |
| CalcR | 5.0.0.0 | neutral | a1690a5ea44bab32 |
| CalcR | 6.0.0.0 | neutral | a1690a5ea44bab32 |
| CRVsPackageLib | 1.0.0.0 | neutral | 4f3430cff154c24c |

*Figure 6-3. Configuring assembly settings in .NET*

## Basic ListView

The ListView control is most often used for a multicolumn list of items. It actually supports four distinct modes that you have probably already seen in Windows Explorer. You specify the mode by setting the ListView.View property to one of the values from the View enumeration.

- **LargeIcon**, which displays full-sized (32 x 32 pixel) icons with a title beneath each one. Items are displayed from left to right, and then on subsequent lines.

- **SmallIcon**, which displays small (16 x 16 pixel) icons with descriptive text at the right. Items are displayed from left to right, and then on subsequent lines.

- **List**, which displays small icons with descriptive text at the right. It's the same as SmallIcon, except it fills items from top to bottom, and then in additional columns. The scrollbar (if needed) is horizontal.

- **Details**, which displays the familiar multicolumn layout. Each item appears on a separate line, and the leftmost column contains a small icon and label. Column headers identify each column, and allow user resizing (and sorting, if the application supports it). The Details view is the only view that supports showing more than an icon and one piece of information per item.

**TIP** *In Visual Studio.NET, the ListView control uses a designer that allows you to add items and subitems. To use it, just click the ellipses (...) next to the Items property in the Property Window. It's quite impressive, but I won't discuss it in this chapter, as pure code gives a clearer understanding of the issues involved.*

To understand the different styles of ListView, it helps to create a simple example. First, create a ListView and two ImageList controls, one to hold any required small icons and one to hold large icons. You can associate the ListView with the corresponding ImageList like this:

```
listAuthors.SmallImageList = imagesSmall
listAuthors.LargeImageList = imagesLarge
```

Once the ImageList is associated, images can be assigned to individual list items by setting a convenient ImageIndex property. You can change the Image-Index at any time to indicate an item that has changed status.

What follows is the code needed to load information into a ListView, in response to a button click. This example relies on a GetProducts() method that returns a DataTable (either by querying a database or by constructing it manually).

```
Private Sub cmdFillList_Click(ByVal sender As System.Object, _
ByVal e As System.EventArgs) Handles cmdFillList.Click

    Dim dt As DataTable = StoreDB.GetProducts()
    Dim dr As DataRow

    For Each dr In dt.Rows
        ' Create the item, with the text from the ModelName field.
        Dim listItem As New ListViewItem((dr(ModelName).ToString())

        ' Give every item the same picture.
        listItem.ImageIndex = 0

        ' Add the item to the ListView.
        listAuthors.Items.Add(listItem)
    Next

End Sub
```

This is ListView code is at its simplest. ListViewItem objects are created, and added to the list. The ListViewItem constructor allows you to specify the default item text (the Text property) and the ImageIndex points to the first picture in the collection. Note that the ImageIndex applies to both the SmallImageList and LargeImageList, meaning that your ImageList objects must use the exact same ordering. The appropriate picture is chosen based on the view style.

Finally, to make the code a little more interesting, a group of radio buttons allows the user to switch between the different view styles. Rather than scatter the code for this in multiple procedures, use a single method that retrieves a tag value:

```
Private Sub NewView(ByVal sender As System.Object, ByVal e As System.EventArgs) _
    Handles optSmallIcon.CheckedChanged, optDetails.CheckedChanged, _
    optLargeIcon.CheckedChanged, optList.CheckedChanged

    ' Set the current view mode based on the number in the tag value of the
    ' selected radio button.

    listAuthors.View = CType(sender, Control).Tag

    ' Display the current view style.
    Me.Text = "Using View: " & listAuthors.View.ToString()

End Sub
```

The tag values can be set at design time or in code when the form is first loaded:

```
optLargeIcon.Tag = View.LargeIcon
optSmallIcon.Tag = View.SmallIcon
optDetails.Tag = View.Details
optList.Tag = View.List
```

If you try this application, you'll see that it doesn't appear to work in details view. The reason is that the ListView only displays information in details view if you have added the appropriate column headers. The example below rewrites the ListView code to fill multiple columns of information. Note, however, that this extra information is ignored in other view styles.

```
Private Sub cmdFillList_Click(ByVal sender As System.Object, _
  ByVal e As System.EventArgs) Handles cmdFillList.Click
    Dim dt As DataTable = StoreDB.GetProducts()
    Dim dr As DataRow

    ' Suspending automatic refreshes as items are added/removed.
    listAuthors.BeginUpdate()

    listAuthors.SmallImageList = imagesSmall
    listAuthors.LargeImageList = imagesLarge
    For Each dr In dt.Rows
        Dim listItem As New ListViewItem(dr("ModelName").ToString)
        listItem.ImageIndex = 0

        ' Add sub-items for Details view.
        listItem.SubItems.Add(dr("ID").ToString())
        listItem.SubItems.Add(dr("Description").ToString())

        listAuthors.Items.Add(listItem)
    Next

    ' Add column headers for Details view.
    listAuthors.Columns.Add("Product", 100, HorizontalAlignment.Left)
    listAuthors.Columns.Add("ID", 100, HorizontalAlignment.Left)
    listAuthors.Columns.Add("Description", 100, HorizontalAlignment.Left)

    ' Re-enable the display.
    listAuthors.EndUpdate()

End Sub
```

When adding a ColumnHeader, you have the chance to specify a width in pixels, a title, and the alignment for values in the column. Figure 6-4 shows the four different view styles. This test program is included with the chapter code with the project name ListView.

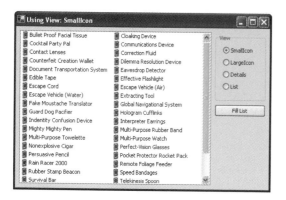

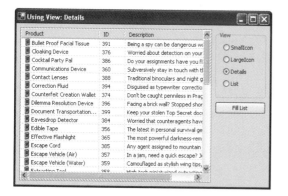

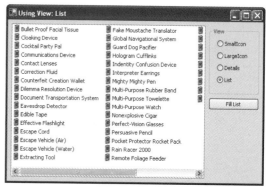

*Figure 6-4. Different view styles with the ListView control*

The ListView is different from almost any other grid control in that it designates every column except the first one as a subitem (Table 6-2). This idiosyncrasy shouldn't trouble you too much, but note that it causes the column header indexes to differ from the subitem indexes. For example, the first subitem is listItem.SubItems.Items(0) while the corresponding column is listAuthors.Columns.Items(1).

> **TIP** *The previous example uses a ListView for its most common task: representing items. However, ListView controls can also represent actions. For example, consider the Control panel, that uses a ListView in LargeIcon view to provide access to a number of different features. Remember, different view styles suggest different uses (and in the case of the Details view, show different information), so you should not allow the user to change the style through a setting in your application. Instead, choose the most suitable style when creating the control.*

*Table 6-2. Basic ListView Members*

| Member | Description |
| --- | --- |
| Columns | Holds the collection of ColumnHeader objects used in Details view. |
| FocusedItem, SelectedItem, and SelectedIndices | Allows you to retrieve the item that currently has focus or the currently selected items (the user can select multiple icons by dragging a box around them or by holding down the Ctrl key). You can also examine the Focused and Selected properties of each ListViewItem. |
| Items | Holds the collection ListViewItem objects displayed in the ListView. |
| LargeImageList and SmallImageList | References the ImageList control that is used for large and small icons. The individual icons are identified by the ListViewItem.ImageIndex property. |
| MultiSelect | When set to False, prevents a user from selecting more than one item at a time. |
| View | Sets the ListView style using the View enumeration. |
| SelectedItemIndexChanged event | Occurs whenever the user selects an item, except when the same item is selected twice in a row. |

## Advanced ListView Tricks

To unlock all the functionality of the ListView control, you need to delve deeper into the .NET classes that support it. Some of the highlights are described in Table 6-3.

*Table 6-3. Advanced ListView Members*

| Member | Description |
|--------|-------------|
| Activation and HoverSelection | Activation determines how items in the ListView are highlighted. If you select OneClick, the mouse cursor becomes a hand icon when it hovers over an item. The HoverSelection property, when set to True, automatically selects an item when the user hovers over it. This formerly cutting-edge feature is now discouraged as being unintuitive (and somewhat "touchy"). |
| Alignment | Sets the side of the ListView that items are aligned against. |
| AllowColumnReorder | When set to True, the user can drag column headers around to rearrange column order in Details view, without requiring any code. |
| AutoArrange and ArrangeIcons() | In SmallIcon and LargeIcon view, this property determines whether icons automatically snap to a grid, or can be positioned anywhere by the user. |
| CheckBoxes, CheckedIndices, and CheckedItems | When CheckBoxes is True, every item will have a checkbox next to it. The state of the checkbox is reflected in the ListViewItem.Checked property of each item. You can also retrieve checked items directly (using CheckedItems) or their index values (CheckedIndices). |
| FullRowSelect | When set to True, the entire row will be highlighted when you select an item in Details view, not just the first column. It's a useful setting for database applications that are using the ListView as a grid control. |
| GridLines | Displays attractive column and row gridlines in Details view. Useful if you are displaying many rows of complex or hard to read information. |

*Table 6-3. Advanced ListView Members (Continued)*

| Member | Description |
|---|---|
| HeaderStyle | Allows you to configure whether column headers respond to clicks (Clickable) or ignore them (Nonclickable). |
| LabelEdit | When set to True, ListViewItem text can be modified by the user or in code using the BeginEdit() method. |
| LabelWrap | Allows the text label to wrap in one of the icon views. |
| Sorting | Allows you to specify an ascending or descending sort order, which considers the main text of the ListViewItem only (not any sub-items). |
| BeginUpdate() and EndUpdate() | Allows you to temporarily suspend the ListView drawing, so that you can add or modify several items at once. |
| EnsureVisible() | Scrolls to make sure a specified ListViewItem is visible. You indicate the item by its zero-based row index. |
| GetItemAt() | Retrieves the ListViewItem at the given X and Y coordinate. Useful for hit testing and drag-and-drop operations. |
| AfterLabelEdit, and BeforeLabelEdit events | Events that fire before and after a label is modified. Both events provide the index to the appropriate ListViewItem, and a property that allows you to cancel the edit. |
| ColumnClick event | Occurs when a user clicks a column. Could be used for programmatic sorting by column, but the current ListView class does not support it. |
| ItemCheck event | Occurs when the state of a checkbox next to an item is changed. |

If you decide to use the ListView as a grid control, you can use a few useful properties to fine-tune the display by adding gridlines and row selection (rather than single-column value selection):

```
listAuthors.GridLines = True
listAuthors.FullRowSelect = True
```

You probably also want to add the ability to sort and rearrange columns. If you only need to sort using the ListItem.Text property, you can make use of the Sorting property.

```
listAuthors.Sorting = SortOrder.Ascending
```

If you want to provide column sorting in details view, life is a little more difficult. The ListView control has no intrinsic support for sorting by column. However, you can easily develop a custom IComparer sorting class to handle the task. This class has a simple responsibility: examine two ListView objects, and return a 1, 0, or –1 depending on how they compare.

The best option is to create an IComparer class that stores a column index as a public member variable, allowing it to provide sorting for any column. In addition, the example includes a Boolean member variable called Alphabetic that allows two types of sorting: numeric or letter-by-letter alphabetic. For simplicity's sake, this class doesn't use any type of error checking.

```
Public Class CompareListViewItems
    Implements IComparer

    ' This index identifies the column that is used for sorting
    Public ReadOnly Column As Integer

    ' Is the sort alphabetic or number?
    Public ReadOnly Alphabetic As Boolean

    Public Sub New(ByVal columnIndex As Integer, ByVal alphabetic As Boolean)
        Me.Column = columnIndex
        Me.Alphabetic = alphabetic
    End Sub

    Public Function Compare(ByVal x As Object, ByVal y As Object) As Integer _
      Implements System.Collections.IComparer.Compare

        ' Convert the items that must be compared into ListViewItem objects.
        Dim ListX As ListViewItem = CType(x, ListViewItem)
        Dim ListY As ListViewItem = CType(y, ListViewItem)
```

```
    ' Sort using the specified column and specified sorting type.
    If Alphabetic Then
        If ListX.SubItems(Column).Text > ListY.SubItems(Column).Text Then
            Return 1
        ElseIf ListX.SubItems(Column).Text = ListY.SubItems(Column).Text Then
            Return 0
        Else
            Return -1
        End If
    Else
        If Val(ListX.SubItems(Column).Text) > _
          Val(ListY.SubItems(Column).Text) Then
            Return 1
        ElseIf Val(ListX.SubItems(Column).Text) = _
          Val(ListY.SubItems(Column).Text) Then
            Return 0
        Else
            Return -1
        End If
    End If

  End Function

End Class
```

Now, you can easily create a ListView that re-sorts itself as a column header when it is clicked by handling the ColumnClicked event, generating a new CompareListViewItems object, and calling the ListView.Sort() method:

```
Private Sub listAuthors_ColumnClick(ByVal sender As Object, _
  ByVal e As ColumnClickEventArgs) Handles listAuthors.ColumnClick

    ' Specify an alphabetic sort based on the column that was clicked.
    listAuthors.ListViewItemSorter = New CompareListViewItems(e.Column, True)

    ' Perform the sort.
    listAuthors.Sort()

End Sub
```

Another interesting trick is column reordering. This allows the user to rearrange columns by dragging the column header. This technique takes place automatically, if you set the AllowColumnReorder property to True. Unfortunately, there is no easy way to save these view settings and apply them later. To manage this type of advanced data display, you may want to consider the DataGrid control described in Chapter 9.

## Label Editing

The ListView includes an automatic label-editing feature that you have probably already witnessed in Windows Explorer. You trigger the label editing by clicking a selected item once. This automatic editing is confusing to many new users. If you use it, you should also provide another way for the user to edit the corresponding information.

To enable label editing, set the LabelEdit property to True. You can programmatically start label editing for a node using the node's BeginEdit() method.

```
Private Sub cmdStartEdit_Click(ByVal sender As System.Object, _
  ByVal e As System.EventArgs) Handles cmdStartEdit.Click

    ' The user clicked a dedicated "Edit" button.
    ' Put the label of the first selected item into edit mode.
    If list.SelectedItems.Count > 0 Then
        list.SelectedItems(0).BeginEdit()
    End If

    ' (You might also want to disable other controls until the user completes
    ' the edit and the AfterLabelEdit event fires.)

End Sub
```

In addition, you can prevent certain nodes from being edited by handling the BeforeLabelEdit event and setting the Cancel flag to True. You can also fix up any invalid changes by reacting to the AfterLabelEdit event.

> **TIP**  *If you want to use the BeginEdit() method but prevent users from modifying the label by clicking it, you must set the LabelEdit property to True. To prevent users from editing labels directly set a special form-level property (like AllowEdit) before you use the BeginEdit() method, and check for this property in the BeforeLableEdit event. If it has not been set, and the user has started the edit, then you should cancel it.*

## Adding Information to a ListView

There are three ways that you can add additional information to a ListView control to represent custom data.

- Assign a DataRow object to the Tag property of a ListViewItem. The advantage of this technique easily accommodates any type of data, and doesn't require modifications if the data fields change (information is held in a weakly typed name/value collection of fields).

- Assign a custom data object to the Tag. This allows you to wrap all the data-related functionality you need into a neat object. The disadvantage is that it requires more steps. For example, if you are retrieving your data from a database, you need to create the corresponding object, initialize its data, and then assign it to the Tag property.

- Derive a custom ListViewItem, and add the properties you need for your particular type of data. Though this is the only approach directly explained in the MSDN reference, it is probably the least convenient because it tightly integrates details about the structure of your data into the user interface code. That means that you need to modify these classes if the data changes or if you move to a different type of control (like the TreeView).

Chapter 9 introduces a reusable pattern that allows a control to interact with data objects without needing to know their database-specific internals. It also provides the flexibility to change data access strategies or the display control.

## Basic TreeView

The TreeView is a hierarchical collection of elements, which are called nodes. This collection is provided through the TreeView.Nodes property. With this collection, it's quite easy to add a few basic nodes:

```
treeFood.Nodes.Add("Apple")
treeFood.Nodes.Add("Peach")
treeFood.Nodes.Add("Tofu")
```

In this example, three nodes are added with descriptive text. If you've worked with the TreeView before through its ActiveX control, you might notice that the .NET implementation dodges a few familiar headaches, because it doesn't require a unique key for relating parent nodes to child nodes. This means it's easier to quickly insert a new node. It also means that unless you take specific steps to record a unique identifier with each item, you won't be able to distinguish duplicates. For example, the only difference between the two "Apple" entries in the example is their respective position in the list.

To specify more information about a node, you have to construct a TreeNode object separately, and then add it to the list. In the example that follows, a unique identifier is stored in the Tag property.

```
Dim newNode As New TreeNode()
newNode.Text = "Apple"
newNode.Tag = 1
treeFood.Nodes.Add(newNode)
```

In this case, a simple integer is used, but the Tag property can hold any type of object if needed, even a reference to a corresponding database record.

```
Dim drFood As DataRow
For Each drFood In dtFoods.Rows
    Dim newNode As New TreeNode()
    newNode.Text = drFoods("Name")
    newNode.Tag = drFood
    treeFood.Nodes.Add(newNode)
Next
```

## TreeView Structure

Nodes can be nested in a complex structure with a virtually unlimited number of layers. Adding subnodes is similar to adding submenu items. First you find the parent node, and then you add the child node to the parent's Nodes collection.

```
Dim node As TreeNode

node = treeFood.Nodes.Add("Fruits")
node.Nodes.Add("Apple")
node.Nodes.Add("Peach")

node = treeFood.Nodes.Add("Vegetables")
node.Nodes.Add("Tomato")
node.Nodes.Add("Eggplant")
```

The Add() method always returns the newly added node object. You can then use this node object to add child nodes. If you wanted to add child nodes to the

Apple node you would follow the same pattern, and catch the node reference returned by the Add() method.

This code produces a hierarchical tree structure as shown in Figure 6-5.

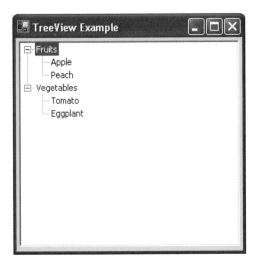

*Figure 6-5. A basic TreeView*

Microsoft suggests that the preferred way to add items to a TreeView is by using the AddRange() method to insert an entire block of nodes at once. It works similarly, but requires an array of node objects.

```
Dim nodes(1) As TreeNode

nodes(0) = New TreeNode("Fruits")
nodes(0).Nodes.Add("Apple")
nodes(0).Nodes.Add("Peach")

nodes(1) = New TreeNode("Vegetables")
nodes(1).Nodes.Add("Tomato")
nodes(1).Nodes.Add("Eggplant")

treeFoods.Nodes.AddRange(nodes)
```

By using this technique, you ensure that the TreeView is updated all at once, improving performance dramatically. You can achieve a similar performance gain by using the BeginUpdate() and EndUpdate() methods, which suspends the graphical refresh of the TreeView control, allowing you to perform a series of operations at once.

```
' Suspend automatic refreshing.
treeFood.BeginUpdate()

' Add or remove several nodes here.

' Enable automatic refreshing.
treeFood.EndUpdate()
```

## TreeView Navigation

The TreeView's multileveled structure can make it difficult to navigate through your tree structure to perform common tasks. For example, you might want to use a TreeView to provide a hierarchical list of check box settings (as Windows does for the View tab in its Folder Options, shown in Figure 6-6). You can configure the TreeView to display check boxes next to each node by setting a single property:

```
treeSettings.CheckBoxes = True
```

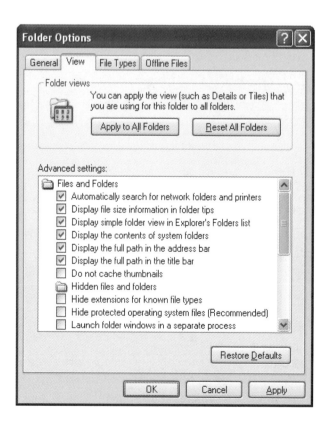

*Figure 6-6. Using a TreeView to configure settings*

When the OK or Apply button is clicked, you then search through the list of settings and make the corresponding changes.

The following section of code might seem like a reasonable attempt, but it won't work:

```
Dim node As TreeNode
For Each node In treeSettings.Nodes
    ' Process node here.
Next
```

The problem is that the TreeView.Nodes collection only contains the first level of the nodes hierarchy, which in this case corresponds to the main groupings (like "Files and Folders.") The correct code would go another level deep:

```
Dim node, nodeChild As TreeNode
For Each node In treeSettings.Nodes
    ' Process parent node here.
    For Each nodeChild in node.Nodes
        ' Process node here.
    Next
Next
```

Alternatively, if you have a less structured organization where similar types of elements are held at various levels, you need to search through all the nodes recursively. The following code calls a ProcessNodes procedure recursively until it has walked through the entire tree structure.

```
Private Sub cmdOK_Click()
    ' Start the update.
    ProcessNodes(treeSettings.Nodes)
End Sub

Private Sub ProcessNodes(ByVal nodes As TreeNodeCollection)
    Dim node As TreeNode
    For Each node In nodes
        ProcessNode(node)
        ProcessNodes(node.Nodes)
    Next
End Sub

Private Sub ProcessNode(ByVal node As TreeNode)
    ' Check if the node interests us.
    ' If it does, process it.
    ' To verify that this routine works, display the node text.
    MessageBox.Show(node.Text)
End Sub
```

> **TIP** *To count all the nodes in your tree, you don't need to enumerate through the collections and sub-collections. Instead, you can use the TreeView.GetNodeCount() method. Make sure you specify True for the required parameter—this indicates that you want to count the items in subtrees. Each TreeNode object also provides a GetNodeCount() method, allowing you to count the items in selected branches of a tree.*

You can also use relative-based navigation. In this model, you don't iterate through the whole collection. Instead, you go from a current node to another node.

```
currentNode = currentNode.Parent.Parent.NextNode
```

This example takes the current node, finds its parent (by moving one level up the hierarchy), then finds the parent's parent, and then moves to the next sibling (the next node in the list that is at the same level). If there is no next node, a null reference (Nothing) is returned. If one of the parents is missing, an error occurs. Table 6-4 lists the relative-based navigation properties you can use.

*Table 6-4. Relative-based Navigation Properties*

| Node Property | Moves... |
| --- | --- |
| Parent | One level up the hierarchy, to the node that contains the current node. |
| FirstNode | One level down the node hierarchy, to the first node in the current node's Nodes collection. |
| LastNode | One level down the node hierarchy, to the last node in the current node's Nodes collection. |
| PrevNode | To the node at the same level, but just above the current node. |
| NextNode | To the node at the same level, but just below the current node. |

The next example shows how you could use the relative-based navigation to walk over every node in a tree.

```
Private Sub cmdOK_Click(ByVal sender As Object, ByVal e As EventArgs)
    ' Start the update.
    ProcessNodes(treeUsers.Nodes.Item(0))
End Sub

Private Sub ProcessNodes(ByVal nodeStart As TreeNode)
    Do
        ProcessNode(nodeStart)
        If nodeStart.Nodes.Count > 0 Then
            ProcessNodes(nodeStart.FirstNode)
        End If
        nodeStart = nodeStart.NextNode()
    Loop Until nodeStart Is Nothing

End Sub

Private Sub ProcessNode(ByVal node As TreeNode)
    ' Check if the node interests us.
    ' If it does, process it.
    ' To verify that this routine works, display the node text.
    MessageBox.Show(node.Text)
End Sub
```

This type of navigation is generally less common in .NET programs, because the collection-based syntax is more readable and easier to deal with.

> **NOTE**   *The Nodes collection is not read-only. That means that you can safely delete and insert nodes while enumerating through the Nodes collection.*

## Manipulating Nodes

Now that you have a good idea of how to add nodes and find them in the tree structure, it's time to consider how nodes can be deleted and rearranged. Once again, you use the methods of the Nodes collection.

Generally, the best way to delete a node is by first obtaining a reference to the node. You could also remove a node using its index number, but index numbers can change as nodes are removed or if sorting is used, so they raise the potential for unexpected problems.

Once again, consider our tree of food products:

```
Dim node As TreeNode

node = treeFood.Nodes.Add("Fruits")
node.Nodes.Add("Apple")
node.Nodes.Add("Peach")

node = treeFood.Nodes.Add("Vegetables")
node.Nodes.Add("Tomato")
node.Nodes.Add("Eggplant")
```

You can now search for the "Fruits" node in the collection and delete it. Note that when you use the Remove() method, all the child nodes are automatically deleted as well.

```
For Each node In treeFood.Nodes
    If node.Text = "Fruits" Then
        treeFood.Nodes.Remove(node)
    End If
Next
```

You can use the Remove() method to delete a node that exists several layers down the hierarchy. What that means is that if you obtain a reference to the "Apple" node, you can delete it directly from the treeFood.Nodes collection even though the collection doesn't really contain that node.

```
Dim nodeApple, nodeFruits As TreeNode
nodeFruits = treeFood.Nodes.Add("Fruits")
nodeApple = nodeFruits.Nodes.Add("Apple")

' This works. It finds the nodeApple in the nodeFruits.Nodes sub-collection.
treeFood.Nodes.Remove(nodeApple)

' This also works. It directly removes the apple from nodeFruits.Nodes.
nodeFruits.Nodes.Remove(nodeApple)
```

The Nodes property provides an instance of the TreeNodeCollection. Table 6-5 lists a few more of its node manipulation features. Some, like the ability to Clear() all child nodes and Insert() a node at a specific position, are particularly useful.

*Table 6-5. Useful TreeNodeCollection Methods*

| Method | Description |
|---|---|
| Add() | Adds a new node at the bottom of the list. |
| AddRange() and CopyTo() | Allows you to copy node objects to and from an array. This technique can be used to update a TreeView in a single batch operation, and thereby optimize performance. The CopyTo() method copies the entire tree into an array, which allow you to easily transfer it to another TreeView control or serialize it to disk. |
| Clear() | Clears all the child nodes of the current node. Any sublevels are also deleted, meaning that if you call this method for the TreeView the whole structure is cleared. |
| Contains() | Returns True or False, depending on whether a given node object is currently part of the Nodes collection. If you want to provide a search that is more than one level deep, you need write your own method and use recursion, as shown in the previous examples. |
| IndexOf() | Returns the current (zero-based) index number for a node. Remember, node indexes change as nodes are added and deleted. This method returns –1 if the node is not found. |
| Insert() | This method allows you to insert a node in a specific position. It's similar to the Add() method, but it takes an additional parameter specifying the index number where you want to add the node. The node that is currently there is shifted down. Unlike the Add() method, the Insert() method does not return the node reference. |
| Remove() | Accepts a node reference and removes the node from the collection. All subsequent tree nodes are moved up one position. |

.NET provides another way to manipulate nodes—using their own methods. For example, you can delete a node without worrying about what TreeView it belongs to by using the Node.Remove() method. This shortcut is extremely convenient.

```
nodeApple.Remove()
```

Nodes also provide a built-in clone method that copies the node *and* any child nodes. This can allow you to transfer a batch of nodes between TreeView controls without needing to iterate over the Nodes collection. (A node object cannot be assigned to more than one TreeView control.)

```
' Select the first node.
Dim node As TreeNode = treeOrigin.Nodes(0)

' Clone it and all the sub-levels.
Dim nodeNew As TreeNode = node.Clone()

' Add the nodes to a new tree.
treeDestination.Add(nodeNew)
```

## Selecting Nodes

On their own, TreeNode objects don't raise any events. The TreeView control, however, provides notification about important node actions like selections and expansions. Each of these actions is composed of two events: a "Before" event that occurs before the TreeView display is updated, and an "After" event that allows you to react to the event in the traditional way when it is completed. (You'll see in some of the advanced examples how the "Before" event can allow you to perform just-in-time node additions. This technique is used in Chapter 7 with a directory tree and Chapter 9 with a database-browser application.) Table 6-6 lists the key TreeView events.

Every custom event in the TreeView is node-specific, and provides a reference to the relevant node. The TreeView control also inherits some generic events that allow it to react to mouse-clicks and other actions that occur to any part of the control, but these are generally not very useful.

*Table 6-6. TreeView Node Events*

| Event | Description |
|---|---|
| BeforeCheck and AfterCheck | Occurs when a user clicks to select or deselect a check box. |
| BeforeCollapse and AfterCollapse | Occurs when a user collapses a node, either by double-clicking it or by using the plus/minus box. |
| BeforeExpand and AfterExpand | Occurs when a user expands a node, either by double-clicking it or by using the plus/minus box. |
| BeforeSelect and AfterSelect | Occurs when a user clicks a node. This event can also be triggered for other reasons. For example, deleting the currently selected node causes another node to be selected. |

These TreeView node-based events provide a special TreeViewEventArgs object. This object has two properties: a Node property that provides the affected node, and an Action property that indicates how the action was triggered. The Action property uses the TreeViewAction enumeration, and can indicate whether an event was caused by a key press, mouse-click, or a node expansion/collapse.

The next example reacts to the AfterSelect event and gives the user the chance to remove the selected node. You'll notice that when a node is deleted, the closest node is automatically selected.

```
Private Sub treeUsers_AfterSelect(ByVal sender As Object, _
 ByVal e As System.Windows.Forms.TreeViewEventArgs) Handles treeUsers.AfterSelect
    Dim Message As String
    Message = "You selected " & e.Node.Text & " with this action: "
    Message &= e.Action.ToString & vbCr & vbCr & "Delete it?"

    Dim Result As New DialogResult()
    Result = MessageBox.Show(message, "Delete", MessageBoxButtons.YesNo)
    If Result = DialogResult.Yes Then
        e.Node.Remove()
    End If
End Sub
```

Depending on your TreeView, just having a reference to the node object may not be enough. For example, you might add duplicate node entries into different subgroups. This technique isn't that unusual: for example, you might have a list of team members subgrouped by role (programmer, tester, documenter, and so on). A single team member might play more than one role. However, depending on what subgroup the selected node is in, you might want to perform a different action.

In this case, you need to determine where the node is positioned. You can use the node relative properties (like Parent) to move up the tree, or you can retrieve a string that represents the full path from the node's FullPath property. A few possible values for the FullPath property are:

```
Fruits
Fruits\Peach
Country\State\City\Street
```

In these examples, a backslash is used to separate each tree level, although you can set a different delimiter by setting the TreeView.PathSeparator property.

## Advanced TreeView Tricks

The TreeView is a sophisticated control, and it provides a great deal of possible customization. Some of the additional appearance-related properties are described in Table 6-7.

*Table 6-7. TreeView Appearance Properties*

| Property | Description |
|----------|-------------|
| CheckBoxes | Set this to True to display a check box next to each node. |
| FullRowSelect | When set to True, selecting a node shows a highlight box that spans the full width of the tree. |
| HotTracking | When set to True, the text in a node changes to a highlighted hyperlink style when the user positions the mouse over it. |
| Indent | Specifies the left-to-right distance between each level of items in the tree, in pixels. |

*Table 6-7. TreeView Appearance Properties (Continued)*

| Property | Description |
|---|---|
| ShowLines, ShowPlusMinus, and ShowRootLines | Boolean properties that configure the appearance of lines linking each node, the plus/minus box that allows users to easily expand a node, and the root lines that connect the first level of objects together. |
| Sorted | When set to True, nodes are sorted in each group alphabetically using their text names. There is no way to specify a custom sort order, other than to add the nodes in a pre-determined order. |

The TreeNode also provides some useful properties that haven't been discussed yet. Mainly, these properties allow you to determine the state of node (Table 6-8). Additional properties exist that let you modify a node's background and foreground color, and determine its relatives, as you saw earlier.

*Table 6-8. TreeNode State Properties*

| Property | Description |
|---|---|
| Checked | True if you are using a TreeView with check box nodes, and the node is checked. |
| IsEditing | True if the user is currently editing this node's label. Label editing is explained later in this section. |
| IsExpanded | True if this node is expanded, meaning its child nodes are displayed. |
| IsSelected | True if this is the currently selected node. Only one node can be selected at a time, and you can control which one is using the TreeView.SelectedNode property. |
| IsVisible | True if the node is currently visible. A node is be visible if its parent is collapsed, or if you need to scroll up or down to find it. To programmatically show a node, use its EnsureVisible() method. |

## Node Pictures

One frequently used feature is the ability to assign icons to each node. As with all modern controls, this works by using a paired ImageList control.

```
treeFood.ImageList = imagesFood
```

You can assign a default picture index that will be used by any node that does not specifically override it:

```
treeFood.ImageIndex = 0
```

You can set an image for each individual node through the properties of the TreeNode object. Each node can have two linked images: a default image, and one that is used when the node is selected.

```
Dim node As New TreeNode("Apples")
node.ImageIndex = 1
node.SelectedImageIndex = 2
treeFood.Nodes.Add(node)
```

## Expanding and Collapsing Levels

You've already learned how to react when the user expands and collapses levels. However, you can also programmatically expand and collapse nodes. There are many uses for this trick:

- Restoring a TreeView control to its "last viewed" state, so users can continue right where they left off with the control in the exact same state.

- Ensuring that a particular node or set of nodes is visible to correspond with another activity. For example, the user might have made a selection in a different part of the window, or might be using a wizard that is stepping them through the process.

- Configuring the TreeView when the window is first loaded so that the user sees the most important (or most commonly used) nodes.

.NET provides a few ways to accomplish these tasks. First, every node provides four useful methods: Collapse(), Expand(), ExpandAll(), and Toggle(). The Expand() method acts on the immediate children, while ExpandAll() expands the node and all subnodes. To expand or collapse the entire tree, you can use one of the TreeView methods: ExpandAll() or CollapseAll().

```
node.Expand()        ' Expand the node to display its immediate children.
node.Toggle()        ' Switches the node: it was expanded, so now it is collapsed.
node.ExpandAll()     ' Expand all nodes and sub-nodes.
tree.ExpandAll()     ' Expand the entire tree.
```

You can also use a node's EnsureVisible() method. This extremely useful method expands whatever nodes are required to make a node visible, and scrolls to the appropriate location. This is extremely useful if you are iterating through a tree looking for a node that matches certain criteria.

```
' Search the first level of a TreeView control.
For Each node in tree.Nodes
    If CType(node.Tag, Integer) = 12 Then
        ' Collapse the whole tree to hide unimportant nodes.
        tree.CollapseAll()

        ' Expand just the node that interests the user.
        node.EnsureVisible()
        Exit For
    End If
Next
```

The TreeView control also provides a TopNode property that references the first fully visible node at the top of the current display window. It also provides a VisibleCount property that identifies the maximum number of nodes that can be displayed at a time in the TreeView at its current height.

## TreeView Drag-and-Drop

TreeView controls can support drag-and-drop operations just as easily as any other .NET control. However, when information is dragged onto a TreeView, you generally need to determine what node it was "dropped" on. To perform this magic, you need to perform your own hit testing, with a little help from the TreeView.GetNodeAt() method.

The following example presents a form with two TreeViews. The user can drag a node from one TreeView to the other TreeView, or to another location in the same TreeView (see Figure 6-7). When a node is dropped, its content is copied, and the original branch is left untouched. Best of all, the code is generic, meaning that one set of event handlers responds to the events from both trees.

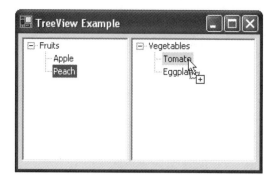

*Figure 6-7. Drag-and-drop operations with a TreeView*

To start, you need to make sure that both TreeView controls can receive drag-and-drop events. At the same time, disable the HideSelection property so that you can highlight the node that will be the drop target, even if the TreeView doesn't have the focus.

```
treeOne.AllowDrop = True
treeTwo.AllowDrop = True
treeOne.HideSelection = False
treeTwo.HideSelection = False
```

The step is to create the MouseDown event handling logic that starts the drag-and-drop operation. This code needs to investigate whether there is a node under the mouse pointer. If there is, the node is copied (along with all subnodes) and a drag-and-drop operation is started.

```
Private Sub tree_MouseDown(ByVal sender As System.Object, _
  ByVal e As System.Windows.Forms.MouseEventArgs) _
  Handles treeOne.MouseDown, treeTwo.MouseDown

    ' Get the tree.
    Dim tree As TreeView = CType(sender, TreeView)

    ' Get the node underneath the mouse.
    Dim node As TreeNode
    node = tree.GetNodeAt(e.X, e.Y)
    tree.SelectedNode = node
```

```
' Start the drag-and-drop operation with a cloned copy of the node.
If Not node Is Nothing Then
    tree.DoDragDrop(node.Clone(), DragDropEffects.Copy)
End If
```

End Sub

Next, both trees need to handle the DragOver event. Note that you use this event, instead of the DropEnter event, because the operation is permitted or allowed based on whether there is a node under the current mouse pointer.

```
Private Sub tree_DragOver(ByVal sender As System.Object, _
  ByVal e As System.Windows.Forms.DragEventArgs) _
  Handles treeOne.DragOver, treeTwo.DragOver

    ' Get the tree.
    Dim tree As TreeView = CType(sender, TreeView)

    ' Drag and drop denied by default.
    e.Effect = DragDropEffects.None

    ' Is it a valid format?
    If Not e.Data.GetData(GetType(TreeNode)) Is Nothing Then

        ' Get the screen point.
        Dim pt As New Point(e.X, e.Y)

        ' Convert to a point in the TreeView's coordinate system.
        pt = tree.PointToClient(pt)

        ' Is the mouse over a valid node?
        Dim node As TreeNode = tree.GetNodeAt(pt)
        If Not node Is Nothing Then
            e.Effect = DragDropEffects.Copy
            tree.SelectedNode = node
        End If

    End If

End Sub
```

Note that the drag-and-drop events provide mouse coordinates in the screen's frame of reference (measuring from the top left corner of the desktop). In order to perform the hit testing, you need to convert this point to a point in the TreeView control's coordinate system (which measures from the top left of the control).

Finally, the actual copied node is inserted by a DragDrop event handler. The node that contains the added node is expanded to ensure that the addition is visible.

```
Private Sub tree_DragDrop(ByVal sender As System.Object, _
    ByVal e As System.Windows.Forms.DragEventArgs) _
    Handles treeOne.DragDrop, treeTwo.DragDrop

    ' Get the tree.
    Dim tree As TreeView = CType(sender, TreeView)

    ' Get the screen point.
    Dim pt As New Point(e.X, e.Y)

    ' Convert to a point in the TreeView's coordinate system.
    pt = tree.PointToClient(pt)

    ' Get the node underneath the mouse.
    Dim node As TreeNode = tree.GetNodeAt(pt)

    ' Add a child node.
    node.Nodes.Add(e.Data.GetData(GetType(TreeNode)))

    ' Show the newly added node if it is not already visible.
    node.Expand()

End Sub
```

You can try this example in the TreeViewDragAndDrop project. This example doesn't provide any restrictions—it allows you to copy nodes anywhere you want. Most programs probably add more restrictive logic in the DragOver event handler. In addition, you might want to create a tree where dragging and dropping moves items instead of copies them. In this case, the easiest approach is to store a reference to the original node object (without cloning it):

```
tree.DoDragDrop(node, DragDropEffects.Copy)
```

The DragDrop event handler would then remove the node from the source tree, and add it to the target tree. However, you would typically need to perform some validation to ensure that the dragged node is an allowed child of the target node.

```
Dim nodeDragged As TreeNode = e.Data.GetData(GetType(TreeNode))

' Copy to new position.
node.Nodes.Add(nodeDragged.Clone())

' Remove from original position.
nodeDragged.Remove()
```

> **TIP** *For even more advanced drag-and-drop possibilities, you can use the DoDragDrop() method with an instance of a custom class that encapsulates all the relevant information, instead of just the TreeView object.*

## Taming the TreeView

The TreeView control provides a sophisticated infrastructure that allows it to be used in countless different ways. Each individual TreeView, however, is generally only used in a specific set of limited ways, depending on the underlying data it represents. That means that the TreeView is an ideal control for subclassing.

## *A Project Tree*

You can easily create custom TreeView classes that are targeted for a specific type of data. Consider the ProjectTree class that follows:

```
Public Class ProjectTree
    Inherits TreeView

    ' Use an enumeration to represent the three types of nodes.
    ' Specific numbers correspond to the database field code.
    Public Enum StatusType
        Unassigned = 101
        InProgress = 102
        Closed = 103
    End Enum

    ' Store references to the three main node branches.
    Private nodeUnassigned As New TreeNode("Unassigned", 0, 0)
    Private nodeInProgress As New TreeNode("In Progress", 1, 1)
    Private nodeClosed As New TreeNode("Closed", 2, 2)
```

```
' Add the main level of nodes when the control is instantiated.
Public Sub New()
    MyBase.New()
    MyBase.Nodes.Add(nodeUnassigned)
    MyBase.Nodes.Add(nodeInProgress)
    MyBase.Nodes.Add(nodeClosed)
End Sub

' Provide a specialized method the client can use to add nodes.
Public Sub AddProject(ByVal name As String, ByVal status As StatusType)
    Dim nodeNew As New TreeNode(name, 3, 4)
    nodeNew.Tag = status

    Select Case status
        Case StatusType.Unassigned
            nodeUnassigned.Nodes.Add(nodeNew)
        Case StatusType.InProgress
            nodeInProgress.Nodes.Add(nodeNew)
        Case StatusType.Closed
            nodeClosed.Nodes.Add(nodeNew)
    End Select
End Sub

End Class
```

When you use this class in a program, you don't add nodes objects; instead, you add projects. The only variable elements for a project are the name and the status. Once your class has these two pieces of information, it can automatically add a node to the correct branch with the correct icon. (The icons are identified by numbers and only come into effect if an appropriately configured ImageList is attached to the ImageList property. This detail could be incorporated in the ProjectTree class, but it would require more work and wouldn't produce any obvious benefits.)

The client might use this custom TreeView as follows:

```
treeProjects.ImageList = imagesProjects
Dim dtProjects As DataTable = GetAllProjects()
Dim drProject As DataRow
For Each drProject In dtProjects.Rows
    treeProjects.AddProject(drProject("Name"), drProject("Status"))
Next
```

The resulting display is shown in Figure 6-8.

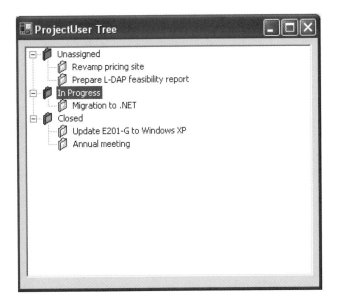

*Figure 6-8. A custom TreeView*

The appeal of this approach is that the appropriate user interface class wraps many of the extraneous details and makes the rest of the code more readable. Depending on your application, you might want to develop a custom TreeView like this into a separate assembly you can reuse in different products.

There's no limit to the possible features you can add to a TreeView class. For example, you can add special methods for finding nodes or presenting context menus. The danger is that you will make the control too specific, locking functionality into places where it can't be reused. Remember to think of your custom TreeView as a generic TreeView designed for a specific type of data. However, it should allow many different possible uses of that data. For example, if you determine that a user action should result in a database select or update, you must raise an event from the TreeView, and allow the code receiving that event to take care of the data layer.

## A Data-Aware TreeView

Another approach is to create a custom TreeView that recognizes the appropriate DataRow objects natively. When an item is selected, the custom class raises a specialized event that is more useful than the generic AfterSelect event. A different event is raised depending on the type of selected item, and the original DataRow object is returned as an argument.

```
Public Class ProjectUserTree
    Inherits TreeView

    ' Use an enumeration to represent the three types of nodes.
    Public Enum NodeType
        Project
        User
    End Enum

    ' Define a new type of higher-level event for node selection.
    Public Delegate Sub ItemSelectEventHandler(ByVal sender As Object, _
      ByVal e As ItemSelectEventArgs)
    Public Class ItemSelectEventArgs
        Inherits EventArgs

        Public Type As NodeType
        Public ItemData As DataRow
    End Class

    ' Define the events that use this signature and event arguments.
    Public Event UserSelect As ItemSelectEventHandler
    Public Event ProjectSelect As ItemSelectEventHandler

    ' Store references to the two main node branches.
    Private nodeProjects As New TreeNode("Projects", 0, 0)
    Private nodeUsers As New TreeNode("Users", 1, 1)

    ' Add the main level of nodes when the control is instantiated.
    Public Sub New()
        MyBase.New()
        MyBase.Nodes.Add(nodeProjects)
        MyBase.Nodes.Add(nodeUsers)
    End Sub

    ' Provide a specialized method the client can use to add projects.
    ' Store the corresponding DataRow.
    Public Sub AddProject(ByVal project As DataRow)
        Dim nodeNew As New TreeNode(project("Name"), 2, 3)
        nodeNew.Tag = project
        nodeProjects.Nodes.Add(nodeNew)
    End Sub

    ' Provide a specialized method the client can use to add users.
    ' Store the correspnding DataRow.
```

```
Public Sub AddUser(ByVal user As DataRow)
    Dim nodeNew As New TreeNode(user("Name"), 2, 3)
    nodeNew.Tag = user
    nodeUsers.Nodes.Add(nodeNew)
End Sub

' When a node is selected, retrieve the DataRow and raise the event.
Protected Overrides Sub OnAfterSelect(ByVal e As TreeViewEventArgs)
    MyBase.OnAfterSelect(e)

    Dim Arguments As New ItemSelectEventArgs()
    Arguments.ItemData = CType(e.Node.Tag, DataRow)

    If e.Node.Parent Is nodeProjects Then
        Arguments.Type = NodeType.Project
        RaiseEvent ProjectSelect(Me, Arguments)
    ElseIf e.Node.Parent Is nodeUsers Then
        Arguments.Type = NodeType.User
        RaiseEvent UserSelect(Me, Arguments)
    End If
End Sub

End Class
```

This technique of intercepting events and providing more useful, higher-level events is quite useful, and provides an easier model to program against.

> **TIP** *Chapter 9 shows an example of how a TreeView can interact without ADO.NET data objects, without needing to understand the underlying field structure. Look for the Decoupled TreeView example toward the end of the chapter.*

## Unusual Trees

Another reason you might want to create a custom TreeView is to create an unusual tree like the one Windows uses for print settings (see Figure 6-9).

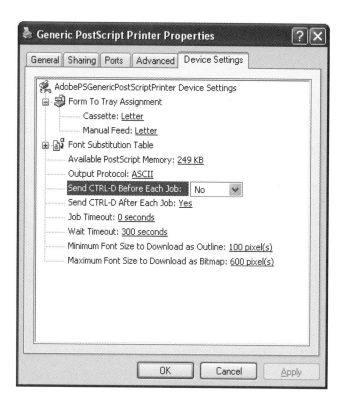

*Figure 6-9. Windows print settings*

When a node is clicked in this window, an edit control (like a text box) is provided allowing information to be added in-place. Implementing a design like this, as long as you define clear rules, is fairly straightforward. You could store a collection of controls, or even store a control in each node's Tag property. In the OnAfterSelect() method, check to see if the node has a corresponding control, and if it does, display it next to the node.

## Design-Time Support for the Custom TreeView

You'll notice that your custom control class isn't added to the Toolbox. To accomplish that, you need to create a separate control project, as explained in Chapter 8. However, there's no reason that you can't use the custom TreeView class by instantiating manually in your code:

```
Dim tree As New ProjectTree()
tree.ImageList = imagesTree
Me.Controls.Add(tree)
```

Another approach that works well for derived controls is to create a more basic, related control, and then modify the designer code in your form so that it creates your control instead. Then, you'll find that you can work with your control at design time, even setting its properties through the Properties window, without needing to create a separate project.

In this example, you create a standard TreeView. Then, replace the following two lines (found at different places in the designer code):

```
Friend WithEvents tree As System.Windows.Forms.TreeView
Me.tree = New System.Windows.Forms.TreeView()
```

With these lines (where CustomTreeView is the namespace of your project):

```
Friend WithEvents tree As CustomTreeView.ProjectTree
Me.tree = New CustomTreeView.ProjectTree()
```

The tree even appears in the designer with its three main branches. Unfortunately, it also develops the nasty habit of adding its basic set of nodes twice: one at design-time, which is serialized in the form's designer code, and again at runtime. Chapter 8 explains how to code around these quirky behaviors. You can also refer to the CustomTreeView project included with the online samples.

## The ToolBar

The ToolBar control represents a strip of buttons that gives access to various features in an application. Conceptually, toolbars play the same role as menus. The difference is that toolbars are only a single level deep and are often restricted to the most important functions. Menus use a multilayered hierarchical structure that provides a single point of access to all features in an application.

Toolbar buttons can include text and variable-size pictures. You can layer several toolbars on a form, and attach drop-down menus to a button. Figure 6-10 shows some common toolbar button styles.

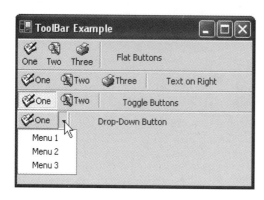

*Figure 6-10. Toolbar styles*

Unfortunately, .NET does not currently provide any way to create a "cool bar," the snap-in toolbar strip used in applications like Microsoft Word that can include other controls (like drop-down list boxes) and can be manually detached by the user into floating tool windows. This is likely to change with future .NET framework releases (or third-party development). Until then, you can start to create your own using the information in Chapter 7 and Chapter 8, or use ActiveX interop with the components provided with Visual Studio 6.

Most of the ToolBar properties are appearance-related (see Table 6-9).

*Table 6-9. Appearance-related ToolBar Properties*

| Member | Description |
|---|---|
| Appearance | ToolBarAppearance.Normal makes buttons appear three-dimensional, like command buttons. ToolBarAppearance.Flat gives toolbar buttons a more modern look. They begin flat, and appear raised when the mouse moves over them. Separators on a toolbar with the Appearance property set to Flat appear as etched lines rather than spaces. |
| AutoSize | When True (the default), the toolbar sizes itself to accommodate the toolbar buttons, based on the button size, the number of buttons, and the DockStyle of the toolbar. |

*Table 6-9. Appearance-related ToolBar Properties (Continued)*

| Member | Description |
|---|---|
| BorderStyle | When set to BorderStyle.Fixed3D the toolbar has a sunken, three-dimensional appearance. With BorderStyle.FixedSingle, the toolbar has a flat thin border around it. |
| ButtonSize | A size structure specifying a size for each button. If a size is not set, the default is used (24 pixels by 22 pixels), or a size is assigned that is large enough to accommodate the image and text for the button. |
| Divider | The default, True, displays a raised edge along the top of the toolbar to help separate it (typically from a menu). |
| DropDownArrows | When False, no down arrow is shown for toolbars that have linked menus (although the drop-down menu is still shown when the button is clicked). When set to True, drop-down buttons provide an arrow that the user must click to show the menu. |
| ImageList | The attached ImageList used for button pictures. |
| ShowToolTips | If set to True, you can set the ToolTipText property of each button object to assign a tooltip (the ToolTipProvider extender control is not used). |
| TextAlign | Sets the alignment for the button text on the toolbar. The options are underneath the image or to the right of the image. |
| Wrappable | If True (the default), and the toolbar becomes too small to display all the buttons on the same line, the toolbar is broken into additional lines, with the breaks occurring at the separators. |

The most important part of a ToolBar is its Buttons property, which contains the collection of button controls. As with the TreeView and ListView, you can add individual ToolBarButton objects using a special designer in Visual Studio.NET (shown in Figure 6-11), or through code.

*Figure 6-11. Toolbar designer*

Each ToolBarButton provides its own set of important properties, as listed in Table 6-10.

*Table 6-10. ToolBarButton Properties*

| Member | Description |
|---|---|
| DropDownMenu | References a ContextMenu object that contains the drop-down menu that is shown for the button. You also must set the Style for the button to DropDown. |
| Enabled and Visible | When not enabled, the button appears dimmed (greyed out) and does not respond to button clicks. Buttons that are not visible do not appear in the toolbar. |
| ImageIndex | Assigns a picture from the ImageList bound to the toolbar. |

*Table 6-10. ToolBarButton Properties (Continued)*

| Member | Description |
|---|---|
| PartialPush and Pushed | You can set Pushed to True to indent a button. This is typically used with toggle buttons, which can be pushed and unpushed by the user. PartialPush shows a dimmed pushed button, which is meant to show a combination of the pushed and unpushed states (for example, a Bold button might appear partially pushed if the current selection has both bold and normal text). |
| Style | Configures the type of button from the ToolBarButtonStyle enumeration. You can use PushButton for the standard button, Separator for an etched line between buttons (or just a space, depending on the ToolBar.Appearance setting), or ToggleButton for a button that appears sunken when clicked and retains the sunken appearance until clicked again. |
| Tag | Allows you to attach other information to a ToolBarButton. This property needs to be specifically added to this class by the .NET framework, as ToolBarButton does not inherit from the base Control class. |
| Text | The text that appears on the button face. |
| ToolTipText | The tooltip that is shown for the button, if the ToolBar.ShowToolTips property is True. |

Reacting to button clicks is not much different than reacting to a menu. You can handle each ToolBarButton.Click event separately, or you can handle them with the same event handler, and inspect the object reference to determine which button was clicked.

## Synchronizing the ToolBar

Usually, a toolbar duplicates functionality that is available in a window's menu. This can result in some rather tiresome state management code that has to carefully disable or enable menu items and the corresponding toolbar button at the same time. To simplify this process, you can create a customized menu class that automatically forwards its state to a linked toolbar control.

This custom control project is a little trickier than some of the previous examples. For one thing, it limits your ability to use the menu designer, because the custom menu items need to be created and added through code.

There's also more than one way to approach this problem. One possibility is to create a custom MenuItem class that stores a reference to a linked toolbar button.

```
Public Class LinkedMenuItem
    Inherits MenuItem

    Public LinkedButton As ToolBarButton

    ' To save space, only one of the original constructors is used.
    Public Sub New(ByVal text As String)
        MyBase.New(text)
    End Sub

    Public Shadows Property Enabled() As Boolean
        Get
            Return MyBase.Enabled
        End Get
        Set(ByVal Value As Boolean)
            MyBase.Enabled = Value
            If Not LinkedButton Is Nothing Then
                LinkedButton.Enabled = Value
            End If
        End Set
    End Property

End Class
```

On the downside, this technique requires you to shadow the Enabled property (because it is not overridable), which is a sleight of hand that can further hamper design-time support for the menu. On the other hand, this is an extremely flexible approach. You could even replace LinkedButton with a collection that provides a whole series of controls that could be automatically enabled or disabled in the Enabled property procedure. Note that defensive programming is used to test the LinkedButton property before attempting to configure the referenced control, in case it has not been set.

The client program can create a linked menu using this class like this:

```
Dim menuMain As New MainMenu()
Me.Menu = menuMain

Dim menuItem1 = New LinkedMenuItem("File")
Dim menuItem2 = New LinkedMenuItem("Exit")

' This ToolBarButton is defined as a form-level variable.
menuItem2.LinkedButton = Me.ToolBarButton2

menuMain.MenuItems.Add(menuItem1)
menuItem1.MenuItems.Add(menuItem2)

' Both the ToolBarButton and MenuItem are disabled at once.
menuItem2.Enabled = False
```

Another approach is to create a special MainMenu class. This class could provide an additional method that disables controls in tandem, without forcing you to observe this practice if you want to deal with MenuItem objects on your own. On the downside, you could forget to use the appropriate methods, and end up in an unsynchronized state. On the other hand, this approach provides you with more freedom. Figure 6-12 illustrates the difference.

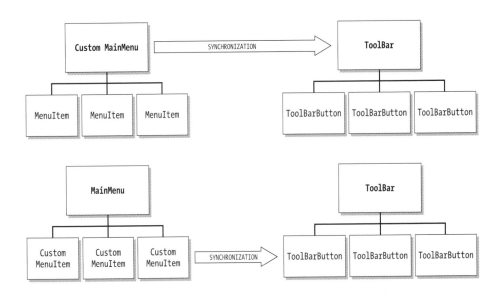

*Figure 6-12. Two ways to synchronize a menu and toolbar*

The link is performed simply by setting the Tag property of the ToolBarItem to reference the appropriate MenuItem, but there are other possibilities. The LinkedMainMenu needs to iterate over all the buttons to find the matching one.

```
Public Class LinkedMainMenu
    Inherits MainMenu

    Public LinkedToolbar As ToolBar

    Public Sub Enable(ByVal item As MenuItem)
        Call SetEnabled(True, item)
    End Sub

    Public Sub Disable(ByVal item As MenuItem)
        Call SetEnabled(False, item)
    End Sub

    Private Sub SetEnabled(ByVal State As Boolean, ByVal item As MenuItem)
        item.Enabled = State
        If Not LinkedToolbar Is Nothing Then
            Dim TButton As ToolBarButton
            For Each TButton In LinkedToolbar.Buttons
                If CType(TButton.Tag, MenuItem) Is item Then
                    TButton.Enabled = State
                End If
            Next
        End If
    End Sub


End Class
```

And the client would follow this pattern:

```
Dim menuMain As New LinkedMainMenu()
menuMain.LinkedToolbar = MyToolBar     ' MyToolBar is a form-level variable
Me.Menu = menuMain

Dim menuItem1 = New MenuItem("File")
Dim menuItem2 = New MenuItem("Exit")

menuMain.MenuItems.Add(menuItem1)
menuItem1.MenuItems.Add(menuItem2)
```

```
' (Create toolbar buttons as usual.)
ExitToolBarButton.Tag = menuItem2

' Both the ToolBarButton and MenuItem are disabled at once.
menuMain.Disable(menuItem2)
```

In this case, I walked through two different approaches to creating a custom control. The following chapters won't have the luxury to be quite as discursive, but it's important that you start to think about *all* the different possibilities for enhancing, customizing, and integrating controls. This is one of the most exciting aspects of .NET user interface programming.

## The StatusBar

The StatusBar control is used to display brief information throughout the life of the application. This information should never be critical or take the place of informative messages or progress indicators, as many users won't notice it. This information should also be kept to a minimum to prevent a cluttered interface. Some possible status bar information includes:

- **Information about the application mode or operating context.** For example, if your application can be run by many different types of users, you might use a status bar panel to provide information about the current user level (e.g., Administrator Mode). Similarly, a financial application might provide a label indicating U. S. Currency Prices if it's possible to switch regularly between several different pricing modes.

- **Information about the application status.** For example, a database application might start by displaying Ready or Connected To… when you first log in, and then display Record Added when you update the database. This technique avoids stalling advanced users with a confirmation window where they need to click an OK button, but it can also easily be missed, leaving it unsuitable for some situations.

- **Information about a background process.** For example, Microsoft Word provides some information about print operations while they are being spooled in its status bar.

- **Information about the current document.** For example, most word processors use a status bar to display the current page count and the user's position in the document. Windows Explorer uses the status bar to display ancillary information like the total number of files in a folder.

These are some of the most useful ways to use a status bar. Status bars should never be used to display the current time. This common default is essentially useless, because the current time is always displayed in the system tray anyway.

Although a status bar can be docked to any side (as set by the Dock property), it is always placed at the bottom of the window by convention.

## Basic StatusBar

There are two ways to use a status bar. You can display a single piece of text, or a combination of panels that can contain text or icons. To use a simple status bar, just set the ShowPanels and Text properties. This doesn't provide any border around the status bar (see Figure 6-13), so you might want to add an extra horizontal line above using a group box control.

```
statusBar.ShowPanels = False
statusBar.Text = "Ready"
```

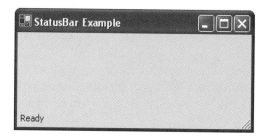

*Figure 6-13. The simplest possible status bar*

You can also tweak the Font for the current text and the SizingGrip property, which enables or disables the grip lines on the bottom right corner of the status bar (where the user can grab to resize the form).

Alternatively, you can create a status bar that contains different pieces of information. This information is represented as a collection of StatusBarPanel objects in the Panels property. You can configure this collection at design-time using the custom designer, or at runtime in code.

```
Dim pnlNew As New StatusBarPanel()
pnlNew.Text = "Ready"
statusBar.Panels.Add(pnlNew)
```

The StatusBarPanel object provides several appearance-related properties (see Table 6-11).

*Table 6-11. StatusBarPanel Properties*

| Property | Description |
|---|---|
| Alignment | Determines how the text is aligned. The default is HorizontalAlignmnent.Left. |
| AutoSize | Determines how the panel should be sized using one of the values from the StatusBarPanelAutoSize enumeration. Contents means the panel is automatically sized to fit the text length. None means that the panel is fixed in size (based on its Width property). Spring means that the panel takes up all available space. You can use this for the last panel, or you can set several panels to spring (and grow proportionately as the status bar is expanded). |
| BorderStyle | Each panel can be displayed with the default sunken border, a different border, or no border at all. |
| Icon | You can display an icon in a panel along with its text by setting this property to a valid Icon object. The icon appears at the left of the panel. |
| MinWidth | If you are using autosizing, this is the minimum width the panel is given. |
| Text | The text that appears in the panel. |
| ToolTipText | The tooltip that appears when the user hovers the mouse over the panel. |
| Width | The current width of the panel, in pixels. |

The code that follows creates a more sophisticated multipaneled status bar, shown in Figure 6-14:

```
Dim pnlStatus As New StatusBarPanel()
pnlStatus.Text = "Ready"
pnlStatus.Icon = New Icon(Application.StartupPath & "\active.ico")
pnlStatus.AutoSize = StatusBarPanelAutoSize.Contents

Dim pnlConnection As New StatusBarPanel()
pnlConnection.Text = "Connected to " & ServerName
pnlConnection.AutoSize = StatusBarPanelAutoSize.Spring

statusBar.Panels.Add(pnlStatus)
statusBar.Panels.Add(pnlConnection)
```

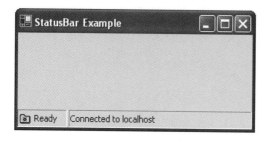

*Figure 6-14. A status bar with panels*

The StatusBar raises a PanelClick event that provides information about the mouse position and the StatusBarPanel object that was clicked. You can respond to this event to create system tray-like functionality. For example, you could add an icon that can be clicked to change modes. This technique can be neat, but it is often not obvious to the average end user.

> **TIP** *You will probably want to use form-level variables to store a reference to the StatusBarPanel objects that you need to update regularly.*

## Synchronizing the StatusBar to a Menu

There is no automatic way to connect menu item Help text to a status bar panel (some C++ programmers may remember this was a feature of the MFC application wizard). Before I tell you how you can do this, I should warn you why you might not want to.

The problem with putting menu Help text in the status bar is that even advanced users rarely associate two controls together when they are separated by so much physical space. In other words, those who need the Help text will have no idea that it is there. Even worse, most users don't understand that they can hover over a menu item to select it, and probably just understand clicking a menu item, which immediately activates without providing the helpful information. Many critics complain that the status bar Help text feature is just a gambit to use up extra space in the status bar (see Figure 6-15).

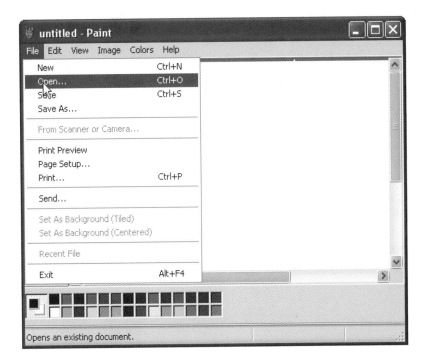

*Figure 6-15. An unhelpful status bar in Microsoft Paint*

If you still want to create this interface, all you need to do is handle the MenuItem.Select method. This technique is very similar to the example shown in Chapter 4. However, the MenuItem class doesn't provide any Tag property where you can store additional information (like the Help text). Instead, you have to keep a hashtable collection handy, and use the control reference to look up the Help string.

```
Private Sub mnu_Click(ByVal sender As System.Object, _
  ByVal e As System.EventArgs) Handles mnuOpen.Click, mnuNew.Click, mnuSave.CLick

    Status.Text = HelpCollection(sender)

End Sub
```

You could also perform the same trick using a custom menu control, and overriding the OnSelect() method. It's similar to the technique used in the previous examples for the MenuItem interaction with a ToolBar. Chapter 7 shows a third way to implement this type of design—this time using a custom extender provider.

## The TabControl

The TabControl is another staple of Windows development—it groups controls into multiple "pages." The technique has become remarkably successful because it allows a large amount of information to be compacted into a small, organized space. It's also easy to use because it recalls the tabbed pages of a binder or notebook. Over the years, the tab control has evolved into today's form, which is sometimes called property pages.

In .NET, you create a TabControl object, which contains a collection of TabPage objects in the TabPages property. Individual controls are then added to each TabPage object. The example that follows shows the basic approach, assuming your form contains a TabControl called tabProperties.

```
Dim pageFile As New TapPage("File Locations")
Dim pageUser As New TapPage("User Information")

' Add controls to the tab pages.
' The code for creating and configuring the child controls is omitted.
pageUser.Controls.Add(txtFirstName)
pageUser.Controls.Add(txtLastName)
pageUser.Controls.Add(lblFirstName)
pageUser.Controls.Add(lblLastName)tabProperties.TabPages.Add(pageFile)
tabProperties.TabPages.Add(pageUser)
```

The output for this code is shown in Figure 6-16.

*Figure 6-16. The TabPage control*

**NOTE** *Chapter 11 presents an example that allows you to add controls to a TabPage without needing to supply a Location property. Instead, the layout is managed automatically.*

The TabControl is easy to work with, and usually configured at design time. Some of its members are described in Table 6-12. TabPage properties are shown in Table 6-13.

*Table 6-12. TabControl Members*

| Member | Description |
|---|---|
| Alignment | Sets the location of the tabs. With very few exceptions, this should always be TabAlignment.Top, which is the standard adopted by almost all applications. |
| Appearance | Allows you to configure tabs to look like buttons that stay depressed to select a page. This is another unconventional approach. |
| HotTrack | When set to True, the text in a tab caption changes to a highlighted hyperlink style when the user positions the mouse over it. |
| ImageList | You can bind an ImageList to use for the caption of each tab page. |
| Multiline | When set to True, allows you to create a tab control with more than one row of tab pages. |
| Padding | Configures a minimum border of white space around each tab caption. This does not effect the actual tab control, but it is useful if you need to add an icon to the TabPage caption and need to adjust the spacing to accommodate it properly. |
| RowCount and TabCount | Retrieves the number of rows of tabs and the number of tabs. |
| SelectedIndex and SelectedTab | Retrieves the index number for the currently selected tab, or the tab as a TabPage object, respectively. |

*Table 6-12. TabControl Members (Continued)*

| Member | Description |
|---|---|
| ShowToolTips | Enables or disables tooltip display for a tab. This property is usually set to False. |
| SizeMode | Allows you to configure tab captions to be a fixed size, expand to the width of the contents, or match the size of the contents. |
| SelectedIndexChanged event | Occurs when the SelectedIndex property changes, usually as a result of the user clicking on a different tab. |

*Table 6-13. TabPage Properties*

| Property | Description |
|---|---|
| ImageIndex | The image shown in the tab. |
| Text | The text shown in the tab. |
| ToolTipText | The tooltip shown when the user hovers over the tab, if the TabControl.ShowToolTips property is True. No ToolTipProvider is used. |

# The NotifyIcon

In past programming frameworks, it's been difficult to use a system tray icon. In .NET it's as easy as adding a simple NotifyIcon control (Table 6-14).

*Table 6-14. NotifyIcon Members*

| Member | Description |
|---|---|
| ContextMenu | The ContextMenu linked the system tray. It is displayed automatically when the user right-clicks the icon. |
| Icon | The graphical icon that appears in the system tray (as an Icon object). |
| Text | The tooltip text that appears above the system tray icon. |

*Table 6-14. NotifyIcon Members (Continued)*

| Member | Description |
| --- | --- |
| Visible | Set this to True to show the icon. It defaults to False, giving you a chance to set up the rest of the required functionality. |
| Click, DoubleClick, MouseDown, MouseMove, and MouseUp events | These events work the same as the Control class events with the same name. They allow you to respond to the mouse actions. |

**NOTE** *Like almost all invisible controls, the NotifyIcon doesn't inherit from the Control class. In other words, the list of members in Table 6-14 is essentially all you have to work with.*

The NotifyIcon is an invisible control that appears in the component tray when added at design time. In many cases, it's more useful to create the NotifyIcon dynamically at runtime. For example, you might create a utility application that loads into the system tray and waits quietly, monitoring for some system event or waiting for user actions. In this case, you need to be able to create the system tray icon without displaying a form. A complete example of this technique is shown in Chapter 11.

## The Last Word

In this chapter you've toured some of the most important controls used in typical Windows user interfaces. Even as I've introduced these staples, I've already started to show you how you can tweak and extend them with custom control classes. Developing custom controls is one of the key ways to tame these full-featured controls. You'll see more examples throughout the book, including Chapter 7, where you will tackle a directory browser TreeView that reads information from the underlying file system automatically.

# Custom Controls

CUSTOM CONTROLS ARE a key theme in .NET development. They can help your programming style by improving encapsulation, simplifying a programming model, and making user interface more "pluggable" (i.e., making it easier to swap out one control and replace it with a completely different one without rewriting your form code). Of course, custom controls can have other benefits, including the ability to transform a generic window into a state-of-the-art modern interface. Generally, developers tackle custom control development for one of three reasons:

- To create controls that abstract away unimportant details and are tailored for a specific type of data. You saw this model in Chapter 6, with custom ListView and TreeView examples.

- To create controls that provide entirely new functionality, or just combine existing UI elements in a unique way. An example of this is the directory browser control developed in this chapter.

- To create controls with a distinct original look, or ones that mimic popular controls in professional applications (like Microsoft's Outlook bar) that aren't available to the masses. This topic is considered briefly in this chapter, and returned to in Chapter 13, with GDI+.

Creating custom controls in .NET is far easier than it has been in languages like C++ or VB, where you typically need to embrace the ActiveX model to create a truly shareable component. As most developers have found, ActiveX controls can be difficult to distribute because every version needs to be registered. Creating ActiveX controls also requires a bit of wizardry, with special care taken to handle property pages, design-time versus runtime appearance, and state management.

In .NET, creating a custom control is as easy as creating an ordinary class. You simply inherit from the best possible ancestor and add the specific features you need. Best of all, you can create a custom control class as part of an existing project, and then decide later to place it in a separate assembly that can be shared with other programmers.

This chapter introduces the different types of custom controls, and the types of problems they can solve. You will look at several key examples, including a thumbnail image viewer and a masked text box, and consider advanced techniques like creating multithreaded controls. However, you won't learn how to make these controls behave happily in Visual Studio .NET. That topic, as well other issues like control distribution and licensing, are picked up in the next chapter.

## Types of Custom Controls

Developers often make a distinction between three or four types of controls:

- User controls are the simplest type of control. They inherit from the System.Windows.Forms.UserControl class, and follow a model of composition. Usually, user controls combine more than one control in a logical unit (like a group of text boxes for entering address information).

- Inherited controls are generally more powerful and flexible. With an inherited control, you choose the existing .NET control that is closest to what you want to provide. Then, you derive a custom class that overrides or adds properties and methods. The examples you've looked at so far in this book, including the custom TreeViews and ListViews, have all been inherited controls.

- Owner-drawn controls generally use GDI+ drawing routines to generate their interfaces from scratch. Because of this, they tend to inherit from a base class like System.Windows.Forms.Control. Owner-drawn controls require the most work and provide the most customizable user interface. You'll see them in Chapter 13.

- Additionally, in this chapter you consider extender providers, which aren't necessarily controls at all. These components add features to other controls on a form, and provide a remarkable way to implement extensible user interface.

The distinction above is slightly exaggerated. For example, you can create a user control that uses GDI+ drawing with other contained controls. Similarly, instead of inheriting from Control, UserControl, or a full-fledged .NET class, you can inherit from one of the intermediary classes to get a different level of support. For example, a control that contains other controls but handles its own output could inherit from ContainerControl, while a control that needs to provide scrolling might inherit from ScrollableControl.

## User Controls

Typically, user controls are created as a group of ordinary controls that are related in some way. For example, you might include a simple record browser, or related customer input fields that provide their own validation. The .NET documentation assumes that user controls are the most common type of custom control project, although they suffer from some serious drawbacks:

- User controls tend to combine your business logic with an inflexible block of user interface. For example, if the application programmer doesn't like the way individual text boxes are arranged in an address user control, there's no way to change it. Similarly, if the underlying business logic needs to change, the control itself needs to be rebuilt and redistributed. It's also hard to make a useful derived control based on an existing user control. In other words, user controls tend to be fragile.

- Unless you take additional steps, user controls hide all the properties and methods of their child controls. This is similar to the way ActiveX controls were created in Visual Basic 6.

That said, user controls are useful for quickly solving certain problems, or just creating composite controls.

## Creating User Controls

To add a user control to a .NET project, right-click the Solution Explorer window and select Add User Control. Figure 7-1 shows a user control in the Solution Explorer.

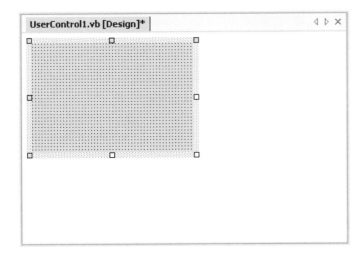

*Figure 7-1. A user control at design-time*

You'll notice from the designer that a user control is halfway between an ordinary control and a form. It helps to imagine that a user control is just a reusable portion of a form—more flexible than the visual inheritance you used in Chapter 5, but more limiting than inherited controls. In fact, user controls inherit from all the same base classes as forms, as shown in Figure 7-2.

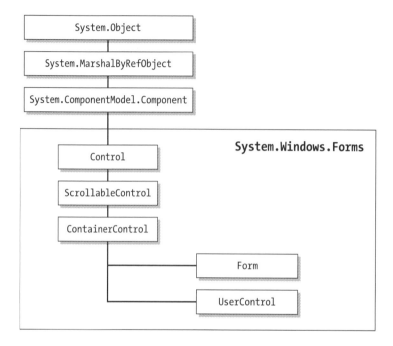

*Figure 7-2. User control inheritance*

To add a control, just draw it onto the design surface in the same way as you would a form. You can (and should) use anchoring and docking with the controls in your user control. That ensures that they always resize to fit the bounds of their container. Remember, the size of the user control is dictated by the application programmer.

If you add a form and a user control to the same project, Visual Studio .NET thoughtfully adds your user control to the toolbar so that you can drag-and-drop it onto your form. In many ways, user controls have the most convenient design-time support, and don't require any additional work from the programmer. Do note, however, that as with visual inheritance, if you change the user control you need to recompile before the change will appear in any form that hosts it. Just right-click the project in the Solution Explorer and choose Build.

To understand the strengths and limitations of user controls, it helps to consider a couple of examples.

## The Progress User Control

The first user control you'll consider is a simple coupling of a ProgressBar and Label control. This control solves a minor annoyance associated with the ProgressBar—there is no way to show the standard text description about the percent of work complete. You can easily get around this limitation by adding a label to every form that uses the ProgressBar, and manually synchronizing the two. Even better, the Progress user control implements a standard, reusable solution.

To begin, the user control is created with a label and progress bar, as shown in Figure 7-3.

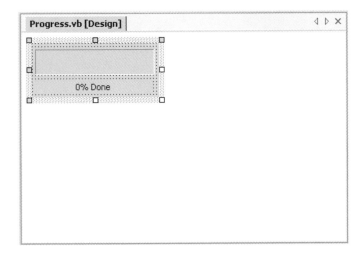

*Figure 7-3. The progress control at design-time*

If you try to use the Progress control directly in a project, you'll discover that you can't access the label or the bar. Instead, the only properties and methods that are available are those of the user control itself, allowing you to modify the default font and background color (as you can with a form), but not much more. To actually make the Progress user control functional, you need to replicate all the important methods and properties. Then, in each method or property procedure for your user control, you simply call the corresponding method or property procedure in the label or progress bar.

This delegation pattern can add up to a lot of extra code for an advanced control! Fortunately, when you create a user control you will usually restrict and simplify the interface so that it is more consistent and targeted for a specific use. In the Progress user control, for example, don't worry about allowing the user to set a font or background color for the label control.

> **TIP** *If your user control contains several controls with the same properties (like Font), you need to decide whether to provide individual user control properties (NameFont, AddressFont, etc.) or set them all at once in a single property procedure. The UserControl class makes your job a little easier. It defines Font and ForeColor properties that are automatically applied to all the composite controls unless they specify otherwise. (This is similar to how a form works.) The UserControl class also provides BackColor and BackImage properties that configure the actual user control drawing surface.*

The Progress user control provides access to three properties from the ProgressBar control (Value, Maximum, and Step), and one method (PerformStep).

```
Public Class Progress
    Inherits System.Windows.Forms.UserControl

    Friend WithEvents Bar As System.Windows.Forms.ProgressBar
    Friend WithEvents lblProgress As System.Windows.Forms.Label
    ' (Designer code omitted.)

    Property Value() As Integer
        Get
            Return Bar.Value
        End Get
        Set(ByVal Value As Integer)
            Bar.Value = Value
            UpdateLabel()
        End Set
    End Property
```

```
Property Maximum() As Integer
    Get
        Return Bar.Maximum
    End Get
    Set(ByVal Value As Integer)
        Bar.Maximum = Value
    End Set
End Property

Property [Step]() As Integer
    Get
        Return Bar.Step
    End Get
    Set(ByVal Value As Integer)
        Bar.Step = Value
    End Set
End Property

Public Sub PerformStep()
    Bar.PerformStep()
    UpdateLabel()
End Sub

Private Sub UpdateLabel()
    lblProgress.Text = ((Bar.Value * 100) \ Bar.Maximum).ToString()
    lblProgress.Text &= "% Done"
End Sub

End Class
```

There are a few interesting details in this code:

- Every time the progress bar changes (either by modifying the Value or invoking the PerformStep() method), the code calls a special private method, UpdateLabel. This ensures that the label always remains completely synchronized.

- The word "Step" is a special Visual Basic keyword that can be used in For/Next loops. Thus, it must be enclosed in square brackets to tell the compiler that it is just a variable name.

Testing this control is easy. All you need is a simple form that hosts the Progress user control, and increments its value. In this case, a timer is used for this purpose. Each time the timer fires, the PerformStep() method increments the counter by its Step value.

```
Private Sub tmrIncrementBar_Tick(ByVal sender As System.Object, _
  ByVal e As System.EventArgs) Handles tmrIncrementBar.Tick

    Status.PerformStep()
    If Status.Maximum = Status.Value Then tmrIncrementBar.Enabled = False

End Sub
```

The timer itself is enabled in response to a button click, which also configures the user control's initial settings:

```
Private Sub cmdStart_Click(ByVal sender As System.Object, _
  ByVal e As System.EventArgs) Handles cmdStart.Click

    tmrIncrementBar.Enabled = False

    Status.Value = 0
    Status.Maximum = 20
    Status.Step = 1

    tmrIncrementBar.Enabled = True

End Sub
```

Figure 7-4 shows the Progress control in the test application.

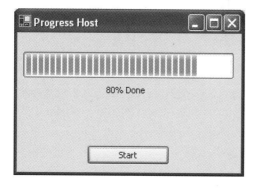

*Figure 7-4. The Progress user control in action*

Incidentally, the user can access one back door in the Progress user control: the Controls collection. If you search for the ProgressBar control by name, and modify it through the Controls collection, the label will not be refreshed. This technique relies on a string name, and is therefore not type-safe. It is strongly discouraged.

When creating any custom control, it helps to remember that you are designing a genuine class. As with any class, you should decide how it will communicate with other code, and how it can encapsulate its private data *before* you begin writing the code. The best approach is to start by designing the control's interface. Figure 7-5 presents a UML (Unified Modeling Language) diagram that defines the interface for the Progress user control.

*Figure 7-5. The Progress control in UML*

There are no clear rules for designing custom controls. Generally, you should follow the same guidelines that apply to any type of class in a program. Some of the basics include the following:

- Always use properties in place of public class variables. Public variables don't offer any protection and won't appear in the Properties window.

- If you provide a property, try to make it both readable and writable, unless there is a clear reason not to. Make sure that properties that can affect the control's appearance trigger a refresh when they are altered.

- Don't expose your basic control methods. Instead, expose higher-level methods that call these lower-level methods as required. One difference is that private methods often need to be used in set ways, while public methods should be able to work in any order. Hide details that aren't important or could cause problems if used incorrectly.

- Wrap errors in custom exception classes that provide additional information to the application programmer about the mistake that was made.

- Always use enumerations when allowing the user to choose between more than one option (never fixed constant numbers of strings). Wherever possible, code so that invalid input can't be entered.

- When all other aspects of the design are perfect, streamline your control for performance. This means reducing the memory requirements, adding threading if it's appropriate, and applying updates in batches to minimize refresh times.

## The Bitmap Thumbnail Viewer

The next example of user control development is a little more ambitious. It creates a series of thumbnails that show miniature versions of all the bitmap files found in a specific directory. This type of control could be created in a more flexible way, and with much more code, by using the GDI+ drawing features. Instead, this example uses control composition, and dynamically inserts a PictureBox control for every image. This makes it easier to handle image clicks and support image selection. It also previews the techniques you'll see in Chapter 11, where user interface is generated out of controls dynamically at runtime.

Possibly the best aspect of the BitmapViewer user control is that it communicates with your program in both directions. You can tailor the appearance of the BitmapViewer by setting properties, and the BitmapViewer notifies your code when a picture is selected by raising an event.

The design-time appearance of the BitmapViewer is unremarkable (see Figure 7-6). It contains a Panel where all the picture boxes will be added. Alternatively, the picture boxes could be added directly to the Controls collection of the user control, but the Panel allows for an attractive border around the control. It also allows automatic scrolling support—as long as AllowScroll is set to True, scrollbars are provided as soon as the image thumbnails won't fit in the Panel. As with our previous example, the Panel is anchored to all sides for automatic resizing.

> **NOTE**  *The size of the user control in the user control designer sets the initial size that is used when the control is added to a form. This size can be changed by the user, but think of it as a best recommendation.*

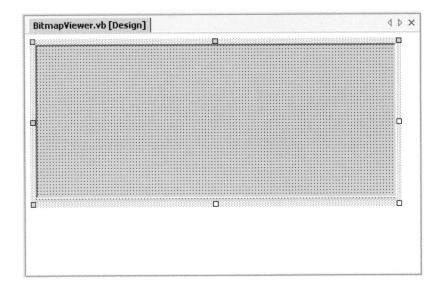

*Figure 7-6. The BitmapViewer at design-time*

Unlike the Progress control, the BitmapViewer cannot just hand off its property procedures and methods to members in one of the composite controls. Instead, it needs to retain a fair bit of its own information. The following code shows the key private variables:

```
' The directory that will be scanned for image.
Private _Directory As String

' Each picture box will be a square of _Dimension X _Dimension pixels.
Private _Dimension As Integer

' The space between the images and the top, left, and right sides.
Private _Border As Integer = 5

' The space between each image.
Private _Spacing As Integer

' The images that were found in the selected directory.
Private Images As New ArrayList()
```

Some of the values are user configurable, while some are not. For example, the collection of images is drawn from the referenced directory. The property procedures for the modifiable values are shown here:

```
Public Property Directory() As String
    Get
        Return _Directory
    End Get
    Set(ByVal Value As String)
        _Directory = Value
        GetImages()
        UpdateDisplay()
    End Set
End Property

Public Property Dimension() As Integer
    Get
        Return _Dimension
    End Get
    Set(ByVal Value As Integer)
        _Dimension = Value
        UpdateDisplay()
    End Set
End Property

Public Property Spacing() As Integer
    Get
        Return _Spacing
    End Get
    Set(ByVal Value As Integer)
        _Spacing = Value
        UpdateDisplay()
    End Set
End Property
```

> **NOTE**  *For simplicity's sake, this code doesn't provide any error-handling logic. For example, all the integer properties in the BitmapViewer should be restricted to positive numbers. Ideally, the property procedure code should refuse negative numbers and raise an error to alert the control user.*

Notice that every time a value is modified, the display is automatically regenerated by calling the UpdateDisplay() method. A more sophisticated approach might make this logic depend on a property like AutoRefresh. That way, the user could temporarily turn off the refresh, make several changes at once, and then re-enable it.

The set procedure for the Directory property also calls a special GetImages() method, which inspects the directory, and populates the Images collection. You might expect that the Images collection contains Image objects, but this is not the case. To provide useful event information, the BitmapViewer actually tracks the file name of every image it displays. To do this, a special NamedImage class is defined:

```
Private Class NamedImage
    Public Image As Image
    Public FileName As String

    Public Sub New(ByVal image As Image, ByVal fileName As String)
        Me.Image = image
        Me.FileName = fileName
    End Sub
End Class
```

The NamedImage class is a private class nested inside the BitmapViewer control class. This means that NamedImage is used exclusively by the BitmapViewer, and not made available to the application using the BitmapViewer control.

The GetImages() method uses the standard .NET file and directory classes to retrieve a list of bitmaps. For each bitmap, a NamedImage object is created, and added to the Images collection.

```
Private Sub GetImages()

    If Directory = "" Then Exit Sub

    Dim Dir As New DirectoryInfo(Directory), File As FileInfo
    For Each File In Dir.GetFiles("*.bmp")
        Images.Add(New NamedImage(Bitmap.FromFile(File.Name), File.Name))
    Next

End Sub
```

The bulk of the work for the BitmapViewer takes place in the UpdateDisplay() method, which generates the picture boxes, adds them to the panel, and sets their tag property with the name of the corresponding file for later reference. The BitmapViewer is filled from left to right, and then row-by-row.

```vb
Private Sub UpdateDisplay()

    ' Clear the current display.
    pnlPictures.Controls.Clear()

    ' Row and Col will track the current position where pictures are
    ' being inserted. They begin at the top-left corner.
    Dim Row As Integer = _Border, Col As Integer = _Border

    ' Iterate through the Images collection, and create PictureBox controls.
    Dim Image As NamedImage
    For Each Image In Images

        Dim pic As New PictureBox()
        pic.Image = Image.Image
        pic.Tag = Image.FileName
        pic.Size = New Size(_Dimension, _Dimension)
        pic.Location = New Point(Col, Row)
        pic.BorderStyle = BorderStyle.FixedSingle

        ' StrechImage mode gives us the "thumbnail" ability.
        pic.SizeMode = PictureBoxSizeMode.StretchImage

        ' Display the picture.
        pnlPictures.Controls.Add(pic)

        ' Move to the next column.
        Col += _Dimension + _Spacing

        ' Move to next line if no more pictures will fit.
        If (Col + _Dimension + _Spacing + _Border) > Me.Width Then
            Col = _Border
            Row += _Dimension + _Spacing
        End If

    Next

End Sub
```

> **TIP**  *This code could be optimized for speed. For example, all the picture boxes could be created and then added to the Panel control using the Controls.AddRange() method, ensuring that the control won't be updated and refreshed after each new picture is inserted.*

This code is also provided to the user through the public RefreshImages() method. This allows the user to trigger a refresh without needing to modify a property if the directory contents have changed.

```
Public Sub RefreshImages()
    GetImages()
    UpdateDisplay()
End Sub
```

The OnSizeChanged() method is also overriden to ensure that the pictures are redrawn when the user control size changes. This ensures that the pictures are automatically adjusted (in rows and columns) to best fit the new size.

```
Protected Overrides Sub OnSizeChanged(ByVal e As System.EventArgs)
    UpdateDisplay()
    MyBase.OnSizeChanged(e)
End Sub
```

Figure 7-7 shows a stripped-down UML diagram for the BitmapViewer control, in keeping with my philosophy of clearly defining the interfaces for custom controls. This diagram omits private members and members that have been inherited. It also shows two other class dependencies: the private NamedImage class and the PictureSelectedEventArgs class, which is introduced shortly as a means of passing event data to the application that hosts the BitmapViewer.

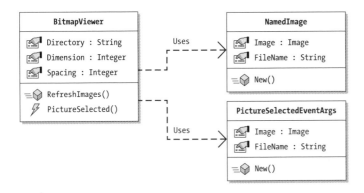

*Figure 7-7. The BitmapViewer in UML*

## Testing the BitmapViewer

To see the final BitmapViewer control, all you need to do is add it to a form and set the appropriate properties, like Directory, Dimension, and Spacing. In Figure 7-8, a dimension of 80 and spacing of 10 is used. The BitmapViewer is anchored to the form so you can change the size and see the image thumbnails being reorganized.

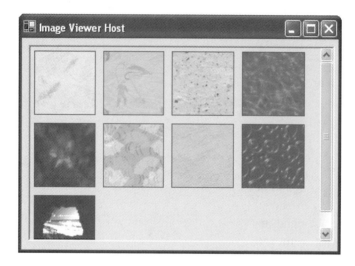

*Figure 7-8. The BitmapViewer in action*

## BitmapViewer Events

To make the BitmapViewer more useful, you can add an event that fires every time a picture box is selected. Because the BitmapViewer is built entirely from PictureBox controls, which natively provide a Click event, no hit testing is required. All you need to do is register to handle the Click even when the picture box is first created in the UpdateDisplay() method.

```
AddHandler pic.Click, AddressOf pic_Click
```

To send an event to the application, the event must first be defined in the user control class. In this case, the event is named PictureSelected. In true .NET style, it passes a reference to the event sender and a custom EventArgs object that contains additional information.

```
Event PictureSelected(ByVal sender As Object, _
  ByVal e As PictureSelectedEventArgs)
```

The custom PictureSelectedEventArgs object follows. It provides the file name of the picture that was clicked, which allows the application to retrieve it directly for editing or some other task. Note that this class should not be private, as the client must use it to retrieve the event information.

```
Public Class PictureSelectedEventArgs
    Inherits EventArgs

    Public FileName As String
    Public Image As Image

    Public Sub New(ByVal fileName As String, ByVal image As Image)
        Me.FileName = fileName
        Me.Image = Image
    End Sub

End Class
```

The PictureBox.Click event handler changes the border style of the clicked picture box to make it appear "selected." If you were using GDI+, you could draw a more flexible focus cue, like a brightly colored outline rectangle. The PictureBox.Click event handler then fires the event, with the required information.

```
Private picSelected As PictureBox

Private Sub pic_Click(ByVal sender As Object, ByVal e As System.EventArgs)

    ' Clear the border style from the last selected picture box.
    If Not picSelected Is Nothing Then
        picSelected.BorderStyle = BorderStyle.FixedSingle
    End If

    ' Get the new selection.
    picSelected = CType(sender, PictureBox)
    picSelected.BorderStyle = BorderStyle.Fixed3D

    ' Fire the selection event.
    Dim Args As New PictureSelectedEventArgs(picSelected.Tag, picSelected.Image)
    RaiseEvent PictureSelected(Me, Args)

End Sub
```

The application can now handle this event. In the example shown here (and pictured in Figure 7-9), a message box is displayed with the file name information.

```
Private Sub BitmapViewer1_PictureSelected(ByVal sender As Object, _
  ByVal e As BitmapThumbnailViewer.PictureSelectedEventArgs) _
  Handles BitmapViewer1.PictureSelected

    MessageBox.Show("You chose " & e.FileName)

End Sub
```

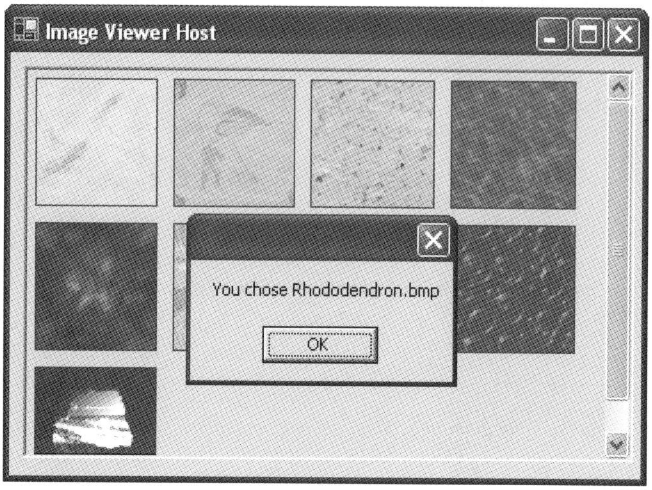

Figure 7-9. A BitmapViewer event

## BitmapViewer Enhancements and Threading

If you use the bitmap viewer with a directory that contains numerous large images, you start to notice a performance slowdown. One of the problems is that in its current form, the BitmapViewer stores the entire image in memory, even though it only displays a thumbnail. A better approach would be to scale the image immediately when it is retrieved. This is accomplished using the Image.GetThumbnail() method.

In the code that follows, the GetImages() method has been rewritten to use this more memory-friendly alternative.

```
Private Sub GetImages()
    If Directory = "" Then Exit Sub

    Dim ThumbNail As Image
    Dim Dir As New DirectoryInfo(Directory), File As FileInfo
    For Each File In Dir.GetFiles("*.bmp")
        ThumbNail = Bitmap.FromFile(File.Name).GetThumbnailImage( _
                    Dimension, Dimension, Nothing, Nothing)
        Images.Add(New NamedImage(ThumbNail, File.Name))
    Next
End Sub
```

This technique also frees you up to use a simpler control than the PictureBox to contain the Image (or even draw it directly on the form surface), because the control no longer has to perform the scaling. However, it also means that you need to update the Dimension property procedure to call the GetImages() method—otherwise, the image objects won't be the correct size.

```
Public Property Dimension() As Integer
    Get
        Return _Dimension
    End Get
    Set(ByVal Value As Integer)
        _Dimension = Value
        GetImages()
        UpdateDisplay()
    End Set
End Property
```

Assuming that the GetImages() method takes a significant amount of time, you might want to change the BitmapViewer to use multithreading. With this design, the GetImages() code runs on a separate thread, and then automatically calls the UpdateDisplay() method when it is completed. That way, the user interface wouldn't be tied up in the meantime. The remainder of this section walks you through the process.

First, change every property procedure that calls GetImages() so that it doesn't call UpdateDisplay(). An example is shown here with the Dimension() property.

```
Public Property Dimension() As Integer
    Get
        Return _Dimension
    End Get
    Set(ByVal Value As Integer)
        _Dimension = Value
        GetImages()
    End Set
End Property
```

Next, modify the GetImages() method so it actually starts the *real* ReadImagesFromFile() method on a separate thread.

```
Private Sub GetImages()

    Dim GetThread As New Threading.Thread(AddressOf ReadImagesFromFile)
    GetThread.Start()

End Sub
```

Finally, modify the file reading code and place it in the ReadImagesFromFile() method:

```
Private Sub ReadImagesFromFile()

    SyncLock Images
        If Directory = "" Then Exit Sub

        Dim ThumbNail As Image
        Dim Dir As New DirectoryInfo(Directory), File As FileInfo
        For Each File In Dir.GetFiles("*.bmp")
            ThumbNail = Bitmap.FromFile(File.Name).GetThumbnailImage( _
                    Dimension, Dimension, Nothing, Nothing)
            Images.Add(New NamedImage(ThumbNail, File.Name))
        Next
    End SyncLock

    ' Update the display on the UI thread.
    pnlpictures.Invoke(AddressOf UpdateDisplay)

End Sub
```

Threading introduces numerous potential pitfalls and isn't recommended unless you really need it. When implementing the preceding example, you have to be careful that the UpdateDisplay() method happens on the user interface thread, not the ReadImagesFromFile() thread. Otherwise, a strange conflict could emerge in real-world use. Similarly, the SyncLock statement is required to make sure that no other part of the control code attempts to modify the Images collection while the ReadImagesFromFile() method is in progress.

## Inherited Controls

Inherited controls are an ideal way to take functionality from the .NET base classes, and extend it. An inherited control can be dramatically different than its predecessor, or it may just add a few refinements. The .NET class library is filled with examples of inherited controls. For example, LinkLabel derives from Label and CheckedListBox derives from ListBox.

Unlike user controls, there is no design-time support for creating an inherited control. You simply create a class that derives from your selected control type and add the features you need. You'll also find that inherited controls are awkward to use in Visual Studio .NET. For example, it's difficult to add inherited controls to a form except through code. You overcome these difficulties in the next chapter by creating custom designers.

Inherited controls are generally more powerful than user controls, and more likely to be used across applications (and even organizations, if you are a tool vendor), not just between different windows in the same program. Some of the reasons that programmers develop inherited controls are to set defaults (for example, a control that automatically configures its appearance in its constructor) or to add features.

So far in this book, you've seen the following examples of inherited controls:

- In Chapter 2, you saw how to make an inherited text box that only accepts numeric input.

- In Chapter 4, you saw an inherited menu control that handles its own drawing to allow custom fonts and embedded thumbnail images.

- In Chapter 5, you saw inherited Form controls with visual inheritance.

- In Chapter 6, you saw custom ListView and TreeView examples that support specific types of data.

In this chapter, I'll present two more advanced inherited control examples.

## Inherited Controls or User Controls?

So, how do you know when to create a user control, and when you need a full-fledged inherited control? It's not always an easy question to answer, because most problems can be solved with either approach. However, here are a few pointers that you should consider before embarking on a custom control project:

- User controls are easier and faster to program. If you don't anticipate reusing the control frequently in different scenarios and different programs, a user control may suffice.

- If your control closely resembles an existing .NET control, it's probably best to create an inherited control. With a user control, you may need to spend a fair amount of effort creating new properties and methods to allow access to the members of the original control.

- Inherited controls provide a fine-grained level of reuse. User controls typically provide only a few members, and thus are not as configurable. Tool vendors who wish to sell their controls will always use inherited controls.

- User controls are well suited if you want to ensure that a block of interface is recreated *exactly* in more than one situation. Because a user control usually provides less flexible configuration, it guarantees a more standardized appearance.

If you want to integrate more than one control, you have two choices: you can use composition with a user control, or you can develop two separate inherited controls. The latter approach gives you the freedom to link controls (like a TreeView and ListView), but make the links optional. The application programmer can then use them separately or together, and has complete freedom about how to integrate them into a user interface. With user controls, however, the application programmer can only control the size taken by the full user control.

## The DirectoryTree Control

The DirectoryTree control inherits from the standard TreeView and adds the features needed to display a hierarchical view of directories. .NET does not include any type of native directory control, so this TreeView is genuinely useful.

Perhaps most important, it fills itself by reading subdirectories "just in time." That means that the control operates very quickly, even if the drive has tens of thousands of subdirectories. Only the expanded directory levels are actually shown. The collapsed branches all have a dummy node inserted. Every time a directory branch is expanded, the inherited control checks if a dummy node is present, and, if it is, the dummy node is removed and the directories are read from the disk. (You see a variation of this technique to allow efficient data access in Chapter 9).

The full code listing follows. Notice that the currently selected drive is stored as a single character string (technically, a Char). Another approach would be to use an instance of the System.IO.DirectoryInfo class to track or set the currently highlighted directory. That approach would provide better control for the application programmer, but it would complicate design-time support.

```
Imports System.IO

Public Class DirectoryTree
    Inherits TreeView

    Event DirectorySelected(ByVal sender As Object, _
      ByVal e As DirectorySelectedEventArgs)

    Private _Drive As Char
    Public Property Drive() As Char
        Get
            Return _Drive
        End Get
        Set(ByVal Value As Char)
            _Drive = Value
            RefreshDisplay()
        End Set
    End Property

    ' This is public so a Refresh can be triggered manually.
    Public Sub RefreshDisplay()
        ' Erase the existing tree.
        Me.Nodes.Clear()

        ' Set the first node.
        Dim RootNode As New TreeNode(_Drive & ":\")
        Me.Nodes.Add(RootNode)

        ' Fill the first level and expand it.
        Fill(RootNode)
        Me.Nodes(0).Expand()
    End Sub
```

```
Private Sub Fill(ByVal DirNode As TreeNode)
    Dim Dir As New DirectoryInfo(DirNode.FullPath)
    Dim DirItem As DirectoryInfo

    ' An exception could be thrown in this code if you don't
    ' have sufficient security permissions for a file or directory.
    ' You can catch and then ignore this exception.

    For Each DirItem In Dir.GetDirectories
        ' Add node for the directory.
        Dim NewNode As New TreeNode(DirItem.Name)
        DirNode.Nodes.Add(NewNode)
        NewNode.Nodes.Add("*")
    Next
End Sub

Protected Overrides Sub OnBeforeExpand(ByVal e As TreeViewCancelEventArgs)
    MyBase.OnBeforeExpand(e)
    ' If a dummy node is found, remove it and read the real directory list.
    If e.Node.Nodes(0).Text = "*" Then
        e.Node.Nodes.Clear()
        Fill(e.Node)
    End If
End Sub

Protected Overrides Sub OnAfterSelect(ByVal e As TreeViewEventArgs)
    MyBase.OnAfterSelect(e)
    ' Raise the DirectorySelected event.
    RaiseEvent DirectorySelected(Me, _
        New DirectorySelectedEventArgs(e.Node.FullPath))
End Sub

End Class
```

The base class events are handled by overriding the corresponding method (the recommended approach). The OnAfterSelect event is turned into a more useful DirectorySelected event, which provides a custom DirectorySelectedEventArgs class.

```
Public Class DirectorySelectedEventArgs
    Inherits EventArgs

    Public DirectoryName As String

    Public Sub New(ByVal directoryName As String)
        Me.DirectoryName = directoryName
    End Sub

End Class
```

## Testing the DirectoryTree

To test the directory tree, you can programmatically add it to a form. Make sure to set the initial drive. The following code snippet creates, configures, and displays the DirectoryTree control on a form. Figure 7-10 shows the results.

```
Private Sub Form1_Load(ByVal sender As System.Object, _
  ByVal e As System.EventArgs) Handles MyBase.Load

    Dim DirTree As New DirectoryTree()
    DirTree.Size = New Size(Me.Width - 30, Me.Height - 60)
    DirTree.Location = New Point(5, 5)
    DirTree.Drive = "C"
    Me.Controls.Add(DirTree)

End Sub
```

Another option is to add an ordinary TreeView to your project and then modify the designer code, so that the reference that defines and creates the System.Windows.Forms.TreeView becomes a reference to the [ProjectName].DirectoryTree class. This allows you to see the DirectoryTree at design time, and even configure it with the Properties window.

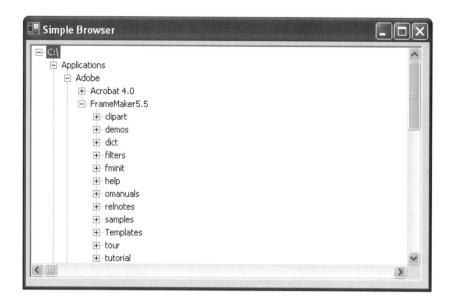

*Figure 7-10. The DirectoryTree in action*

The DirectoryTree could have been created as a user control, but the inheritance approach provides far more flexibility. For example, all the original TreeView events, properties, and methods are still available to the client code. Images can be assigned, the Nodes collection can be traversed, and restricted directories could have their nodes removed. Best of all, you don't need to write any code to delegate the properties of your custom control class to an underlying control. Clearly, inherited controls provide a far greater level of flexibility.

## A Masked TextBox Control

The final inherited control example is for a custom masked text box. A masked text box is one that automatically formats the user's input into the correct format. For example, it may add dashes or brackets to make sure it looks like a phone number. This task is notoriously difficult, and no clear standard has ever been defined. One useful tool is Microsoft's masked edit text box, which is provided as an ActiveX control with previous versions of Visual Studio.

The example of a masked text box is important because it demonstrates how features (rather than data) might be added to an existing control by subclassing. The example I provide is still quite limited—notably, it restricts deletions and the use of the arrow keys. Tracking the cursor position, which is required to allow inline masked edits, results in a good deal of tedious code that only obscures the point.

Here's the full class code for the masked text box:

```
Public Class MaskedTextBox
    Inherits TextBox

    Private _Mask As String
    Public Property Mask() As String
        Get
            Return _Mask
        End Get
        Set(ByVal Value As String)
            _Mask = Value
            Me.Text = ""
        End Set
    End Property

    Protected Overrides Sub OnKeyPress(ByVal e As KeyPressEventArgs)
        If Mask = "" Then Exit Sub

        ' Suppress the typed character.
        e.Handled = True

        Dim i As Integer
        Dim NewText As String = Me.Text

        ' Loop through the mask, adding fixed characters as needed.
        ' If the next allowed character matches what the user has
        ' typed in (a number or letter), that is added to the end.
        For i = Me.SelectionStart To _Mask.Length - 1
            Select Case _Mask.Chars(i)
                Case "#"
                    ' Allow the keypress as long as it is a number.
                    If Char.IsDigit(e.KeyChar) = True Then
                        NewText &= e.KeyChar.ToString()
                        Exit For
                    Else
                        ' Invalid entry; exit and don't change the text.
                        Exit Sub
                    End If
                Case "."
                    ' Allow the keypress as long as it is a letter.
                    If Char.IsLetter(e.KeyChar) = True Then
                        NewText &= e.KeyChar.ToString()
                        Exit For
```

```
                    Else
                        ' Invalid entry; exit and don't change the text.
                        Exit Sub
                    End If
                Case Else
                    ' Insert the mask character.
                    NewText = NewText & _Mask.Chars(i)
            End Select
        Next

        ' Update the text.
        Me.Text = NewText
        Me.SelectionStart = Me.Text.Length

    End Sub

    Protected Overrides Sub OnKeyDown(ByVal e As KeyEventArgs)
        ' Stop special characters.
        e.Handled = True
    End Sub

End Class
```

To use the masked control, the application programmer chooses a mask and applies it to the Mask property of the control. The number sign (#) represents any number, and the period (.) represents any letter. All other characters in the mask are treated as fixed characters, and are inserted automatically when needed. For example, in the phone number mask (###) ###-#### the first bracket is inserted automatically when the user types the first number. Figure 7-11 shows this mask in action.

```
Private Sub Form1_Load(ByVal sender As System.Object, _
  ByVal e As System.EventArgs) Handles MyBase.Load

    Dim txtMask As New MaskedTextBox()
    txtMask.Location = New Point(10, 10)
    txtMask.Mask = "(###) ###-####"
    Me.Controls.Add(txtMask)

End Sub
```

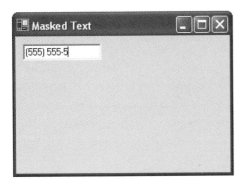

*Figure 7-11. The MaskedTextBox in action*

## Custom Extender Providers

Extender providers were first introduced in Chapter 4 as interesting components that extend other controls. Examples are the ToolTipProvider, which displays a tooltip next to other controls; the ErrorProvider, which displays an error icon; and the HelpProvider, which invokes context-sensitive Help on a control's behalf when the F1 key is pressed. Providers tend to be specialized solutions, and you may design dozens of custom controls before even contemplating a custom provider.

Nonetheless, custom providers can achieve some remarkable tricks. In this section, I demonstrate two extender providers, one that mimics the old-fashioned MFC behavior of menu Help text, and another that displays a clickable Help icon. Both of these classes are found in the ExtenderProvider project provided with the online samples. The test applications can be found in the ExtenderProviderHost project.

> **TIP** *To create an extender provider, it's easiest to create the custom provider class in a class library project, compile it into a DLL file, and then reference the DLL file from another project by choosing Customize Toolbox. (In fact, this approach is generally the easiest way to integrate inherited controls.) When you add the reference to the extender provider assembly, any associated extender control automatically appears in the ToolBox.*

## The Menu Text Provider

The MenuTextProvider extends ordinary menus by associating each item with a unique Help string. When the user hovers over a menu item, the MenuTextProvider displays the appropriate Help string. This is a common user interface convention I've mentioned before, and while it's not very useful for the average user, it does provide a good introduction to extender providers.

### Choosing a base class

The first step when creating an extender provider is to create a class that implements the IExtenderProvider interface and uses the ProvideProperty attribute (both of these types are found in the System.ComponentModel interface). This can be any type of class, including a user control, inherited control, or just a basic Component class that doesn't derive from any control. The type of class depends on the type of provider you are creating.

A control-based provider, like the MenuTextProvider, uses a dedicated control to display information in a specific location on a form. In this example, the MenuTextProvider inherits from the StatusBar class. This means you can add the MenuTextProvider to any form, and it will act as an ordinary status bar and update its display to provide the appropriate text automatically. Another possible approach would be to derive the provider from the StatusBarPanel class. You could then add it to an existing status bar.

### Choosing the object to extend

Once you've decided what type of provider you are creating, your next decision is to determine the type of object that you are extending. Many providers extend any type of Windows control, while some are limited to specific classes. To specify the appropriate type of object, you need to handle the IExtenderProvider.CanExtend() method. In this method, you look at the supplied type of object, and then make a decision about whether or not it can be extended by your provider. To make this decision you can evaluate any information about the target, including the type (the most common criteria), whether it is hosted in another control or on a form, and even its name. You return True if the object can be extended.

The MenuTextProvider only extends the MenuItem object. Here's the code that enforces this restriction:

```
Public Class MenuTextProvider
    Inherits StatusBar
    Implements IExtenderProvider

    Public Function CanExtend(ByVal extendee As Object) As Boolean _
      Implements System.ComponentModel.IExtenderProvider.CanExtend
        If extendee Is GetType(MenuItem) Then
            Return True
        Else
            Return False
        End If
    End Function

End Class
```

### Providing an extended property

The next step is to identify the property that will be assigned to all extended controls. You do this by adding a ProvideProperty attribute just before your class declaration. The ProvideProperty attribute identifies the property name and the data type.

```
<ProvideProperty("HelpText", GetType(String))> _
Public Class MenuTextProvider
```

Once you've specified a property in this fashion, you need to provide corresponding Get and Set methods that perform the actual work when the property is changed. These members are preceded with "Get" or "Set" and use the same name you identified in the ProvidePoperty attribute. These methods must be public.

```
Public Sub SetHelpText(ByVal extendee As Object, ByVal value As String)
    ' (Code omitted.)
End Sub

Public Function GetHelpText(ByVal extendee As Object) As String
    ' (Code omitted.)
End Function
```

Note that the GetProperty() method accepts a reference to the target and the SetProperty() method accepts a reference to the target and a value for the property. Keep in mind that a single instance of your extender can be reused to extend dozens of controls (and, conversely, two similar providers can extend the same control). That means that you need to keep track of all the extended controls in a collection. Our examples use the Hashtable class for this purpose, because it allows the object reference to be used as a key. (Remember, MenuItem objects are not controls, and do not have a unique Name property that can be used as a key).

### The completed provider

To complete the MenuTextProvider, create a collection to store the Help text values for every extended control, and add the implementation logic for the SetHelpText() and GetHelpText() methods.

When the Help text is set, the provider registers to receive the Select event from the MenuItem and stores the Help text in the collection under the name of the control. When the Select event occurs, the Help text is retrieved and displayed in the status bar panel. We could just as easily monitor different events (like key presses, as the HelpProvider control does).

Here's the complete code:

```
<ProvideProperty("HelpText", GetType(String))> _
Public Class MenuTextProvider
    Inherits StatusBar
    Implements IExtenderProvider

    Private HelpText As New Hashtable()

    Public Function CanExtend(ByVal extendee As Object) As Boolean _
      Implements System.ComponentModel.IExtenderProvider.CanExtend
        If extendee Is GetType(MenuItem) Then
            Return True
        Else
            Return False
        End If
    End Function
```

```
Public Sub SetHelpText(ByVal extendee As Object, ByVal value As String)
    ' Specifying an empty value removes the extension.
    If value = "" Then
        HelpText.Remove(extendee)
        RemoveHandler CType(extendee, MenuItem).Select, AddressOf MenuSelect
    Else
        HelpText(extendee) = value
        AddHandler CType(extendee, MenuItem).Select, AddressOf MenuSelect
    End If
End Sub

Public Function GetHelpText(ByVal extendee As Object) As String
    If Not HelpText(extendee) Is Nothing Then
        Return HelpText(extendee).ToString()
    Else
        Return String.Empty
    End If
End Function

Private Sub MenuSelect(ByVal sender As System.Object, _
  ByVal e As System.EventArgs)
    Me.Text = HelpText(sender).ToString()
End Sub

End Class
```

**NOTE** *With extender providers, calling a Set method with an empty string is assumed to mean removing the extension. In the preceding example, this call causes the MenuHelpProvider to detach its event handler.*

You can set the Help text for a menu item with the SetHelpText() method (see Figure 7-12):

```
MenuTextProvider1.SetHelpText(mnuNew, _
  " Create a new document and abandon the current one.")
```

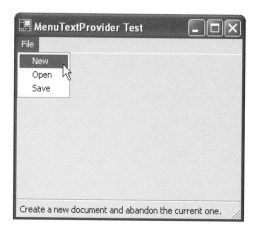

*Figure 7-12. The MenuTextProvider in action*

## The Help Icon Provider

In many ways, the next example is a more typical provider because it extends other controls without being a control itself. Instead, it derives from the System.ComponentModel.Component class.

The HelpIconProvider retrieves a reference to the form that contains the control and adds a miniature PictureBox control with a question mark icon in it. It also registers for the DoubleClick event for the picture box. If this occurs, a Help file is launched, with the specified context identifier for the control. The name of the Help file is global to the provider, and specified through a standard HelpFile property. To further refine the control, you could handle more events from the dynamically generated picture box, perhaps tailoring the mouse cursor when it is positioned over it.

```
<ProvideProperty("HelpID", GetType(String))> _
Public Class HelpIconProvider
    Inherits Component
    Implements IExtenderProvider

    Private ContextID As New Hashtable()
    Private Pictures As New Hashtable()
    Private _HelpFile As String

    Public Function CanExtend(ByVal extendee As Object) As Boolean _
      Implements System.ComponentModel.IExtenderProvider.CanExtend
        If extendee Is GetType(Control) Then
            If CType(extendee, Control).FindForm Is Nothing Then
                Return False
```

```
        Else
            Return True
        End If
    Else
        Return False
    End If
End Function


Public Property HelpFile() As String
    Get
        Return _HelpFile
    End Get
    Set(ByVal Value As String)
        _HelpFile = Value
    End Set
End Property


Public Sub SetHelpID(ByVal extendee As Object, ByVal value As String)
    Dim ctrl As Control = CType(extendee, Control)

    ' Specifying an empty value removes the extension.
    If value = "" Then
        ContextID.Remove(extendee)

        ' Remove the picture.
        Dim pic As PictureBox = CType(Pictures(extendee), PictureBox)
        RemoveHandler pic.DoubleClick, AddressOf PicDoubleClick

        pic.Parent.Controls.Remove(pic)
        Pictures.Remove(extendee)
    Else
        ContextID(extendee) = value

        ' Create new icon.
        Dim pic As New PictureBox()
        pic.Image = Image.FromFile("Help.gif")

        ' Store a reference to the related control in the PictureBox.
        pic.Tag = extendee

        pic.Size = New Size(16, 16)
        pic.Location = New Point(ctrl.Right + 10, ctrl.Top)
        ctrl.Parent.Controls.Add(pic)
```

```
                        ' Register for DoubleClick event.
                        AddHandler pic.DoubleClick, AddressOf PicDoubleClick

                        ' Store a reference to the PictureBox so it can be easily
                          removed if needed.
                        Pictures(extendee) = pic
                    End If
                End Sub


                Public Function GetHelpID(ByVal extendee As Object) As String
                    If Not ContextID(extendee) Is Nothing Then
                        Return ContextID(extendee).ToString()
                    Else
                        Return String.Empty
                    End If
                End Function


                Public Sub PicDoubleClick(ByVal sender As Object, ByVal e As EventArgs)
                    ' Invoke help for control.
                    Dim ctrlRelated As Control = CType(CType(sender, Control).Tag, Control)
                    Help.ShowHelp(ctrlRelated, _HelpFile, HelpNavigator.Topic, _
                        ContextID(ctrlRelated).ToString())
                End Sub

            End Class
```

You will find out much more about the Help class this control uses to invoke the Help engine in Chapter 14.

To use the HelpIconProvider,, just specify a global Help file for the provider and set a Help context ID for a specific control. In order to test the control, you must have a valid help file with a known topic ID, otherwise the ShowHelp() method will be ignored. In the online samples, the code adds a debug message box to inform you when the picture is double-clicked and the help should be triggered.

```
Private Sub HelpIconHost_Load(ByVal sender As System.Object, _
  ByVal e As System.EventArgs) Handles MyBase.Load

    HelpIconProvider1.HelpFile = "myhelp.hlp"
    HelpIconProvider1.SetHelpID(TextBox1, "10001")
    HelpIconProvider1.SetHelpID(TextBox2, "10002")

End Sub
```

Figure 7-13 shows the HelpIconProvider in action.

*Figure 7-13. A HelpIconProvider extending two text boxes*

One limitation with this provider is that it reads the image it displays from a file. That means that every client who uses the provider control also requires the Help icon picture in the project directory directory. The next chapter demonstrates a better approach that embeds the picture as a resource, so it can't be lost.

## The Last Word

This chapter considered one of the most important ingredients in advanced user interfaces: custom controls. You learned how to master user interface controls, and equip them with useful properties, methods, and events. You also learned about inherited controls and the different model they provide.

One topic that hasn't been considered in great detail is Visual Studio .NET's sometimes quirky design-time support of custom controls. In order to improve on this, I take the same collection of controls to the next chapter, and develop the designers and type editors that allow them to behave properly in the IDE.

# CHAPTER 8

# Design-Time Support for Custom Controls

THE CUSTOM CONTROLS you have explored so far are full of promise. Being able to drop a tool-like directory browser or thumbnail viewer directly into your application without writing a single line of extra code is a remarkable advantage. However, there is one caveat. Though your custom controls perform wonders at runtime, many of them act oddly while a form is being designed. By default, only user controls appear in the Toolbox, and even they only appear with a generic icon. Inherited controls need to be created in code, unless you create a similar control and manually edit the hidden designer instructions. Even if you use this trick, the results aren't always what you expect.

In this chapter, I sort through these quirks and show you how to create a control that behaves properly at design time. Some of the topics this chapter tackles include:

- Using attributes to classify and describe properties and other aspects of your control.

- Adding your control to the toolbox—with an icon.

- Using prebuilt UITypeEditor classes that allow directory names, collections, and other property types to be edited at design time.

- Creating your own UITypeEditor classes that allow your control to be configured with custom dialog windows.

- Using control designers to filter out unused properties, add designer wizards, and other tricks.

- Licensing your controls.

This chapter explores these topics, and uses them to revise some of the examples introduced in the Chapter 7.

# Control Projects

Before beginning, it helps to review a few best practices for creating custom controls. In the previous chapter, you created controls and test forms in the same project. In this chapter, you'll alter your approach, and put each control in a dedicated project. Every project that needs to use the control then needs to add a reference to the compiled assembly. This approach makes it easier to test the design-time abilities of a control.

## The Class Library Project

Typically, you'll create your control as either a Class Library Project (for most custom control projects) or a Windows Control Project (for user controls). The choice you make doesn't make much difference—essentially all the project type does is configure the default references and the namespaces that are initially imported into your project. The important fact is that you are creating a library project, which creates a DLL assembly, instead of a stand-alone executable. This DLL can then be shared with any other project that needs to use the control. Figure 8-1 shows the option you must select to create a Class Library project.

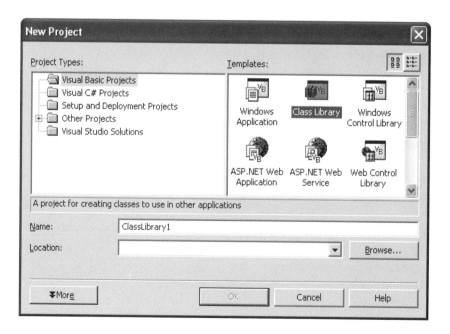

*Figure 8-1. Creating a control project*

When you begin your control project, you will probably find that you need to add a few assembly references and import some namespaces. If you try to use a standard type and you receive an error, the problem is probably a missing reference.

Typically, you need to add references to the System.Windows.Form.dll, System.Drawing.dll, and System.Design assemblies. Just right-click the project in the Solution Explorer and select Add Reference (see Figure 8-2).

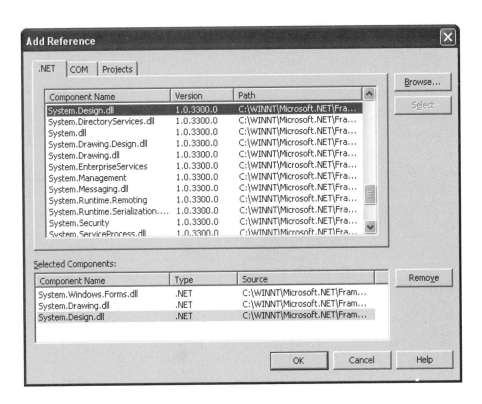

*Figure 8-2. Adding required assemblies*

Having accomplished this step, you'll probably want to import some project-wide namespaces so you don't have to type fully qualified names (like System.Windows.Forms.Form instead of just Form). You can add these by right-clicking your project and choosing Properties. Look under the Common Properties ➤ Build node (see Figure 8-3). Useful namespaces include System.Windows.Forms, System.ComponentModel, and System.Drawing. Remember, importing namespaces isn't required—it's just a convenience that helps trim long lines of code.

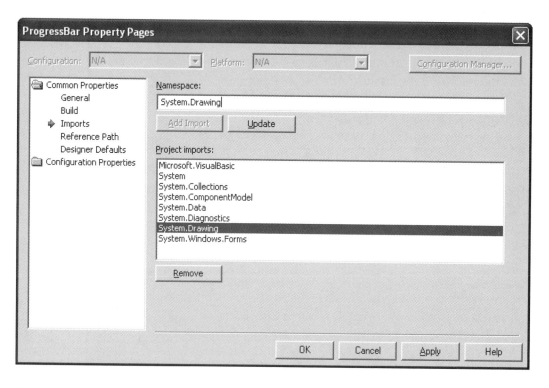

*Figure 8-3. Importing useful namespaces*

You can then create your custom control classes. Generally, you place each control in a separate file, although this approach isn't required. You can create a class library project that contains several files and multiple controls, or you can create a separate project and assembly for each custom control you make. To build your project at any time, right-click it in the Solution Explorer and choose Build. The DLL file will be placed in the bin subdirectory of your project directory.

## Referencing a Custom Control

For other projects to use your control, they need a reference to the compiled assembly. When you add a reference, Visual Studio .NET stores the location of the file. Every time you rebuild your client project, Visual Studio copies the latest version of the dependent assembly from its source directory into the client project's bin directory, where the client executable resides. That ensures that you are always testing against the most recent build of a control.

To add a reference to a control, right-click the Toolbox, and choose Customize. Then, select the .NET Framework Components tab, and click the Browse button. Once you select the appropriate assembly, all controls are added to the list, and checkmarked automatically (see Figure 8-4).

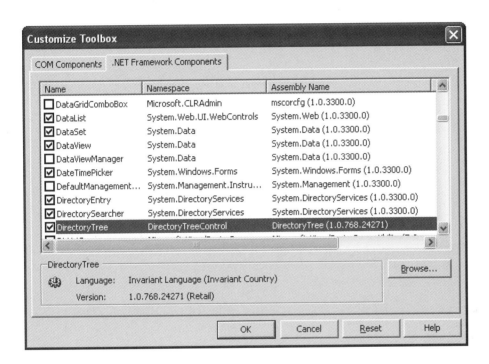

*Figure 8-4. Referencing an assembly with controls*

When you click OK, your control is added to the bottom of the Toolbox alongside its .NET counterparts (see Figure 8-5). If you haven't configured a custom icon, it appears with the default gear icon. You can then create instances of this control by drawing on the design surface.

*Figure 8-5. Your custom control in the Toolbox*

When you actually deploy an application that uses a custom control, all you need to do is ensure that the required control DLL is in the same directory as the application executable. When you copy these files to another computer, you do not need to worry about registering them or performing any additional steps. This is the infamous zero-touch deployment that is heavily hyped with .NET.

## The GAC

If multiple applications need to use the same control, you can copy the appropriate assembly to each application directory. This gives you the freedom to update some applications with additional functionality without worrying about backward compatibility. It also only requires a minuscule amount of disk space, and is thus the favored approach.

Another option is to install your component to the Global Assembly Cache (the same repository that contains the core .NET assemblies). The Global Assembly Cache (or GAC) also allows multiple versions of a component to be installed side-by-side. The GAC also ensures that every application uses the version of a control that it was compiled with, which almost completely eliminates versioning headaches. The only disadvantage to using the GAC is that you need to sign your versioned assembly using a private key to ensure that it has a unique identifier (and can't conflict with other components), and to ensure that no other organization can release a new control that claims to be your own. This process is the same for any shared component, whether it is a control or a business object.

Many factors that required a central repository for components in the old world of COM don't apply with .NET. If you just want to share a control between specific applications, you probably don't need the additional complexity of the GAC. On the other hand, if you are a tool vendor who creates, sells, and distributes custom controls, you will almost certainly want to use it. This process is well documented in the MSDN reference, but the essential steps are explained in the following three sections.

> **TIP** *You don't need to install your control to the GAC in order to use licensing (which is described at the end of this chapter).*

## Creating a key

The first step for installing a control into the GAC is to use the sn.exe command-line utility included with the .NET framework. To create a key, you use the –k parameter, and specify the name for your key:

```
sn -k MyKey.snk
```

Each .snk file contains a private and a public key. Private and public keys provide a special type of encryption. Anything encrypted with a private key can be read only with the corresponding public key. Anything encrypted with a private key, however, can only be read with the corresponding private key. The public key is typically made available to the world. The private key is carefully guarded.

In .NET, the private key is used to compile the assembly, and the public key is embedded inside the assembly. When an application uses your control, the Common Language Runtime uses the public key to decode information from the manifest. Thus, no one else can create an update to your assembly, because they need to have your original private key to encode it successfully.

## Applying a key to a control

To add the key to a control project, you need to add an Assembly attribute to the AssemblyInfo.vb file that identifies the file.

```
<Assembly: AssemblyKeyFile("c:\KeyFiles\MyKey.snk")>
```

The next time you compile the project, the key information is added to the assembly. .NET also supports delayed assembly signing, which allows you to add the strong name just before shipping the control. This is useful in a large organization, because it allows you to debug the control without requiring the private key. The assembly can then be signed just before it is released by the individual who guards the private key. Delayed assembling assignment requires a little more grunt-work, and is described in the MSDN reference.

## Installing a control to the GAC

Now that your control is signed, you can install it to the GAC using a dedicated setup program or the GACUtil.exe utility. You can event drag-and-drop the assembly to the C:\[WindowsDir]\Assembly directory in Windows Explorer, which installs it automatically. At this point, life couldn't be easier.

If you install later versions of the same assembly in the GAC, the original version remains. Clients automatically use the latest assembly that shares the same major and minor and version number as the one they were compiled with. In other words, if you compile an application that uses version 1.2.0.0 of your control, the application automatically upgrades itself to version 1.2.1.0 if it exists in the GAC. However, it won't support version 1.3.0.0.

When dealing with assemblies, you have many more options for configuring version policies. You should consult the MSDN reference or a book about .NET fundamentals for more information.

## Control Designer Basics

Adding a basic level of design-time support to your controls is easy. In this section you learn how you can outfit your control with a custom toolbox icon, resource files, and support for the Properties window.

## Attributes

Designer attributes are the first line in custom control support. They instruct the IDE how to treat various parts of your control. Attributes are a unique development in .NET programming. To specify this type of information about a custom control in another programming language, you would either need to create a separate file in a proprietary format (and learn a new syntax), or use some sort of visual tool. With attributes, the information that describes your control can be easily created and edited alongside your code, but it is still cleanly separated from the logic that generates the user interface.

The previous chapter developed a Progress user control that displayed a synchronized label paired with a progress bar. To make it work three properties were added: Value, Step, and Maximum. You may have noticed that these properties appear in the design window grouped under the generic "Misc" category without any additional information (see Figure 8-6).

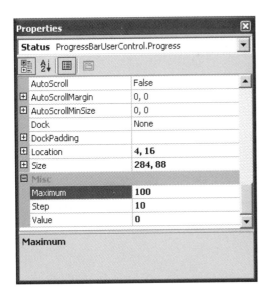

*Figure 8-6. Nondescript properties*

You can improve on this situation using attributes. The example below adds a Description, Category, and DefaultValue attribute to the Value property. Note that when you use more than one attribute, they are all enclosed between angled brackets, and separated with commas. The underscore character is used to spread the attributes over several lines for better readability.

```
<Description("The current value (between 0 and Maximum)" & _
            "which sets the position of the progress bar"), _
 Category("Behavior"), _
 DefaultValue(0)> _
Property Value() As Integer
    Get
        Return Bar.Value
    End Get
    Set(ByVal Value As Integer)
        Bar.Value = Value
        UpdateLabel()
    End Set
End Property
```

The result of applying these attributes is shown in Figure 8-7.

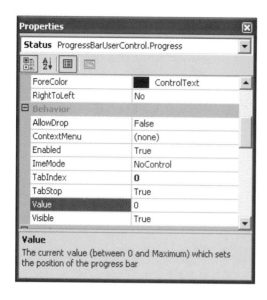

*Figure 8-7. A property configured with attributes*

All these attributes are found in the System.ComponentModel namespace, along with many more that allow you to configure aspects of your control's design-time behavior. Table 8-1 lists the most useful attributes you can use to configure properties.

*Table 8-1. Basic Control Property Attributes*

| Attribute | Description |
| --- | --- |
| AmbientValue(True\|False) | Indicates that the value for a property is derived from the control's parent. For example, most controls have an ambient Font and BackColor property—if these values are not set, the Font and BackColor of the parent is used automatically. |
| Browsable(True\|False) | If False, indicates that a property should not be shown in the Properties window. However, the property is still accessible through code. |

*Table 8-1. Basic Control Property Attributes (Continued)*

| Attribute | Description |
|---|---|
| Category("") | Sets the category under which the property appears in the Properties window. If a category with this name doesn't exist, it is created. |
| DefaultValue() | Sets the initial value that will be used for this property when the control is created. |
| Description("") | Specifies the text description that will be displayed for this property in the Object Browser of Properties window. |
| DesignOnly(True\|False) | When set to True, this property is only available at design time. This is typically used with special properties that configure how a control behaves at design time (like a SuppressUI property), and don't correspond to a "real" piece of information about the control. |
| ImmutableObject(True\|False) | When set to True on an object property, this attribute ensures that the sub-properties of this object is displayed as read-only. For example, if you apply this to a property that uses a Point object, the X and Y subproperty will be read-only. |
| Localizable(True\|False) | When set to True, the design-time value for this property is stored in a resource file instead of in the generated code. This makes it easy to swap the value later by introducing a new resource file. When the user configures properties that don't use this attribute, the appropriate code is inserted in the hidden designer region of the form, unless it requires a special data type (like an image) that must be stored in a resource file. |

*Table 8-1. Basic Control Property Attributes (Continued)*

| Attribute | Description |
|---|---|
| MergableProperty(True\|False) | Configures how the Properties window behaves when more than one instance of this control are selected at once. If False, the property is not shown. If True (the default), the property can be set for all selected controls at once. |
| NotifyParentProperty(True\|False) | Set this to True to indicate that a parent property should receive notification about changes to the property's value (and update its display accordingly). For example, the Size property has two nested properties: Height and Width. These nested properties should be marked with this attribute. |
| ParenthesizePropertyName(True\|False) | When True, indicates that the property should be displayed with brackets around it in the Properties window (like the Name property). |
| ReadOnly(True\|False) | When True, this property is read-only in the Properties window at design time. |
| RefreshProperties() | You use this attribute with a value from the RefreshProperties enumeration. It specifies whether the rest of the Properties window must be updated when this property is changed (for example, if one property procedure could change another property). |

A few attributes can be applied to your custom control class declaration, rather than a specific property. These include two attributes that set the default event and property. Here's how you could use these attributes with the DirectoryTree developed in the previous chapter:

```
<DefaultEvent("DirectorySelected"), _
 DefaultProperty("Drive")> _
Public Class DirectoryTree
    Inherits TreeView
```

Table 8-2 lists the useful designer attributes that you can apply to the class definition.

*Table 8-2. Basic Control Class Attributes*

| Attribute | Description |
|---|---|
| DefaultEvent | When the application programmer double-clicks your control, Visual Studio .NET automatically adds an event handler for the default event. |
| DefaultProperty | The DefaultProperty is the property that is highlighted in the Properties window by default, the first time the control is selected. |

You can also use some advanced attributes to support licensing and custom windows for property settings. You'll learn about these topics a little later in this chapter.

## Basic Serialization

When creating a property, you can add additional methods to configure its default value, and specify whether changes should be serialized to the Windows designer code in the form. You add this extra logic by creating two optional methods for each property: ShouldSerialize*PropertyName*() and Reset*PropertyName*().

For example, if you have a property named Drive, you could add the following methods:

```
Public Sub ResetDrive()
    ' (Reset code goes here.)
End Sub

Public Function ShouldSerializeDrive() As Boolean
    ' (Determine if serialization is needed here.)
End Sub
```

Visual Studio .NET automatically invokes the ResetDrive() method when the control is first created (to set a default value), or whenever the user right-clicks the property in the Properties window and chooses Reset. If you don't use the ResetDrive() method, Visual Studio .NET uses whatever value is specified in the DefaultValue attribute applied to the Drive property. Thus, you should use either a DefaultValue attribute or the custom ResetDrive() method, not both.

One reason that you might want to use the custom ResetDrive() method instead of a DefaultValue attribute is so that you can make a runtime decision about what value to use. For example, you could set this property in accordance with other control properties, or by examining the hard drive to determine what drive letters are valid.

The ShouldSerializeDrive() method performs a slightly different task. It returns True or False to indicate whether Visual Studio .NET should generate the commands required to commit this change to the designer code. If you don't include this method, Visual Studio .NET always generates the designer code in response to the values chosen by the user at design-time. One reason that the ShouldSerialize*PropertyName*() method is often used is to avoid serializing information when this information corresponds to the default value. This results in more economical code.

Here's a complete example for the Drive property:

```
Private _Drive As Char
Public Property Drive() As Char
    Get
        Return _Drive
    End Get
    Set(ByVal Value As Char)
        _Drive = Value
        RefreshDisplay()
    End Set
End Property


Public Sub ResetDrive()
    _Drive = "C"
End Sub


Public Function ShouldSerializeDrive() As Boolean
    ' Serialize the change as long as it does not equal the default value.
    Return Not (_Drive = "C")
End Sub
```

## The Toolbox Bitmap

Adding a toolbox icon is refreshingly easy. All you need to do is add a bitmap to your project and ensure it has the same file name as your custom control class. This bitmap must meet a few basic criteria:

- It must be 16 pixels by 16 pixels. Otherwise, Visual Studio .NET attempts to scale it and the results will be ugly.

- It must use only 16 colors.

Once you add the file, use the Properties window to set the Build Action for it to Embedded Resource. Then, recompile the control project. Figure 8-8 shows an example: the DirectoryTree control project with the required image file.

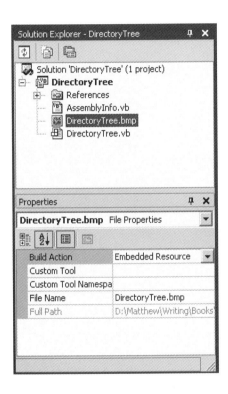

*Figure 8-8. Configuring a toolbox bitmap*

When you add the control to a client project, the embedded bitmap appears in the toolbox, as shown in Figure 8-9.

*Figure 8-9. A custom toolbox bitmap*

## Resource Files

The previous chapter developed an extender provider that displayed a custom Help icon next to ordinary .NET controls. One of the flaws in the design was that the icon was read from a file. This means it has to be in the current directory of the program that is using the HelpIconProvider.

A better approach is to embed the binary data for the icon as a resource in the compiled DLL. In .NET, this is accomplished using .resx files. Visual Studio .NET creates a .resx file automatically for every form, and uses it to store images (or other binary data) that you set at design time.

To see the .resx files in your project, select Project ➤ Show All Files from the Visual Studio .NET menu. A .resx file appears under each form node in the Solution Explorer, as shown in Figure 8-10.

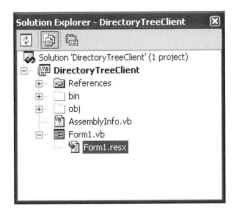

*Figure 8-10. A resource file*

If you opened a .resx file in Notepad or a similar text editor, you would discover that it is actually an XML file that contains a name/value pair for each resource. For example, the snippet that follows defines the binary data for a picture in a PictureBox control.

```
<data name="PictureBox1.Image" type="System.Drawing.Bitmap, System.Drawing,
 Version=1.0.3300.0, Culture=neutral, PublicKeyToken=b03f5f7f11d50a3a"
 mimetype="application/x-microsoft.net.object.bytearray.base64">
```

```
<value>          R0lGODlhEAAQAPcAAP7+/f/99fLy8+7z/O7x9ubt++jt9uPp8+Dm8///
7vLx70zt7uPj5Mbz/9vq/9rj
9Nfh8s7p/93i7dTe8cre/8rY89Hc783U4MfQ48bP4dzd39LS0sDJ28rKysbIysLCwqjd/qnU/73J4JjP
/3HJ/7vG3brBz6G555Gt6Iev7LG7yqi1z6Kxz5qv2ZCo2J+v1Zar1JWkwoGaz7u7u70zs6qssaysrJid
ppOZpZqamnGy/3mk9muY9Xuc4Hea4kyL/3CS2X+c12mO2GaM2myKyWqGwl2H3n2BiVJ/10Bx0Fl+x1F5
xz1z4DZx5itn4jNr2zlsODRpOzpszTRozjJmzTNjxSxizCpfyiNbyytfxSRZwCBWxBVU0RpVyR1VxRFM
wz1luSVXuRFIuRZNtw5JvQ1GugExvX19fXJycm9zeWxsbGNjY1lZWlJSUk50TgAAAAAAAAAAAAAAAAAA
AAAAAAAAAAAAAAAAAAAAAAAAAAAAAAAAAAAAAAAAAAAAAAAAAAAAAAAAAAAAAAAAAAAAAAAAAAAAAAAA
AAAAAAAAAAAAAAAAAAAAAAAAAAAAAAAAAAAAAAAAAAAAAAAAAAAAAAAAAAAAAAAAAAAAAAAAAAAAAAAA
AAAAAAAAAAAAAAAAAAAAAAAAAAAAAAAAAAAAAAAAAAAAAAAAAAAAAAAAAAAAAAAAAAAAAAAAAAAAAAAA
AAAAAAAAAAAAAAAAAAAAAAAAAAAAAAAAAAAAAAAAAAAAAAAAAAAAAAAAAAAAAAAAAAAAAAAAAAAAAAAA
AAAAAAAAAAAAAAAAAAAAAAAAAAAAAAAAAAAAAAAAAAAAAAAAAAAAAAAAAAAAAAAAAAAAAAAAAAAAAAAA
AAAAAAAAAAAAAAAAAAAAAAAAAAAAAAAAAAAAAAAAAAAAAAAAAAAAAAAAAAAAAAAAAAAAAAAAAAAAAAAA
AAAAAAAAAAAAAAAAAAAAAAAAAAAAAAAAAAAAAAAAAAAAAAAAAAAAAAAAAAAAAAAAAAAAAAAAAAAAAP//
```

```
/yH5BAEAACQALAAAAAAAQABAAAAj8AEkIBPBggoWDEyQIEMiQxIAJBwBIlIhggoaGDyU2ADFiRAiJEzwM
nAAggo4UEhQg2PGDAoAJHUg8IODgh5EEAE4ACMCkyQAENxiQ5OGEyAEkZoIAGMLFBwAONiAUeBLlCpYu
XzAASIJFCgALah5UwEKFipUtKwDO8GIlC4EJbQp6KYulCAAUX6yOFQDBDQQAVbBMwULkARSyXpYAyNCG
pAsyeqUIuWLlyhgRBnCsWfBXSZkvMQAA+VJGBgAIbHIAuHAggIwxYFpoCfMiwIMOaC4KMPEAAAMWMEoo
         4HtEzQyGDGpggPCgOQQVbNDQaEhiwQc1bdxob3NmA8OAADs=
```

    </value>
    </data>

You can also view the .resx file in Visual Studio .NET by double-clicking it. It displays the list of pairs in a special dataset view (see Figure 8-11).

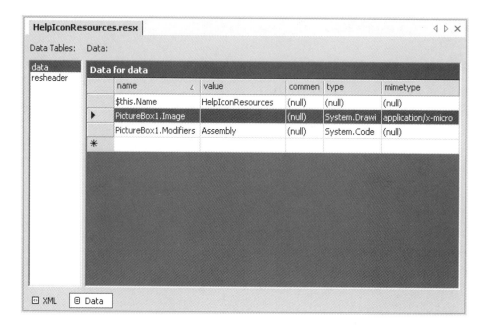

*Figure 8-11. A .resx file in Visual Studio .NET*

When a project is compiled, the .resx is converted to a binary .resources file. This file is then embedded in the compiled assembly (DLL or executable file) for the application. That guarantees that the required information is always available, without needing to rely on an external file that could be moved or deleted.

It is possible to create .resx files programmatically by hand, but the process is labor intensive. With custom control development, you can take a simple shortcut that reaps the same benefits. The process works like this:

1. Add a new form to your control project. This form will not be shown; its purpose is to store resources that your control will use. For the HelpIconProvider, you might create a form called HelpIconResources.

2. Create picture boxes for the images you need to access and load the appropriate image into each picture box at design time. Behind the scenes, Visual Studio .NET creates a .resx file for the form and adds the binary data for each picture.

3. Read through the form's designer region to find the code that reads the images from the resource file.

```
Dim resources As System.Resources.ResourceManager
resources = New System.Resources.ResourceManager(GetType(HelpIconResources))

Me.PictureBox1 = New System.Windows.Forms.PictureBox()
Me.PictureBox1.Image = CType(Resources.GetObject("PictureBox1.Image"), _
                  System.Drawing.Bitmap)
```

4. Use this code to read the appropriate resource in your control class. For example, consider the original HelpIconProvider code:

```
Dim pic As New PictureBox()
pic.Image = Image.FromFile("Help.gif")
```

This can be replaced with the following code that retrieves the picture from the resource file:

```
Dim pic As New PictureBox()
Dim resources As System.Resources.ResourceManager
resources = New System.Resources.ResourceManager(GetType(HelpIconResources))
pic.Image = CType(Resources.GetObject("PictureBox1.Image"), _
                  System.Drawing.Bitmap)
```

It's important to realize that every code file in Visual Studio .NET has an associated .resx file, even if does not correspond to a form. For example, you can add resources directly to a HelpIconProvider.resx file by adding picture boxes to the design portion of the HelpIconProvider.vb file (see Figure 8-12).

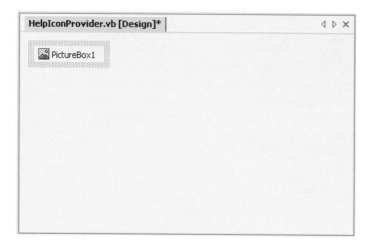

*Figure 8-12. Adding resources to an ordinary code file*

The fact that HelpIconProvider.vb doesn't have a graphical display doesn't stop you from adding resources. In fact, the appropriate designer code is added directly to a collapsed "Component Designer generated code" region in your control class! The approach you take is up to you. You can refer to the ExtenderProvider project, which is included with the online samples for Chapter 7, to see one example of how a resource file can be embedded in a custom control. As you become more comfortable with the .resx format, you may even want to create your .resx files by hand. Refer to the MSDN documentation for the System.Resources namespace for more information.

## Testing Custom Controls

Testing custom controls can sometimes be a little awkward. Visual Studio .NET provides several options:

- You can add test forms directly to your control class projects and remove them when they are no longer needed (or just set the Build Action to None instead of Compile, so that they are retained but not added to the compiled DLL).

- You can create a solution with two projects: one that tests the control, and one that uses the control. However, you may find that you need to close the solution and reopen it to see changes to the control's design-time behavior.

- You can open two instances of Visual Studio .NET, one with the control project, and one with the control test project. Once again, you may need to close and reopen the client project to see changes in a control's design-time behavior.

• You can use the specialized PropertyGrid control examined in this section.

Even if you don't follow one of these specialized approaches, if an error occurs in your custom control code and the .vb source file is available, Visual Studio .NET automatically loads the file and enters break mode, pausing execution on the offending line.

## Debugging Design-Time Support

If you test your custom control in a project with the control source code, you are able to set breakpoints and use other debugging tricks. However, these breakpoints are ignored at design-time, and only have an effect while the control is running "live."

This limitation can hamper your testing to a certain extent. Developing good design-time support for your control requires a different set of considerations than creating its basic functionality. One solution to this problem is to debug the IDE itself. To accomplish this, add your control to the toolbox, and then configure your custom control project to start Visual Studio .NET when you run it (see Figure 8-13). You can now set breakpoints in your control code or custom designer code that are triggered as the control is manipulated in the IDE.

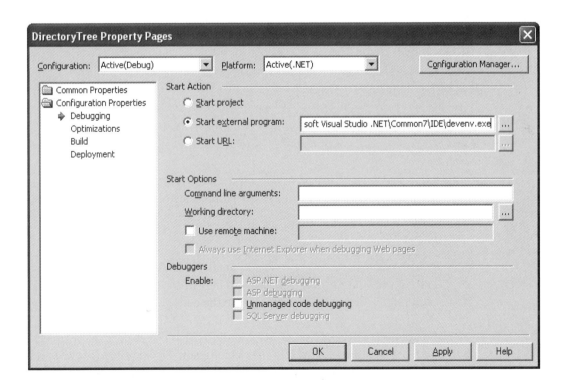

*Figure 8-13. Debugging design-time support*

## Testing for Design Mode

You may also notice some quirky design-time behavior that doesn't occur if the control is added programmatically. For example, if you add the DirectoryBrowser at design time, you'll discover some quirky behavior.

At first, it seems straightforward enough—once you set the Drive property, the corresponding directory tree appears. You can even expand nodes and browse the directory structure at design time, as shown in Figure 8-14.

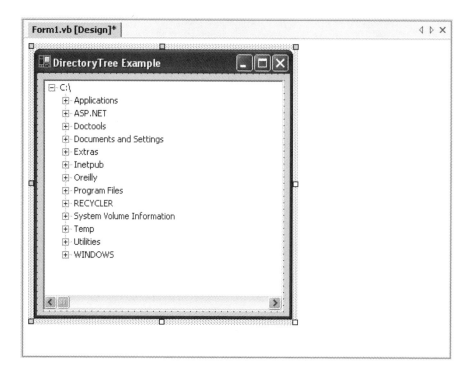

*Figure 8-14. The DirectoryTree at design time*

However, when you start your program, a second set of identical directory nodes appears. The problem is that the nodes you create at design time are automatically serialized to the form's designer code. At runtime, the control is recreated, the directory nodes are rebuilt when the drive property is set, and then the serialized nodes are added.

There are several ways you can resolve this problem. First, you could change the order of the form designer lines so that the Drive property is configured after the serialized nodes are added (setting the Drive property automatically clears the current list of nodes). Alternatively, you could create a custom designer, as you do later in this chapter. The simplest approach, however, is just to configure DirectoryTree control so that it doesn't provide its directory Node display at design-time. You can do this by explicitly checking what mode the control is in before refreshing the display.

```
Public Property Drive() As Char
    Get
        Return _Drive
    End Get
    Set(ByVal Value As Char)
        _Drive = Value
        If Not Me.DesignMode Then RefreshDisplay()
    End Set
End Property
```

## The PropertyGrid Control

Another way to test your control is using .NET's specialized PropertyGrid control. This control is actually an exact replica of the Properties window contained in the Visual Studio .NET environment. You can add this control to a form, and use it to run your custom control through its paces by modifying any of its properties. This is a good practice to get into—if you try to set invalid property values, you'll probably discover that your control isn't as successful as you expect at rejecting them.

By default, the PropertyGrid control doesn't appear in the toolbox. To add it, you need to choose Customize Toolbox and find it in the list. The PropertyGrid provides properties that allow you to format its appearance and configure its display. The most important property, however, is SelectedObject. When you set the SelectedObject to an instance of a control, the grid automatically fills with a list of all the available properties. When you change a property in the grid, it is applied to the control immediately. Figure 8-15 shows a test project that combines an instance of the DirectoryTree control with a PropertyGrid. This example is included with online samples for this chapter as the project named DirectoryTreeClient.

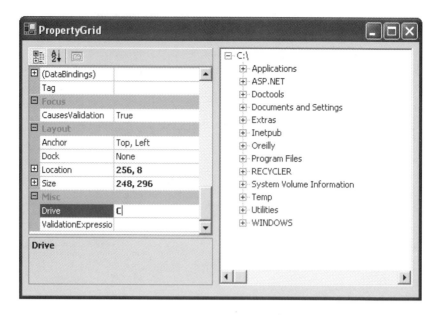

*Figure 8-15. The PropertyGrid control*

TIP   *Interestingly, you can use the PropertyGrid control with any object, regardless of whether it is a control, component, or simple class. The PropertyGrid allows you to modify any public property exposed by the class.*

## Custom Designers

One of the problems with traditional ActiveX control development is that details about a control's design-time behavior are mingled with details about its runtime behavior. With .NET control development, this problem is neatly sidestepped by a new feature called a control designer.

A control designer provides the design-time behavior for a control. The .NET framework provides a basic control designer in the System.Windows.Forms.Design.ControlDesigner class, and some derived classes that add support for child control containment and scrolling. Figure 8-16 shows the hierarchy.

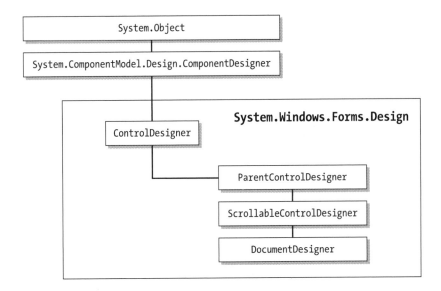

*Figure 8-16. Control designer classes*

Controls can also derive their own custom designers. Why would you create your own designer?

- To add special designer tools, like context menu options.

- To remove inappropriate events or properties from view (or add design-time only events or properties).

- To add support for controls that contain other controls (like the toolbar) or controls with special needs (like menus).

The next few sections consider all these topics by designing and enhancing a DirectoryTreeDesigner class that works with the DirectoryTree control.

## Filtering Properties and Events

Sometimes, an event or property needs to be hidden from a control, but not removed entirely. For example, the ProgressBar control provides a Text property, which it inherits from the base Control class. This property can be used at the programmer's discretion, but it does not have any visible text because the ProgressBar doesn't provide a caption. For this reason, the Text property should be hidden from the Properties window.

If you are defining or overriding a property, you can use the Browsable attribute to keep it from appearing in the Properties window. However, consider the TreeView control, which provides a Nodes collection. You may have noticed that the DirectoryTree displays the Nodes property in the designer, and allows it to be modified, even though the display is built automatically at runtime based on the Drive property. The TreeView.Nodes property is not overridable, so you can't use the Browsable attribute. However, you can create a custom designer that ensures it won't appear aT design-time.

Designers provide six methods from the IDesignerFilter interface that you can override to filter properties, events, and attributes. These methods are listed in Table 8-3.

*Table 8-3. ControlDesigner Filtering Methods*

| Method | Description |
| --- | --- |
| PostFilterAttributes | Overrides this method to remove unused or inappropriate attributes. |
| PostFilterEvents | Overrides this method to remove unused or inappropriate events. |
| PostFilterProperties | Overrides this method to remove unused or inappropriate properties. |
| PreFilterAttributes | Overrides this method to add attributes. |
| PreFilterEvents | Overrides this method to add events. |
| PreFilterProperties | Overrides this method to add properties. |

To use filtering with the DirectoryTree, create a custom designer class that derives from ControlDesigner. In this designer, you can override the PostFilterProperties() method, and use the provided properties collection to remove properties that you don't want displayed. You remove them by name.

```
Public Class DirectoryTreeDesigner
    Inherits ControlDesigner

    Protected Overrides Sub PostFilterProperties( _
      ByVal properties As System.Collections.IDictionary)

        properties.Remove("Nodes")

    End Sub

End Class
```

The next step is to link the custom designer to the DirectoryTree control. To do this, you use the Designer attribute, and specify the appropriate designer type.

```
<Designer(GetType(DirectoryTreeDesigner))> _
Public Class DirectoryTree
    Inherits TreeView
```

Now, when you recompile the control and test it in the client, you'll notice that the Nodes property does not appear in the Properties window. However, the Nodes property is still accessible in code. This allows clients to perform other useful tasks (like enumerating through the collection of nodes) at their discretion.

## Designer Verbs

You can also use a custom designer to add to the context menu that is displayed when a programmer right-clicks your control in the design environment. This menu contains some standard options provided by Visual Studio .NET, but it can also contain your commands (technically known as verbs).

To add verbs, you need to override the Verbs property in your custom designer, create a new DesignerVerbCollection, and add the appropriate DesignerVerb object entries. Your control designer handles the verb click event, generally by updating the associated control.

The following example retrieves a list of all the drives on the current computer, and adds a context menu entry for each one. The user can click the appropriate entry to set the Drive property of the control.

```
Public Class DirectoryTreeDesigner
    Inherits ControlDesigner

    Private _Verbs As New DesignerVerbCollection()

    Public Sub New()
        ' Configure the designer verb collection.
        Dim Drives() As String = System.IO.Directory.GetLogicalDrives()
        Dim Drive As String
        For Each Drive In Drives
            _Verbs.Add(New DesignerVerb("Set Drive " & Drive, _
                        New EventHandler(AddressOf OnVerb)))
        Next
    End Sub

    Public Overrides ReadOnly Property Verbs() As DesignerVerbCollection
        Get
            Return _Verbs
        End Get
    End Property

    Protected Sub OnVerb(ByVal sender As Object, ByVal e As EventArgs)
        ' Retrieve the selected drive.
        Dim DriveLetter As Char = CType(sender, DesignerVerb).Text.Chars(10)

        ' Adjust the associated control.
        CType(Me.Control, DirectoryTree).Drive = DriveLetter
    End Sub

End Class
```

The resulting context menu for the DirectoryTree control is shown in Figure 8-17.

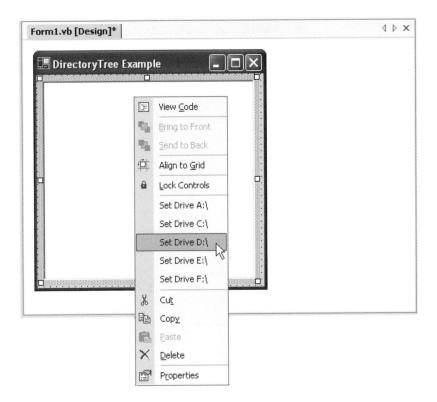

*Figure 8-17. Designer verbs*

Generally, you won't use your designer verbs to provide settings for a simple property. A more interesting technique is to provide higher-level configuration operations that adjust several properties at once. One example of this is found in the ASP.NET Calendar control, which allows the user to choose a theme from a list of preset choices (see Figure 8-18). When a theme is selected, several properties are modified in conjunction.

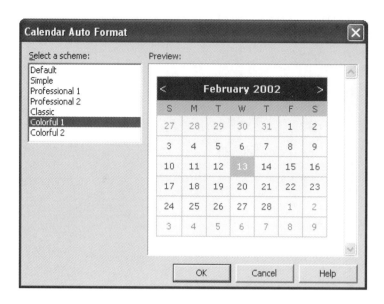

*Figure 8-18. The Calendar themes*

Implementing this design is refreshingly easy. Just add a Windows form to your project and display it when the appropriate designer verb is selected. Here's another simple example using the DirectoryTree. This time, only a single verb is available, which then displays a window that allows the user to choose a drive. When a drive is chosen, a public form-level variable is set and retrieved by the designer, which applies the change. This approach is more manageable than the previous design, and doesn't clutter the context menu with drive letters.

```
Public Class DirectoryTreeDesigner
    Inherits ControlDesigner

    Private _Verbs As New DesignerVerbCollection()

    Public Sub New()
        _Verbs.Add(New DesignerVerb("Set Drive", _
                    New EventHandler(AddressOf OnVerb)))
    End Sub

    Public Overrides ReadOnly Property Verbs() As DesignerVerbCollection
        Get
            Return _Verbs
        End Get
    End Property
```

```vbnet
    Protected Sub OnVerb(ByVal sender As Object, ByVal e As EventArgs)
        ' Show the form.
        Dim frm As New SelectDrive()
        frm.DriveSelection = CType(Me.Control, DirectoryTree).Drive
        frm.ShowDialog()

        ' Adjust the associated control.
        CType(Me.Control, DirectoryTree).Drive = frm.DriveSelection
    End Sub

End Class
```

The SelectDrive form is quite simple:

```vbnet
Public Class SelectDrive
    Inherits System.Windows.Forms.Form

    ' (Designer code omitted.)
    Public DriveSelection As Char

    Private Sub SelectDrive_Load(ByVal sender As System.Object, _
      ByVal e As System.EventArgs) Handles MyBase.Load

        Dim Drives() As String = System.IO.Directory.GetLogicalDrives()
        lstDrives.DataSource = Drives

        ' Select the current drive.
        lstDrives.SelectedIndex = lstDrives.FindString(DriveSelection)

        ' Attach the event handler.
        ' This step is performed after the selected index is set,
        ' to prevent it from being overwritten as the list is built.
        AddHandler lstDrives.SelectedIndexChanged, _
          AddressOf lstDrives_SelectedIndexChanged

    End Sub

    Private Sub lstDrives_SelectedIndexChanged(ByVal sender As System.Object, _
      ByVal e As System.EventArgs)
        DriveSelection = lstDrives.Text.Chars(0)
    End Sub

End Class
```

Figure 8-19 shows the drive selection window that appears when the user edits the Drive property.

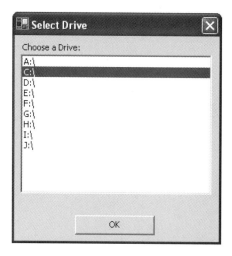

*Figure 8-19. A custom drive selection window*

One quirk remains in the control designer. When the DirectoryTree.Drive property is modified by the designer, the Properties window is not updated until the control is deselected and then reselected. To correct this defect, you need to explicitly notify the IDE that a change has been made.

The rewritten OnVerb() method handles this detail:

```
Protected Sub OnVerb(ByVal sender As Object, ByVal e As EventArgs)
    ' Show the form.
    Dim frm As New SelectDrive()
    frm.DriveSelection = CType(Me.Control, DirectoryTree).Drive
    frm.ShowDialog()

    ' Adjust the associated control.
    CType(Me.Control, DirectoryTree).Drive = frm.DriveSelection

    ' Notify the IDE that the Drive property has changed.
    Dim Properties As PropertyDescriptorCollection
    Properties = TypeDescriptor.GetProperties(GetType(DirectoryTree))
    Dim ChangedProperty As PropertyDescriptor = Properties.Find("Drive", False)
    Me.RaiseComponentChanged(ChangedProperty, "", frm.DriveSelection)

End Sub
```

The final designer code for this example can be found in the DirectoryTree project with the online samples for this chapter.

> **NOTE**   *When you add a form to a control project in this way, the client is able to see the form class in your designer and create and display instances of it. If this isn't the behavior you want, you need to nest your form class inside your control class and make it private or protected. Unfortunately, if you do this you have to forego Visual Studio .NET's design-time support for the form and manually copy the form code into the class.*

## Control Designer Notifications

Visual Studio .NET only creates one instance of a control designer per form. For example, if you create a custom DirectoryTreeDesigner class and add three DirectoryTree controls to a form, the single DirectoryTreeDesigner instance is reused to provide the behavior for all three trees. This detail can usually be ignored, unless you are designing controls that contain other special controls. For example, the TabControl class is designed to host one or more TabPage controls. Every time a TabPage is added, the TabControl needs to update its visual appearance (for example, the tab strip at the top) accordingly.

To perform this sort of functionality, you need to create a control class that derives from ControlDesignerParent, and then access the features of the IComponentChangeService. Luckily, the ControlDesigner class provides a GetService() method to help you out. Here's an example that uses the GetService() method to register for notifications when child components have been added:

```
Public Sub New()

    Dim Service As IComponentChangeService
    Service = GetService(GetType(IComponentChangeService))
    AddHandler Service.ComponentAdded, AddressOf ComponentAdded

End Sub
```

You should place this constructor inside your custom designer class, so that the designer registers for child control notifications as soon as it is created.

This book doesn't consider custom container controls, and so none of the examples use the IComponentChangeService. However, if it's something you would like to explore, start with the overview of key events in Table 8-4.

*Table 8-4. IComponentChangeService Methods*

| Event | Description |
| --- | --- |
| ComponentAdded | Triggered when a component is added to the control at design time. |
| ComponentAdding | Triggered when a component is in the process of being added to the control at design time. |
| ComponentChanged | Triggered when a contained component has changed at design time. |
| ComponentChanging | Triggered when a component is in the process of changing at design time. |
| ComponentRemoved | Triggered when a component is removed at design time. |
| ComponentRemoving | Triggered when a component is in the process of being removed. |

## Data Types and UITypeEditors

The Properties window does a solid job of providing support for all common data types. Basic data types like strings and numbers are all seamlessly supported. If you create a property that uses a custom enumeration, the Properties window automatically provides a drop-down list with the values from the enumeration.

For example, consider the DisplayStyle property shown here:

```
Public Enum Display
    Standard
    SpecialDirectoryPictures
    AllDirectoryPictures
End Enum
```

```
Private _DisplayStyle As Display
Public Property DisplayStyle() As Display
    Get
        Return _DisplayStyle
    End Get
    Set(ByVal Value As Display)
        _DisplayStyle = Value
    End Set
End Property
```

The enumerated values are shown in the Properties window (see Figure 8-20).

*Figure 8-20. Enumerations in the Properties window*

**NOTE**   *Remember, even if you use an enumerated value, you still need to perform some error-checking in your property procedure. Though programmers won't be able to submit an invalid value through the Properties window, nothing prevents them from using code to directly set an integer value that doesn't correspond to a valid value in the enumeration.*

In addition to this basic level of support, you may have noticed that some richer object types have additional design-time support. For example, if you create a Property that has a Font or Color data type, a special color picker or font selection dialog is used in the Properties window. Similar magic happens if you create a Collection property. This support is provided through .NET UITypeEditor classes, which are special components that provide the design-time user interface that allows the programmer to set complex properties.

## Using Prebuilt UITypeEditors

The base UITypeEditor class is found in the System.Drawing.Design namespace. You can inherit from this class to create your custom UITypeEditors, or you can use one of the derived classes that are provided with the .NET framework. These classes are listed in Table 8-5 (UITypeEditors that are only usable with specific web controls have been omitted).

*Table 8-5. UITypeEditors in the .NET Framework*

| Class | Description |
| --- | --- |
| System.ComponentModel.Design.ArrayEditor | Edits an array by allowing the programmer to enter a list of strings. Used automatically for supported arrays. |
| System.Drawing.Design.FontEditor | Allows the programmer to select and configure a font. Used automatically for font properties. |
| System.Drawing.Design.ImageEditor | Allows the programmer to create an Image object by selecting a bitmap from an open file dialog. Used automatically for image types. |
| System.Web.UI.Design.WebControls.RegexTypeEditor | Allows the programmer to choose a regular expression from a list of common choices. This UITypeEditor works with string properties. |
| System.Windows.Forms.Design.AnchorEditor | Allows the Anchor property to be set at design time. |
| System.Windows.Forms.Design.FileNameEditor | Allows a fully qualified filename to be set by choosing a file from an open file dialog box. This UITypeEditor works with string properties. |

Depending on the data type of your property, .NET may use the corresponding UITypeEditor automatically (for example, with a Font). On the other hand, some UITypeEditors do not have dedicated types. An example is the RegExTypeEditor, which allows the programmer to choose a common regular expression for a control property. The regular expression is stored as an ordinary string, so it needs to be explicitly associated with the appropriate UITypeEditor.

You associate a property with a UITypeEditor using the Editor attribute. Consider this example:

```
Public _RegEx As String = ""
<Editor(GetType(System.Web.UI.Design.WebControls.RegexTypeEditor), _
 GetType(UITypeEditor))> _
Public Property ValidationExpression() As String
    Get
        Return _RegEx
    End Get
    Set(ByVal Value As String)
        _RegEx = Value
    End Set
End Property
```

When the programmer clicks this property in the Properties window, an ellipsis (...)appears next to the property name. If the programmer clicks the ellipsis button, a full dialog appears with common regular expression choices (see Figure 8-21).

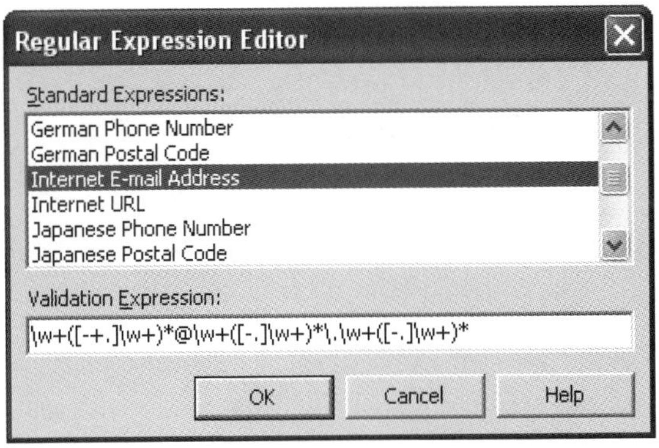

*Figure 8-21. The RegexTypeEditor*

> **NOTE**  *Interestingly, this type editor is originally designed for the validation controls provided with ASP.NET, and is provided alongside the web controls in the .NET namespaces. However, it works equally well with a Windows control.*

## Custom UITypeEditors

You can also develop custom UITypeEditor classes to allow special settings to be configured. For example, consider the TreeView control. Its Nodes property is a collection, but it doesn't use the standard collection editor (which only allows strings to be entered). Instead, it uses its specialized UITypeEditor.

To create a custom type editor, you must first create a class that derives from System.Drawing.Design.UITypeEditor. You can then override the four methods shown in Table 8-6.

*Table 8-6. UITypeEditor Overridable Methods*

| ClassMethod | Description |
|---|---|
| EditValue() | Invoked when the property is edited. Generally, this is where you would create a special dialog box for property editing. |
| GetEditStyle() | Specifies whether the type editor is a DropDown (provides a list of specially drawn choices), Modal (provides a dialog box for property selection), or None (no editing supported). |
| GetPaintValueSupported() | Use this to return True if you are providing a PaintValue() implementation. |
| PaintValue() | Invoked to paint a graphical thumbnail that represents the value in the property grid. |

The PaintValue() supported technique requires a little GDI+ wizardry, and you consider an example that uses it in Chapter 13. The next example, however, uses the EditValue() method with the DirectoryTree control. It allows editing of the Drive property by presenting the dialog box developed earlier.

```vb
Public Class DriveEditor
    Inherits UITypeEditor

    Public Overloads Overrides Function GetEditStyle( _
      ByVal context As System.ComponentModel.ITypeDescriptorContext) _
      As System.Drawing.Design.UITypeEditorEditStyle

        ' We will use a window for property editing.
        Return UITypeEditorEditStyle.Modal

    End Function

    Public Overloads Overrides Function EditValue( _
      ByVal context As System.ComponentModel.ITypeDescriptorContext, _
      ByVal provider As System.IServiceProvider, ByVal value As Object) As Object

        Dim frm As New SelectDrive()

        ' Set current drive in window.
        frm.DriveSelection = value
        frm.ShowDialog()

        ' Return the new value.
        Return frm.DriveSelection

    End Function

    Public Overloads Overrides Function GetPaintValueSupported( _
      ByVal context As System.ComponentModel.ITypeDescriptorContext) As Boolean

        ' No special thumbnail will be shown for the grid.
        Return False

    End Function

End Class
```

The type editor is attached to the appropriate property using an Editor attribute:

```vb
<Editor(GetType(DriveEditor), GetType(UITypeEditor))> _
 Public Property Drive() As Char
```

One benefit to this design is that you can reuse this UITypeEditor with any drive property in any control. It's specific to the property data type, not the control.

An alternative approach is to use a DirectoryInfo object to represent the drive instead of an underlying char. Because the property editing is now handled by the UITypeEditor, there's no need to choose a basic type that can be edited with the default design-time support built into the property grid. That would also give you the freedom to enhance the control so it could be set to initially display a specific subdirectory, for example.

## Licensing Custom Controls

Licensing in the .NET world is far more customizable and far less painful than it was with ActiveX controls. The .NET framework provides several licensing classes in the System.ComponentModel namespace. By using and extending these classes, you can grant or allow access to your control, using ordinary .NET code to check external resources like the Windows registry, an XML file, or even a remote web service for registration information.

### Simple LIC File Licensing

To best understand .NET licensing, it helps to start with a simple example using the LicFileLicenseProvider class. This class doesn't provide any real protection, but it's a stepping-stone to the more advanced licensing strategies you look at next.

The LicFileLicenseProvider searches for a text file in the same directory as the control assembly. This LIC file uses the control's fully qualified class name for a filename, so the DirectoryTree control requires a license file named DirectoryTreeControl.DirectoryTree.LIC. Inside this file is a simple predefined text string in the format "[Component] is a licensed component."

Thus, the contents of the DirectoryTreeControl.DirectoryTree.LIC file would be:

```
DirectoryTreeControl.DirectoryTree is a licensed component.
```

This file must be placed in the client project's bin directory (where Visual Studio .NET compiles the final exe just prior to launching it).

> **NOTE** *It's worth noting that these LIC files don't need to be distributed with a client application. When you compile a Windows program, a license.licx file is created with all the licensing information for all license controls. This file is compiled as a binary resource and embedded in the final client assembly. However, if another developer wants to create a client application with your control, a LIC source file is needed.*

To enforce LIC file licensing, you need to add a LicenseProvider attribute to your control class that tells .NET to use the LicFileProvider class to validate licenses.

```
<LicenseProvider(GetType(LicFileLicenseProvider))> _
Public Class DirectoryTree
```

Additionally, you need to create the license when the control is created, using the shared Validate() method of the LicenseManager Help class:

```
Private _License As License

Public Sub New()
    _License = LicenseManager.Validate(Me.GetType, Me)
End Sub
```

The Validate() method throws a LicenseException if it doesn't find the correct string in the LIC file, and refuses to create your control. This restriction applies both to design time and runtime control creation.

Finally, you need to dispose of the license when the control is disposed.

```
Protected Overloads Overrides Sub Dispose(ByVal dispoing As Boolean)

    If Not (_License Is Nothing) Then
        _License.Dispose()
    End If
    MyBase.Dispose(disposing)

End Sub
```

## Custom LIC File Licensing

Clearly, simple LIC file licensing doesn't offer much in the way of protection. Any user who knows a little about the .NET framework will realize the generic format that must be created for a LIC file. However, you can add more stringent requirements by creating a custom license provider based on the LicFileLicenseProvider.

All you need to do is inherit from the class and override the IsValid() method. The IsValid() method receives the contents of the LIC file, and returns True or False to indicate if the contents are correct. Thus, you could use the IsValid() method to check a license number against a company-specific algorithm.

The example below extracts the first three characters from the license file, and verifies that they correspond to a number that is divisible by 7.

```
Public Class FileLicenseProvider
    Inherits LicFileLicenseProvider

    Protected Overrides Function IsKeyValid(ByVal key As String, _
      ByVal type As System.Type) As Boolean

        Dim Code As Integer = Val(key.Substring(0, 3))
        If Code <> 0 Then
            If Math.IEEERemainder(Code, 7) = 0 Then
                Return True
            Else
                Return False
            End If
        Else
            Return False
        End If

    End Function

End Class
```

## Advanced License Providers

Control licensing doesn't need to be based on LIC files. In fact, you can create any type of licensing scheme imaginable. You can even perform tremendously annoying tricks like only allowing controls to be registered to specific computers. To implement a custom licensing scheme, you need to create two classes: a custom license provider, and a custom license.

The custom license is the easiest ingredient. It simply derives from the base License class, overrides the LicenseKey property and Dispose() method, and adds properties for any required pieces of information. You also need to add a constructor that configures the license, as the LicenseKey property is read-only.

```
Public Class CustomLicense
    Inherits License

    Private _Key As String

    Public Overrides ReadOnly Property LicenseKey() As String
        Get
            Return _Key
        End Get
    End Property

    Public Sub New(ByVal key As String)
        _Key = key
    End Sub

    Public Overrides Sub Dispose()
        ' This method must be overriden.
    End Sub

End Class
```

The custom LicenseProvider plays the same role as the LicFileLicenseProvider. It provides a GetLicense() method, which the .NET framework calls to validate the control. For example, when you use the LicenseManager.Validate() method in the constructor for the DirectoryTree control, .NET uses the LicenseProvider.GetLicense() method to retrieve the license.

In the GetLicense() method, you may want to examine whether the component is in design-time or runtime mode, and apply different rules. Additionally, you may want to return a valid license object, nothing at all, or throw a LicenseException to indicate that the control should not be created. The LicFileProvider throws a LicenseException to indicate when a LIC file is not valid.

The example that follows looks for a predefined registry entry at design time. At runtime, it first examines the current context, and then defaults to the registry if a compiled license key can't be found. The registry value is stored under a predefined company name, followed by the fully qualified name of the control. The key is validated as long as it matches the string "1234567890" and a CustomLicense object encapsulating this key is returned.

```vb
Public Class RegistryLicenseProvider
    Inherits LicenseProvider

    Public Overrides Function GetLicense( _
      ByVal context As System.ComponentModel.LicenseContext, _
      ByVal type As System.Type, _
      ByVal instance As Object, ByVal allowExceptions As Boolean) _
      As System.ComponentModel.License

        Dim Key As String

        If context.UsageMode = LicenseUsageMode.Runtime Then
            ' Try to find key in current context.
            Key = context.GetSavedLicenseKey(type, Nothing)
        End If

        ' Always look in the registry at design time.
        ' If the key wasn't found in the current context at runtime,
        ' we can also look in the registry.
        ' Another option might be to always allow the control at runtime,
        ' and just restrict it at design time.
        If Key = "" Then
            ' A debugging hint (remove when you perfect the licensing scheme):
            MessageBox.Show("Performing registry lookup.", _
                            "RegistryLicenseProvider")

            Dim rk As RegistryKey
            rk = Registry.LocalMachine.OpenSubKey("Software\MyCompany\" & _
                type.ToString())
            If Not rk Is Nothing Then
                Key = rk.GetValue("LicenseKey", "")
            End If

            ' Save key in current context.
            If Key <> "" Then context.SetSavedLicenseKey(type, Key)
        End If

        ' Check if key is valid.
        If Not IsValid(Key) Then
            If Not allowExceptions Then Throw New LicenseException(type)
        End If
```

```
    ' Return the license object.
    Return New CustomLicense(Key)
End Function

Private Function IsValid(ByVal key As String) As Boolean
    If key = "1234567890" Then
        Return True
    Else
        Return False
    End If
End Function
```

```
End Class
```

The GetLicense() method is provided with a fair bit of information, including the current LicenseContext, the type of the component that is requesting the license, and a reference to instance of the component. This means you can easily create a single LicenseProvider that could handle the licensing for all different types of controls. Custom licensing schemes are limited only by your imagination, and can become quite complex. The material presented here is only a basic introduction for what a component vendor might do.

## The Last Word

This chapter covered a lot of ground with custom controls. The story doesn't end here, however. In the coming chapters you continue to look at how custom controls can solve all kinds of programming problems, and handle everything from data access to rich graphics. In all these cases, knowing how to match custom controls with an appropriate level of design-time support will simplify your life immensely. If you are planning to develop and sell your components, it's indispensable.

To see what other developers are creating, you can take your search online and begin working with the latest user interface elements. And if you develop your own controls, feel free to send me an email with the details. I can't critique your code creations, but I just might provide a link from this book's web site (www.prosetech.com) if there's enough interest.

# Data Controls

I'ts OFTEN REMARKED that a large percentage of Windows applications are little more than attractive window dressings over a relational database. This is especially true of the internal software that powers most businesses. The chief responsibility of this type of software is to allow highly structured data entry and provide report-generating modules that summarize vast quantities of information. As a result, a great deal of thought (and code) is usually concentrated in the user interface tier.

Of course, databases aren't only used for workflow and administrative software. Almost every application needs to connect to a data source and retrieve, format, and display information at some point. Even an Internet e-commerce site is really just an interactive product catalog that draws information from one table and logs transactions in another. The situation becomes more complicated with Windows applications, which provide a wide range of user interface options for displaying data.

This chapter considers how you can use Windows controls with data. I'll also share some advice about how to do it without hopelessly intermingling details about your data source in your user interface code. You'll consider three fundamental topics:

- How to use .NET's data-binding framework with any generic control. You'll also learn about the specialized DataGrid control.

- How to create "data aware" controls—controls that interact efficiently and intelligently with data sources without requiring data binding.

- How to use adapter classes and miscellaneous wizardry to help automate the shuffle of information through the levels of your application, and write more focused code.

## Introducing Data Binding

Traditionally, data binding has been viewed with a great deal of suspicion. Many developers feel that it's an inflexible, clumsy tool favored by beginning programmers. For the most part, they have been right.

Data binding usually suffers from several well-known problems:

- **It's inflexible.** For example, you can only bind special controls to special objects—and when you do, you usually lose control of the process. In many cases, you need to either enable or disable features like data editing completely, as data controls don't allow you to participate in their work.

- **It's ugly.** When you bind to data, you often have to display all available rows, and sacrifice any ability to format details like column widths or order. And if you hoped to convert a field made up of numeric constants into a friendlier representation, forget it.

- **It's fragile.** Data binding doesn't follow classic three-tier design. Instead, it binds database details directly to user interface logic. If the data source changes, or you need to create functionality that should be shared among different applications or environments, you are entirely on your own.

- **It's proprietary.** A fine-tuned data binding solution is great—until your organization decides to upgrade to a newer programming tool or change programming languages. At this point, there is generally no migration path, because much of the logic is hard-coded in proprietary designer or project files. If you've used Visual Basic 6 data binding (or even worse, created VB 6 data environment projects), you may be in this difficult position right now.

.NET provides some remarkable data binding enhancements that just might change your mind. The first two obstacles—lack of flexibility in programming and display—are completely removed and replaced with an elegant, extensible framework. The questions of application design and proprietary standards may still apply, depending on your goals. Certainly, .NET allows programmers in several different languages to share components and classes, but heavy use of data binding still makes it extremely difficult to port your code to a non-Microsoft platform.

## Basic Data Binding

Almost every control in .NET supports data binding in one form or another. However, different controls support data binding in different ways. For example, when binding to a text box, button, or image control, you will usually bind to the TextBox.Text, Button.Text, or PictureBox.Image property (although there are other possibilities, as you'll discover shortly). Each of these properties can bind to a single piece of information at a time. On the other hand, a control like ListBox or CheckedListBox can hold an entire list of data or the contents of a single field from a database. Last, there are rich controls like DataGrid that can display all the information from a DataSet on their own.

You don't need to create any database code to start working with data binding. .NET allows controls to bind to any class that implements the IList interface. Possible data sources include the following:

- **Arrays.** You can use the ArrayList, Visual Basic's default Collection class, and a custom collection class that derives from System.Collections.CollectionBase. Other collection types (like queues and hastables) are not supported.

- **ADO.NET data objects.** Technically, you can only directly bind to a DataColumn, DataView, or DataViewManager object. However, when you bind to a DataTable, .NET automatically uses the corresponding default DataView it provides. Similarly, when binding to a DataSet .NET automatically uses the default DataViewManager.

- **Your custom classes.** You have two options—you can create custom collections that implement IList or, more likely, you can just add your objects to an array or collection class, and use the collection object as a data source.

Figure 9-1 shows the relationship between data providers and data consumers.

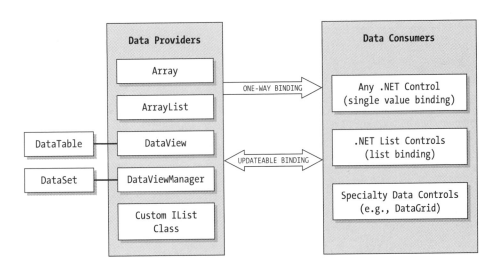

*Figure 9-1. Information flow in .NET data binding*

## Simple List Binding

Binding to a list is one of the most common data binding tasks. All the basic .NET list controls supply a DataSource property that accepts a reference to any IList data source. To test out simple data binding, create and fill an array, and bind it to a list using the DataSource property:

```
Dim CityChoices() As String = {"Seattle", "New York", "Tokyo", "Montreal"}
lstCity.DataSource = CityChoices
```

The list appears with the items from the array preloaded (see Figure 9-2).

*Figure 9-2. Binding a list to an array of strings*

There are two caveats: First, the Items collection of the list control is now read-only and can't be modified in your code. Second, if you change the contents of the array, the modifications do not appear in the list unless you clear the current binding and then rebind the list to the array.

```
Dim CityChoices() As String = {"Seattle", "New York", "Tokyo", "Montreal"}
lstCity.DataSource = CityChoices

' This change will not appear in the list.
CityChoices(3) = "Toronto"

' To update the list, you must rebind it.
lstCity.DataSource = Nothing
lstCity.DataSource = CityChoices
```

If you want to provide for more flexibility, you can circumvent data binding and just copy the array items into the list:

```
Dim CityChoices() As String = {"Seattle", "New York", "Tokyo", "Montreal"}
lstCity.Items.AddRange(CityChoices)
```

Though this approach appears to be equivalent, there are several differences. First, existing entries in the list remain in place. Second, you are free to modify the Items collection of the list. However, the most important differences may not appear until you begin to bind multiple controls simultaneously, as you see a little later in this chapter.

## Binding Lists to Complex Objects

You can also bind a list control to a more complex object that provides several different fields of data. In this case, you still bind to the entire data source, but the DisplayMember property configures what text is used for each list entry.

DisplayMember accepts a string that identifies a property in the data source. For example, you could create an array of special City objects and bind it to a list. You would then specify the property from the City class that should be used for the text. Note that the DisplayMember *cannot* be a public member variable. Instead, it must be a full property procedure. Consider the sample City class shown in the code that follows. It defines two properties and a constructor for easy initialization.

```
Public Class City

    Private _Name As String
    Private _Country As String

    Public Property Name() As String
        Get
            Return _Name
        End Get
        Set(ByVal Value As String)
            _Name = Value
        End Set
    End Property
```

```
Public Property Country() As String
    Get
        Return _Country
    End Get
    Set(ByVal Value As String)
        _Country = Value
    End Set
End Property

Public Sub New(ByVal name As String, ByVal country As String)
    Me.Name = name
    Me.Country = country
End Sub
```

End Class

You could bind this in an array as follows:

```
Dim CityChoices() As City = {New City("Seattle", "U.S.A."), _
    New City("New York", "U.S.A."), New City("Tokyo", "Japan"), _
    New City("Montreal", "Canada")}

lstCity.DataSource = CityChoices
lstCity.DisplayMember = "Name"
```

The list looks and behaves exactly the same as the simple array example. The only difference is that when you retrieve the currently selected item, you find that it's a full City object, complete with all the City properties. That allows you to store your data directly in a control, without needing to worry about retaining other collections. To test this out, add the following code, which reacts when an item is double-clicked in the list:

```
Private Sub lstCity_DoubleClick(ByVal sender As Object, _
    ByVal e As System.EventArgs) Handles lstCity.DoubleClick

    MessageBox.Show(CType(lstCity.SelectedItem, City).Country)

End Sub
```

One interesting thing to note is what happens if you don't set the DisplayMember property. In this case, .NET simply calls the ToString() method of each object, and uses that to provide the text. Typically, this is the fully qualified class named, which means that every list appears exactly the same, as shown in Figure 9-3.

*Figure 9-3. Binding to an array of objects without DisplayMember*

However, you can put this behavior to good use by creating an object with an overriden ToString() method. This method could return some more useful information or a combination of different properties. Here's an example:

```
Public Class City

    Public Name As String
    Public Country As String

    Public Sub New(ByVal name As String, ByVal country As String)
        Me.Name = name
        Me.Country = country
    End Sub

    Public Overrides Function ToString() As String
        Return Name & ", " & Country
    End Function

End Class
```

You then bind it without setting the DisplayMember property.

```
Dim CityChoices() As City = {New City("Seattle", "U.S.A."), _
    New City("New York", "U.S.A."), New City("Tokyo", "Japan"), _
    New City("Montreal", "Canada")}

lstCity.DataSource = CityChoices
```

The result of this code, using the overridden version of the ToString() method, is shown in Figure 9-4.

*Figure 9-4. Overriding ToString() in a data bound object*

> **TIP** *The advantages that can be gained by these two techniques are remarkable. You can bind data without being forced to adopt a specific data access technology. If you don't like ADO.NET, it's easy to design your own business objects and use them for binding. Best of all, they remain available through the Items collection of the list, which means you don't need to spend additional programming effort tracking this information.*

## Single-Value Binding

.NET list controls are designed for this type of data binding and provide a helpful DataSource property that's inherited from the base ListControl class. Other controls, like text boxes and buttons, don't add this feature. However, every control gains basic single-value data binding ability from the Control.DataBindings collection.

Using this collection, you can link any control property to a field in a data source. To connect a text box to an array, you can use the following syntax:

```
Dim CityChoices() As String = {"Seattle", "New York", "Tokyo", "Montreal"}
txtCity.DataBindings.Add("Text", CityChoices, "")
```

The first parameter is the name of the control property as a string. (.NET uses reflection to find the matching property, but it does not detect your mistakes at compile time.) The second parameter is the data source. The third parameter is the property or field in the DataSource that is used for the binding. In this case, the data source only has one set of information, so an empty string is used.

The results of this code are a little perplexing. The text for the first city appears in the text box, but there won't be any way to move to other items.

Programmers who are familiar with traditional data binding will probably expect that they need to add a clumsy workaround to the form, like a special navigation control. This isn't the case. Instead, you have two options—controlling navigation programmatically, which you look at a little later, or adding a list control to provide simple navigation. For example, you can combine the list control example and the text box example to try out multiple control binding. Whatever item is selected in the list box appears in the text box. You'll also notice that the text in the text box is still editable, although the changes have no effect (see Figure 9-5).

*Figure 9-5. Binding to two controls*

> **TIP** *The .NET list controls also provide a DataBindings collection. You can use this collection with single-value data binding. Just fill the list manually, and then bind to the SelectedValue property. This allows you to create a list control that can be used to update data (instead of one that is used for navigation).*

The nicest thing about single-value binding is that it can be used with almost any property. For example, you could set the background color of a text box, or specify the font. Unfortunately, there is no implicit type conversion when setting these specialized properties, which means you can't easily convert a string representing a font name into an actual font object. The code example that follows demonstrates some of the extra effort you need to go through if you want to bind one of these properties. It makes for an interesting example of extreme data binding, too. In order for it to work, the System.Drawing namespace must be imported.

```
' These are our final data sources: two ArrayList objects.
Dim FontObjList As New ArrayList()
Dim ColorObjList As New ArrayList()


' The InstalledFonts collection allows us to enumerate installed fonts.
' Each FontFamily needs to be converted to a genuine Font object
' before it is suitable for data binding to the Control.Font property.
Dim Family As FontFamily
Dim InstalledFonts As New System.Drawing.Text.InstalledFontCollection()
For Each Family In InstalledFonts.Families
    Try
        FontObjList.Add(New Font(Family, 12))
    Catch
        ' We end up here if the font could not be created
        ' with the default style.
    End Try
Next


' In order to retrieve the list of colors, we need to first retrieve
' the strings for the KnownColor enumeration, and then convert each one
' into a suitable color object.
Dim ColorNames(), ColorName As String
ColorNames = System.Enum.GetNames(GetType(KnownColor))
Dim cnvrt As TypeConverter = TypeDescriptor.GetConverter(GetType(KnownColor))

For Each ColorName In ColorNames
    ColorObjList.Add(Color.FromKnownColor(cnvrt.ConvertFromString(ColorName)))
Next


' We can now bind both our list controls.
lstColors.DataSource = ColorObjList
lstColors.DisplayMember = "Name"
lstFonts.DataSource = FontObjList
lstFonts.DisplayMember = "Name"
```

```
' The label is bound to both data sources.
lblSampleText.DataBindings.Add("ForeColor", ColorObjList, "")
lblSampleText.DataBindings.Add("Font", FontObjList, "")
```

You'll notice that the ForeColor and Font properties of the text box are simultaneously bound to two different data sources, which doesn't require any additional code. Some work is involved, however, to retrieve the list of currently installed fonts and named colors. The application is shown in Figure 9-6.

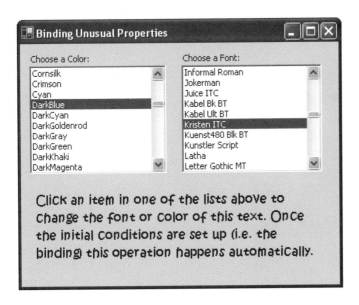

*Figure 9-6. Data binding with other text box properties*

> **NOTE** *The code examples up to this point can all be found in the DataBinding101 project included with the online samples for this book.*

## ADO.NET Data Binding

One of the most common applications of data binding is with ADO.NET data objects. This type of binding is easy, painless, and built on one of .NET's core standards.

The basic principle is the same for binding collections of custom objects. However, instead of specifying a property name with the DisplayMember, you use it to indicate the database field name. The following example uses this technique to bind to the ModelName column in a DataTable. It uses information drawn from Microsoft's sample IBuySpy e-commerce Web application. The result is shown in Figure 9-7.

```
Dim dsStore As New DataSet()
dsStore.ReadXmlSchema(Application.StartupPath & "\store.xsd")
dsStore.ReadXml(Application.StartupPath & "\store.xml")

lstName.DataSource = dsStore.Tables("Products")
lstName.DisplayMember = "ModelName"
```

*Figure 9-7. Binding to a DataView*

**NOTE** *The ADO.NET examples in this chapter read DataSets from XML, as this approach doesn't clutter the examples with data access logic, and doesn't require any special relational database product. The "data aware" control examples later in this chapter separate the data logic into a discrete class, which allows this code to be completely independent of the data-binding logic.*

In this example, the code appears to bind to a DataTable object, but it actually binds to the DataTable.DefaultView property. This property provides a DataView object that implements the required IList interface. For the most part, you can ignore this lower-level reality, unless you want to use the DataView object to customize the displayed data. For example, the code that follows doesn't change the actual information in the DataTable, but it does ensure that only a subset of it will be shown in the list control:

```
Dim dsStore As New DataSet()
dsStore.ReadXmlSchema(Application.StartupPath & "\store.xsd")
dsStore.ReadXml(Application.StartupPath & "\store.xml")
dsStore.Tables("Products").DefaultView.RowFilter = "UnitCost < 5"

lstName.DataSource = dsStore.Tables("Products")
lstName.DisplayMember = "ModelName"
```

Figure 9-8 shows the filtered list.

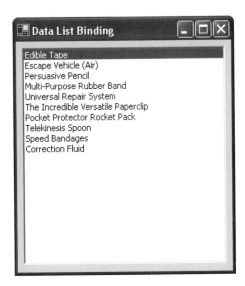

*Figure 9-8. Binding to a filtered DataView*

The DataView class provides other properties that allow you to implement sorting, and to specify whether the data-bound collection allows deletions, additions, and modifications (these properties don't apply to the list control, which never allows the modification of a bound data source). Taken together, these options provide an extra layer of indirection, which allows your code to be more flexible

Table 9-1 shows useful DataView members and a description of each.

*Table 9-1. Useful DataView Members*

| Member | Description |
|--------|-------------|
| RowFilter | A string that allows you to filter the results based on any field. This string works like a tiny snippet of SQL code, meaning that string values must be enclosed in single quotes, and you can use the operators like =, <, and >. |
| RowStateFilter | A combination of the values from DataViewRowState enumeration. This allows you to display rows that have been scheduled for deletion in the DataSet, pending the next update (deleted rows are usually hidden). |
| Sort | Allows you to configure the sort order for the DataView. You can enter a combination of columns, separated by commas (as in "CategoryID, ModelName"). Append a space and the letters DESC after a column name to indicate descending (reverse) sort order. |
| Table | The DataTable object that contains the data used by this DataView. |

**TIP** *As you might imagine, you can even create multiple DataView objects, allowing you to show data from the same underlying DataSet in multiple controls, but with different filtering or sorting options.*

You can also bind to a list control with the following syntax. The result is the same, but in this case the DataSet.DefaultViewManager is used for the data binding. This property contains a DataViewManager object for the entire DataSet. The DisplayMember property then specifies the appropriate table and field.

```
Dim dsStore As New DataSet()
dsStore.ReadXmlSchema(Application.StartupPath & "\store.xsd")
dsStore.ReadXml(Application.StartupPath & "\store.xml")

lstName.DataSource = dsStore
lstName.DisplayMember = "Products.ModelName"
```

**NOTE** *All the ADO.NET code examples can be found in the ADO.NET Binding project included with the online samples for this book.*

## Multiple Control Binding

The next example shows a more practical use of data binding. The information from a product record is displayed on a form using a combination of three labels and a drop-down list control. This list control allows navigation—when the user selects a different model name, the other data bound controls are updated automatically without requiring any code.

Here's the complete code for this example:

```
Public Class MultipleControlBinding
    Inherits System.Windows.Forms.Form

    ' (Windows designer code omitted.)

    Friend WithEvents cboModelName As System.Windows.Forms.ComboBox
    Friend WithEvents lblDescription As System.Windows.Forms.Label
    Friend WithEvents lblUnitCost As System.Windows.Forms.Label
    Friend WithEvents lblModelNumber As System.Windows.Forms.Label

    Private Sub MultipleControlBinding_Load(ByVal sender As System.Object, _
      ByVal e As System.EventArgs) Handles MyBase.Load
        Dim dsStore As New DataSet()

        dsStore.ReadXmlSchema(Application.StartupPath & "\store.xsd")
        dsStore.ReadXml(Application.StartupPath & "\store.xml")

        cboModelName.DataSource = dsStore.Tables("Products")
        cboModelName.DisplayMember = "ModelName"

        lblModelNumber.DataBindings.Add("Text", _
          dsStore.Tables("Products"), "ModelNumber")
        lblUnitCost.DataBindings.Add("Text", _
          dsStore.Tables("Products"), "UnitCost")
        lblDescription.DataBindings.Add("Text", _
          dsStore.Tables("Products"), "Description")

    End Sub

End Class
```

Figure 9-9 shows the resulting form.

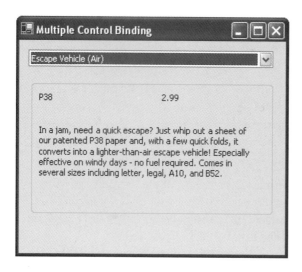

*Figure 9-9. Multiple binding with ADO.NET*

**TIP** *In this example, the list control is really a navigation control that allows the user to access any record. In some cases this isn't the behavior you want. For example, in a form that allows the user to create a new product record, you might want to bind to a list of options for the field, but you wouldn't want selections in this control to affect the other controls. In this case, you would copy the items out of the array and into the list control with the AddRange() method, as described earlier, and then use simple binding with the list control's SelectedIndex or Text property.*

## Updating with Data Binding

As was described earlier, you can perform basic binding with any IList data source. However, data sources that implement additional interfaces can gain some extra features. Four such interfaces are listed in Table 9-2.

*Table 9-2. Interfaces Used with Data Binding*

| Interface | Description |
|-----------|-------------|
| IList | Allows simple data binding to a collection of identical types. (For example, you cannot bind to an ArrayList with different types of objects in it.) |
| IBindingList | Provides additional features for notification, both for when the list itself has changed (for example, the number of items in the list increases), as well as when the list items themselves change (for example, the third item in a list of customers has a change to its FirstName field). |
| IEditableObject | Allows permanent changes. For example, this allows a data-bound control to commit its changes back to the source DataSet. This implementation provides BeginEdit, EndEdit, and CancelEdit methods. |
| IDataErrorInfo | Allows data sources to offer error information that a control can bind to. This information consists of two strings: the Error property, which returns general error message text (for example, "An error has occurred") and the Item property, which returns a string with a specific error message from the column (for example, "The value in the Cost column cannot be negative"). |

The DataView, DataViewManager, and DataRowView ADO.NET objects work together to implement all these interfaces. This means that when you bind to a DataSet, you acquire a much greater level of functionality. For example, if you modify the multiple control sample to use input controls, you will be able to make changes that permanently modify the DataSet. When you navigate to a changed record, you will see that its change persists. Furthermore, if multiple controls display the same data (for example, if you use a list control for navigation and allow the same field to be modified in a text box) they will all be updated with the new content when you browse back to the record. You can see this behavior with the product name field in the following example.

```
Dim dsStore As New DataSet()
dsStore.ReadXmlSchema(Application.StartupPath & "\store.xsd")
dsStore.ReadXml(Application.StartupPath & "\store.xml")
```

```
cboModelName.DataSource = dsStore.Tables("Products")
cboModelName.DisplayMember = "ModelName"

txtModelName.DataBindings.Add("Text", dsStore.Tables("Products"), "ModelName")
txtModelNum.DataBindings.Add("Text", dsStore.Tables("Products"), "ModelNumber")
txtUnitCost.DataBindings.Add("Text", dsStore.Tables("Products"), "UnitCost")
txtDesc.DataBindings.Add("Text", dsStore.Tables("Products"), "Description")
```

The code is largely unchanged. The key difference is that the Label controls are replaced with TextBox controls. Figure 9-10 shows the corresponding form.

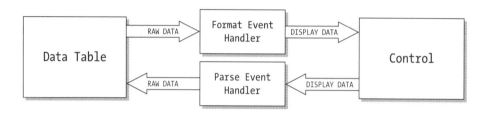

*Figure 9-10. An editable bound data source*

Of course, changes made to the data set won't affect the original data source (whether it is a database or an XML file, as it is in this case). Remember, the DataSet is always disconnected by nature. To commit changes, you need to add something like an update button, which would then use the WriteXml() method (in your example), or the DataAdapter.Update() method (to update a relational database). But because this book only covers the user interface aspect of your code, I won't explore these options.

## Formatting Data Before Binding

One limitation in your current example is that there is no way to handle data that needs to be formatted before it can be displayed. (Occasionally, you may have values that come out of a database in a less-than-professional looking state. For example, certain fields might use hard-coded numbers that are meaningless to the user, or use a confusing short form.) There's also no way to do the converse—take user supplied data, and convert it to a representation suitable for the appropriate field.

Luckily, both tasks are easy, provided you handle the Format and Parse events for the Binding object. Format gives you a chance to modify values as they exit the database (before they appear in a data bound control). Parse allows you to take a user-supplied value and modify it before it is committed to the data source. Figure 9-11 shows the process.

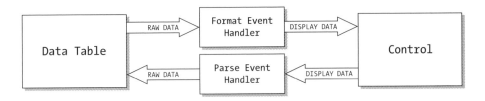

*Figure 9-11. Formatting data*

Here's an example that works with the UnitCost variable. It formats the numeric (decimal) value as a currency string when it's requested for display in a text box. The reverse process ensures that the final committed value doesn't use the currency symbol. To connect this logic, you need to create the Binding object, register to receive its events, and then add it to the DataBindings collection. Notice that the following code adds a trick—it registers for the DataTable's ColumnChanged event. This way, you can verify what value is actually inserted into the DataSet.

```
Dim dsStore As New DataSet()
dsStore.ReadXmlSchema(Application.StartupPath & "\store.xsd")
dsStore.ReadXml(Application.StartupPath & "\store.xml")

cboModelName.DataSource = dsStore.Tables("Products")
cboModelName.DisplayMember = "ModelName"

' Create the binding.
Dim CostBinding As New Binding("Text", dsStore.Tables("Products"), "UnitCost")

' Connect the methods for formatting and parsing data.
AddHandler CostBinding.Format, AddressOf DecimalToCurrencyString
AddHandler CostBinding.Parse, AddressOf CurrencyStringToDecimal

' Add the binding.
txtUnitCost.DataBindings.Add(CostBinding)

' Register an event handler for changes to the DataTable.
AddHandler dsStore.Tables("Products").ColumnChanged, AddressOf TableChanged
```

The event-handling code for formatting simply returns the new converted value by setting the e.Value property.

```
Private Sub DecimalToCurrencyString(ByVal sender As Object, _
  ByVal e As ConvertEventArgs)

    If e.DesiredType Is GetType(String) Then
        ' Use the ToString method to format the value as currency ("c").
        e.Value = CType(e.Value, Decimal).ToString("c")
    End If

End Sub


Private Sub CurrencyStringToDecimal(ByVal sender As Object, _
  ByVal e As ConvertEventArgs)

    If e.DesiredType Is GetType(Decimal) Then
        ' Convert the string back to decimal using the shared Parse method.
        e.Value = Decimal.Parse(e.Value.ToString, _
                    Globalization.NumberStyles.Currency, Nothing)
    End If

End Sub
```

The DataTable.ColumnChanged event handler is quite straightforward. It notes the changes by updating a label.

```
Private Sub TableChanged(ByVal sender As Object, _
  ByVal e As System.Data.DataColumnChangeEventArgs)

    lblStatus.Text = "Detected change. Column " & e.Column.ColumnName
    lblStatus.Text &= " updated to " & e.ProposedValue & "."

End Sub
```

Figure 9-12 shows the form after changing a value.

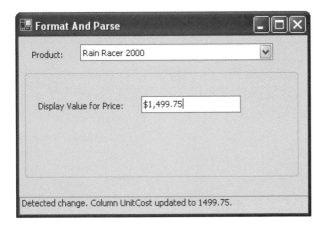

*Figure 9-12. Formatting numbers to strings*

> **NOTE** *Be warned, this approach can lead you to mingle too many database details into your code. A better approach is to handle the problem at the database level, if you can. For example, if you use a list of numeric constants, create a table in the database that maps the numbers to text descriptions. Then use a Join query when retrieving the data to get it in the form you need for your interface. Or, try to encapsulate the details as much as possible using a dedicated database resource class.*

## Advanced Conversions

You can use a similar technique to handle more interesting conversions. For example, you could convert a column value to an appropriate string representation, straighten out issues of case, or ensure the correct locale-specific format for dates and times. Here's one example that compares hard-coded integers from the database against an enumeration:

```
Private Sub ConstantToString(ByVal sender As Object, _
  ByVal e As ConvertEventArgs)

    If e.DesiredType Is GetType(String) Then
        Select Case e.Value
            Case ProjectStatus.NotStarted
                e.Value = "Project not started."
            Case ProjectStatus.InProgress
                e.Value = "Project in progress."
            Case ProjectStatus.Complete
                e.Value = "Project is complete."
        End Select
    End If

End Sub
```

Now let's look at an additional trick that's useful when storing records that link to pictures. When storing a record that incorporates a graphic, you have two options. You can store the image as binary information in the database (which is generally less flexible but more reliable), or you can store the filename, and ensure that the file exists in the appropriate project directory. The next example uses the Format event to convert a picture name to the required Image object.

Unfortunately, data binding is always a two-way street, and if you implement a Format event handler, you need to create a corresponding Parse event handler to reverse your change. In our example, the Format event handler takes the filename, and inserts the corresponding picture into a PictureBox. In the event handler, the code needs to take the picture, change it to the appropriate filename string, and insert this into the DataTable. This bidirectional conversion is required even though the application doesn't offer any way for the user to choose a new picture file, and the content in the PictureBox can't be changed.

To make matters more complicated, there's no way to convert an image object back to the filename, so we have to fall back on another trick: storing the actual filename in the control, for retrieval later.

Here's the data binding code:

```
Dim PictureBinding As New Binding("Image", dsStore.Tables("Products"), _
  "ProductImage")
AddHandler PictureBinding.Format, AddressOf FileToImage
AddHandler PictureBinding.Parse, AddressOf ImageToFile

picProduct.DataBindings.Add(PictureBinding)
```

And here is the formatting code (note that it requires the System.Drawing namespace to be imported):

```
Private Sub FileToImage(ByVal sender As Object, ByVal e As ConvertEventArgs)

    If e.DesiredType Is GetType(Image) Then
        ' Store the filename.
        picProduct.Tag = e.Value

        ' Look up the corresponding file, and create an Image object.
        e.Value = Image.FromFile(Application.StartupPath & "\" & e.Value)
    End If

End Sub

Private Sub ImageToFile(ByVal sender As Object, ByVal e As ConvertEventArgs)

    If e.DesiredType Is GetType(String) Then
        ' Substitute the filename.
        e.Value = picProduct.Tag
    End If

End Sub
```

This can only be considered a "conversion" in the loosest sense. What's really happening here is a file lookup. The process, however, is completely seamless. If you allow the user to dynamically choose a picture (maybe from a file or the clipboard), you could even create a corresponding Parse event handler that saves it to the appropriate directory with a unique name and then commits that name to the database (Figure 9-13).

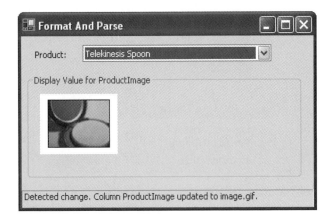

*Figure 9-13. "Converting" file names to image objects*

## Row Validation and Changes

Now that you realize how easy it is to commit changes to a bound DataSet, you are probably wondering what you can do to restrict the user's update ability—making sure some fields are read-only and others are bound by specific rules. This validation can be performed in exactly the same way it always is—by handling events like KeyPress in a text box, or using the validation techniques described in Chapter 4. These controls behave exactly like ordinary .NET controls—the only difference is that their changes are stored in the DataSet as soon as the user navigates to another record.

Resist the urge to enter error-handling code into the Parse event handler. This method is purely designed to convert a value before attempting to store it. Instead, you can handle ordinary DataTable events like ColumnChanging. Here is an example that uses the ColumnChanging event, and refuses to allow a change to the UnitCost column if the number is negative. Instead, it substitutes the existing value, effectively canceling the change.

```
Private Sub TableChanging(ByVal sender As Object, _
  ByVal e As System.Data.DataColumnChangeEventArgs)

    If e.ProposedValue < 0 Then
        e.ProposedValue = e.Row(e.Column.ColumnName)
    End If

End Sub
```

To use this code, you need to connect the event handler (typically at the same time you add the data binding):

```
AddHandler dsStore.Tables("Products").ColumnChanging, AddressOf TableChanging
```

This code is useful as a basic level of error protection, but it doesn't provide an easy way to notify the user about the error, because the user has more than likely already moved to another record. In some cases you may need to prevent the user from navigating to a new record after making invalid changes. To apply this logic, you need to take manual control of record navigation. This technique is explored in the next section.

The interesting question in these multiple control examples is how the controls work in conjunction with each other. If you know a little about ADO.NET, you'll remember that the DataSet is always disconnected for the data source, and doesn't provide any cursor or bookmark to store a current position (unlike the traditional ADO Recordset). Similarly, ordinary classes like arrays and ArrayList collections certainly don't have this capability. So where does it come from? The next section considers what's really at work in data binding, and shows how you can interact with it programmatically.

## Data Binding Exposed

The secret behind data binding lies in two objects that you don't ordinarily see: BindingContext and CurrencyManager. Every Windows Form provides a BindingContext object. In turn, every BindingContext provides a collection of zero or more CurrencyManager objects. Both objects are contained in the System.Windows.Forms namespace.

The CurrencyManager object shoulders the responsibility for tracking the user's position in the bound data and synchronizing all the controls that are bound to it. To this end, the CurrencyManager provides a small set of properties, including Count, and the ever-important Position, which indicates an integer row index. It performs its work automatically.

The BindingContext object, on the other hand, creates CurrencyManager objects as required. Depending on how you configure your form, you could have several different CurrencyManager objects, allowing you to bind to different data sources (or different positions in the same data source). Figure 9-14 diagrams this relationship.

There are really only three reasons that you might want to access the data binding objects:

- To programmatically control record navigation.

- To programmatically react to record navigation.

- To create a new BindingContext that allows you to store a different position to the same data.

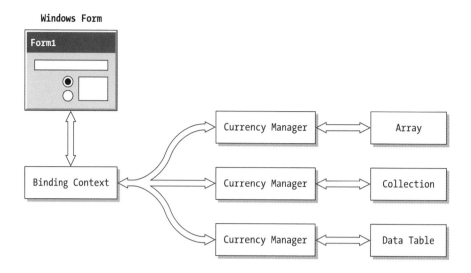

*Figure 9-14. Data binding under the hood*

## Navigation with Data Binding

To navigate programmatically you need to access the form's BindingContext object, and modify its Position property. Unfortunately, to find the correct BindingContext object, you need to submit the data source object. That means you either need to store the data source in a form-level variable, or create a form-level variable to track the binding object. The following example demonstrates the second technique with the DataSet product example.

First, create the variable for storing the BindingContext object:

```
Public StoreBinding As BindingManagerBase
```

Next, in the Form.Load event handler create the bindings and store a reference to the binding object. The only new line is highlighted in bold.

```
Private Sub MultipleControlBinding_Load(ByVal sender As System.Object, _
  ByVal e As System.EventArgs) Handles MyBase.Load

    Dim dsStore As New DataSet()
    dsStore.ReadXmlSchema(Application.StartupPath & "\store.xsd")
    dsStore.ReadXml(Application.StartupPath & "\store.xml")
```

```
cboModelName.DataSource = dsStore.Tables("Products")
cboModelName.DisplayMember = "ModelName"

lblModelNumber.DataBindings.Add("Text", dsStore.Tables("Products"), _
                                "ModelNumber")
lblUnitCost.DataBindings.Add("Text", dsStore.Tables("Products"), "UnitCost")
lblDescription.DataBindings.Add("Text", dsStore.Tables("Products"), _
                                "Description")

StoreBinding = Me.BindingContext(dsStore.Tables("Products"))

End Sub
```

Now you can control the position through the StoreBinding object. Here's an example with Previous and Next buttons that allows the user to browse through the data (see Figure 9-15):

```
Private Sub cmdPrev_Click(ByVal sender As System.Object, _
  ByVal e As System.EventArgs) Handles cmdPrev.Click
    StoreBinding.Position -= 1
End Sub

Private Sub cmdNext_Click(ByVal sender As System.Object, _
  ByVal e As System.EventArgs) Handles cmdNext.Click
        StoreBinding.Position += 1
End Sub
```

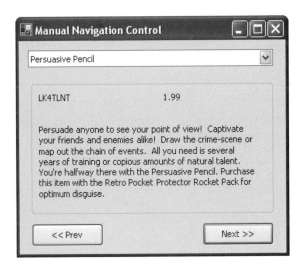

*Figure 9-15. Data binding with custom navigation controls*

## *Reacting to Record Navigation*

As it stands, the navigation controls harmlessly fail to work if you try to browse past the bounds of the data source (for example, click the Previous button on the first record). However, a more intuitive approach would be to disable the controls at this position. You can accomplish this by reacting to the Binding.PositionChanged event.

First, you connect the event handler (after binding the data source):

```
StoreBinding = Me.BindingContext(dsStore.Tables("Products"))
AddHandler StoreBinding.PositionChanged, AddressOf Binding_PositionChanged
```

The PositionChanged event doesn't provide you with any useful information (such as the originating page). But it does allow you to respond and update your controls accordingly. In the example below, the previous and next buttons are disabled when they don't apply.

```
Private Sub Binding_PositionChanged(ByVal sender As Object, ByVal e As EventArgs)

    If StoreBinding.Position = StoreBinding.Count -1 Then
       cmdNext.Enabled = False
    Else
       cmdNext.Enabled = True
    EndIf

    If StoreBinding.Position = 0
       cmdPrev.Enabled = False
    Else
      cmdPrev.Enabled = True
    End If

End Sub
```

If you want to be able to track the previous record, you need to add a form-level variable, and track it in the PositionChanged event handler. This technique has a few interesting uses, including validation (which you examine later in this chapter).

```
Dim CurrentPage As Integer

Private Sub Binding_PositionChanged(ByVal sender As Object, ByVal e As EventArgs)
    ' At this point, CurrentPage holds the previous page number.
    ' Now we update CurrentPage:
    CurrentPage = StoreBinding.Position
End Sub
```

## Creating Master-Detail Forms

Another interesting use of the PostionChanged event is to create master-detail forms. The concept is simple: you bind two controls to two different tables. When the selection in one table changes, you update the second by modifying the set of displayed rows with the RowFilter property.

This example uses two list controls, one that displays categories and one that displays the products in a given category. The lists are filled in the normal manner:

```
Private CategoryBinding As BindingManagerBase
Private dsStore As New DataSet()

Private Sub MasterDetail_Load(ByVal sender As System.Object, _
  ByVal e As System.EventArgs) Handles MyBase.Load

    dsStore.ReadXmlSchema(Application.StartupPath & "\store.xsd")
    dsStore.ReadXml(Application.StartupPath & "\store.xml")

    lstCategory.DataSource = dsStore.Tables("Categories")
    lstCategory.DisplayMember = "CategoryName"

    lstProduct.DataSource = dsStore.Tables("Products")
    lstProduct.DisplayMember = "ModelName"

    CategoryBinding = Me.BindingContext(dsStore.Tables("Categories"))

    AddHandler CategoryBinding.PositionChanged, AddressOf Binding_PositionChanged

End Sub
```

Now, when the PositionChanged event is detected for the category binding, the current view of products is automatically modified:

```
Private Sub Binding_PositionChanged(ByVal sender As Object, ByVal e As EventArgs)

    Dim Filter As String
    Dim SelectedRow As DataRow

    ' Find the current category row.
    SelectedRow = dsStore.Tables("Categories").Rows(CategoryBinding.Position)

    ' Create a filter expression using its CategoryID.
    Filter = "CategoryID='" & SelectedRow("CategoryID").ToString() & "'"

    ' Modify the view onto the product table.
    dsStore.Tables("Products").DefaultView.RowFilter = Filter

End Sub
```

The result is a perfectly synchronized master-detail list, as shown in Figure 9-16.

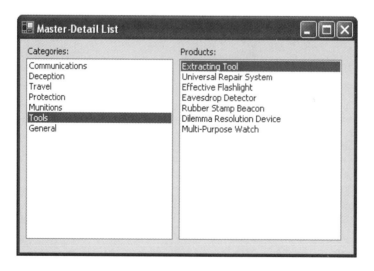

*Figure 9-16. Data binding with a master-detail list*

## Creating a New Binding Context

In the previous example, both controls were synchronized separately and had separate binding contexts because they were bound to two different tables (and hence two different DataViewManager objects). In some cases, however, you might want the ability to bind to two different positions in the same table (or any other data source). To accomplish this, you need to manually create an extra binding context.

The last task is easy. All you need to do is place the controls that you want in different binding contexts into different container controls (like a group box). Before you bind the data to the controls in the group boxes, manually create a new BindingContext object for one of them. Voila— you have two sets of controls that are synchronized separately.

The code that follows carries out this operation for two list controls in different group boxes. .

```
' Create a separate binding context for the controls in the
' category group box.
grpCategory.BindingContext = New BindingContext()

Dim dsStore As New DataSet()
dsStore.ReadXmlSchema(Application.StartupPath & "\store.xsd")
dsStore.ReadXml(Application.StartupPath & "\store.xml")

lstCategory.DataSource = dsStore.Tables("Categories")
lstCategory.DisplayMember = "CategoryName"

lstProduct.DataSource = dsStore.Tables("Categories")
lstProduct.DisplayMember = "CategoryName"
```

Figure 9-17 shows the separately synchronized panels.

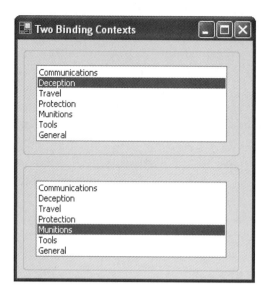

*Figure 9-17. Separately synchronized view of the same data*

## The DataGrid Control

The DataGrid is perfect for those who want a single data control that can do everything on its own. Even with some impressive column mapping features, it's still not as customizable or flexible as the approaches you've looked at so far, and the visual appearance doesn't provide much variety (multiline text columns, for example, are not supported except when editing a row). If you need a perfect super-grid control, you are likely to find that many custom options will soon appear on the network, and these third-party controls are likely to have a far wider range of features and much more customizability. Still, the DataGrid control is useful in the true, rapid application design spirit. It even provides simple user-editing functionality.

To use the DataGrid, you only need to assign a table or DataSet to its DataSource property. If you use an entire DataSet, the DataGrid provides special navigation links that allow you to browse to any of the tables it contains (see Figure 9-18).

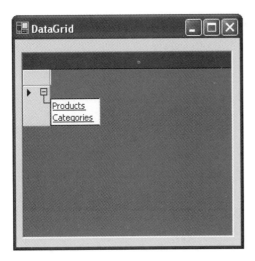

*Figure 9-18. DataGrid navigation links*

## DataGrid Relations

You can also make use of these navigation links to create a master-detail list. All you need to do is create the appropriate table relations first.

```
' Create a relation between categories and products.
Dim dr As New DataRelation("Products in this category", _
  dsStore.Tables("Categories").Columns("CategoryID"), _
  dsStore.Tables("Products").Columns("CategoryID"))

' Add the relation to the DataSet.
dsStore.Relations.Add(dr)

' Bind the data grid.
DataGrid1.DataSource = dsStore.Tables("Categories")
```

It's not as flexible as our custom solution for master-detail forms, but it works well with little tweaking required. Figure 9-19 shows the master-details list.

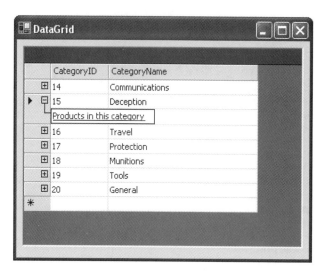

*Figure 9-19. DataGrid master-detail lists*

## DataGrid Column Mapping

Ordinarily, the DataGrid uses default header text and column widths and adds every field from the data source. In typical use, however, you may need to change cryptic field names, expand some columns to fit data, hide others, and choose the order they are displayed in.

To do this, you need to create a DataGridTableStyle collection, and add column objects that represent every column you want displayed. When you add this collection to the DataGrid.TableStyles property, the DataGrid changes its default behavior, and only displays the columns contained in the collection. It also abides by all the column settings you have configured.

Here is an example that configures a DataGrid to show only one field:

```
' Create the column collection.
Dim Columns As New DataGridTableStyle()
Columns.MappingName = "Products"

' Create and configure the columns you want to display.
Dim DescriptionCol As New DataGridTextBoxColumn()
DescriptionCol.HeaderText = "Description of Product"
DescriptionCol.Width = 500
DescriptionCol.MappingName = "Description"
```

```
' Add the columns to the collection.
Columns.GridColumnStyles.Add(DescriptionCol)

' Configure the DataGrid to use these column settings.
DataGrid1.TableStyles.Add(Columns)

' Bind the grid.
DataGrid1.DataSource = dsStore.Tables("Products")
```

## Creating Custom DataGrid Column Styles

The DataGrid only provides two types of columns: one for text data and one for True/False Boolean Fields. These column types correspond to the .NET column classes DataGridBoolColumn and DataGridTextBoxColumn.

It doesn't take much experimentation with the DataGrid control to realize that there are many types of data that don't suit either column type. The usual solution is to provide a read-only text field, or try to code innovative algorithms in the Format and Parse event handlers that can perform the required conversions. However, you can derive your own custom classes from the DataGridColumnStyle class, and use them to support other types of data. Table 9-3 lists the methods you need to override to create a custom DataGridColumnStyle.

*Table 9-3. Overridable DataGridColumnStyle Methods*

| Method | Description |
| --- | --- |
| Abort(), Commit(), and Edit() | These methods are triggered in response to column editing. Edit occurs when the user clicks in a cell to start editing. Commit happens when the user navigates to a new cell (another field or another record) and the change is to be committed. If Commit returns False, the change is not made—instead, the Abort method gets a chance to roll it back. If you want to make a read-only column, you don't need to do anything in these methods, but you still need to override them. |
| GetMinimumHeight(), GetMinimumSize(), and GetPreferredHeight() | Gets the dimensions of the row, both as the minimum allowed, and the preferred (default). |
| Paint() | Displays the data in the column. |

Support for unusual data types isn't the only reason to create a DataGridColumnStyle. You might just want to tweak the display for a specific field. For example, you might want to display an icon in a field that indicates something about the status of a given record (for example, a graphical "New!" starburst next to a recently added product).

The next example presents a custom DataGridColumnStyle that's designed to show prices—with a twist. Prices that are lower than the indicated "special" price are displayed with a happy icon next to them.

Start by defining the basic class, with a public member for the threshold price:

```
Public Class DataGridPriceIconColumn
    Inherits DataGridColumnStyle

    Public NicePrice As Decimal
    Public Sub New(ByVal nicePrice As Decimal)
        Me.NicePrice = nicePrice
    End Sub

End Class
```

Next, the editing methods are overridden. No actual code is added, as this column only supports read-only use.

```
Protected Overrides Sub Abort(ByVal rowNum As Integer)
    ' Do nothing.
End Sub

Protected Overrides Function Commit(ByVal dataSource As CurrencyManager, _
  ByVal rowNum As Integer) As Boolean
    Return True
End Function

Protected Overloads Overrides Sub Edit(ByVal source As CurrencyManager, _
  ByVal rowNum As Integer, ByVal bounds As System.Drawing.Rectangle, _
  ByVal [readOnly] As Boolean, ByVal instantText As String, _
  ByVal cellIsVisible As Boolean)
    ' Do nothing.
End Sub

Protected Overloads Overrides Sub Edit(ByVal source As CurrencyManager, _
  ByVal rowNum As Integer, ByVal bounds As System.Drawing.Rectangle, _
  ByVal [readOnly] As Boolean)
    ' Do nothing.
End Sub
```

```
Protected Overloads Overrides Sub Edit(ByVal source As CurrencyManager, _
   ByVal rowNum As Integer, ByVal bounds As System.Drawing.Rectangle, _
   ByVal [readOnly] As Boolean, ByVal instantText As String)
      ' Do nothing.
End Sub
```

Next, the code is added to return size information:

```
Protected Overrides Function GetMinimumHeight() As Integer
      Return 20
End Function

Protected Overrides Function GetPreferredHeight( _
   ByVal g As System.Drawing.Graphics, ByVal value As Object) As Integer
      Return 20
End Function

Protected Overrides Function GetPreferredSize( _
   ByVal g As System.Drawing.Graphics, _
   ByVal value As Object) As System.Drawing.Size
      Return New Size(100, 20)
End Function
```

Finally, the interesting code is added. This code uses some basic GDI+ techniques to draw an icon and the actual price text in the provided rectangle (which represents the cell). Notice that there are three versions of the Paint() method, and you need to implement them all. In this sample implementation, the versions with fewer parameters simply call the fullest Paint() method with some logical defaults.

```
Protected Overloads Overrides Sub Paint(ByVal g As System.Drawing.Graphics, _
    ByVal bounds As System.Drawing.Rectangle, ByVal source As CurrencyManager, _
    ByVal rowNum As Integer, ByVal backBrush As System.Drawing.Brush, _
    ByVal foreBrush As System.Drawing.Brush, ByVal alignToRight As Boolean)

      ' Clear the cell.
      g.FillRegion(backBrush, New Region(bounds))

      Dim Price As Decimal = CType(Me.GetColumnValueAtRow(source, rowNum), Integer)
      Dim PriceIcon As Icon
      If Price < NicePrice Then
          PriceIcon = New Icon(Application.StartupPath & "\happy2.ico")

          ' Draw the optional "nice price" icon.
          g.DrawIcon(PriceIcon, New Rectangle(bounds.X, bounds.Y, 16, 16))
      End If
```

```
                ' Draw the text.
            g.DrawString(Price.ToString("C"), New Font("Tahoma", 8.25), _
                    Brushes.Black, bounds.X + 20, bounds.Y + 2)

    End Sub

    Protected Overloads Overrides Sub Paint(ByVal g As System.Drawing.Graphics, _
      ByVal bounds As System.Drawing.Rectangle, ByVal source As CurrencyManager, _
      ByVal rowNum As Integer, ByVal alignToRight As Boolean)

        Me.Paint(g, bounds, source, rowNum, Brushes.White, Brushes.Black, _
            alignToRight)

    End Sub

    Protected Overloads Overrides Sub Paint(ByVal g As System.Drawing.Graphics, _
      ByVal bounds As System.Drawing.Rectangle, ByVal source As CurrencyManager, _
      ByVal rowNum As Integer)

        Me.Paint(g, bounds, source, rowNum, Brushes.White, Brushes.Black, False)

    End Sub
```

Figure 9-20 shows the custom DataGridPriceIconColumn in action.

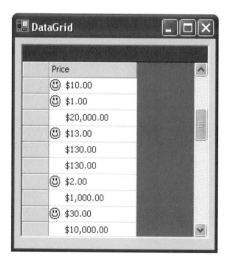

*Figure 9-20. A custom DataGrid column*

This design could also be implemented using a separate column. For example, you could bind a Price column to a normal DataGridTextBoxColumn and to a custom DataGridPriceIconColumn to show the icon. You could then place the DataGridPriceIcon column at the beginning of the row.

## Encapsulation with Data Controls

With this exhaustive look at data binding, you now know how to tailor data for your user interface without writing manual code to loop through records and commit changes. However, all this functionality comes at a price. Namely, if you use data binding in the way I've described, you'll soon end up with a tangle of database-specific details (such as formatting and field names) directly in your form code. What's worse, this code is fragile and loosely typed—meaning that if a field name changes in the database, your user interface code needs immediate modifications to survive.

This state of affairs is far from ideal. Luckily, there are a few ways to minimize the problem. One way is not to use data binding at all. Instead, create a database table with three columns: FormName, ControlName, and DataField. You can then fill this table with content that maps individual controls to specific data fields. A simple helper function in a database adapter class can then manage the information transfer:

```
Public Class DBHelper

    Public Shared Sub FillForm(ByVal formToBind As Form, _
      ByVal mappings As DataTable)

        Dim RowMatch() As DataRow

        Dim ctrl As Control
        For Each ctrl In formToBind.Controls
            ' See if this menu item has a corresponding row.
            RowMatch = mappings.Select("ControlName = '" & ctrl.Text & "'")

            ' If it does, configure the binding accordingly.
            If RowMatch.GetLength(0) > 0 Then
                Dim FieldToUse As String = RowMatch(0)("DataField")
                ' We assume the text property is the one to be filled.
                ' Alternatively, we could add a database field with
                ' this information.
                ctrl.Text = dt.Rows(FieldToUse)
            End If
```

```
        Next

    End Sub

End Class
```

This technique works well because it establishes an extra layer of indirection between the database and the controls. It's easy to modify this table if field names or user interface elements change. Best of all, the routine to fill the user interface is quite generic. Of course, you need to manually call this method every time the user moves to a new row to ensure that control synchronization occurs as naturally as it does with data binding.

> **NOTE** *Variations on this theme are examined in Chapter 11, which considers dynamic user interfaces, and Chapter 14, which shows you how to use a database to roll your own context-sensitive Help.*

Another way to help separate your database from your user interface code is by keeping database-specific content like field names and constants (used in the Parse and Format methods) in a separate resource class. The next example, which shows how you can use proper validation with data binding, demonstrates a perfect example of this technique with validation.

## Validating Bound Data

Earlier in this chapter, you learned that one problem with ADO.NET data binding is validation. You can write specific error-handling code for each control, which is often a good approach, but one that creates extra code and ends up importing database details into your form code. Another approach is to handle the DataTable events like ColumnChanging, ColumnChanged, RowChanging, and RowChanged. The potential problem here is that the user may browse to another record, not realizing that invalid data has been rejected.

Taking control of data binding navigation allows you to provide a more elegant solution. First, you create two form-level variables: one that tracks the current page, and the other that tracks the validity of the current record.

```
Private CurrentPage As Integer
Private ErrFlag As Boolean
```

You also need to hook up the events for column changes and position changes.

```
AddHandler StoreBinding.PositionChanged, AddressOf Binding_PositionChanged
AddHandler dsStore.Tables("Products").ColumnChanged, AddressOf TableChanging
```

Next, you make the record navigation conditional on the current record being valid. If the ErrFlag member variable is set to True, the user is automatically sent back to the original page.

```
Private Sub Binding_PositionChanged(ByVal sender As Object, ByVal e As EventArgs)

    If ErrFlag = True Then
        StoreBinding.Position = CurrentPage
    Else
        CurrentPage = StoreBinding.Position
    End If

End Sub
```

Next, you add the validation code, which occurs in response to a table change. This event is fired when the user tabs to a new field after making a modification, or tries to browse to a new record after making a modification. It always occurs before the PositionChanged event.

```
Private Sub TableChanging(ByVal sender As Object, _
  ByVal e As System.Data.DataColumnChangeEventArgs)

    Dim Errors As String = DBStore.ValidateProduct(e.Row)

    If Errors = "" Then
        ErrFlag = False
    Else
        ErrFlag = True
    End If

    lblErrorSummary.Text = Errors
End Sub
```

You'll notice that so far this form doesn't contain any database-specific code. Instead, the validation is performed by passing the current row to a special shared method provided by a database class. This method returns an error string, or an empty string if the validation succeeded.

```
Public Class DBStore

    Public Shared Function ValidateProduct(ByVal row As DataRow) As String
        Dim Errors As String

        If row("UnitCost") <= 0 Then
            Errors &= "* UnitCost value too low" & NewLine
        End If
        If row("ModelNumber") = "" Then
            Errors &= "* You must specify a ModelNumber" & NewLine
        End If
        If row("ModelName") = "" Then
            Errors &= "* You must specify a ModelName" & NewLine
        End If


        Return Errors
    End Function

End Class
```

The error message is displayed in the window. Everything works nicely together. Database validation code is in a database component, but record navigation is halted immediately if an error is found.

Figure 9-21 shows the final application detecting an error.

## Data-Aware Controls

Not all controls work well with data binding. For example, the popular TreeView and ListView controls need to be filled manually. In other circumstances, you may have controls that support data binding, but you want to take control of the entire process. Maybe you want to create a control that can't be filled all at once, but uses partial data reads or just-in-time queries to allow a user to browse through a large amount of data.

.NET provides many opportunities for data integration without data binding. One handy technique is using the Tag property. Every control provides the Tag property, but the .NET framework doesn't use it. Instead, you can use the Tag property to store any information or object you need. For example, you could use this property to store the relevant business object with each node in a TreeView, or a DataRow object with each row in a ListView.

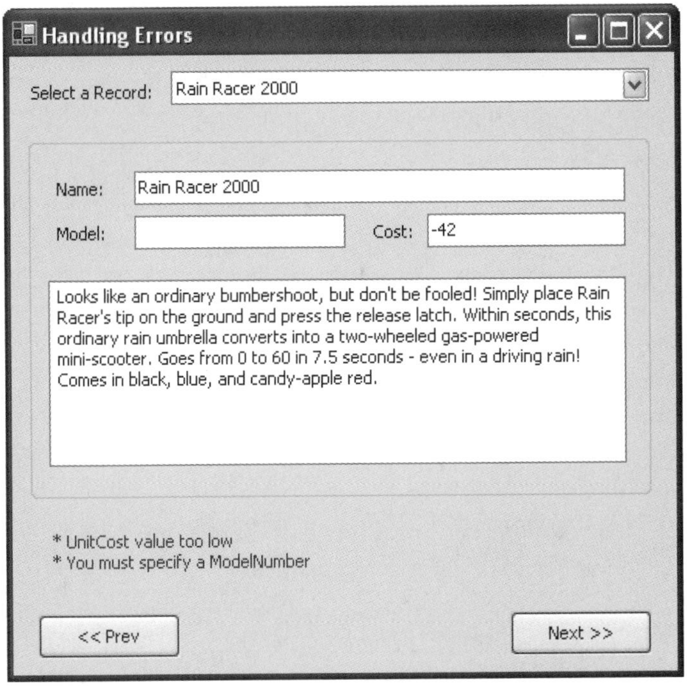

*Figure 9-21. Custom row validation with data binding*

The next example shows a TreeView that embeds the data it needs use the Tag property of each node. Here's the code needed to fill the TreeView (which could be placed in the Form.Load event handler):

```
Dim dsStore As New DataSet()

dsStore.ReadXmlSchema(Application.StartupPath & "\store.xsd")
dsStore.ReadXml(Application.StartupPath & "\store.xml")

' Define the relation.
Dim relCategoryProduct As New DataRelation("Products in this category", _
  dsStore.Tables("Categories").Columns("CategoryID"), _
  dsStore.Tables("Products").Columns("CategoryID"))
dsStore.Relations.Add(relCategoryProduct)

Dim nodeParent, nodeChild As TreeNode
Dim rowParent, rowChild As DataRow
For Each rowParent In dsStore.Tables("Categories").Rows
```

```
' Add the category node.
nodeParent = treeDB.Nodes.Add(rowParent("CategoryName"))

' Store the disconnected category information.
nodeParent.Tag = rowParent

For Each rowChild In rowParent.GetChildRows(relCategoryProduct)
    ' Add the product order node.
    nodeChild = nodeParent.Nodes.Add(rowChild("ModelName"))

    ' Store the disconnected product information.
    nodeChild.Tag = rowChild
Next
Next
```

When a node is selected, a generic code routine reads the accompanying DataRow and displays all the information it contains in a label.

```
Private Sub treeDB_AfterSelect(ByVal sender As System.Object, _
  ByVal e As System.Windows.Forms.TreeViewEventArgs) Handles treeDB.AfterSelect

    lblInfo.Text = ""
    Dim row As DataRow = CType(e.Node.Tag, DataRow)
    Dim Field As Object
    For Each Field In row.ItemArray
        lblInfo.Text &= Field.ToString & vbNewLine
    Next

End Sub
```

The result, shown in Figure 9-22, is a TreeView that has easy access to the information for each node.

## A Decoupled TreeView with Just-in-Time Nodes

The preceding TreeView example requires very little information about the data source. Instead, it loops through the available fields to display a list of information. However, in doing so the control also gives up the ability to format the data in a more acceptable format. For example, fields that aren't important are always displayed, and the field order is fixed.

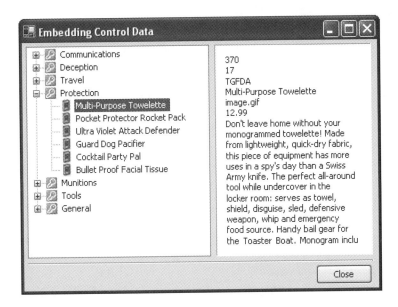

*Figure 9-22. A TreeView with embedded data*

There is an elegant way to solve this problem. The next example shows a TreeView that still embeds data, but relies on a ProductDatabase class to transform the DataRow fields into display information. An instance of the ProductDatabase class is created as form-level variable:

```
Private DataClass As New ProductDatabase()
```

Thanks to the ProductDatabase class, the TreeView doesn't need to handle the table hierarchy. Instead, it begins by filling the tree with a list of categories and adds dummy nodes under every level.

```
Private Sub Form1_Load(ByVal sender As Object, ByVal e As System.EventArgs) _
    Handles MyBase.Load

    Dim nodeParent As TreeNode, row As DataRow

    For Each row In DataClass.GetCategories.Rows
        ' Add the category node.
        nodeParent = treeDB.Nodes.Add(row(ProductDatabase.CategoryField.Name))
        nodeParent.ImageIndex = 0
```

```
                    ' Store the disconnected category information.
                    nodeParent.Tag = row

                    ' Add a "dummy" node.
                    nodeParent.Nodes.Add("*")
            Next

        End Sub
```

When a node is expanded, the TreeView calls the ProductDatabase with the expanded node, and requests more information. The ProductDatabase then returns the information needed to add the appropriate child nodes.

```
Private Sub treeDB_BeforeExpand(ByVal sender As Object, _
   ByVal e As System.Windows.Forms.TreeViewCancelEventArgs) _
   Handles treeDB.BeforeExpand

     Dim nodeSelected, nodeChild As TreeNode
     nodeSelected = e.Node
     If nodeSelected.Nodes(0).Text = "*" Then
         nodeSelected.Nodes.Clear()
         Dim row As DataRow
         For Each row In DataClass.GetProductsInCategory(nodeSelected.Tag)
             nodeChild = nodeSelected.Nodes.Add(row(DataClass.ProductField.Name))

             ' Store the disconnected product information.
             nodeChild.Tag = row
             nodeChild.ImageIndex = 1
             nodeChild.SelectedImageIndex = 1
         Next
     End If

End Sub
```

When an item is selected, the TreeView again relies on the ProductDatabase class to "translate" the embedded DataRow (Figure 9-23):

```
Private Sub treeDB_AfterSelect(ByVal sender As System.Object, _
   ByVal e As System.Windows.Forms.TreeViewEventArgs) Handles treeDB.AfterSelect

   lblInfo.Text = DataClass.GetDisplayText(e.Node.Tag)

End Sub
```

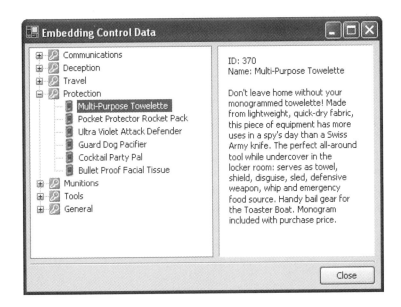

*Figure 9-23. A decoupled TreeView*

This pattern allows the ProductDatabase to handle its own data access strategy—it can fetch the information as needed with miniqueries every time a node is expanded, or it can retain it in memory as a private member variable (as it does in this example). Even better, the ProductDatabase code is extremely simple because it doesn't need to convert ADO.NET objects into "business" objects. The TreeView can use and embed the ADO.NET objects natively, without needing to know anything about their internal field structures.

```
Public Class ProductDatabase

    Public Class Tables
        Public Const Product As String = "Products"
        Public Const Category As String = "Categories"
    End Class

    Public Class ProductField
        Public Const Name As String = "ModelName"
        Public Const Description As String = "Description"
    End Class

    Public Class CategoryField
        Public Const Name As String = "CategoryName"
    End Class
```

```
        Private dsStore As DataSet
        Dim relCategoryProduct As DataRelation

        Public Sub New()
            dsStore = New DataSet()

            dsStore.ReadXmlSchema(Application.StartupPath & "\store.xsd")
            dsStore.ReadXml(Application.StartupPath & "\store.xml")

            ' Define the relation.
            relCategoryProduct = New DataRelation("Prod_Cat", _
              dsStore.Tables("Categories").Columns("CategoryID"), _
              dsStore.Tables("Products").Columns("CategoryID"))
            dsStore.Relations.Add(relCategoryProduct)
        End Sub

        Public Function GetCategories() As DataTable
            Return dsStore.Tables("Categories")
        End Function

        Public Function GetProductsInCategory(ByVal rowParent As DataRow) _
          As DataRow()
            Return rowParent.GetChildRows(relCategoryProduct)
        End Function

        Public Function GetDisplayText(ByVal row As DataRow) As String
            Dim Text As String
            Select Case row.Table.TableName
                Case Tables.Product
                    Text = "ID: " & row(0) & vbNewLine
                    Text &= "Name: " & row(ProductField.Name) & vbNewLine & vbNewLine
                    Text &= row(ProductField.Description)
            End Select
            Return Text
        End Function

End Class
```

The ProductDatabase methods could easily be used with other controls. None of them are specific to the TreeView.

## Can There Be a Data-Bound ListView Control?

It seems like dealing with data is always a compromise. You can have a full-featured control that supports flexible data binding and lacks user interface niceties, like the DataGrid, or a more attractive ListView or TreeView that doesn't have any intrinsic support to display information from a data source. Wouldn't an ideal solution combine both of these worlds and create a ListView or TreeView that can bind to any data source?

The short answer is no. Programmers have developed ListView controls that can automatically display DataTable information, and TreeView controls that can accept DataSets and show a master-details list by inspecting the table relations. But these custom controls are rarely flexible enough to be used in a real application. Their intelligence is remarkable, but once you start to work with them, you repeatedly stumble across basic limitations. For example, in a data-bound ListView there would be no easy way to set column widths and ordering. This type of information can't be stored in a DataSet or DataTable object, and even if it could, it might vary with the display font or the current user's preferences. Similarly, a data-bound TreeView would have no support for multiple groupings. A just-in-time node solution (like you saw in the previous example) can't be implemented because the data-bound TreeView requires a completely configured DataSet.

These limitations are not trivial. The DataGrid solves them partially by providing another layer of indirection with DataGridColumnStyle classes. These styles allow you to configure the display appearance of the data separately from the data itself. Even still, the DataGrid lacks many formatting and display niceties. To work with a richer control like the TreeView would require the development of a similar framework. As an undertaking, it would be far more difficult than creating a customized TreeView that's tailored for your type of data.

In short, the best approach is to design your control to suit your data strategy. No single control can support every type of data, and no data-binding framework can accommodate every possible way data binding can be used. If you are creating a control that needs to support several different ways of interacting with data, follow the design explained with the decoupled TreeView. This control allows you a maximum of programming convenience, with the flexibility to change your controls or your data access strategy later.

## The Last Word

This chapter has provided an in-depth examination of the inner workings of data binding. It has also considered the best practices you need to use for data binding without crippling your code and tying it too closely to the specific data source details. In Chapter 11 you revisit this issue with a twist, and examine a case where tight coupling is exactly what you want!

The chapter also considered some useful examples about how to sidestep data binding and create custom controls that are data-aware. These smart controls are invaluable in cleaning up tangled messes of code, and provide an excellent solution when you want to use controls that don't support data binding well, like the ListView and TreeView.

# CHAPTER 10

# MDI Interfaces and Workspaces

MULTIPLE DOCUMENT INTERFACE (MDI) represents one of the most common user interface designs on the Windows platform. MDI interfaces provide a single application window that contains multiple child windows (and optionally other windows like toolbars and floating palettes). MDI windows turn up in some form or another in most complex applications, and Visual Studio .NET is no exception.

In this chapter, you learn how to create an MDI application in .NET, and see how it's dramatically easier to use and more flexible than in previous programming toolkits. You also learn basic window management and synchronization with the document-view architecture. Finally, toward the end of the chapter, you explore one of the trickiest aspects of MDI interfaces with dockable windows.

## The Story of MDI

MDI windows have been the de facto standard for user interfaces for the past several years, although their dominance is fading. Newer Windows applications sometimes use multiple independent SDI (single-document interface) windows instead. For example, Internet Explorer is an SDI application—if you want to open several pages at once, the pages appear in several windows, each of which is shown on the taskbar. Microsoft Word has also become an SDI application, although it was one of the earliest MDI examples in the Windows world. Most other word processors and document applications use MDI interfaces, and Visual Studio .NET is irredeemably MDI. Though it provides a unique user interface with tabbed and grouped windows, the basic principle—hosting several different windows in one large container—remains unchanged.

The debate between SDI versus MDI is sometimes heated. There is no clear standard, although Microsoft officially states that SDI is easier to use and preferred. The best design depends on the purpose of your application and the user it is designed to serve. If you are dealing with advanced users who need to manage several views simultaneously, an MDI interface is usually better than scattering multiple windows across the taskbar. On the other hand, if you are creating a simple editor for a novice user, it's probably clearer to follow a simpler SDI design like that used in Microsoft Paint of WordPad.

## Types of MDI Applications

There are essentially two types of MDI applications:

- **Document applications.** These applications use a single application window to contain multiple identical document windows. In a word processing program, this might provide a simple way for a user to work with several files at once.

- **Workspace applications.** These applications provide several different windows (which correspond to different features) that can all be displayed simultaneously. For example, you might create a project management program that allows you to simultaneously browse through a list of users, enter new projects, and report software bugs. This could be modeled in an Explorer-style SDI interface application, but the user would only be able to perform one task at a time.

## MDI Essentials

In .NET, there is no sharp distinction between ordinary windows and MDI windows. In fact, you can transform any window into an MDI parent at design-time or runtime by setting the IsMdiContainer container. You can even change a window back and forth at will, which is a mind-expanding trick never before allowed.

```
Me.IsMdiContainer = True
```

When displayed as an MDI container, the form's surface becomes a dark gray open area where other windows can be hosted. To add a window as an MDI child, you simply set the form's MdiParent property on startup:

```
Dim frmChild As New Child()
frmChild.MdiParent = Me
frmChild.Show()
```

Ideally, you perform this task before you display the window, but with .NET you don't need to. In fact, you can even have more than one MDI parent in the same project, and move a child from one parent to the other by changing the MdiParent property.

Figure 10-1 shows two different views of an MDI parent with a contained MDI child.

*Figure 10-1. An MDI Child*

One of the most unusual features of .NET MDI parents is that they can display any type of control. Traditionally, MDI parents only support docked controls like toolbars, status bars, and menus. With an MDI parent created in .NET, however, you can add any other type of control, and it remains fixed in place (or anchored and docked), suspended "above" any other windows.

This trick can be used to create a bizarre window like that shown in Figure 10-2, or a unique type of floating tool window (although you need to add the "fake" drag-and-drop support, as described in Chapter 4).

*Figure 10-2. Suspended controls*

> **TIP**  *MDI child forms can be minimized or maximized. When maximized, they take up the entire viewable area, and the title name appears in square brackets in the MDI container's title bar. When minimized, just the title bar portion appears at the bottom of the window. You can prevent this behavior by disabling the ShowMaximize or ShowMinimize properties for the child form.*

## Finding Your Relatives

If you display multiple windows in an SDI application, you need to carefully keep track of each one, usually by storing a form reference in some sort of shared application class. With MDI interfaces, you don't need to go to this extra work. That's because it's easy to find the currently active MDI window, the MDI parent, and the full collection of MDI children.

Consider the next example, which provides a toolbar with two buttons: New and Close. The New button creates an MDI child window, while the Close button always closes the currently active window (see Figure 10-3). You don't need to write any extra code to track the currently active child. Instead, it is provided through the MDI container's ActiveMdiChild property.

```
Private Sub ToolBar1_ButtonClick(ByVal sender As Object, _
  ByVal e As System.Windows.Forms.ToolBarButtonClickEventArgs) _
  Handles ToolBar1.ButtonClick

    If e.Button Is cmdNew Then
        Dim frmChild As New Child()
        frmChild.MdiParent = Me
        frmChild.Show()
    ElseIf e.Button Is cmdClose Then
        Me.ActiveMdiChild.Close()
    End If

End Sub
```

> **TIP**  *You can also set the active MDI form using the Form.Activate() method. This is similar to setting the focus for a control. It automatically moves the appropriate child form to the top of all other child forms, and sets the focus to the most recently selected control on that form. You can also find the control that has focus on an MDI form by reading the ActiveControl property.*

*Figure 10-3. Working with the active child*

## Synchronizing MDI Children

The MdiParent property allows you to find the MDI container from any child. The ActiveMdiChild property allows you to find the active child from the parent form. The only remaining gap to fill is retrieving the full list of all MDI children. This can be accomplished using the MdiChildren property, which provides an array of form references. (That's right, an array—not a collection, which means you can't use methods like Add() and Remove() to manage MDI children.)

The next example shows how you can use the MdiChildren collection to synchronize MDI children. In this example, every child shows a text box with the same content. If the text box content is modified in one window, the custom Refresh-Children() method is called in the parent form.

```
Private IsUpdating As Boolean

Private Sub TextBox1_TextChanged(ByVal sender As System.Object, _
    ByVal e As System.EventArgs) Handles TextBox1.TextChanged

    If Not MdiParent Is Nothing And Not IsUpdating Then
        ' The reference to the MDI parent must be converted to the appropriate
        ' form class in order to access the custom RefreshChildren() method.
        CType(Me.MdiParent, Parent).RefreshChildren(Me, TextBox1.Text)
    End If

End Sub
```

The RefreshChildren() method steps through all the child windows, and updates each one, except the original sender. It also stores the current text in a private member variable, so it can assign it automatically to newly created windows.

```
Private SynchronizedText As String

Public Sub RefreshChildren(ByVal sender As Child, ByVal text As String)
    ' Store text for use when creating a child form, or if needed later.
    SynchronizedText = text

    ' Update children.
    Dim frm As Child
    For Each frm In Me.MdiChildren
        If Not frm Is sender Then
            frm.RefreshText(text)
        End If
    Next
End Sub
```

The refreshing is performed through the RefreshText() method provided by each child window. It takes special care to avoid triggering another refresh by disabling the event handler for the duration of the task.

```
Public Sub RefreshText(ByVal text As String)
    ' Disable the event to prevent an endless string of updates.
    IsUpdating = True

    ' Update the control.
    TextBox1.Text = text

    ' Re-enable the event handler.
    IsUpdating = False
End Sub
```

This example shows how synchronization can be implemented using the MdiChildren property. However, the potential drawback of this technique is that it forces every window to be updated even if the change only affects one or two. This is suitable if all windows are linked together, but is not useful if the user is working in multiple independent windows. A more scalable approach is introduced later when you explore document-view architecture.

## MDI Layout

By convention, MDI applications often provide a menu that lists all the open document windows, and provides options for automatically tiling or cascading them. Adding these features in .NET is easy.

To create an MDI child window list, simply add a top-level menu item (usually named Window), and set the MdiList property to True. The Windows Forms engine will then automatically add one item to the bottom of the submenu for each child window (using the title bar for the menu text), and place a check mark next to the window that is currently active (see Figure 10-4). The user can also use the menu to move from window to window, without any required code.

*Figure 10-4. The MDI child list*

If you want to add support for tiling and cascading windows, you'll probably also add these options to this menu. Every MDI container supports a LayoutMdi() method that accepts a value from the MdiLayout enumeration, and arranges the windows automatically.

For example, here's the code to tile windows horizontally:

```
Private Sub mnuTileH_Click(ByVal sender As System.Object, _
    ByVal e As System.EventArgs) Handles mnuTileH.Click

    Me.LayoutMdi(MdiLayout.TileHorizontal)

End Sub
```

Of course, it's just as easy to create your own custom layout logic. Here's the code for a menu option that minimizes all the open windows:

```
Private Sub mnuMinimizeAll_Click(ByVal sender As System.Object, _
    ByVal e As System.EventArgs) Handles mnuMinimizeAll.Click

    Dim frm As Form
    For Each frm In Me.MdiChildren
        frm.WindowState = FormWindowState.Minimized
    Next

End Sub
```

Figure 10-5 summarizes some of the layout options.

## Merging Menus

Another unique characteristic of MDI applications is their treatment of menus. If you create a child form with a menu, that menu is added to the main menu when the child form is displayed. This behavior allows you to provide different options depending on the current view, but presents a centralized menu to the user.

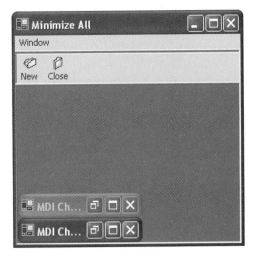

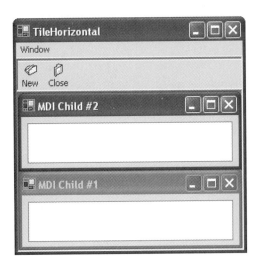

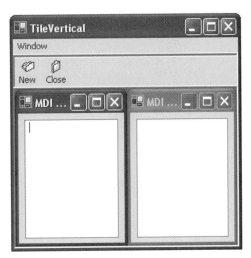

*Figure 10-5. Different layout options*

Using the default menu behavior, menu items from the child form are added
to the right of the standard menu items. Figure 10-6 shows an example with a child
menu named Document. However, you can configure this behavior to a certain
extent using the MergeStyle and MergeOrder properties.

*Figure 10-6. Merged menus*

- To add a child menu in front of a parent menu, set the MergeOrder for the child menu to 0 (the default) and change the MergeOrder in the parent menu items to 1, or any larger number.

- To ensure that a child menu does *not* appear when displayed in an MDI container, set the MergeStyle for the menu item to Remove.

- To merge similar menus together (for example, the entries under two top-level File menus), make sure that the MergeOrder for both is the same, and set the MergeStyle of each one to MergeItems. Without this step, you would end up with two identically named items, one with the child menu items and one with the parent items.

> **NOTE** *.NET does not automatically merge toolbars (or any other type of control you dock to the MDI parent form). If this is the behavior you want, you will have to write the code to perform this task manually.*

## Managing Interface State

When creating MDI applications, you'll often find that you have more than one control with equivalent functionality. The most common example is the toolbar, which usually replicates options in the main menu.

You can handle this duplication fairly easily in code. One technique is to hand off the work to another method. Thus, both the toolbar button-click and the menu-click event handler forward requests for a new document to a form-level or application class method like NewDocument(). Here's how it works:

```
Public Class MDIParent
    Inherits Form
    ' Designer code omitted.

    Private Sub ToolBar1_ButtonClick(ByVal sender As Object, _
      ByVal e As System.Windows.Forms.ToolBarButtonClickEventArgs) _
      Handles ToolBar1.ButtonClick
        If e.Button Is cmdOpen Then
            ApplicationTasks.NewDocument(Me)
        End If
    End Sub

    Private Sub mnuNew_Click(sender As Object, e As EventArgs)
        ApplicationTasks.NewDocument(Me)
    End Sub

End Class


Public Class ApplicationTasks

    Public Shared Sub NewDocument(parent As Form)
        ' (Code implementation here.)
    End Sub

End Class
```

Life becomes a little trickier when you need to handle the enabled/disabled state for these controls. For example, rather than performing error checking to verify there is an active document when the user clicks Save, you should disable the Save button and menu option unless a document is available. The problem is that you not only have to disable the menu option, but you need to ensure that the corresponding toolbar button (or any other control that provides the same functionality) becomes disabled or enabled at the same time. Otherwise, mysterious bugs can creep into your application, where controls allow a function to be attempted when the document is in an invalid state. If you are performing all your testing with the menu bar, you might not even notice this vulnerability, because it's exposed solely through the toolbar.

Generally, you'll need a dedicated controller class (often called a state management class) to assume this responsibility. One option is to provide higher-level methods or properties in the controller class that automatically disable or enable related controls. Then your code will call one of these methods instead of manually interacting with the appropriate controls.

Here's how a controller class like this might look:

```
Public Class MDIMainController

    Public MDIMain As Form

    Public Property NewEnabled() As Boolean
        Get
            Return MDIMain.mnuNew.Enabled
        End Get
        Set(ByVal Value As Boolean)
            MDIMain.mnuNew.Enabled = Value
            MDIMain.cmdNew.Enabled = Value
        End Set
    End Property

End Class
```

This is typical of many programming solutions: it works by adding another layer of indirection. The MDIMainController acts as a layer between the form and the user interface code. When you want to remove the ability for the user to create new documents, you simply use a single line of code:

```
ControllerInstance.NewEnabled = False
```

As with many programming tasks, the trick is in managing the details. The controller class technique works well and helps tame the inevitable complexity of an interface. However, you need to design with this technique in mind from the beginning, even if the interface only exposes a few simple options.

## Document-View Architecture

Many developers will recognize document-view architecture as a staple of MFC design. In .NET, the emphasis is less critical because custom form classes can be equipped with most of the intelligence they need (as you saw in our refresh example), and don't require an additional separation between the document and the view. Tasks that typically required views, like scrolling, are dealt with effortlessly with the built-in smarts of most .NET controls.

On the other hand, there are several scenarios that are particularly well suited to a dedicated document-view architecture:

- When you are using complex documents.

- When you are providing more than one view of the same document.

- When you want the flexibility to provide different views in separate windows or in a single window.

When discussing MDI interfaces, a *document* is the actual underlying data. For example, with Microsoft Word the document is the memo, report, or résumé the user is composing. The *view* is a window onto the document. For example, the view in Microsoft Word might just include the page that is currently being edited (which can be scrolled to different pages).

A typical document-view application uses the following ingredients:

- A document class.

- A document view class that references an instance of a document.

- An MDI child class that hosts the view.

- An MDI container that holds all the MDI children.

Why would a document require more than one view? It's easy to think of a view as a window into a different part of a document, but a view can also correspond to a *representation* of the document. For example, you could have an editing view where changes are made and a print preview that shows the final layout. Both views represent the same data in different ways and must be synchronized. However, they can't be cleanly dealt with in a single class. Similarly, you might have a document object that corresponds to a large amount of information from a database. You could simultaneously view this as a grid of records and as a diagram with two different views. Yet another example is an HTML file, which can be viewed as straight text or marked-up content.

## A Document-View Ordering Program

Our next example presents a fairly sophisticated model that supports real-time previews using the document-view architecture. It includes the following ingredients:

- An Order document object that contains a list of OrderItem objects.

- Two view objects: OrderPrintPreview and OrderGridView. Both derive from the UserControl class, but they could be implemented just as easily using a Panel or some other control.

- A Child form class, which can display either of the two view objects.

- A main Parent class, which provides a toolbar and the event handling logic that creates the document objects and displays the child windows.

- Resource classes, like Product, which represents an individual product, and PriceList, which provides a shared GetItem() method that accepts a product ID and returns a Product object with product information.

Figure 10-7 shows the relationship of some of the classes in this example.

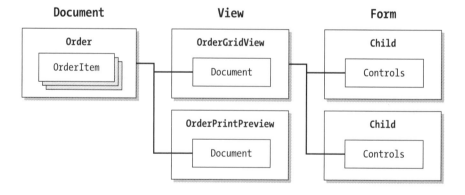

*Figure 10-7. The document-view architecture in the ordering program*

## Document Class

The heart of this application is the document class called Order, which represents a collection of items in a sales order. Because this is a fairly long piece of code, it helps to attack it piecemeal. The first ingredient is the Product class, which represents a single item that can be ordered from the product catalog.

```
Public Class Product
    Public Name As String
    Public Description As String
    Public Price As Decimal

    Public Sub New(ByVal name As String, ByVal description As String, _
      ByVal price As Decimal)
        Me.Name = name
        Me.Description = description
        Me.Price = price
    End Sub
End Class
```

In an order, each product is identified solely by product ID. Here's the OrderItem class, which represents a line item in an order:

```
Public Class OrderItem
    Public ID As Integer

    Public Sub New(ID As Integer)
        Me.ID = ID
```

Next is the Order class, which is created as a custom collection by deriving from the CollectionBase class. This trick provides an added benefit to all clients, ensuring that they can easily iterate through the order items using For/Each syntax. It also prevents deficient code from trying to add any objects other than OrderItem instances.

Here's the basic framework for the Order class:

```
Public Class Order
    Inherits CollectionBase

    Event DocumentChanged(ByVal sender As Object, ByVal e As EventArgs)

    Private _LastFilename As String = "[New Order]"
```

```
Public Property LastFileName() As String
    Get
        Return _LastFilename
    End Get
    Set(ByVal Value As String)
        _LastFilename = Value
    End Set
End Property


Public Sub Add(ByVal item As OrderItem)
    Me.List.Add(item)
    OnDocumentChanged(New EventArgs())
End Sub


Public Sub Remove(ByVal Index As Integer)
    ' Check to see if there is an item at the supplied index.
    If Index > Count - 1 Or Index < 0 Then
        Throw New System.IndexOutOfRangeException()
    Else
        List.RemoveAt(Index)
    End If
    OnDocumentChanged(New EventArgs())
End Sub


Public ReadOnly Property Item(ByVal Index As Integer) As OrderItem
    Get
        ' The appropriate item is retrieved from the List object and
        ' explicitly cast to the OrderItem type.
        Return CType(List.Item(Index), OrderItem)
    End Get
End Property


Protected Sub OnDocumentChanged(ByVal e As EventArgs)
    ' Note that this currently occurs as items are added or removed,
    ' but not when they are edited. To overcome this would require adding
    ' an additional OrderItem change event.
    RaiseEvent DocumentChanged(Me, e)
End Sub
End Class
```

The OnDocumentChanged() method is a critically important ingredient. This is the key that allows other views to update themselves when the list of items in the order is changed (either by adding a new item or removing an existing one).

The Order class also includes two additional document-specific methods, Save and Open, which transfer the data to and from a file:

```
Public Sub Open(ByVal filename As String)
    Dim s As New FileStream(filename, FileMode.Open)
    Dim r As New StreamReader(s)

    Do
        Me.Add(New OrderItem(CType(r.ReadLine, Integer)))
    Loop Until r.Peek() = -1

    r.Close()
    s.Close()

    ' By placing this last we ensure that the file will not be updated
    ' if a load error occurs.
    Me.LastFileName = filename
End Sub

Public Sub Save(ByVal filename As String)
    Dim s As New FileStream(filename, FileMode.Create)
    Dim w As New StreamWriter(s)

    Dim Item As OrderItem
    For Each Item In Me.List
        w.WriteLine(Item.ID)
    Next

    w.Close()
    s.Close()

    ' Note: a real pricing program would probably store the price in the file
    ' (required for orders) but update it to correspond with the current
    ' price for the item when the file is opened.

    ' By placing this last we ensure that the file will not be updated
    ' if a save error occurs.
    Me.LastFileName = filename
End Sub
```

All in all, the Order class is really built out of three parts: It contains data (the collection or OrderItem objects), it provides the functionality for saving and opening files, and it provides the DocumentChanged event that will prompt the appropriate views to update themselves when any changes are detected.

### OrderGridView class

The OrderGridView presents a ListView that displays all the order items and provides support for adding and removing items. The view is created as a user control, which allows it to hold various combined controls and be tailored at design-time. The ListView is anchored so that it grows as the dimensions of the user control expand (see Figure 10-8).

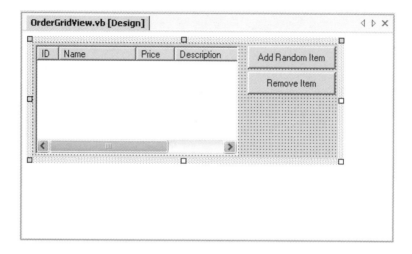

*Figure 10-8. The OrderGridView*

```
Public Class OrderGridView
    Inherits System.Windows.Forms.UserControl
    ' (Designer code omitted.)

    Public WithEvents Document As Order

    Public Sub New(ByVal document As Order)
        ' This is required to make sure the controls that were added at
        ' design-time are actually rendered.
        Me.New()

        ' Store a reference to the document and refresh the display.
        Me.Document = document
        RefreshList(Me, Nothing)
    End Sub
```

```vbnet
' Update the ListView control with the new document contents.
Private Sub RefreshList(ByVal sender As Object, _
  ByVal e As System.EventArgs) Handles Document.DocumentChanged
    If Not list Is Nothing Then

        ' For best performance, disable refreshes while updating the list.
        list.SuspendLayout()

        list.Items.Clear()

        ' Step through the list of items in the document.
        Dim Item As OrderItem
        Dim ItemProduct As Product
        Dim ItemDisplay As ListViewItem
        For Each Item In Me.Document
            ItemDisplay = list.Items.Add(Item.ID)
            ItemProduct = PriceList.GetItem(Item.ID)
            ItemDisplay.SubItems.Add(ItemProduct.Name)
            ItemDisplay.SubItems.Add(ItemProduct.Price)
            ItemDisplay.SubItems.Add(ItemProduct.Description)
        Next

        list.ResumeLayout()
    End If

End Sub

Private Sub cmdAdd_Click(ByVal sender As System.Object, _
  ByVal e As System.EventArgs) Handles cmdAdd.Click
    ' Add a random item.
    Dim RandomItem As New Random()
    Document.Add(New OrderItem(RandomItem.Next(1, 4)))
End Sub

Private Sub cmdRemove_Click(ByVal sender As System.Object, _
  ByVal e As System.EventArgs) Handles cmdRemove.Click
    ' Remove the current item.
    ' The ListView Is configured for single-selection only.
    Document.Remove(list.SelectedIndices(0))
End Sub

End Class
```

Our simple example doesn't provide an additional product catalog—instead, a random order item is added every time the Add button is clicked. It also doesn't include any code for editing items. None of these details would change the overall model being used.

You should also notice that the RefreshList() method handles the DocumentChanged event, ensuring that the list is rebuilt if any change is made by any view (or even through code).

### OrderPrintPreview class

The OrderPrintPreview class is also a user control, but it only contains a single instance of the PrintPreview control. Once again, this example has been left intentionally crude. You could easily add other controls for zooming, moving from page to page, and otherwise configuring the print preview. Similarly, the printed output is very basic, and doesn't include details like an attractive title or letterhead. Figure 10-9 shows the OrderPrintPreview view in action.

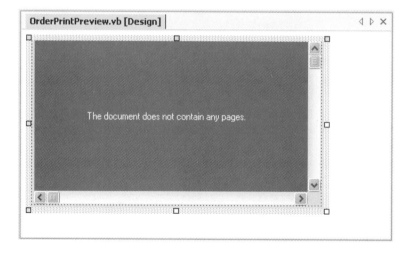

*Figure 10-9. The OrderPrintPreview*

The OrderPrintPreview class follows a similar design to the OrderGridView. A reference to the document is set in the constructor, and the RefreshList() method handles the DocumentChanged event. The only difference is that the RefreshList() needs to initiate printing using a PrintDocument instance. The PrintDocument.PrintPage event handler writes the output to the preview window.

```vb
Imports System.Drawing.Printing

Public Class OrderPrintPreview
    Inherits System.Windows.Forms.UserControl
    ' (Designer code omitted.)

    Public WithEvents Document As Order
    Public WithEvents PrintDoc As New PrintDocument()

    Public Sub New(ByVal document As Order)
        ' This is required to make sure the controls that were added at
        ' design-time are actually rendered.
        Me.New()

        ' Store a reference to the document and refresh the display.
        Me.Document = document
        RefreshList(Me, Nothing)
    End Sub

    Private Sub RefreshList(ByVal sender As Object, _
      ByVal e As System.EventArgs) Handles Document.DocumentChanged
        ' Setting this property starts the preview,
        ' even if the PrintDoc document is already assigned.
        Preview.Document = PrintDoc
    End Sub

    ' Tracks placement while printing.
    Private ItemNumber As Integer

    ' The print font.
    Private PrintFont As New Font("Tahoma", 14, FontStyle.Bold)

    Private Sub PrintDoc_PrintPage(ByVal sender As Object, _
      ByVal e As System.Drawing.Printing.PrintPageEventArgs) _
      Handles PrintDoc.PrintPage
        ' Tracks the line position on the page.
        Dim y As Integer = 70

        ' Step through the items and write them to the page.
        Dim Item As OrderItem
        Dim ItemProduct As Product
        For ItemNumber = ItemNumber To Document.Count - 1
```

```
                    Item = Document.Item(ItemNumber)
                    e.Graphics.DrawString(Item.ID.ToString(), PrintFont, _
                                    Brushes.Black, 70, y)
                    ItemProduct = PriceList.GetItem(Item.ID)
                    e.Graphics.DrawString(ItemProduct.Name, PrintFont, _
                                    Brushes.Black, 120, y)
                    e.Graphics.DrawString(ItemProduct.Price.ToString(), PrintFont, _
                                    Brushes.Black, 350, y)

                    ' Check if more pages are required.
                    If (y + 30) > e.MarginBounds.Height And _
                      ItemNumber < (Document.Count - 1) Then
                        e.HasMorePages = True
                        Exit Sub
                    End If

                    ' Move to the next line.
                    y += 20

            Next

            ' Printing is finished.
            ItemNumber = 0
            e.HasMorePages = False
        End Sub

    End Class
```

> **TIP**  *Printing operations are threaded asynchronously, which allows you to code lengthy RefreshList() code without worrying. However, if you create other views that need to perform time-consuming work in their automatic refresh routines (like analyzing statistical data), you should perform the work on a separate thread, and callback at the end to display the final results. Chapter 7 shows an example of this technique with the BitmapViewer custom control.*

## Child form class

So far, everything is designed according to the document-view ideal. Most of the data manipulation logic is concentrated in the Order class, while most of the presentation logic is encapsulated in the view classes. All that's left for the child form is to create the appropriate view and display it. This is implemented by adding an additional constructor to the form class that accepts an Order document object.

```
Public Class Child
    Inherits System.Windows.Forms.Form
    ' (Designer code omitted.)

    Enum ViewType
        ItemGrid
        PrintPreview
    End Enum

    Public Document As Order

    Public Sub New(ByVal doc As Order, ByVal viewType As ViewType)
        ' This is required to make sure the controls that were added at
        ' design-time are actually rendered.
        Me.New()

        ' Configure the title.
        Me.Text = doc.LastFileName
        Me.Document = doc

        ' Create a reference for the view.
        ' This reference can accomodate any type of control.
        Dim View As Control

        ' Instantiate the appropriate view.
        Select Case viewType
            Case viewType.ItemGrid
                View = New OrderGridView(doc)
            Case viewType.PrintPreview
                View = New OrderPrintPreview(doc)
        End Select

        ' Add the view to the form.
        View.Dock = DockStyle.Fill
        Me.Controls.Add(View)
    End Sub

End Class
```

One advantage to this design is that you could easily create a child window that hosts a combination of views (for example, grid views for two different orders, or a grid view and print preview for the same document). This could even provide the flexibility to change the interface to an SDI style.

## The Parent form class

The MDI parent provides a toolbar with basic options, and the typical event handling logic that allows users to open, close, and save documents. This code follows true "switchboard" style, and relies heavily on the other classes to actually perform the work.

```
Public Class Parent
    Inherits System.Windows.Forms.Form
    '(Designer code omitted.)

    Private LastDir As String = "C:\Temp"

    Private Sub ToolBar1_ButtonClick(ByVal sender As Object, _
      ByVal e As System.Windows.Forms.ToolBarButtonClickEventArgs) _
      Handles ToolBar1.ButtonClick

        ' Show open dialog and allow user to open an existing order.
        If e.Button Is cmdOpen Then
            Dim dlgOpen As New OpenFileDialog()
            dlgOpen.InitialDirectory = LastDir
            dlgOpen.Filter = "Order Files (*.ord)|*.ord"

            ' Show open dialog and allow user to open an existing order.
            If dlgOpen.ShowDialog() = DialogResult.OK Then
                Dim Doc As New Order()

                Try
                    Doc.Open(dlgOpen.FileName)
                Catch err As Exception
                    ' All exceptions bubble up to this level.
                    MessageBox.Show(err.ToString())
                    Exit Sub
                End Try
```

```vb
            Dim frmChild As New Child(Doc, Child.ViewType.ItemGrid)
            frmChild.MdiParent = Me
            frmChild.Show()
        End If

    ' Create new order.
    ElseIf e.Button Is cmdNew Then
        Dim doc As New Order()
        Dim frmChild As New Child(Doc, Child.ViewType.ItemGrid)
        frmChild.MdiParent = Me
        frmChild.Show()

    ' Save current order.
    ElseIf e.Button Is cmdSave Then
        If Not Me.ActiveMdiChild Is Nothing Then
            Dim dlgSave As New SaveFileDialog()
            Dim Doc As Order = CType(Me.ActiveMdiChild, Child).Document
            dlgSave.FileName = Doc.LastFileName
            dlgSave.Filter = "Order Files (*.ord)|*.ord"

            If dlgSave.ShowDialog() = DialogResult.OK Then
                Try
                    Doc.save(dlgSave.FileName)
                    Me.ActiveMdiChild.Text = dlgSave.FileName
                Catch err As Exception
                    ' All exceptions bubble up to this level.
                    MessageBox.Show(err.ToString())
                    Exit Sub
                End Try
            End If
        End If

    ' Close the active order.
    ElseIf e.Button Is cmdClose Then
        If Not Me.ActiveMdiChild Is Nothing Then
            Me.ActiveMdiChild.Close()
        End If

    ' Launch a print preview child for the active order.
    ElseIf e.Button Is cmdPreview Then
        If Not Me.ActiveMdiChild Is Nothing Then
            Dim Doc As Order = CType(Me.ActiveMdiChild, Child).Document
```

```
                        Dim frmChild As New Child(Doc, Child.ViewType.PrintPreview)
                        frmChild.MdiParent = Me
                        frmChild.Show()
                    End If
                End If

            End Sub

        End Class
```

One interesting detail is the event handling code for the preview button. It determines whether there is a current document, and if there is, it opens a preview window with the same underlying document object.

Figure 10-10 shows the finished application with its synchronized views. You can peruse the full code in the DocumentView project included with the samples for this chapter.

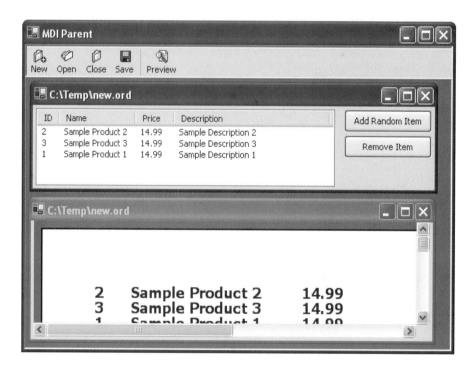

*Figure 10-10. Synchronized views on the same document*

# Floating Windows and Docking

Everyone expects an MDI interface to sport dockable windows and toolbars—floating controls that can be latched into place or left hovering above your application. Unfortunately, designing this type of interface is surprisingly awkward. Windows (and previous application frameworks) do not provide native support for most of these features. Instead, the developer has to resort to some creative coding to implement a solution. As a side effect, docked and floating windows never look exactly the same in any two Windows applications—even if those two applications are both written by Microsoft programmers. Every solution has drawbacks and advantages.

## *Floating Toolbars*

By default, when you create a toolbar it is automatically docked to the top of the form. However, it doesn't need to be—as with any .NET control, you can set the Dock property to modify this behavior.

To create a toolbar that can float, you need to add some additional logic to the mouse events that detect if the toolbar is clicked and "pulled" downward or rightward. In the next example, the toolbar is disconnected after 20 pixels of a movement in either direction. Then other event-handling logic comes into play, which allows the control to be dragged around the surface of the MDI container.

Here's the code that needs to be added to the Form class to support this design. It's similar to the dragging code developed in Chapter 4, as it combines MouseDown, MouseMove, and MouseUp event handlers to manage the process of moving the floating control.

```
Private DraggingToolbar As Boolean
Private DraggedFrom As Point

Private Sub ToolBar1_MouseDown(ByVal sender As Object, _
  ByVal e As System.Windows.Forms.MouseEventArgs) Handles ToolBar1.MouseDown
    DraggingToolbar = True
    DraggedFrom = New Point(e.X, e.Y)
    ToolBar1.Capture = True
End Sub

Private Sub ToolBar1_MouseMove(ByVal sender As Object, _
  ByVal e As System.Windows.Forms.MouseEventArgs) Handles ToolBar1.MouseMove
    If DraggingToolbar Then
        If ToolBar1.Dock = DockStyle.Top Then
```

```
                    ' Check it the dragging has reached the threshold.
                    If (DraggedFrom.X < e.X - 20) Or (DraggedFrom.Y < e.Y - 20) Then
                        DraggingToolbar = False

                        ' Disconnect the toolbar.
                        ToolBar1.Dock = DockStyle.None
                        ToolBar1.Location = New Point(10, 10)
                        ToolBar1.Size = New Size(200, 100)
                        ToolBar1.BorderStyle = BorderStyle.FixedSingle
                    End If

            ElseIf ToolBar1.Dock = DockStyle.None Then
                ToolBar1.Left = e.X + ToolBar1.Left - DraggedFrom.X
                ToolBar1.Top = e.Y + ToolBar1.Top - DraggedFrom.Y
            End If
        End If
End Sub

Private Sub ToolBar1_MouseUp(ByVal sender As Object, _
   ByVal e As System.Windows.Forms.MouseEventArgs) Handles ToolBar1.MouseUp
     DraggingToolbar = False
     ToolBar1.Capture = False
End Sub
```

Figure 10-11 shows the toolbar in its "floating" state.

*Figure 10-11. Creating a floating toolbar*

A key technique in this example is the use of the Control.Capture property. By setting this property to True, the code ensures that mouse events will be received, even if the mouse moves off the control. This allows the user to drag the toolbar from its docked position by clicking at the bottom of the control and dragging down *off* the surface of the toolbar. This step wasn't required for our simple dragging examples in Chapter 4, because the control was never fixed. Instead, it always moved to keep under the mouse pointer.

There's still one aspect missing from the draggable toolbar: it doesn't automatically reattach itself. To accomplish this, you simply need to add some code in the MouseMove event that checks how close the toolbar is to top of the form. If it is within a given threshold, the toolbar should return to its fixed position.

Here's the rewritten mouse move code that allows automatic docking to the top or left sides.

```
Private Sub ToolBar1_MouseMove(ByVal sender As Object, _
  ByVal e As System.Windows.Forms.MouseEventArgs) Handles ToolBar1.MouseMove
    If DraggingToolbar Then
        If ToolBar1.Dock = DockStyle.Top Then

            ' (Code for undocking omitted.)

        ElseIf ToolBar1.Dock = DockStyle.None Then
            ToolBar1.Left = e.X + ToolBar1.Left - DraggedFrom.X
            ToolBar1.Top = e.Y + ToolBar1.Top - DraggedFrom.Y

            If ToolBar1.Top < 5 Then
                DraggingToolbar = False

                ' Re-dock the control.
                ToolBar1.Dock = DockStyle.Top
                ToolBar1.BorderStyle = BorderStyle.None
            ElseIf ToolBar1.Left < 5 Then
                DraggingToolbar = False

                ' Re-dock the control.
                ToolBar1.Dock = DockStyle.Left
                ToolBar1.BorderStyle = BorderStyle.None
            End If
        End If
    End If
End Sub
```

These techniques are simple building blocks that can lead to a fairly sophisticated interface. You can experiment with the FloatingToolbar project, which is included with the samples for this chapter.

## Unusual controls

The preceding example also paves the way to creating your own "coolbar" type of control that provides other .NET controls (like drop-down list controls) in a dockable toolbar. All you need to do is create a custom user control that contains a Panel control and the controls you want to use. You can then use that control with exactly the same docking code used for the toolbar example. Remember, in .NET any type of control can be dragged over the surface of an MDI container.

> **TIP**   *With several dockable controls, you'll want to rewrite the code to be more generic, so that it automatically works with the sender control, instead of assuming a specific control. You would also add docking information to a hash table collection, indexed under the control reference.*

## Dockable Windows

Dockable windows use a similar concept to floating toolbars, but require a little more finesse. The problem is that window movement is handled automatically by Windows, and can't be easily altered in your code.

A typical approach to create a dockable window is to create a toolbox-border window, and then check its position in the Form.LocationChanged or Form.Move event handler. If you find that it is within certain range from one of the form sides, you could then manually move it to so that it sits flush against the border.

Unfortunately, several problems arise with this approach. It's possible to react after the position of a window has changed, but it's not possible to prevent attempted changes (and thus "fix" a window into place). Generally, a docked window should only move if the user clicks and drags it beyond a specified threshold. However, if the user has configured their system settings to show window contents while dragging, there could be a significant amount of flicker as the window battles between the user's movement and the code's attempt to resist. It's for this reason that the Visual Studio .NET dockable windows (and those in earlier Visual Studio versions) never show their contents while dragging. All you see is a grey transparent outline, regardless of your system settings.

## Dockable windows with owner-drawn controls

One of the ways that you can create fake dockable windows is to create your own owner-drawn control that attempts to look as much like a window as possible. This fake window can use the technique you applied with the floating toolbar, which allows you to drag it across the surface of an MDI container and automatically latch it onto a side. Best of all, you have complete control over when the window does and doesn't move. Unfortunately, you will have to take some effort to ensure that your control mimics a real window closely enough, and takes into account the current system colors and font. This painful approach is used in many modern Windows applications, although this chapter won't attempt it.

## Dockable windows with timers

One of the key problems you'll face while trying to create dockable windows is the fact that forms don't fire MouseUp events when the user finishes dragging them (instead, mouse events are reserved for actions in the client area). Typically, you would use a MouseUp event handler to dock the control.

You can code around this limitation with a little desperate ingenuity, by manually polling the state of the mouse when a dock is potentially about to take place. That's the technique used in your next example, which provides two forms: MDIMain and Floater, the dockable window.

When the program first starts, MDIMain creates an instance of the Floater window and displays it. Note that the Floater is not a child window but an owned form. That means it can be moved anywhere on the screen, but will always appear above the MDIMain form. This is simply a design decision—the Floater window could also be created as a child window.

```
Private Sub MDIMain_Load(ByVal sender As System.Object, _
  ByVal e As System.EventArgs) Handles MyBase.Load

    Dim frmFloat As New Floater()
    frmFloat.Owner = Me
    frmFloat.Show()

End Sub
```

Some of the most interesting code takes place in the Move event handler for the floating window. Here, the current position of the form is examined:

```
Dim DockTestAt As Point

Private Sub Floater_Move(ByVal sender As Object, ByVal e As System.EventArgs) _
   Handles MyBase.Move

   ' Determine the current location in parent form coordinates.
Dim MouseAt As Point =Me.Owner.PointToClient(Me.Location)

' Dertimine if the floater is close enough to dock.
    If MouseAt.X < 5 And MouseAt.X > -5 Then
        If Me.MouseButtons And MouseButtons.Left = MouseButtons.Left Then
            DockTestAt = MouseAt

            ' Show dock focus rectangle.
            CType(Me.Owner, MDIMain).DrawDockRectangle = True

            ' Reset timer to poll for MouseUp event.
            tmrDock.Enabled = False
            tmrDock.Enabled = True

        End If
    End If
End Sub
```

If the floating window is within a predefined threshold of the left border of the owner form, the floating window instructs the owner to draw a dock cue: a grey rectangle in the spot where the dock will be performed. This is performed by setting the custom MDIMain.DrawDockRectangle property.

```
Public Property DrawDockRectangle() As Boolean
    Get
        Return pnlDock.Visible
    End Get
    Set(ByVal Value As Boolean)
        pnlDock.Visible = Value
    End Set
End Property
```

All this property does is hide or show a Panel control. The panel provides its own logic to draw a hatched border outline, as shown in Figure 10-12.

```
Private Sub pnlDock_Paint(ByVal sender As System.Object, _
  ByVal e As System.Windows.Forms.PaintEventArgs) Handles pnlDock.Paint

    Dim DockCueBrush As New HatchBrush(HatchStyle.LightDownwardDiagonal, _
                                       Color.White, Color.Gray)
    Dim DockCuePen As New Pen(DockCueBrush, 10)
    e.Graphics.DrawRectangle(DockCuePen, _
                             New Rectangle(0, 0, pnlDock.Width, pnlDock.Height))


End Sub
```

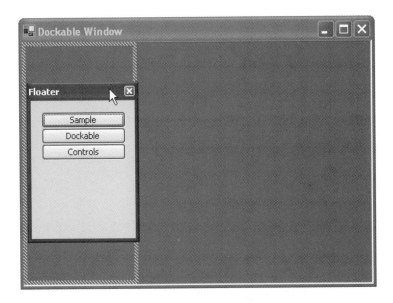

*Figure 10-12. A dock cue*

This isn't the only action that's taken when the floating window is in a valid dock position. The floating window also begins polling to check if the mouse button is released by enabling a timer.

```
Private Sub tmrDock_Tick(ByVal sender As System.Object, _
  ByVal e As System.EventArgs) Handles tmrDock.Tick

    If DockTestAt.X = Me.Owner.PointToClient(Me.Location).X _
      And DockTestAt.Y = Me.Owner.PointToClient(Me.Location).Y Then
```

```
            If Me.MouseButtons = MouseButtons.None Then
                ' Dock in place.
                tmrDock.Enabled = False
                CType(Me.Owner, MDIMain).AddToDock(Me)
            End If


        Else
            ' Mouse has moved. Disable this dock attempt.
            tmrDock.Enabled = False
            CType(Me.Owner, MDIMain).DrawDockRectangle = False
        End If

End Sub
```

If the form is moved, the polling is disabled, and the dock cue is hidden. If the mouse button is released while the form is still in the same place, docking is initiated using the MDIMain.AddToDock() method.

```
Public Sub AddToDock(ByVal frm As Form)
    ' Allow the form to be contained in a container control.
    frm.TopLevel = False
    pnlDock.Controls.Add(frm)

    ' Don't let the form be dragged off.
    frm.WindowState = FormWindowState.Maximized
End Sub
```

This is one of the most unusual pieces of code in this example. It works by adding the form to the Controls collection of another container, and maximizing it so that it can't be moved. This seemingly bizarre approach is possible as long as you disable the TopLevel property of the form. The docked window is shown in Figure 10-13.

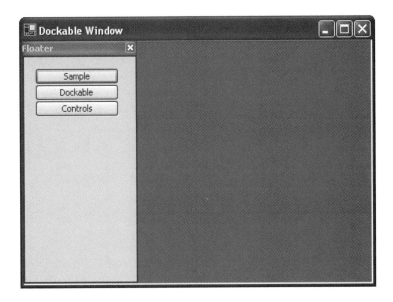

*Figure 10-13. A docked window*

One benefit of this approach is that it is fairly easy to create a system with multiple dockable windows, just by adding separate Panel for each form into one fixed Panel control. You can set the Dock property for each form-containing panel to Top or Fill, ensuring that they automatically adjust their sizes to accommodate one another. You could even add splitter bars so the user could alter the relative size of each panel, as demonstrated in Chapter 5.

However, this simple example is a long way away from the docking intelligence of Visual Studio. To perfect this system requires a lot of mundane code and tweaking. For example, in Visual Studio .NET forms aren't pulled out of a docked position based on the amount they are dragged, but also the speed at which the user drags them. Thus, a quick jerk will dislodge a docked form, while a slow pull will leave it in place. Try it out on your own—you'll find a lot of thought has been put in to this behavior. Unfortunately, docked windows are a nonstandardized area of Windows programming, and one where the .NET framework still comes up short.

## The Last Word

This chapter explored MDI programming and design. The chapter began with an introduction to .NET's effortless MDI features, and showed how to use menu merging, simple synchronization, and MDI layout styles. It continued in more detail with a sophisticated example of document-view architecture, which provides the freedom to create multiple synchronized views hosted in separate windows or the same window. Finally, the chapter ended by delving into one of MDI design's hottest topics with an introduction to coding your own dockable windows.

# CHAPTER 11

# Dynamic User Interface

IN VISUAL BASIC PROGRAMMING, one of the most common questions is how can a control be added to a form through code at runtime? The answer is fairly simple, but it becomes more complex—and clumsy—as the programmer tries to add licensed ActiveX controls or handle the events of the newly created control.

In .NET programming, the story is dramatically different. In fact, every .NET control is already created through code. When you add a control to a form and configure its properties using the design editor, Visual Studio .NET generates the appropriate code and adds it to a collapsed region of your Form class. By studying this region of your code, you can quickly learn how to create and add any control you need at runtime.

Of course, creating dynamic user interface is about much more than defining a control class at runtime. It's also a philosophy that breaks free of the shackles of visual design tools and allows you to generate interfaces based on database records, user preferences, or localization needs. This chapter examines some innovative techniques you can use to dynamically generate user interface. It starts with the mandatory button generators, and moves to drawing tools, document applications, and the question of localization. It even considers how you can create a custom form layout engine.

## The Case for Dynamic User Interface

One theme you see in this chapter is the recurring question—how dynamic should a dynamic user interface be? You'll see examples that do little more than add a few simple elements to a form, and others that build the Window dynamically from scratch. So which approach is best?

As usual, it all depends on your project and design goals. To determine where dynamic user interface fits in, you need to consider the role of the user interface designer. Some of the reasons that programmers rely on Visual Studio .NET to create their interface include the following:

- **To design a static interface.** It's far easier to create an interface that won't change for long periods of time with perfect precision and cosmetic appeal using the IDE.

- **It hides the ugly code details.** These are difficult to manage due to the sheer number of lines. .NET controls do not provide constructors that allow important properties to be set, so you need to fall back on multiple property set statements to fully configure your controls.

- **It saves time.** The design-time environment makes it faster to create and maintain an interface. Changes can be applied directly, with little chance of error.

On the other hand, there are some things that user interfaces designed in the IDE don't handle well:

- **If the interface must change according to certain distinct rules.** In this case, you may find yourself writing a great deal of "control tweaking" code. One example of this situation is with a program that needs to have all its text translated to different languages. In this case, it may be a good point to consider a more radical solution that builds the whole interface dynamically. It takes longer to code initially, but it may end up being more manageable.

- **If you need to standardize the consistency of similar but not identical visual elements** (like a common dialog box format). Visual inheritance and user controls may help a little, but their range is limited compared to creating a custom form layout engine.

- **If you want to create a program that allows the user to create an interface.** In some cases, your product might be so customizable that you need to include a separate administrative module that allows a non-programmer to define or modify some aspects of the interface.

- **If you are designing a drawing or diagramming tool.** You could use the GDI+ drawing features described later in this book. However, allowing a user to create a "drawing" out of control objects is a simple shortcut to a vector-based diagramming tool.

These are the types of problems that the discussion centers on in this chapter.

## Creating Controls at Runtime

Creating a control at runtime involves a few simple steps:

1. Create the control object as you would any other class.

2. Set the properties for the control (including basics like size and position).

3. Add the control object to the Controls collection of a container control, like a Form, GroupBox, Panel, or TabPage.

4. If you want to handle any of the control's events, use the AddHandler statement to hook up your code.

To demonstrate this process, consider the sample button generator program shown in Figure 11-1. This program creates a button at the specified position every time the user clicks the Create button. An event handler is attached to every new button's Click event, ensuring that .NET can capture user clicks (and display a brief user message at the bottom of the window).

```vb
Public Class ButtonMaker
    Inherits System.Windows.Forms.Form

    ' (Windows designer code omitted.)

    Private ButtonCount As Integer = 0

    Private Sub cmdCreate_Click(ByVal sender As System.Object, _
      ByVal e As System.EventArgs) Handles cmdCreate.Click
        ButtonCount += 1

        Dim NewButton As New Button()
        NewButton.Text = "Button " & ButtonCount.ToString()
        NewButton.Left = Val(txtLeft.Text)
        NewButton.Top = Val(txtTop.Text)

        AddHandler NewButton.Click, AddressOf ButtonHandler

        Me.Controls.Add(NewButton)
    End Sub

    Private Sub ButtonHandler(ByVal sender As System.Object, _
      ByVal e As System.EventArgs)
        Status.Text = " You clicked ... "
        Status.Text &= CType(sender, Button).Text
    End Sub

End Class
```

*Figure 11-1. A ButtonMaker program*

## A System Tray Application

Sometimes the only reason you create a control at runtime is for cleaner, more logical code. One example is found with "invisible" controls that don't really appear on a form. These include the standard dialog controls (for changing colors, choosing fonts, and viewing a print preview) that we saw in Chapter 5. You could add these controls to a form at design-time, but why bother? Code that creates it dynamically is more readable. On the other hand, if the control is a part of the form (for example, the PrintPreviewControl instead of a PrintPreviewDialog) it makes sense to create and configure it when you are designing the form.

One common example of creating runtime controls for convenience occurs with system tray applications. Often, a system tray application is designed to run quietly in the background, waiting for user interaction or a specific operating system event. This application might even be configured to start every time the computer is logged on. Applications such as this should start minimized in the system tray. You don't want to force the user interact with any unnecessary windows when the application first loads up.

If you build this program by adding a NotifyIcon control to a form at design time, your program will need to load the corresponding form before the icon system tray will appear. If you create the icon in a startup routine at runtime, however, no such limitation applies.

The next example demonstrates exactly such an application. When it first loads, it creates a system tray icon (see Figure 11-2), attaches two menu items to it, and begins monitoring the file system for changes (using the System.IO.FileSystemWatcher class). No windows are displayed.

*Figure 11-2. A dynamic system tray icon*

Here's the essential code for the dynamic system tray icon:

```
Public Module App

    ' Define the system tray icon control.
    Private AppIcon As New NotifyIcon()

    ' Define the menu.
    Private SysTrayMenu As New ContextMenu()
    Private WithEvents DisplayFiles As New MenuItem("Display New Files")
    Private WithEvents ExitApp As New MenuItem("Exit")

    ' Define the file system watcher, and a list to store filenames.
    Private WithEvents Watch As New FileSystemWatcher()
    Private NewFiles As New ArrayList()

    Public Sub Main()
        ' Configure the system tray icon.
        Dim ico As New Icon("icon.ico")
        AppIcon.Icon = ico
        AppIcon.Text = "My .NET Application"

        ' Place the menu items in the menu.
        SysTrayMenu.MenuItems.Add(DisplayFiles)
        SysTrayMenu.MenuItems.Add(ExitApp)
        AppIcon.ContextMenu = SysTrayMenu
```

```
        ' Show the system tray icon.
        AppIcon.Visible = True

        ' Hook up the file watcher.
        Watch.Path = "c:\"
        Watch.IncludeSubdirectories = True
        Watch.EnableRaisingEvents = True

        ' Because no forms are being displayed, you need this
        ' statement to stop the application from automatically ending.
        Application.Run()
    End Sub

End Module
```

This presents the basic application class framework. In order to log newly created files, you need to handle the FileSystemWatch.Created event, and simply add the name of the new file to the ArrayList.

```
Private Sub Watch_Created(ByVal sender As Object, _
  ByVal e As System.IO.FileSystemEventArgs) Handles Watch.Created
    NewFiles.Add(e.Name)
End Sub
```

To enable the system tray icon menu, you also need to add two more event handlers. The menu only provides two options: exit the application or display another window that lists the name of changed files (shown in Figure 11-3).

```
Private Sub ExitApp_Click(ByVal sender As Object, _
  ByVal e As System.EventArgs) Handles ExitApp.Click
    Application.Exit()
End Sub

Private Sub DisplayFiles_Click(ByVal sender As Object, _
  ByVal e As System.EventArgs) Handles DisplayFiles.Click
    Dim frmFileList As New FileList()
    frmFileList.FillList(NewFiles)
    frmFileList.Show()
End Sub
```

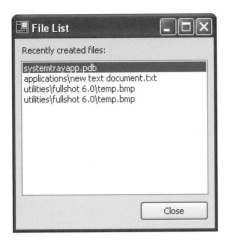

*Figure 11-3. A list of changed files*

Finally, the following code is used in the FileList form to display the ArrayList information. Figure 11-3 shows how the list of changed files might look.

```
Public Class FileList
    Inherits System.Windows.Forms.Form
    ' (Windows designer code omitted.)
    Private Sub cmdClose_Click(ByVal sender As System.Object, _
      ByVal e As System.EventArgs) Handles cmdClose.Click
        Me.Close()
    End Sub

    Public Sub FillList(ByVal List As ArrayList)
        lstFiles.DataSource = List
    End Sub

End Class
```

Of course, though this is a useful example, it's not the only approach to freeing the NotifyIcon from the confines of a form. You could also create the App class as a component by inheriting from System.ComponentModel.Component. (You'll also need to add some additional code to your class, which you can coax Visual Studio .NET into creating by selecting Add ➤ New Component from the Solution Explorer content menu.) Every component has the ability to host design-time controls—just drag-and-drop the control onto the design time view of the class, and Visual Studio .NET will create the code in the special hidden designer region. Using this approach, you could configure the NotifyIcon and the menu items at design-time, without needing to tie them to a form. This is the approach used in Chapter 8 to create a design-time picture box that can store an icon file for the HelpIconProvider control.

> **TIP** *One example of this type of program is a batch file processor. It might scan a directory for files that correspond to work orders or invoices, and immediately add database records, send emails, or perform some other task.*

## Using Controls in a Drawing Program

Drawing programs exist in two basic flavors. Painting programs, like Microsoft Paint, allow users to create a bitmap with static content. Once the user draws a shape or types some text onto the drawing area, it can't be modified or rearranged. In more sophisticated vector-based drawing programs (everything from Adobe Illustrator to Microsoft Visio), the drawing is actually a collection of objects. The user can click and change any object at any time or remove it entirely.

To create a bitmap drawing program is relatively easy, once you learn the appropriate functions for drawing on a form with GDI+. A vector-based drawing or diagramming program, however, is not so easy, because you need to keep track of every object and its location individually. When the user clicks on the drawing surface, you may need some fairly intricate logic to find out which object the user is trying to select, and handle the overlapping painting.

One shortcut to making a drawing program is allowing the user to create drawings out of dynamically generated controls. The next example does exactly that, and demonstrates some fundamentals about handling events and context menus with custom controls.

The basic application (shown in Figure 11-4) allows the user to create squares of any color, and then resize them or move them around the form to any location. The squares are based on label controls with borders, although you could easily add support for additional controls with only a few more lines of code. This drawing program, with a few minor changes, could become an entity diagramming tool for creating class models. It could also become more like a traditional paint program—which is the direction I develop the paint program in through Chapter 13.

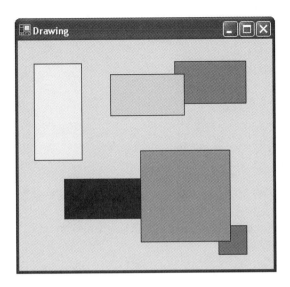

*Figure 11-4. A vector-based drawing application*

The application begins with an empty canvas. To create a square, the user right-clicks the form drawing area, and chooses Create New Square from the context menu. The square then appears (with a default size) at the current mouse location. The code that creates the square is shown in the following:

```
Private Sub mnuNewSquare_Click(ByVal sender As System.Object, _
  ByVal e As System.EventArgs) Handles mnuNewSquare.Click

    ' Create and configure the "square".
    Dim NewLabel As New Label()
    NewLabel.Size = New Size(40, 40)
    NewLabel.BorderStyle = BorderStyle.FixedSingle

    ' To determine where to place the label, you need to convert the
    ' current screen-based mouse coordinates into relative form coordinates.
    NewLabel.Location = Me.PointToClient(Me.MousePosition)

    ' Attach a context menu to the label.
    NewLabel.ContextMenu = mnuLabel
```

```
' Connect the label to all its event handlers.
AddHandler NewLabel.MouseDown, AddressOf lbl_MouseDown
AddHandler NewLabel.MouseMove, AddressOf lbl_MouseMove
AddHandler NewLabel.MouseUp, AddressOf lbl_MouseUp

' Add the label to the form.
Me.Controls.Add(NewLabel)

End Sub
```

There are three things the user can do with a square once it is created:

- Right-click to show its context menu, which provides a single option for changing the color.

- Click and drag it to a new location.

- Click its bottom-right corner and resize it.

All these actions happen in response to the MouseDown event. At this point, the code retrieves a reference that points to the control that fired the event, and then examines whether the right-mouse button was clicked (in which case the menu is shown). If the left mouse button has been clicked, the form switches into resize or drag mode (using one of two Boolean form-level variables), depending on the location of the cursor. Resizing can only be performed from the bottom-right corner.

```
' Keep track of when fake drag or resize mode is enabled.
Private IsDragging As Boolean = False
Private IsResizing As Boolean = False

' Store the location where the user clicked on the control.
Private ClickOffsetX, ClickOffsetY As Integer

Private Sub lbl_MouseDown(ByVal sender As System.Object, _
  ByVal e As System.Windows.Forms.MouseEventArgs)

    ' Retrieve a reference to the active label.
    Dim CurrentCtrl As Control
    CurrentCtrl = CType(sender, Control)
```

```
    If e.Button = MouseButtons.Right Then
        ' Show the context menu.
        CurrentCtrl.ContextMenu.Show(CurrentCtrl, New Point(e.X, e.Y))

    ElseIf e.Button = MouseButtons.Left Then
        ClickOffsetX = e.X
        ClickOffsetY = e.Y

        If (e.X + 5) > CurrentCtrl.Width And (e.Y + 5) > CurrentCtrl.Height Then
            ' The mouse pointer is in the bottom right corner,
            ' so resizing mode is appropriate.
            IsResizing = True
        Else
            ' The mouse is somewhere else, so dragging mode is
            ' appropriate.
            IsDragging = True
        End If
    End If

End Sub
```

The MouseMove event changes the position or size of the square if it is in drag or resize mode. It also changes the cursor to the resize icon to alert the user when the mouse pointer is in the bottom right corner.

```
Private Sub lbl_MouseMove(ByVal sender As Object, _
  ByVal e As System.Windows.Forms.MouseEventArgs)

    ' Retrieve a reference to the active label.
    Dim CurrentCtrl As Control
    CurrentCtrl = CType(sender, Control)

    If IsDragging = True Then
        ' Move the control.
        CurrentCtrl.Left += e.X - ClickOffsetX
        CurrentCtrl.Top += e.Y  - ClickOffsetY

    ElseIf IsResizing = True Then
        ' Resize the control.
        CurrentCtrl.Width = e.X
        CurrentCtrl.Height = e.Y
```

```
    Else
        ' Change the pointer if the mouse is in the bottom corner.
        If (e.X + 5) > CurrentCtrl.Width And (e.Y + 5) > CurrentCtrl.Height Then
            CurrentCtrl.Cursor = Cursors.SizeNWSE
        Else
            CurrentCtrl.Cursor = Cursors.Arrow
        End If
    End If

End Sub
```

Figure 11-5 shows the process of resizing a square.

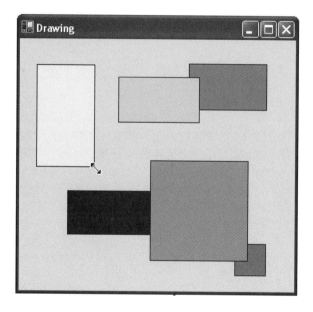

*Figure 11-5. Resizing a square*

The MouseUp event ends the dragging or resizing operation.

```
Private Sub lbl_MouseUp(ByVal sender As System.Object, _
    ByVal e As System.Windows.Forms.MouseEventArgs)
        IsDragging = False
        IsResizing = False
End Sub
```

Finally, the context menu provides a single option which, when clicked, allows the user to change the square's fill color using a common color dialog box. Note that the code retrieves the active control through the SourceControl property of the ContextMenu control.

```
Private Sub mnuColorChange_Click(ByVal sender As System.Object, _
  ByVal e As System.EventArgs) Handles mnuColorChange.Click

    ' Show color dialog.
    Dim dlgColor As New ColorDialog()
    dlgColor.ShowDialog()

    ' Change label background.
    mnuLabel.SourceControl.BackColor = dlgColor.Color

End Sub
```

Figure 11-6 shows how a square's background color can be modified using this color dialog.

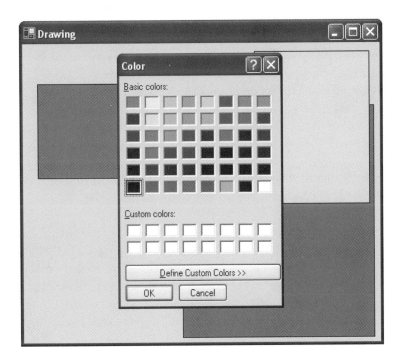

*Figure 11-6. Changing a square's background color*

As written, this simple example could easily grow into a more sophisticated drawing framework. For example, you could add context-menu items that allow the user to set text in the label (and change its font), or configure other properties. You could also change the form's context menu, and add additional options for other controls. You could even use methods like Control.BringToFront and Control.SendToBack to allow squares to be layered in various ways, according to the user's selections. Currently, all the event handlers assume they are dealing with generic control events, and thus work with buttons, text boxes, picture boxes, and just about any other control.

> **TIP** *To make this a perfect drawing program, you would add custom controls that handle their own drawing instead of the label control. That way you could create shaded squares, circles, or other types of shapes. Chapter 12 explains these features with GDI+, and Chapter 13 revisits this program with a more sophisticated example that supports rectangles, ellipses, and triangles.*

## Dynamic Content

When discussing dynamic interfaces, it's useful to draw a distinction between those that generate controls dynamically (like the examples you've just seen), and those that configure their controls dynamically. Dynamic content can appear in just about any situation, but it's most common in these cases:

- Applications that need to be localized or configured for different sets of users.

- Data-driven applications (like product catalogs) that use interfaces designed to closely model the organization of a database.

One simple example of dynamic content is the average About box (shown in Figure 11-7). It rarely makes sense to hard-code information like a program's version directly into the user interface of a window, because it cannot be guaranteed to remain correct (and it can be extremely tedious to synchronize if you use autoincrementing version numbers). Instead, this information should be retrieved dynamically:

```
lblProductName.Text = Application.ProductName
lblProductVersion.Text = "Version: " & Application.ProductVersion.ToString()
lblPath.Text = "Executing in: " & Application.ExecutablePath
```

*Figure 11-7. Dynamic content in the About box*

## Localization

The .NET platform provides considerable support for localizing Windows Forms
through resource files. Using resource files, you ensure that elements that may
change in different product version (for example text labels that need to be translated
into different languages) are embedded in a separate satellite assembly. You can
create different localized versions of your application simply by creating a new
satellite assembly.

The basic process for creating a localizable form is simple:

1. Set the Localizable property for the Form to True using the Properties
   window.

2. Set the Language property of the Form using the Properties window. You'll
   be provided with the full list of recognized local languages, as defined by the
   Windows operating system (see Figure 11-8).

3. Configure the localizable properties of various controls (for example, the
   text of a button). Your settings will be stored in a dedicated resource file
   for this language.

4. Return to step 2 to add information for another language. As soon as you
   change the language, all the localizable properties of the controls on your
   form revert to the settings in the resource file for that language.

*Figure 11-8. Choosing a language when designing a form*

To get a handle on exactly what is going on, select Show All Files from the Projects menu. For every localizable form, you see multiple .resx files with different language identifiers. In fact, there will be one for each language you've configured in the design environment. Figure 11-9 shows an example with two additional languages: German (de) and French (fr).

*Figure 11-9. Multiple .resx files for a form*

When you compile this project, Visual Studio .NET creates a separate directory using the language identifier, and uses it to store the satellite assembly with the localization settings (see Figure 11-10).

The greatest part about this is that you won't have to delete or move files around for different versions. Because of the way probing works with .NET assemblies, you can count on the CLR to automatically inspect the right directory based on the computer's regional settings and load the correct localized text! Or, you can fall back on a code statement like the one that follows to change the program's culture for testing purposes:

```
Thread.CurrentThread.CurrentUICulture = New CultureInfo("fr-FR")
```

*Figure 11-10. Multiple satellite assemblies*

The .NET SDK also ships with a utility called Winres.exe, which is extremely useful for localization. It allows another user to edit the information in an .resx resource file using a scaled down form editor. This is useful because it allows translators and other non-programming professionals to create the locale-specific resource files without allowing them the chance to see sensitive code or inadvertently alter it.

Finally, you should be aware that you can also read and write directly to resource files using the classes in the System.Resources namespace. This is useful if you have localizable strings that can't be configured at design time, like error messages that appear in dialog boxes. This task is beyond the scope of the present discussion.

## A Dynamic Menu Example

Here's an example that demonstrates a simple use of dynamic content. It uses a database table that maps user levels to control access permissions. Depending on the user type, some options may be disabled or hidden entirely.

The database uses three tables (see Figure 11-11). Controls lists the names of available controls in the user interface, Levels lists the supported user levels, and Controls_Levels specifies what controls are allowed for a given user level (using a special State field that indicates 0 for normal, 1 for hidden, and 2 for disabled). All controls are enabled by default, so the only records that need to be added to Controls_Levels are those that specifically hide or disable controls. In a full-blown application, there would probably also be a Users table that indicates what level each user has.

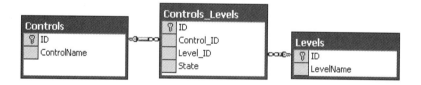

*Figure 11-11. Tables mapping control access permissions*

In this example, the database is configured with the information for two user levels: User and Admin. The different menu structures these users will see are shown in Figure 11-12.

By pulling all the user permission logic out of the user interface and placing it in the database, it becomes very easy to write a small amount of generic code that automatically configures the user interface for the user who is currently logged on:

```
Dim dtPermissions As DataTable

' Get permissions for an Admin-level user.
dtPermissions = DBPermissions.GetPermissions(DBPermissions.Level.Admin)

' Update the menu with these permissions.
SearchMenu(Me.Menu, dtPermissions)
```

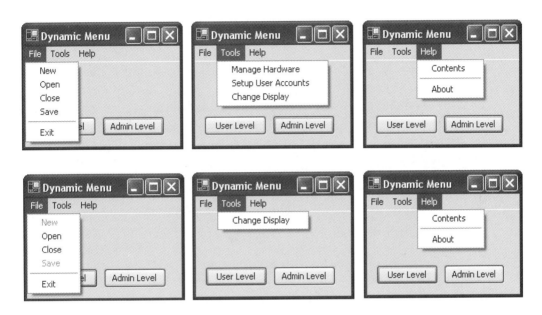

*Figure 11-12. Different menu structures*

The DBPermissions class uses a shared GetPermissions() function that returns a table with all the security information for the specified user level. To remove the chance of errors, it also uses an enumeration that defines the different levels of user access in the database. This is a technique you saw in Chapter 9, where a database class encapsulates all the important information about a database.

```vbnet
Public Class DBPermissions

    Enum State
        Normal = 0
        Disabled = 1
        Hidden = 2
    End Enum

    Enum Level
        Admin
        User
    End Enum

    Private Shared con As New SqlConnection("Data Source=localhost;" & _
     "Integrated Security=SSPI;Initial Catalog=Apress;")

    Public Shared Function GetPermissions(ByVal UserLevel As Level) As DataTable

        con.Open()

        ' Permissions isn't actually actually a table in our data source.
        ' Instead, it's a view that combines the important information
        ' from all three tables using a Join query.
        Dim SelectPermissions As String = "SELECT * FROM Permissions "

        Select Case UserLevel
            Case Level.Admin
                SelectPermissions &= "WHERE LevelName = 'Admin'"
            Case Level.User
                SelectPermissions &= "WHERE LevelName = 'User'"
        End Select

        Dim cmd As New SqlCommand(SelectPermissions, con)
        Dim adapter As New SqlDataAdapter(cmd)
        Dim ds As New DataSet()
        adapter.Fill(ds, "Permissions")

        con.Close()

        Return ds.Tables("Permissions")

    End Function

End Class
```

Finally, the form's SearchMenu() function recursively tunnels through the menu, hiding or disabling controls as indicated in the permissions table.

```
Private Sub SearchMenu(ByVal Menu As Menu, ByVal dtPermissions As DataTable)

    Dim RowMatch() As DataRow

    Dim mnuItem As MenuItem
    For Each mnuItem In Menu.MenuItems

        ' See if this menu item has a corresponding row.
        RowMatch = dtPermissions.Select("ControlName = '" & mnuItem.Text & "'")

        ' If it does, configure the menu item state accordingly.
        If RowMatch.GetLength(0) > 0 Then
            Select Case RowMatch(0)("State")
                Case DBPermissions.State.Hidden
                    mnuItem.Visible = False
                Case DBPermissions.State.Disabled
                    mnuItem.Enabled = False
            End Select
        Else
            ' Default all controls to visible and enabled.
            mnuItem.Visible = True
            mnuItem.Enabled = True
        End If

        ' Search recursively through any submenus.
        If mnuItem.MenuItems.Count > 0 Then
            SearchMenu(mnuItem, dtPermissions)
        End If

    Next

End Sub
```

Best of all, if the permissions need to change or another access level needs to be added, only the database needs to be modified. An application created in this way is easy to maintain without painful recompiles and redeployment.

Our example dynamically configures menus, but there are other approaches. For example, you could disable controls in a form (at which point you would probably want to add a FormName field to the Controls table). Chapter 14 demonstrates a similar technique with dynamic help content. You could also use a similar model to create localizable content for your menus. Instead of mapping controls to user levels with a State field, you would use a Text field that would be applied to the control's Text property.

> **NOTE**  *You could even extend this system to make a radically configurable interface supporting user-selected themes. But beware of going too far. The more variation your application supports, the more difficult it is to create support material and solve problems in the field. This is the classic flexibility versus ease-of-use dilemma.*

## Data-Driven Programming

An extreme example of dynamic content is found in applications that generate their entire interface using the information in a database record. This approach isn't suited for all types of programs, but it can be a lifesaver in certain data-driven applications, saving you hours of recompiling, and providing other non-programmers with the tools they need to modify and configure your program.

Occasionally, a programmer develops a system that allows every aspect of a form to be defined in a database record or XML document. This type of approach is rarely useful because it requires too much code. However, specialized applications might use a scaled down version of these techniques, like a survey-generation tool that allows you to define a collection of forms that represent the questions of a survey. The most common example of all is a pricing application, where the program must match the product catalog as closely as possible. This is the type of application considered in the next section. I don't present any code for creating this program because it's quite similar to the previous example, and is mostly centered on retrieving information from a database. Instead, I will sketch out the basic structure for the whole application in the next section.

## A Data-Driven Pricing Application

The next example demonstrates that, contrary to what three-tier design dictates, tight coupling between the user interface and a data source is acceptable sometimes—in fact, it may be the best approach.

Consider the case where you have a product catalog that changes frequently. The scope of the changes aren't limited to price; new items and categories are regularly added or removed, and different customers enjoy completely different pricing schemes and discount structures. If you write this application ordinarily, you end up creating a great deal of custom code that needs to be tweaked and changed endlessly as the product catalog changes. Sooner or later, these frequent modifications will introduce unexpected errors or make the program difficult to change or extend (for example, if you decide you need to create a new web-based version).

A more successful way to model this problem is to create a program that constructs its interface according to information in a database. So, when adding a product to an order, the user is presented with a list of categories from a list control, with the description for each also read from the database. When the user chooses items from a category, the whole interface is built out of a grid control (in this case, Microsoft's MSFlexGrid ActiveX control that ships with Visual Studio 6), and text boxes are added dynamically for quantity (see Figure 11-13).

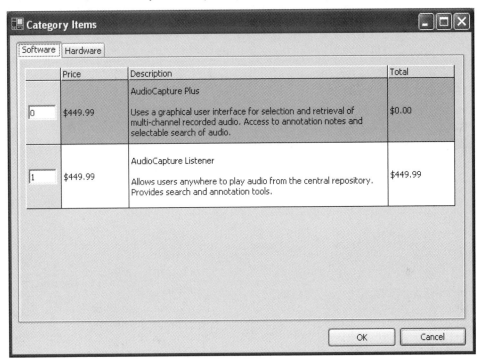

*Figure 11-13. The dynamic ordering window*

The pricing information is also read from a database. However, the pricing is not product-specific. Instead, every product has a basic price (as listed in the Products table). Additionally, a Pricing table lists different pricing schemes, and gives each one a descriptive name. The Pricing_Products table maps these two tables together, assigning each product multiple prices—one for each pricing system. The database structure is diagrammed in Figure 11-14.

*Figure 11-14. Pricing table structure*

This application would typically ship with a special admin tool that is little more than a glorified database editor. It would allow the sales department to modify the list of products, change prices, and add new pricing schemes. This system is great for salespeople, who love to invent new price structures for every customer.

> **NOTE**  *The data-driven design you looked at in this example is even more common in web applications.*

## Control Layout Engines

As you've seen, the .NET forms architecture provides support for laying out controls using coordinates in a grid. This approach, combined with the built-in support for docking and anchoring, gives developers a rich layout environment.

However, there are times when grid layout is not necessarily the best approach. For example, you may need a container control that automatically lays out child controls according to different rules, perhaps adjusting them to accommodate the width of the largest control or shrinking them to fit the size of the container, to name just two possibilities. You could create a custom user control to encapsulate this type of functionality, but that wouldn't let you use the same layout logic in different containers (for example, forms, group boxes, and tabs). To provide a more generic, reusable system, you need to create a layout manager.

A layout manager is a class that dictates the layout of child controls in a container. Ideally, a layout manager can be reused with any type of child control and applied to any type of container.

> **NOTE** *If you've programmed with Java before, the idea of layout managers is nothing new. Some layout managers provided for Java containers sinclude FlowLayout (similar to a word processor), BorderLayout (which divides the screen into five zones), CardLayout (like a stack of cards layered on to of each other), GridLayout (which allows one component per equal-sized cell), and GridBagLayout (which adds support for variable control sizes and location with a grid).*

Generally, a layout manager connects itself to the action by listening for layout events from the container control. It then iterates through all the items in the Controls collection, and arranges them accordingly. Depending on the layout manager, this may mean ignoring the Location property and even the Size property of each control. It could also involve inspecting other extended properties, as I discuss at the end of this section.

## The SingleLineFlow Layout Manager

A good example of a simple layout provider is shown with the following Single-LineFlow example. It lays out one control per line, from top to bottom, and gives each control the width of the container. It's ideal for a property page display (as with a TabPage container control).

```
Public Class SingeLineFlow

    Private WithEvents _Container As Control
    Private _margin As Integer

    Public Sub New(ByVal parent As Control, ByVal margin As Integer)
        _Container = parent
        _margin = margin
        UpdateLayout(Me, Nothing)
    End Sub
```

```
Public Property Margin() As Integer
    Get
        Return _margin
    End Get
    Set(ByVal Value As Integer)
        _margin = Value
    End Set
End Property


' This is public so it can be triggered manually if needed.
Public Sub UpdateLayout(ByVal sender As Object, _
  ByVal e As System.Windows.Forms.LayoutEventArgs) Handles _Container.Layout
    Dim ctrl As Control
    Dim y As Integer
    For Each ctrl In _Container.Controls
        y += Margin
        ctrl.Left = Margin
        ctrl.Top = y
        ctrl.Width = _Container.Width
        ctrl.Height = Margin
    Next
End Sub
```

End Class

The bulk of the work is performed in the UpdateLayout() method, which adjusts the position of the controls in the container. The client doesn't need to call this method manually. Instead, once the layout manager is connected to the correct container, it fires automatically as controls are added or removed. The UpdateLayout() method arranges controls with a fixed height and uses the width of the container. Many more alternatives are possible—for example, you could record the width of the largest contained control, and resize all the other controls and the container itself to match.

The following form code shows how easy it is to use the layout provider. It adds several check box controls to a TabPage container when a form is loaded. Because a layout provider is being used, the client doesn't need to worry about details like the position or size of the child controls—they are organized automatically.

```
Private Sub Form1_Load(ByVal sender As System.Object, _
  ByVal e As System.EventArgs) Handles MyBase.Load

    ' Create and attach the layout manager.
    Dim LayoutManager As New SingleLineFlow (TabPage1, 20)
```

```
    ' Add 10 sample checkboxes.
    Dim chkbox As CheckBox
    Dim i As Integer
    For i = 1 To 10
        chkbox = New CheckBox()
        chkbox.Text = "Setting " & i.ToString()
        TabPage1.Controls.Add(chkbox)
    Next i
End Sub
```

Without the layout manager, all the check boxes would just be layered on top of each other with the default size and the coordinates (0, 0). Figure 11-15 shows the result with the SingleLineFlow layout manager.

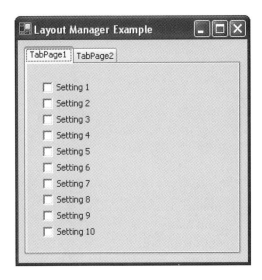

*Figure 11-15. The SingleLineFlow layout manager in action*

You can use the same technique with controls that you add at design-time. However, in this case the layout logic isn't performed until the layout manager class is created. That means that the controls won't be organized in the IDE view at design-time. Instead, they will be reorganized when the program begins and you attach the layout manager.

You could extend this example layout manager so that it creates a tabular layout, or so that it provides a multicolumn single line flow layout. The only limits are time and imagination.

## Control Layout Engines As Extender Providers

In the previous example, the control layout engine treats all controls equally. However, what happens if you need a more customizable layout that allows individual control settings to affect it? For example, the default layout provided by Windows Forms gives every control a Size and a Location property that is used to determine where the control is placed in the container. Is it possible for you to add other layout properties (for example, a Justification or Column property) to standard controls?

The answer is yes—if you develop your layout manager using extender providers. The basic strategy is as follows:

- Create an extender provider for the container control. This will also be the main layout manager class. You can use this extender provider to add properties that configure the layout for all controls (like MarginWidth, or NumberOfColumns).

- Create an extender provider for all other controls. This can add additional properties that configure the position of the control as governed by the layout manager. For example, you might provide a LayoutListPriority property. The smaller the LayoutListPriority, the higher the control would be placed by the SingleLineFlow layout manager. Controls with equal Layout-ListPriority values would be entered in the order they are found in the Controls collection.

These techniques aren't a conceptual leap, but they do require some lengthy trial-and-error coding, and they are a specialty item that won't be of interest to all application programmers. Microsoft provides an interesting article about how custom layout can be developed with extender providers on their MSDN web site (look for it at http://msdn.microsoft.com/library/en-us/dndotnet/html/custlaywinforms.asp). Their approach may be more effort than it's worth for most programmers (which may explain the article's low reader ranking), but it could also form the nucleus for an advanced localization system for a specialized product.

## The Last Word

This chapter considered dynamic user interfaces. But rather than limit the discussion to questions about how to create controls at runtime and hook up their events (which, as you've seen, is relatively trivial once you know how to do it), the chapter examined some more radical approaches. These techniques allow you to dynamically build a vector-based drawing application, or a program that generates its own interfaces using information from a database. It's remarkable what you can accomplish if you surrender the design-time comfort of the Visual Studio .NET IDE.

Many of these applications have specific niches, and the techniques discussed here aren't suitable for all applications. On the other hand, if you need to create a data-driven tool like the product catalogue application in this chapter, you *need* to use a dynamic interface—without it you'll be trapped in an endless cycle of user interface tweaking and recompiling as the underlying data changes. Perhaps best of all, dynamic user interfaces give developers a change to write innovative code—and that is always fun.

# CHAPTER 12

# GDI+ Basics

.NET PROVIDES A new framework of classes for two-dimensional drawing and rendering. Taken together, these classes, found in the five System.Drawing namespaces (and contained in the System.Drawing.dll assembly), represent GDI+.

Technically, GDI+ still relies on the same low-level Windows APIs you may have used in Windows programming of the past. The APIs were often referred to as GDI (Graphics Device Interface). The central idea behind these GDI functions was that the programmer could write text and images to different devices (printers, monitors, and video cards), without needing to understand the underlying hardware. In turn, Windows ensured wide client compatibility, and made use of any optimizations that the hardware might provide. Unfortunately, the GDI functions required a lot of coding wizardry.

The GDI+ types in .NET are object-oriented wrappers over the low-level GDI functions, and, strictly speaking, they don't add any new capabilities. However, the .NET types provide a higher level of abstraction, with convenient support for geometric transformations, antialiasing, and palette blending. Many of these techniques required a painful amount of tiresome coding (and lucky insights) to pull off in the past.

You've already seen GDI+ at work throughout this book. In fact, a number of the more advanced examples would have been impossible without it. A few examples include the following:

- In Chapter 3, you saw many of the basic GDI+ ingredients in the System.Drawing namespace, including objects representing fonts, colors, position (points), and size (rectangles).

- In Chapter 4, you saw an owner-drawn menu that created menu entries using text and a thumbnail icon.

- In Chapter 5, you saw irregularly shaped forms that construct and outline their borders with a graphics path.

- In Chapter 6, you saw how ImageList images could be drawn on a form's surface.

- In Chapter 9, you saw a custom DataGrid column that draws text content and an icon.

This chapter explains the underlying GDI+ framework that makes all this possible.

## Paint Sessions with GDI+

The heart of GDI+ programming is the System.Drawing.Graphics class. The
Graphics class encapsulates a GDI+ drawing surface whether it is a window or
print document. You paint on the GDI+ drawing surface using a combination of
the Graphics class methods.

### Accessing the Graphics Object

There are essentially two ways to access a live instance of the Graphics class. In
many of the examples you've looked at so far, the painting logic is performed
inside a dedicated Paint event handler. In this case, the Graphics object is provided
as a parameter to an event handler.

For example, the code that follows draws a curve onto a form using the
Graphics.DrawArc() method (see Figure 12-1):

```
Private Sub Form1_Paint(ByVal sender As Object, _
  ByVal e As System.Windows.Forms.PaintEventArgs) Handles MyBase.Paint

    Dim DrawingPen As New Pen(Color.Red, 15)
    e.Graphics.DrawArc(DrawingPen, 50, 20, 100, 200, 40, 210)

End Sub
```

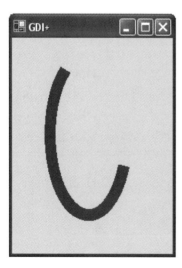

*Figure 12-1. Painting to a GDI+ surface*

You could perform the same task by overriding the OnPaint() method, which is the best approach for an owner-drawn control.

```
Protected Overrides Sub OnPaint(ByVal e As System.Windows.Forms.PaintEventArgs)

    Dim DrawingPen As New Pen(Color.Red, 15)
    e.Graphics.DrawArc(DrawingPen, 50, 20, 100, 200, 40, 210)
    MyBase.Paint(e)

End Sub
```

You don't have to wait for a Paint event to occur. Instead, you can directly obtain the GDI+ Graphics object for a control or an object using the Control.CreateGraphics() method. However, a GDI+ device context uses system resources, and you should make sure to call the Graphics.Dispose() method if you obtain it directly. (In a Paint event handler, you can assume that the .NET framework acquires and disposes of the graphics device context for you.)

Here's an example that draws the same arc shown in Figure 12-1, but this time in response to a button click.

```
Private Sub Button1_Click(ByVal sender As System.Object, _
  ByVal e As System.EventArgs) Handles Button1.Click

    Dim DrawingPen As New Pen(Color.Red, 15)
    Dim GDISurface As Graphics = Me.CreateGraphics()
    GDISurface.DrawArc(DrawingPen, 50, 20, 100, 200, 40, 210)
    GDISurface.Dispose()

End Sub
```

However, this code isn't equivalent in every respect. You'll discover that as soon as you minimize or hide the window, the arc disappears, and is not repainted until you click the button again. To understand why this discrepancy exists, you need to take a closer look at how the Windows operating system handles paint operations.

## Painting and Refreshing

The Windows operating system does not store the graphical representation of a window in memory. This architecture stems from the early days of Windows programming when memory was scarce. Storing a bitmap image of every open Window could quickly consume tens of megabytes, and cripple a computer.

Instead, Windows automatically discards the contents of a window as soon as it is minimized or hidden by another window. When the program window is restored, Windows sends a message to the application, compelling it to repaint itself. In a .NET application, this means that the Paint event will fire. Similarly, if part of a window is obscured, only those controls that are affected fire Paint events when they reappear on the screen.

What this all boils down to is that it's the responsibility of the application (and hence the programmer) to repaint the window when needed. With Paint event handlers, your painting logic will be triggered automatically at the right time. However, if you perform painting inside another method, the result of your work will be lost unless you take specific steps to restore the window after it is hidden or minimized.

The best approach is to code around this limitation so that all painting is performed in the Paint event handler. The examples from Chapter 3 include a FontViewer application that draws text using the GDI+ Graphics class. When the user chooses a different font from the drop-down list box, the window is repainted with an example of the new font (see Figure 12-2). However, though the repainting is triggered by the selection, the code still resides in the Paint event handler.

*Figure 12-2. Painting font text*

Here's how it works. The SelectedIndex event for the list control uses the Control.Invalidate() method. This tells Windows that the window needs to be repainted. It then sends a message to the window, which the .NET framework translates into a paint event.

```
Private Sub lstSize_SelectedIndexChanged(ByVal sender As System.Object, _
    ByVal e As System.EventArgs) Handles lstSize.SelectedIndexChanged

    Me.Invalidate()

End Sub
```

In the Paint event handler, the code reads the font selection and size from the appropriate controls and draws the text in the appropriate font.

```
Private Sub FontViewer_Paint(ByVal sender As Object, _
  ByVal e As System.Windows.Forms.PaintEventArgs) Handles MyBase.Paint

    If lstFonts.SelectedIndex <> -1 Then

        Try
            e.Graphics.DrawString(lstFonts.Text, New Font(lstFonts.Text, _
                            Val(lstSize.Text)), Brushes.Black, 10, 50)
            StatusBar.Panels(0).Text = ""
        Catch err As Exception
            StatusBar.Panels(0).Text = err.Message
        End Try

    End If

End Sub
```

Note that there is no way to "clear" content that you've drawn. You can only paint over it, or invalidate the window, at which point the entire window is repainted from scratch.

In a more complicated application you could use form-level variables to track the drawing content. Then, an event handler can set these variables and invalidate the form, letting the Paint event handler take care of the rest. This technique is demonstrated a little later in this chapter.

> **TIP**   *You should never call the Paint event handler or OnPaint() method directly. This is especially true if your painting logic is complicated or potentially time consuming. If you call the Invalidate() method instead, Windows will queue the paint message if necessary and take care of other critical tasks first if the system is under a heavy load. Calling Invalidate() also allows Windows to save work. If the window is invalidated twice in quick succession, the window may just be repainted once. If you call the OnPaint() method twice, however, your painting code will always execute two times.*

## Optimizing GDI+ Painting

Painting is a performance-sensitive area for any application. Slow rendering may not stop your application from performing its work, but screen flicker and slow painting can make it seem unprofessional. This section considers some techniques that optimize drawing with GDI+ surfaces.

## *Painting and Resizing*

One often-overlooked fact about automatic repainting is that it only affects the portion of the window that is obscured. This is particularly important with Window resizing. For example, consider the slightly modified Paint code that follows, which paints an ellipse that is the same size as the containing window. The result is pictured in Figure 12-3.

```
Private Sub Form1_Paint(ByVal sender As Object, _
  ByVal e As System.Windows.Forms.PaintEventArgs) Handles MyBase.Paint

    Dim DrawingPen As New Pen(Color.Red, 15)
    e.Graphics.DrawEllipse(DrawingPen, New Rectangle(New Point(0, 0), _
                     Me.ClientSize))

End Sub
```

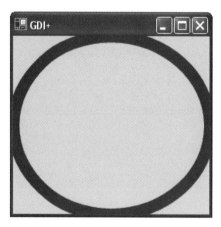

*Figure 12-3. Filling a form with an ellipse*

When you resize this window, you'll discover that the painting code isn't working correctly. The newly exposed portions of the window are filled with the resized ellipse, but rest of the window is not updated, leading to the mess shown in Figure 12-4.

*Figure 12-4. Flawed resizing*

The problem is that Windows assumes that it only needs to repaint the portion of the window that has been hidden or restored. In this case, the *entire* content of the window depends on its dimensions, so the assumption is incorrect.

Fortunately, you can solve this problem by manually invalidating the code whenever the form is resized.

```
Private Sub Form1_Resize(ByVal sender As Object, ByVal e As System.EventArgs) _
  Handles MyBase.Resize

    Me.Invalidate()

End Sub
```

With the addition of this code, the entire form is repainted and the ellipse grows or shrinks to fit the window bounds perfectly. Another option is to set the Form.ResizeRedraw property to True.

## *Painting Portions of a Window*

In some cases, it just doesn't make sense to repaint the entire window when you only need to update a portion of the display. One example is a drawing program.

Consider a simple example program that allows the user to draw squares. When the user clicks with the mouse, a square is created, but not directly drawn. Instead, a rectangle object is added to a special ArrayList collection so it can be tracked, and the form is invalidated.

```
' Store the squares that are painted on the form.
Dim Sqares As New ArrayList()

Private Sub DrawSquare_MouseDown(ByVal sender As Object, _
  ByVal e As System.Windows.Forms.MouseEventArgs) Handles MyBase.MouseDown

        Dim Square As New Rectangle(e.X, e.Y, 20, 20)
        Squares.Add(Square)
        Me.Invalidate()

End Sub
```

The painting logic then takes over, iterating through the collection, and drawing each rectangle. The number of squares that are currently being displayed is also written to a status bar.

```
Private Sub DrawSquare_Paint(ByVal sender As Object, _
  ByVal e As System.Windows.Forms.PaintEventArgs) Handles MyBase.Paint

    Dim DrawingPen As New Pen(Color.Red, 10)
    Dim Square As Rectangle
    For Each Square In Squares
        e.Graphics.DrawRectangle(DrawingPen, Square)
    Next

    pnlSquares.Text = " " & Squares.Count.ToString & " squares"

End Sub
```

The result of a paint operation is shown in Figure 12-5.

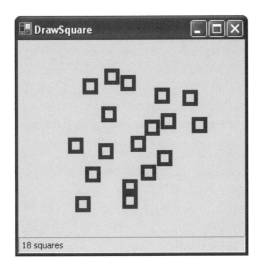

*Figure 12-5. A square painting program*

The problem with this code is that every time a rectangle is created, the entire form is redrawn. This causes noticeable screen flicker as the number of squares advances beyond 100. You can try this out yourself using the GDI+ Basics project included with the code for this chapter.

There are two ways that you can remedy this problem. The fastest solution is to draw the square in two places: in the Paint logic and the MouseDown event handling code. With this approach, the MouseDown event handler does not need to invalidate the form. It draws the square directly, and stores enough information about the new rectangle for it to be successfully repainted if the window is minimized and restored. The potential drawback is that the code becomes significantly more tangled. If you are drawing a more complex object, you might be able to separate the drawing logic into a separate subroutine that accepts a Graphics object and the item to draw, as shown in the following code snippet.

```
' Paint a square in response to a mouse click.
Private Sub DrawSquare_MouseDown(ByVal sender As Object, _
  ByVal e As System.Windows.Forms.MouseEventArgs) Handles MyBase.MouseDown
    Dim Square As New Rectangle(e.X, e.Y, 20, 20)
    Squares.Add(Square)

    Dim g As Graphics = Me.CreateGraphics
    DrawRectangle(Square, g)
    g.Dispose()
End Sub
```

```
' Paint all the squares when the form needs to be refreshed.
Private Sub DrawSquare_Paint(ByVal sender As Object, _
  ByVal e As System.Windows.Forms.PaintEventArgs) Handles MyBase.Paint
    Dim Square As Rectangle
    For Each Square In Squares
        DrawRectangle(Square, e.Graphics)
    Next
End Sub


' This procedure performs the actual drawing, and is called by
' DrawSquare_MouseDown and DrawSquare_Paint.
Private Sub DrawRectangle(ByVal rect As Rectangle, ByVal g As Graphics)
    Dim DrawingPen As New Pen(Color.Red, 10)
    g.DrawRectangle(DrawingPen, rect)
End Sub
```

A simpler approach is to use one of the overloaded versions on the Invalidate()
method. This instructs Windows to repaint only a small portion of the window.
The full painting code still runs (which could slow your application if the painting
is complex), but only the specified region is repainted, thereby improving performance and drastically reducing screen flicker.

```
Private Sub DrawSquare_MouseDown(ByVal sender As Object, _
  ByVal e As System.Windows.Forms.MouseEventArgs) Handles MyBase.MouseDown

    Dim Square As New Rectangle(e.X, e.Y, 20, 20)
    Squares.Add(Square)
    Me.Invalidate(Square)

End Sub
```

Another way to paint just a portion of a window, and achieve better performance,
is to develop owner-drawn controls that override their own OnPaint() methods.

> **TIP** *The framework just discussed could become the basis of a simple GDI+
> drawing application. You would probably add controls that allow the user to
> draw more than one type of object. You would need to add a special class
> (perhaps called DrawnShape) that encapsulates all the details about the drawn
> object, such as size, color, pen width, and so on. Your Paint event handler would
> then iterate through a collection of DrawnShape objects and render all of them
> to the form.*

## Rendering Mode and Antialiasing

One factor that's hampered the ability of drawing tools in other programming frameworks (like Visual Basic) is the lack of control over rendering quality. With GDI+, however, you can enhance the quality of your drawing with automatic antialiasing.

Antialiasing is a technique used to smooth out jagged edges in shapes and text. It works by adding shading at the border of an edge. For example, grey shading might be added to the edge of a black curve to make a corner look smoother. Technically, antialiasing blends a curve with its background. Figure 12-6 shows a close-up of an antialiased ellipse.

*Figure 12-6 Antialiasing with an ellipse*

To use smoothing in your applications, you set the SmoothingQuality property of the Graphics object. You can choose between None, HighSpeed (the default), AntiAlias, and HighQuality (which is similar to AntiAlias but uses other, slower optimizations with LCD screens). The Graphics.SmoothingQuality property is one of the few stateful Graphics class members. That means that you set it before you begin drawing, and it applies to any text or shapes you draw in the rest of the paint session (until the Graphics object is disposed of).

```
e.Graphics.SmoothingMode = Drawing.Drawing2D.SmoothingMode.AntiAlias
```

Figure 12-7 shows a form with several picture boxes. Each picture box handles its own paint event, sets a different smoothing mode, and then draws an ellipse.

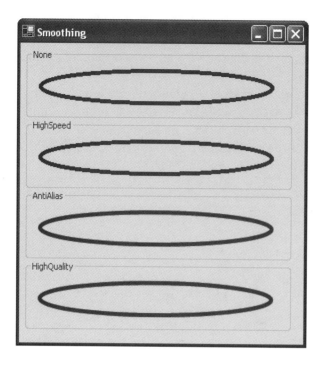

*Figure 12-7 Smoothing modes for shapes*

Antialiasing can also be used with fonts to soften jagged edges on text. The latest versions of the Windows operating system use antialiasing automatically with on-screen fonts. However, you can set the Graphics.TextRenderingHint property to ensure optimized text. You can choose between SingleBitPerPixel-GridFit (fastest performance and lowest quality), AntiAliasGridFit (better quality but slower performance), and ClearTypeGridFit (the best quality on an LCD display). Or, you can use the SystemDefault value to use whatever font smoothing settings the user has configured. Figure 12-8 compares different font smoothing modes.

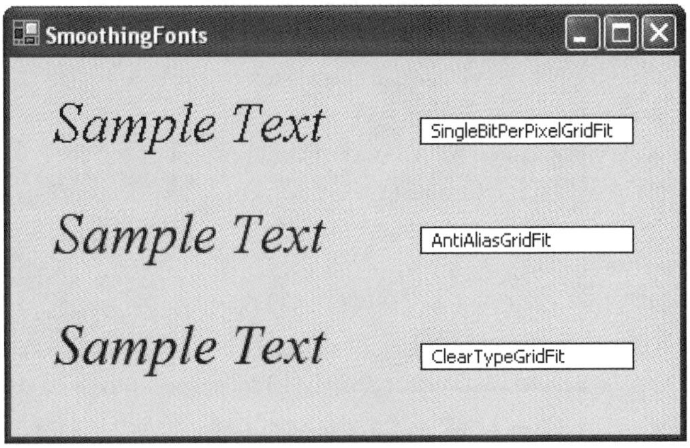

*Figure 12-8 Smoothing modes for fonts*

## Double Buffering

You may notice that when you repaint a window frequently it flickers madly. The flicker is caused by the fact that with each paint event, the image is first erased and then redrawn object by object. The flash you see is the blank background that precedes the redrawn content.

You can reduce flickering by preventing a control or form from drawing its background. If you do, your code must begin by painting a background using one of the fill methods from the Graphics class. Otherwise, the original content remains underneath the new content.

To disable background painting, all you need to do is override the OnPaint-Background() method for the form or control and do nothing. In other words, you *won't* call the base OnPaintBackground() method.

```
Protected Overrides Sub OnPaintBackground( _
  ByVal pevent As System.Windows.Forms.PaintEventArgs)
    ' Do nothing.
End Sub
```

If you are filling a form or control with a custom background color, you should always follow this step, as it can improve performance dramatically. Otherwise, your window will flicker noticeably between the default background color and the color you paint every time you redraw the form.

Disabling the automatic background painting reduces flicker, but the flicker remains. To remove it completely, you can use a technique known as double buffering. With double buffering, an image is built in memory instead of on the surface of a form or control. When the image is completed, it's drawn directly to the form. The process of drawing takes just as long, but the refresh is faster because it is delayed until the image is completely rendered. Hence, there is very little flicker.

To use double buffering, you need to create an Image object. You then draw on the in-memory Image object using the Graphics methods. Finally, you copy the fully rendered image to the form. One good way to test double buffering is to create a form that is frequently refreshed. The next example presents a form with an ellipse that grows and shrinks automatically (see Figure 12-9). The form is redrawn in response to the tick of a Timer control.

Here's the timer code:

```
Private IsShrinking As Boolean
Private ExtraSize As Single

Private Sub tmrRefresh_Tick(ByVal sender As System.Object, _
  ByVal e As System.EventArgs) Handles tmrRefresh.Tick

    ' Change the circle dimensions.
    If IsShrinking Then
        ExtraSize -= 1
    Else
        ExtraSize += 1
    End If

    ' Change the sizing direction if needed.
    If ExtraSize > Me.Width - 150 Then
        IsShrinking = True
    ElseIf ExtraSize < 1 Then
        IsShrinking = False
    End If

    ' Repaint the form.
    Me.Invalidate()
End Sub
```

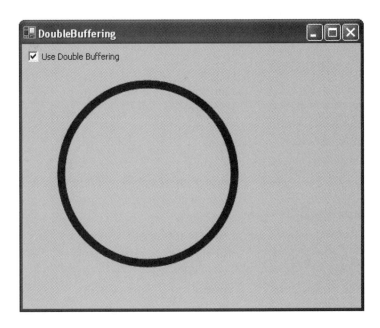

*Figure 12-9. Using double buffering*

The paint code examines the state of a check box and decides whether or not it will implement double buffering.

```
Private Sub DoubleBuffering_Paint(ByVal sender As Object, _
  ByVal e As System.Windows.Forms.PaintEventArgs) Handles MyBase.Paint

    Dim g As Graphics
    Dim Drawing As Bitmap

    ' Check if double buffering is needed, and assign the GDI+ context.
    If chkDoubleBuffer.Checked Then
        Drawing = New Bitmap(Me.Width, Me.Height, e.Graphics)
        g = Graphics.FromImage(Drawing)
    Else
        g = e.Graphics
    End If

    g.SmoothingMode = System.Drawing.Drawing2D.SmoothingMode.HighQuality
```

```
' Draw a rectangle.
Dim DrawingPen As New Pen(Color.Black, 10)
g.FillRectangle(Brushes.White, New Rectangle(New Point(0, 0), Me.ClientSize))
g.DrawEllipse(DrawingPen, 50, 50, 50 + ExtraSize, 50 + ExtraSize)

' If using double buffering, render the final image and dispose of it.
If chkDoubleBuffer.Checked Then
    e.Graphics.DrawImageUnscaled(Drawing, 0, 0)
    g.Dispose()
End If

End Sub
```

When you test this application, you'll see that there is absolutely no flicker in double-buffered mode. There is significant flicker without it.

> **TIP**   *The .NET framework implements its own drawing optimizations. You'll find that if you don't override the OnPaintBackground() method the double buffered method is actually slower than direct drawing, and produces noticeable flicker. However, if you disable background painting and implement double buffering, drawing operations are performed without any detectable flicker.*

## Painting and Debugging

Debugging drawing code can sometimes be frustrating. For example, consider what happens if you set a breakpoint in the painting code. When the breakpoint is reached, the code enters break mode, the IDE appears, and the window is hidden. When you run the next line of code, the program is redisplayed, and a new Paint event is triggered.

To escape this endless sequence of repainting, you can use a couple of tricks:

- If you have a large monitor, you may be able to run your application alongside the program you are testing. Then, when your program enters break mode, the IDE window does not appear on top of your program window, and a repaint is not triggered.

- Alternatively, you can set the TopMost property of your form to True, which keeps it superimposed of your IDE window at all times. This should also avoid a repaint.

## The Graphics Class

The majority of the GDI+ drawing smarts is concentrated in the Graphics class. Table 12-1 describes the basic set of Graphics class members, many of which are explored in detail as the chapter progresses.

*Table 12-1. Basic Graphics Class Members*

| Member | Description |
|---|---|
| CompositingMode and CompositingQuality | CompositingMode determines whether the drawing will overwrite the background or be blended with it. The CompositingQuality specifies the technique that will be used when blending, which determines the quality and speed of the operation. |
| InterpolationMode | Determines how properties are specified between the start point and end point of a shape (for example, when drawing a curve). |
| SmoothingMode and TextRenderingHint | These properties set the rendering quality (and optionally, the antialiasing) that will be used for drawing graphics or text on this GDI+ surface. |
| Clear() | Clears the entire drawing surface and fills it with the specified background color. |
| Dispose() | Releases all the resources held by the graphics object. |
| FromHdc(), FromHwnd(), and FromImage() | These static methods create a Graphics object using either a handle to a device context, handle to a window, or a .NET Image object. |

*Table 12-1. Basic Graphics Class Members (Continued)*

| Member | Description |
| --- | --- |
| GetHdc() and RemoveHdc() | GetHdc() gets the Windows GDI handle that you can use with unmanaged code (for example, methods in the gdi32.dll library). You should use the RemoveHdc() method to release the device context when you are finished, before the Graphics object is disposed of. |
| IsVisible() | Accepts a point object, and indicates whether this point is in a visible portion of the graphics device (not outside the clipping region). This does not depend on whether the window itself is actually visible on the screen. |
| MeasureString() | Returns a Size structure that indicates the amount of space that is required for a given string of text in a given font. This is an extremely important method when handling wrapped printing or drawing a multiline text display. |
| Save() and Restore() | Save() stores the state of the current Graphics object in a GraphicState object. You can use this object with the Restore() method. This is typically used when you are changing the GDI+ surface coordinate systems. |
| SetClip() | Allows you to define the clipping region of this device context using a Rectangle, Region, or GraphicsPath. When you paint content on this surface, the only portions that appear are those that lie inside the clipping region. |

The Graphics class also provides a slew of methods for drawing specific shapes, images, or text. Most of these methods begin with the word "Draw." All shape-drawing methods draw outlines; you need to use the corresponding "Fill" method to paint an interior fill region.

*Table 12-2. Graphics Class Methods for Drawing*

| Method | Description |
|---|---|
| DrawArc() | Draws an arc representing a portion of an ellipse specified by a pair of coordinates, a width, and a height. |
| DrawBezier() and DrawBeziers() | The infamous and attractive Bezier curve, which is defined by four control points. |
| DrawClosedCurve() | Draws a curve, and then closes if off by connecting the end points. |
| DrawCurve() | Draws a curve (technically, a cardinal spline). |
| DrawEllipse() | Draws an ellipse defined by a bounding rectangle specified by a pair of coordinates, a height, and a width. |
| DrawIcon() and DrawIconUnstretched() | Draws the icon represented by an Icon object, and (optionally) stretches it to fit a given rectangle. |
| DrawImage and DrawImageUnscaled() | Draws the image represented by an Image-derived object, and (optionally) stretches it to fit a given rectangle. |
| DrawLine() and DrawLines() | Draws a line connecting the two points specified by coordinate pairs. |
| DrawPath() | Draws a GraphicsPath object, which can represent a combination of curves and shapes. |
| DrawPie() | Draws a "piece of pie" shape defined by an ellipse specified by a coordinate pair, a width, a height. and two radial lines. |
| DrawPolygon() | Draws a multisided polygon defined by an array of points. |
| DrawRectangle() and DrawRectangles() | Draws an ordinary rectangle specified by a starting coordinate pair and width and height. |
| DrawString() | Draws a string of text in a given font. |
| FillClosedCurve() | Draws a curve, closes if off by connecting the end points, and fills it. |

*Table 12-2. Graphics Class Methods for Drawing*

| Method | Description |
| --- | --- |
| FillEllipse() | Fills the interior of an ellipse. |
| FillPath() | Fills the shape represented by a GraphicsPath object. |
| FillPie() | Fills the interior of a "piece of pie" shape. |
| FillPolygon() | Fills the interior of a polygon. |
| FillRectange() and FillRectanges() | Fills the interior of a rectangle. |
| FillRegion() | Fills the interior of a Region object. |

Most of the methods in Table 12-2 are self-explanatory. Two interesting methods that I haven't describde yet include DrawPath() and FillPath(), which work with the GraphicsPath class in the System.Drawing.Drawing2D namespace.

The GraphicsPath class encapsulates a series of connected lines, curves, and text. You used the GraphicsPath class in Chapter 5 to create a shaped form. To build a GraphicsPath object, you simply create a new instance, and use the methods in Table 12-3 to add all the required elements.

```
Dim Path As New GraphicsPath()
Path.AddEllipse(0, 0, 100, 50)
Path.AddRectangle(New Rectangle(100, 50, 100, 50)
```

Optionally, you can also create a solid filled figure out of lines. To do this, you first call the StartFigure() method. Then you add the required curves and lines using the appropriate methods. When finished, you call the CloseFigure() method to close off the shape by drawing a line from the endpoint to the starting point. You can use these methods multiple times to add several closed figures to a single GraphicsPath object.

```
Dim Path As New GraphicsPath()
Path.StartFigure()
Path.AddArc(10, 10, 100, 100, 20, 50)
Path.AddLine(20, 100, 70, 230)
Path.CloseFigure()
```

*Table 12-3. GraphicsPath MethodsMethod*

| GraphicsPath MethodsMethod | Description |
| --- | --- |
| AddArc() | Draws an arc representing a portion of an ellipse specified by a pair of coordinates, a width, and a height. |
| AddBezier() and AddBeziers() | The infamous and attractive Bezier curve, which is defined by four control points. |
| AddClosedCurve() | Draws a curve, and then closes if off by connecting the end points. |
| AddCurve() | Draws a curve (technically, a cardinal spline). |
| AddEllipse() | Draws an ellipse defined by a bounding rectangle specified by a pair of coordinates, a height, and a width. |
| AddLine() and AddLines() | Draws a line connecting the two points specified by coordinate pairs. |
| AddPath() | Adds another GraphicsPath object to this GraphicsPath object. |
| AddPie() | Draws a "piece of pie" shape defined by an ellipse specified by a coordinate pair, a width, a height, and two radial lines. |
| AddPolygon() | Draws a multisided polygon defined by an array of points. |
| AddRectangle() and AddRectangles() | Draws an ordinary rectangle specified by a starting coordinate pair and width and height. |
| AddString() | Draws a string of text in a given font. |
| StartFigure() and CloseFigure() | StartFigure() defines the start of a new closed figure. When you use CloseFigure(), the starting point will be joined to the end point by an additional line. |
| Transform(), Warp(), and Widen() | Used to apply a matrix transform, a warp transform (defined by a rectangle and parallelogram), or an expansion, respectively. |

Optionally, you can create a solid-filled figure out of lines. To do this, you first call the StartFigure() method. Then you add the required curves and lines using the appropriate methods. When finished, you call the CloseFigure() method to close off the shape by drawing a line from the endpoint to the starting point. You can use these methods multiple times to add several closed figures to a single GraphicsPath object.

```
Dim Path As New GraphicsPath()
Path.StartFigure()
Path.AddArc(10, 10, 100, 100, 20, 50)
Path.AddLine(20, 100, 70, 230)
Path.CloseFigure()
```

## Coordinate Systems and Transformations

By default, when you draw GDI+ shapes, you use a coordinate system that designates the top left corner as (0, 0). The *x*-axis value increases as you move to the right, and the *y*-axis value increases as you move down. The point (Me.Width, Me.Height) corresponds to the bottom-right corner of a form (discounting the title bar region). Each unit corresponds to one pixel. This is nothing new—it's the same coordinate system you examined when I introduced control basics in Chapter 3. However, the Graphics class also gives you the flexibility to change the unit of measurement, point of origin, and rotation.

To change the unit of measurement, you simply set the PageUnit property of the Graphics class. You can use one of several values from the GraphicsUnitClass, including Display (1/75 of an inch), Document (1/300 inch), Inch, Millimeter, Pixel (the default), and Point (1/72 of an inch).

```
e.Graphics.PageUnit = Graphics.Inch
```

The ability to change the point of origin is more useful. It uses the Graphics.TranslateTranform() method, which accepts the coordinates of the new point that should become (0,0). Using the code below, the point at (50, 50) will become the new (0,0) origin. Points to the left or right of this origin must be specified using negative values.

```
e.Graphics.TranslateTransform(50, 50)
```

This is a fairly handy trick. For example, it can allow you to perform simple calculations by assuming the top left point of your drawing is (0, 0), but gives you the freedom to add a border between the drawing and the form by translating the coordinate system before you begin to draw. You could even use this method several times with different points and repeat the same drawing code. The figure you are drawing would then appear at several different points in the window, as shown in Figure 12-10.

```
Private Sub Transform_Paint(ByVal sender As Object, _
  ByVal e As System.Windows.Forms.PaintEventArgs) Handles MyBase.Paint

    ' Draw several squares in different places.
    DrawRectangle(e.Graphics)
    e.Graphics.TranslateTransform(180, 60)
    DrawRectangle(e.Graphics)
    e.Graphics.TranslateTransform(-50, 80)
    DrawRectangle(e.Graphics)
    e.Graphics.TranslateTransform(-100, 50)
    DrawRectangle(e.Graphics)

End Sub

Private Sub DrawRectangle(ByVal g As Graphics)
    Dim DrawingPen As New Pen(Color.Red, 30)

    ' Draw a rectangle at a fixed position.
    g.DrawRectangle(DrawingPen, New Rectangle(20, 20, 20, 20))
End Sub
```

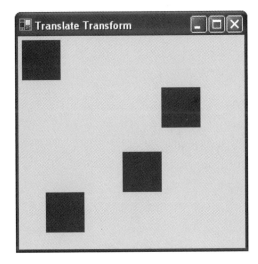

*Figure 12-10. Using translate transforms*

The final transformation considered here is a rotational one. It uses the Graphics.RotateTransform() method, which rotates the coordinate system using an angle or matrix. The important fact to remember is that rotations are performed around the point of origin. If you haven't performed any translation transformations, this will be in the top right corner of the form.

The next example uses a translation transform to move the center point to the middle of the form, and then rotates text around that point with successive rotational transforms. The result is shown in Figure 12-11.

```
Private Sub RotateTransform_Paint(ByVal sender As Object, _
  ByVal e As System.Windows.Forms.PaintEventArgs) Handles MyBase.Paint
    ' Optimize text quality.
    e.Graphics.TextRenderingHint = TextRenderingHint.AntiAliasGridFit

    ' Move origin to center of form so we can rotate around that.
    e.Graphics.TranslateTransform(Me.Width \ 2 - 30, Me.Height \ 2 - 30)

    DrawText(e.Graphics)
    e.Graphics.RotateTransform(45)
    DrawText(e.Graphics)
    e.Graphics.RotateTransform(75)
    DrawText(e.Graphics)
    e.Graphics.RotateTransform(160)
    DrawText(e.Graphics)
End Sub

Private Sub DrawText(ByVal g As Graphics)
    g.DrawString("Text", New Font("Verdana", 30, FontStyle.Bold), _
            Brushes.Black, 0, 10)
End Sub
```

*Figure 12-11. Using rotational transforms*

## Pens

In Chapter 3, you learned about many of the GDI+ basics, including fonts, colors, points, and rectangles. However, GDI+ drawing code also uses other details like brushes and pens.

Pens are used to draw lines when you use the shape or curve drawing methods from the Graphics class. You can retrieve a standard pen using one of the shared properties from the System.Drawing.Pens class. These pens all have a width of 1; they only differ in their color.

```
Dim MyPen As Pen = Pens.Black
```

You can also create a Pen object on your own, and configure all the properties described in Table 12-4.

```
Dim MyPen As New Pen(Color.Red)
MyPen.DashCap = DashCap.Triangle
MyPen.DashStyle = DashDotDot
e.Graphics.DrawLine(MyPen, 0, 0, 10, 0)
```

*Table 12-4. Pen Members*

| Member | Description |
|--------|-------------|
| DashPattern | Defines a dash style for broken lines using an array of dashes and spaces. |
| DashStyle | Defines a dash style for broken lines using the DashStyle enumeration. |
| LineJoin | Defines how overlapping lines in a shape will be joined together. |
| PenType | The type of fill that will be used for the line. Typically this will be SolidColor, but you can also use a gradient, bitmap texture, or hatch pattern by supplying a brush object when you create the pen. You cannot set the PenType through this property, however, as it is read-only. |
| StartCap and EndCap | Determines how the beginning and ends of lines will be rendered. You can also define a custom line cap by creating a CustomLineCap object (typically by using a GraphicsPath), and then assigning it to the CustomStartCap or CustomEndCap property. |
| Width | The pixel width of lines drawn by this pen. |

Figure 12-12 shows different line caps (which determine the appearance of the start and end of a line), while Figure 12-13 shows different dash styles.

> **TIP** *GDI+ differs from the traditional world of GDI programming in that it isn't stateful. That means that you need to keep track of pens on your own, and submit the appropriate pen with every call to a draw method.*

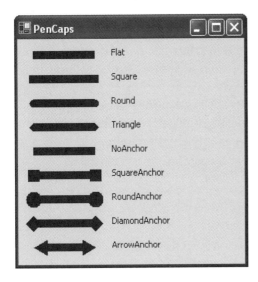

Figure 12-12. Line caps

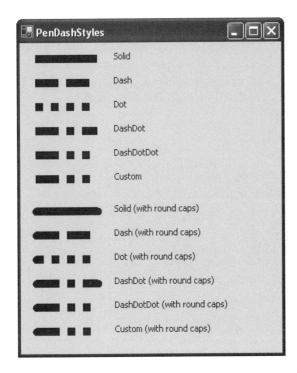

Figure 12-13. Dash styles

## Brushes

Brushes are used to fill the space between lines. Brushes are used when drawing text or when using any of the fill methods of the Graphics class for painting the inside of a shape.

You can quickly retrieve a predefined solid brush using a shared property from the Brushes class, or the SystemBrushes class (which provides brushes that correspond to various Windows color scheme settings, like the control background color or the highlight menu text color).

```
Dim MyBrush As Brush = SystemBrushes.Menu
e.Graphics.FillRectangle(MyBrush, 0,0,50,50)
```

Last, you can create a custom brush. You need to decide what type of brush you are creating. Solid brushes are created from the SolidBrush class, while other classes (HatchBrush, LinearGradientBrush, and TextureBrush) allow fancier options. The next three sections consider these different types of brushes.

> **TIP** *You can also create a pen that draws using the fill style of a brush. This allows you to draw lines that are filled with gradients and textures. To do so, begin by creating the appropriate brush, and then create a new pen. One of the overloaded pen constructor methods accepts a reference to a brush—that's the one you need to use for a brush-based pen.*

### The HatchBrush

A HatchBrush has a foreground color, a background color, and a hash style that determines how these colors are combined. Typically, colors are interspersed using stripes, grids, or dots, but you can even select unusual pattern styles like bricks, confetti, weave, and shingles.

Following is the code for a simple brush demonstration program that displays the available hatch brush styles. Figure 12-14 shows the result.

```
Private Sub HatchBrushes_Paint(ByVal sender As Object, _
  ByVal e As System.Windows.Forms.PaintEventArgs) Handles MyBase.Paint

    Dim MyBrush As HatchBrush
    Dim y As Integer = 20
    Dim x As Integer = 20
```

```
' Enumerate over all the styles.
Dim BrushStyle As HatchStyle
For Each BrushStyle In System.Enum.GetValues(GetType(HatchStyle))

    MyBrush = New HatchBrush(BrushStyle, Color.Blue, Color.LightYellow)
    ' Fill a rectangle with the brush.
    e.Graphics.FillRectangle(MyBrush, x, y, 40, 20)
    ' Display the brush name.
    e.Graphics.DrawString(BrushStyle.ToString(), New Font("Tahoma", 8), _
                    Brushes.Black, 50 + x, y + 5)

    y += 30
    If (y + 30) > Me.ClientSize.Height Then
        y = 20
        x += 180
    End If
Next

End Sub
```

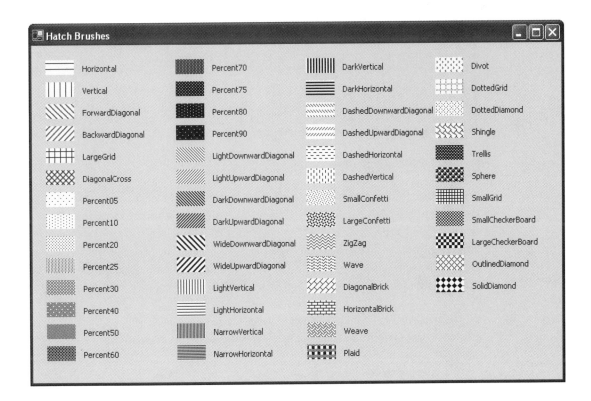

*Figure 12-14. HatchBrush styles*

## The LinearGradientBrush

The LinearGradientBrush allows you to blend two colors in a gradient pattern. You can choose any two colors (as with the hatch brush) and then choose to blend horizontally (from left to right), vertically (from top to bottom), diagonally (from the top-left corner to the bottom-right), or diagonally backward (from the top-right to the bottom-left). You can also specify the origin point for either side of the gradient.

Figure 12-15 shows the different gradient styles.

*Figure 12-15. The LinearGradient brush*

## The TextureBrush

Finally, the TextureBrush attaches a bitmap to a brush. The image is tiled in the painted portion of the brush, whether it is text or a simple rectangle. Here's an example that fills a form with a tiled bitmap. The result is shown in Figure 12-16.

```
Private Sub TextureBrushExample_Paint(ByVal sender As Object, _
  ByVal e As System.Windows.Forms.PaintEventArgs) Handles MyBase.Paint

    Dim MyBrush As New TextureBrush(Image.FromFile("tile.bmp"))
    e.Graphics.FillRectangle(MyBrush, e.Graphics.ClipBounds)

End Sub
```

*Figure 12-16. The TextureBrush*

## Hit Testing

In Chapter 11, you saw how you could build a simple drawing application by dynamically adding controls. An alternative (and potentially more lightweight) approach is to use GDI+ drawing structures. However, squares, ellipses, curves, and other shapes have no ability to capture mouse actions and raise the typical MouseDown and Click events. Instead, you need to intercept these events using the containing object (typically a form), and then manually determine if a shape was clicked. This process is known as hit testing.

.NET provides basic hit testing support through a Contains() method that's built into the Rectangle structure. It examines a supplied *x* and *y* coordinate, Point object, or Rectangle object, and returns True if it is located inside the Rectangle.

However, there are a couple of quirks that take some getting used to with Rectangle hit testing:

- A Rectangle is a combination of points (defined by a top-left corner, width, and height). It doesn't necessarily correspond to a region on the screen—that depends on whether you've drawn some sort of shape based on the Rectangle with one of the GDI+ drawing methods.

- The Rectangle is the only structure that supports hit testing. That means that if you create another shape (like a region or ellipse based on a rectangle), you either need to convert its coordinates into a Rectangle object, or retain the original Rectangle for later use.

The next example uses hit testing with the square-drawing program developed earlier. When the user right-clicks the form, the code loops through the collection of squares, and displays a message box for each one that contains the clicked point (see Figure 12-17).

```
Private Sub DrawSquare_MouseDown(ByVal sender As Object, _
  ByVal e As System.Windows.Forms.MouseEventArgs) Handles MyBase.MouseDown

    If e.Button = MouseButtons.Left Then
        ' Add a square and update the screen.
        Dim Square As New Rectangle(e.X, e.Y, 20, 20)
        Squares.Add(Square)
        Me.Invalidate(Square)
    ElseIf e.Button = MouseButtons.Right Then
        ' Search  for the clicked square.
        Dim Square As Rectangle
        Dim SquareNumber As Integer
        For Each Square In Squares
            SquareNumber += 1
            If Square.Contains(e.X, e.Y) Then
                MessageBox.Show("Point inside square #" & SquareNumber.ToString())
            End If
        Next
    End If
End Sub
```

Once you have determined which square was clicked, you could modify it and then invalidate the form, or allow drag-and-drop as featured in Chapter 11.

> **TIP**  *The Rectangle also provides methods I don't consider here. For example, you can use Intersect() to return a Rectangle representing where two Rectangles intersect, Offset() to move it, and Inflate () to enlarge it.*

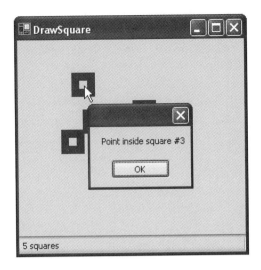

*Figure 12-17. Hit testing with squares*

## Hit Testing Nonrectangular Shapes

.NET does provide some help if you need to perform hit testing with a nonrectangular object. If you use the GraphicsPath object to create a shape (or combination of shapes), you can rely on the indispensable IsVisible() method, which accepts a point and returns True if this point is contained inside a closed figure in the GraphicsPath. This method works equally well, whether you click inside a prebuilt closed figure (like a square, ellipse, polygon, and so on), or if you click inside a figure you created yourself with line segments using the StartFigure() and CloseFigure() methods of the GraphicsPath object.

```
Private Sub GraphicsPathExample_MouseDown(ByVal sender As Object, _
  ByVal e As System.Windows.Forms.MouseEventArgs) Handles MyBase.MouseDown

    If Path.IsVisible(e.X, e.Y) Then
        MessageBox.Show("You clicked inside the figure.")
    End If

End Sub
```

Figure 12-18 shows a successful test of hit-testing with a nonrectangular shape. This technique is expanded in the next chapter into the basic framework for an advanced drawing program.

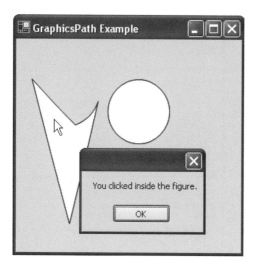

*Figure 12-18. Hit testing a nonrectangular path*

## The ControlPaint Class

Technically, the ControlPaint class isn't a part of GDI+. However, it's an extremely useful tool for custom control developers who use GDI+. It is also a well-kept .NET secret. Essentially, the ControlPaint class offers methods for drawing standard Windows interface elements, like scroll buttons, borders, focus rectangles, and check boxes.

This functionality is tremendously useful. For example, if you want to create a special control that contains a list of items with check boxes, you ordinarily have limited options. You can use control composition (and create contained CheckBox controls), but this limits the ways that you can use the check boxes and tailor the interface. Alternatively, you could attempt to draw your own, and probably end up with a rather crude looking square. With the ControlPaint class, however, you can use the DrawCheckBox() method, and end up with the perfectly shaded Windows standard for free. You can even create a check box of any size you like. Similarly, if you want to create a scroll button, or a button that displays a focus rectangle, you can also turn to the ControlPaint class.

The ControlPaint class consists entirely of the shared methods described in Table 12-5. Here's a line of code that uses it draw a check box:

```
ControlPaint.DrawCheckBox(e.Graphics, New Rectangle(10, 10, 50, 50), _
  ButtonState.Checked)
```

And here's one that draws the familiar dotted focus rectangle:

```
ControlPaint.DrawFocusRectangle(e.Graphics, New Rectangle(130, 80, 20, 20))
```

*Table 12-5. Essential ControlPaint Methods*

| Method | Description |
| --- | --- |
| DrawBorder() and DrawBorder3D() | Draws a border on a button-style control. |
| DrawButton() and DrawCaptionButton() | Draws a standard command button control. |
| DrawCheckBox() | Draws a check box control. |
| DrawComboButton() | Draws the drop-down button for a combo box control. |
| DrawFocusRectangle | Draws a dotted rectangular outline for a focus rectangle. |
| DrawGrid() | Draws a grid of one-pixel dots with the specified spacing, within the specified bounds, and in the specified color. |
| DrawImageDisabled() and DrawStringDisabled() | Draws an image or string of text in a disabled ("greyed out") state. |
| DrawLockedFrame() and DrawSelectionFrame() | Draws a standard selection frame in the specified state, with the specified inner and outer dimensions, and with the specified background color. |
| DrawMenuGlyph() | Draws a menu glyph on a menu item control (for example, a check mark). |
| DrawMixedCheckBox | Draws a three-state check box control. |
| DrawRadioButton() | Draws a standard radio button control. |
| DrawScrollButton | Draws a scroll button on a scroll bar control. |
| DrawSizeGrip() | Draws the sizing grip that appears on the bottom right of some windows. |

Figure 12-19 shows the sample output for several ControlPaint methods, including check boxes of different sizes and states. The next chapter develops a button control that uses ControlPaint to create its basic appearance.

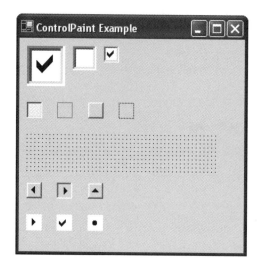

*Figure 12-19. Drawing pictures with ControlPaint*

Remember, this is a picture of a check box, not a check box! If you want it to change its state when the user clicks it, you need to manually repaint a new check box in a different state.

> **NOTE**  *Unfortunately, ControlPaint only supports the standard Windows graphical look. There's no way to draw shaded Windows XP controls on your own.*

## The Last Word

In this chapter you learned how to use .NET's revitalized painting framework, and the optimized techniques that make drawing routines sharp and flicker-free, including double buffering. You also considered topics you need to master if you want to develop your own owner-drawn controls, like hit testing and the ControlPaint class. The next chapter delves into interesting examples of custom control development with GDI+.

## CHAPTER 13

# GDI+ Controls

OWNER-DRAWN CONTROLS are one of the most ambitious projects a developer can undertake. This is not because they are conceptually tricky, but because a moderately sophisticated control needs a great deal of basic code just to handle all aspects of its appearance. If you can create a control using composition (i.e., a user control) or by inheriting from a similar control class, as shown in Chapter 7, you'll save yourself a great deal of effort. On the other hand, if you need complete control over drawing and behavior, or you want to introduce some of the unusual GDI+ features to your user interface, you need to create a control that performs its painting manually.

The prime advantage to GDI+ controls is freedom. The prime disadvantage with GDI+ controls is that they aren't nearly as autonomous as prebuilt controls. For example, with custom GDI+ controls you need to handle the following details manually:

- Scrolling support

- Focus cues (i.e., indicating when the control has focus)

- The "pushed" state appearance for a button control

- Special cues or "hot tracking" appearance changes when the mouse moves over the control

- Hit testing to determine if a click was made in an appropriate area

This chapter introduces several example controls, and shows how they confront these problems and add a few visual treats.

## Simple GDI+ Controls

The first type of GDI+ control that might occur to you to use is one that simply wraps one of the GDI+ drawing features you examined in the previous chapter. For example, you might want to provide a simple shape control that renders a closed figure depending on the properties you set. Or, you might want to create a special type of label that paints itself with a textured brush, or a gradient that the developer can configure through the appropriate properties. That's the type of example considered next with the GradientLabel control.

## A Gradient Label

The first example presents a special label that allows the developer to add a gradient background by choosing two colors. The developer can also specify the usual properties like Text, Font, and ForeColor, and configure the type of gradient fill through an additional property. The GradientLabel control is a quick and painless way to add a label with a gradient background to a splash screen or wizard in your application without having to rewrite the basic GDI+ code.

The GradientLabel class inherits from UserControl and overrides the drawing logic. This isn't necessary—it could simply inherit from the base Control class and incur slightly less of an overhead, but the UserControl approach makes it easy to work with the GradientLabel class in a test project, rather than requiring a separate DLL and client test program.

```
Public Class GradientLabel
    Inherits System.Windows.Forms.UserControl

    ' (Code omitted.)

End Class
```

The first step is to create the required properties. In this case, you need to store information about the text to be displayed on the label, the two colors for the gradient, and the type of gradient to be used.

```
Private _Text As String
Private _ColorA As Color = Color.LightBlue
Private _ColorB As Color = Color.Purple
Private _GradientStyle As LinearGradientMode = LinearGradientMode.ForwardDiagonal
```

Each member variable requires a separate property procedure. For the sake of brevity, I've left out the optional attributes you could use to configure the category and the corresponding description for each property. Note that each property invalidates the display, ensuring that the gradient and text are repainted as needed.

```vb
<Browsable(True), _
 DesignerSerializationVisibility(DesignerSerializationVisibility.Visible)> _
Public Overrides Property Text() As String
    Get
        Return _Text
    End Get
    Set(ByVal Value As String)
        _Text = Value
        Me.Invalidate()
    End Set
End Property


Public Property ColorA() As Color
    Get
        Return _ColorA
    End Get
    Set(ByVal Value As Color)
        _ColorA = Value
        Me.Invalidate()
    End Set
End Property


Public Property ColorB() As Color
    Get
        Return _ColorB
    End Get
    Set(ByVal Value As Color)
        _ColorB = Value
        Me.Invalidate()
    End Set
End Property


Public Property GradientFillStyle() As LinearGradientMode
    Get
        Return _GradientStyle
    End Get
    Set(ByVal Value As LinearGradientMode)
        _GradientStyle = Value
        Me.Invalidate()
    End Set
End Property
```

> **TIP** *Note that the user control class already provides a Text property. However, this Text property will not appear in the Properties window unless you manually override it and set the Browsable attribute to True. Also, this property will not be serialized (stored in the form designer code when configured at design-time) unless you add the DesignerSerializationAttribute. This is a source of much confusion for beginning control developers. Always remember, if you inherit from a control and have trouble storing an existing property, you may need to override it and modify this attribute!*

The final step is to add the drawing logic, which is made up of three separate steps:

- Set the ResizeRedraw property of the control to True so it will be refreshed every time the size changes.

- Override the OnPaintBackground() method, add the code to generate the gradient fill, and don't call the base implementation on the method. This way, the blank grey background is not painted before the gradient, and control drawing or refreshing takes place faster and with less flicker.

- Override the OnPaint() method and add the code needed to paint the label text with the current font and forecolor.

```
' Ensure it will be repainted when resized.
Private Sub GradientLabel_Load(ByVal sender As System.Object, _
  ByVal e As System.EventArgs) Handles MyBase.Load
    Me.ResizeRedraw = True
End Sub

Protected Overrides Sub OnPaintBackground( _
  ByVal e As System.Windows.Forms.PaintEventArgs)
    Dim Brush As New LinearGradientBrush(e.ClipRectangle, _ColorA, _ColorB, _
                                    _GradientStyle)

    ' Draw the gradient background.
    e.Graphics.FillRectangle(Brush, e.ClipRectangle)
End Sub
```

```
Protected Overrides Sub OnPaint(ByVal e As System.Windows.Forms.PaintEventArgs)
    MyBase.OnPaint(e)

    ' Draw the label text.
    e.Graphics.DrawString(_Text, Me.Font, New SolidBrush(Me.ForeColor), 0, 0)
End Sub
```

Figure 13-1 shows the gradient label sized to fill a form.

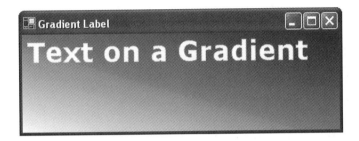

*Figure 13-1. The GradientLabel*

## Improving the GradientLabel's Design-Time Support

As it stands, the GradientLabel works seamlessly. You can easily configure the two colors from an automatically provided color picker at design-time, and the results appear immediately in the IDE.

However, there are a couple of changes you can make to improve the control. First, consider ColorA, ColorB, and GradientFillStyle properties. These properties are really all parts of the same setting, and together they determine the background fill. If you wrapped these three settings into one class, they would be easier to find and set at design time, and easier to reuse in any other control that might need a gradient fill.

Here's how the custom class would look. It uses a special TypeConverter attribute that instructs Visual Studio .NET to expose this object as an expandable set of subproperties in the Properties window.

```
<TypeConverter(GetType(ExpandableObjectConverter))> _
Public Class GradientFill

    Private _ColorA As Color = Color.LightBlue
    Private _ColorB As Color = Color.Purple
    Private _GradientStyle As LinearGradientMode = _
            LinearGradientMode.ForwardDiagonal

    Public Property ColorA() As Color
        Get
            Return _ColorA
        End Get
        Set(ByVal Value As Color)
            _ColorA = Value
        End Set
    End Property

    Public Property ColorB() As Color
        Get
            Return _ColorB
        End Get
        Set(ByVal Value As Color)
            _ColorB = Value
        End Set
    End Property

    <System.ComponentModel.RefreshProperties(RefreshProperties.Repaint)> _
    Public Property GradientFillStyle() As LinearGradientMode
        Get
            Return _GradientStyle
        End Get
        Set(ByVal Value As LinearGradientMode)
            _GradientStyle = Value
        End Set
    End Property

End Class
```

The new GradientLabel control does not define any of these properties. Instead, it now defines a single GradientFill property. Note that this property requires the DesignerSerializationVisibility attribute set to Content. This instructs Visual Studio .NET to serialize all embedded child properties of the GradientFill class. Without it, you'll face the "disappearing configuration" problem all over again.

```
Private _Gradient As New GradientFill()

<DesignerSerializationVisibility(DesignerSerializationVisibility.Content)> _
Public Property GradientFill() As GradientFill
    Get
        Return _Gradient
    End Get
    Set(ByVal Value As GradientFill)
        _Gradient = Value
        Me.Invalidate()
    End Set
End Property
```

This design also provides an opportunity to get a little fancy by creating a custom thumbnail of the gradient in the Properties window. To add this extra bit of finesse, all you need to do is create a UITypeEditor for the GradientFill class, and override the PaintValue() method. Here's the complete code:

```
Public Class GradientFillEditor
    Inherits UITypeEditor

    Public Overloads Overrides Function GetPaintValueSupported( _
      ByVal context As System.ComponentModel.ITypeDescriptorContext) As Boolean
        Return True
    End Function

    Public Overloads Overrides Sub PaintValue( _
      ByVal e As System.Drawing.Design.PaintValueEventArgs)
        Dim Fill As GradientFill = CType(e.Value, GradientFill)
        Dim Brush As New LinearGradientBrush(e.Bounds, Fill.ColorA, _
                                             Fill.ColorB, Fill.GradientFillStyle)
        ' Paint the thumbnail.
        e.Graphics.FillRectangle(Brush, e.Bounds)
    End Sub

End Class
```

Finally, attach the UITypeEditor to the GradientFill class with an Editor attribute, as you did in Chapter 8:

```
<TypeConverter(GetType(ExpandableObjectConverter)), _
Editor(GetType(GradientFillEditor), GetType(UITypeEditor))> _
Public Class GradientFill
```

The GradientLabel now retains its effortless design-time support, with the added frill of a thumbnail gradient in the Properties window next to the GradientFill property (see Figure 13-2). You can also reuse the GradientFill and GradientFillEditor to add similar features to countless other custom control projects.

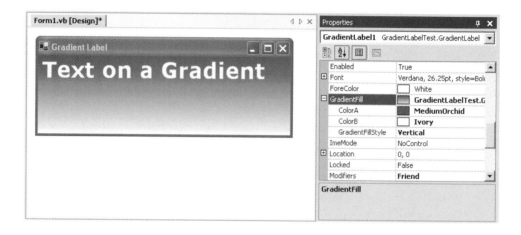

*Figure 13-2. Custom thumbnails with the GradientLabel*

## A Marquee Label

The next example presents another graphical label control—with a twist. This control automatically refreshes its display in response to a timer, scrolling a line of text across the visible area. The code is quite similar to the previous example, except for the fact that it adds double-buffering so that the label can be scrolled smoothly without flicker.

The control uses three significant properties: Text; ScrollTimeInterval, which determines how frequently the timer fires; and ScrollPixelAmount, which determines how much the text is scrolled with every timer tick. An additional private member variable, called _Position, is defined to track how far the text has scrolled. This property is not made available to the client (although it could be if you wanted to allow the text to be set at a specific scroll position).

Here's the property procedure code for the MarqueeLabel control:

```
Private _Text As String
Private _ScrollAmount As Integer = 10
Private _Position As Integer = 0
```

```
<Browsable(True), _
 DesignerSerializationVisibility(DesignerSerializationVisibility.Visible)> _
Public Overrides Property Text() As String
    Get
        Return _Text
    End Get
    Set(ByVal Value As String)
        _Text = Value
        Me.Invalidate()
    End Set
End Property

Public Property ScrollTimeInterval() As Integer
    Get
        Return tmrScroll.Interval
    End Get
    Set(ByVal Value As Integer)
        tmrScroll.Interval = Value
    End Set
End Property

<DefaultValue(10)> _
Public Property ScrollPixelAmount() As Integer
    Get
        Return _ScrollAmount
    End Get
    Set(ByVal Value As Integer)
        _ScrollAmount = Value
    End Set
End Property
```

When the control is instantiated, it checks the current mode. In design mode, it disables the timer. The text still appears on the control, but it is not automatically scrolled (which would be a potentially distracting and CPU-wasting approach).

```
Private Sub MarqueeLabel_Load(ByVal sender As System.Object, _
  ByVal e As System.EventArgs) Handles MyBase.Load
    Me.ResizeRedraw = True
    If Me.DesignMode = False Then
        tmrScroll.Enabled = True
    End If
End Sub
```

At runtime, the timer simply increments the _Position variable and invalidates the display with each tick:

```
Private Sub tmrScroll_Tick(ByVal sender As System.Object, _
  ByVal e As System.EventArgs) Handles tmrScroll.Tick
    _Position += _ScrollAmount
    ' Force a refresh.
    Me.Invalidate()
End Sub
```

The painting logic takes care of the rest. First, the OnPaintBackground() method is overridden to prevent the default grey background from being painted (which would add significant flicker). Next, the OnPaint() method draws the blank background and the scrolled text to an image object in memory, and paints it to the form at once. (This is the double-buffering technique presented in the last chapter.)

```
Protected Overrides Sub OnPaintBackground( _
  ByVal e As System.Windows.Forms.PaintEventArgs)
    ' Do nothing.
    ' To prevent flicker, we will draw both the background and the text
    ' to a buffered image, and draw it to the control all at once.
End Sub

Protected Overrides Sub OnPaint(ByVal e As System.Windows.Forms.PaintEventArgs)
    ' The following line avoids a design-time error that would
    ' otherwise occur when the control is first loaded (but does not yet
    ' have a defined size).
    If e.ClipRectangle.Width = 0 Then Exit Sub

    MyBase.OnPaint(e)
    If _Position > Me.Width Then
        _Position = -e.Graphics.MeasureString(_Text, Me.Font).Width
    End If

    ' Create the drawing area in memory.
    ' Double buffering is used to prevent flicker.
    Dim blt As New Bitmap(e.ClipRectangle.Width, e.ClipRectangle.Height)
    Dim g As Graphics = Graphics.FromImage(blt)

    g.FillRectangle(New SolidBrush(Me.BackColor), e.ClipRectangle)
    g.DrawString(_Text, Me.Font, New SolidBrush(Me.ForeColor), _Position, 0)
```

```
' Render the finished image on the form.
e.Graphics.DrawImageUnscaled(blt, 0, 0)

    g.Dispose()
End Sub
```

If the text has scrolled off the form, the position is reset. However, the new starting position is *not* (0, 0). Instead, the text is moved to the left by an amount equal to its length. That way, when the scrolling resumes, the last letter appears first from the left side of the control, followed by the rest of the text.

The online samples for this chapter include a test program (shown in Figure 13-3) that allows you to try out the marquee control and dynamically modify its scroll speed settings.

*Figure 13-3. The MarqueeLabel test utility*

## Creating Button Controls

The label controls are fairly easy to develop because they are essentially static pieces of user interface. Other controls may need to support user interaction. For example, a button control needs to receive mouse clicks and a text box needs to handle key presses. To create one of these controls can require significant extra code and thorough testing to verify that its behavior is consistent under all circumstances.

To illustrate some of these considerations, the next example presents a button that's been created from scratch by deriving from the base Control class.

## A Hot Tracking Button

This example develops HotTrackButton that displays an image and text. When the mouse is positioned over the image, it appears with a raised border (see Figure 13-4).

*Figure 13-4. The HotTrackButton*

This control project raises some unique, subtle challenges:

- The clickable portion of the button should only include the image. Thus, the control needs to use hit testing when a click is detected, and suppress click events if the text portion is clicked.

- The button can appear in several states, including disabled, selected (when the mouse is positioned above the image), depressed (when the button is pushed), and normal.

- The button must be able to deal with any valid image size.

The first step is to create a control class that provides a member variable to track its current state. In our example, a State enumeration is defined to help track the valid button states.

```
Public Class HotTrackButton
    Inherits Control
```

```
    Public Enum State
        Normal
        MouseOver
        Pushed
    End Enum

    Private _State As State = State.Normal

    ' (Other code omitted.)

End Class
```

Next, you need to create the button's public interface. This includes an Image property to store the picture it will display, and a Text property to store the caption text. Every control automatically inherits the Text property; however, the HotTrackButton class needs to override it to make sure that the control is invalidated (and thus repainted) when the text is changed.

```
Private _Image As Image
Private _Bounds As Rectangle

Public Property Image() As Image
    Get
        Return _Image
    End Get
    Set(ByVal Value As Image)
        _Image = Value
        _Bounds = New Rectangle(0, 0, _Image.Width + 5, _Image.Height + 5)
        Me.Invalidate()
    End Set
End Property

' You must override this property to invalidate the display and
' provide automatic refresh when the property is changed.
Public Overrides Property Text() As String
    Get
        Return MyBase.Text
    End Get
    Set(ByVal Value As String)
        MyBase.Text = Value
        Me.Invalidate()
    End Set
End Property
```

Notice that a private member variable called _Bounds is used to track the drawing area of the control. This rectangle is slightly larger than the image itself, because it needs to accommodate the focus rectangle. When the button changes state in response to a mouse action, the control class code can then invalidate just the region defined by the _Bounds rectangle, guaranteeing a faster refresh.

The next step is to override four mouse-related methods, including OnMouseMove(), OnMouseDown(), OnMouseUp(), and OnMouseLeave(). The code in these methods sets the button state appropriately, and forces a repaint if the state has changed.

```
Protected Overrides Sub OnMouseMove( _
  ByVal e As System.Windows.Forms.MouseEventArgs)
    MyBase.OnMouseMove(e)

    ' Check if the mouse pointer is over the button.
    ' If the mouse moves off the button surface, it will be deactivated,
    ' even if the button is being held in a pressed position.
    ' The code repaints the button only if needed.
    If _Bounds.Contains(e.X, e.Y) Then
        If _State = State.Normal Then
            _State = State.MouseOver
            Me.Invalidate(_Bounds)
        End If
    Else
        If _State <> State.Normal Then
            _State = State.Normal
            Me.Invalidate(_Bounds)
        End If
    End If
End Sub


Protected Overrides Sub OnMouseLeave(ByVal e As System.EventArgs)
    ' Reset the button appearance. This will also deactivate the button
    ' if it has been pressed but not released.
    ' The code repaints the button only if needed.
    If _State <> State.Normal Then
        _State = State.Normal
        Me.Invalidate(_Bounds)
    End If
End Sub
```

```
Protected Overrides Sub OnMouseDown( _
   ByVal e As System.Windows.Forms.MouseEventArgs)
      ' Change the button to a pushed state, provided the mouse pointer is
      ' over the image and the Left mouse button has been clicked
      If _Bounds.Contains(e.X, e.Y) And _
       (e.Button And MouseButtons.Left = MouseButtons.Left) Then
          _State = State.Pushed
          Me.Invalidate(_Bounds)
      End If
End Sub

Protected Overrides Sub OnMouseUp(ByVal e As System.Windows.Forms.MouseEventArgs)
      ' Change the button to a normal state and repaint if needed.
      If Not e.Button And MouseButtons.Left = MouseButtons.Left Then
          _State = State.Normal

          If _Bounds.Contains(e.X, e.Y) Then
              _State = State.MouseOver
          Else
              _State = State.Normal
          End If

          Me.Invalidate(_Bounds)
      End If
End Sub
```

Finally, the paint logic renders the button in the appropriate state and the associated text. It uses a raised three-dimensional border when the mouse is positioned over the button, and a sunken border when it is clicked, which is similar to the image bar style used in Microsoft Outlook. The text is placed to the right of the picture and is vertically centered with the mid-point of the image by measuring the image and font sizes.

```
Protected Overrides Sub OnPaint(ByVal e As System.Windows.Forms.PaintEventArgs)

    If _Image Is Nothing Then
        ' Draw the text without the image.
        e.Graphics.DrawString(Me.Text, Me.Font, New SolidBrush(Me.ForeColor), _
                        10, 0)
    Else
        If Me.Enabled = False Then
            ' Paint the picture in a disabled state.
            ControlPaint.DrawImageDisabled(e.Graphics, _Image, 2, 2, _
                                    Me.BackColor)
```

```
            Else
                ' Paint the image according to the button state.
                Select Case _State
                    Case State.Normal
                        e.Graphics.DrawImage(_Image, 2, 2)
                    Case State.MouseOver
                        ControlPaint.DrawBorder3D(e.Graphics, _Bounds, _
                            Border3DStyle.Raised, Border3DSide.All)
                        e.Graphics.DrawImage(_Image, 2, 2)
                    Case State.Pushed
                        ControlPaint.DrawBorder3D(e.Graphics, _Bounds, _
                            Border3DStyle.Sunken, Border3DSide.All)
                        e.Graphics.DrawImage(_Image, 3, 3)
                End Select
            End If

            ' Paint the caption text next to the image.
            e.Graphics.DrawString(Me.Text, Me.Font, New SolidBrush(Me.ForeColor), _
                _Bounds.Width + 3, (_Bounds.Height - Me.Font.Height) \ 2)

        End If

End Sub
```

The drawing logic benefits from the ControlPaint class, which provides the DrawBorder3D() and the DrawImageDisabled() methods. This class, which was described in the previous chapter, could also help with the DrawFocusRect() method if you wanted to expand the control to be able to handle keyboard events.

The only remaining task is to make sure the click event is only raised when the image is clicked. You can accomplish this by overriding the OnClick() method, and only calling the base implementation (which raises the event) if the mouse is currently positioned over the image.

```
Protected Overrides Sub OnClick(ByVal e As System.EventArgs)

    ' Only propagate the click to the client if it was detected over the image.
    If _State = State.Pushed Then
        MyBase.OnClick(e)
    End If

End Sub
```

There's clearly a lot more you could add to this button control. For example, you could allow the user to change the orientation, place the text under the image, add support for text wrapping, or even create a compound control that contains a collection of images. From a conceptual point of view, these additions are easy. However, you'll find that the code can grow quite lengthy with the additional commands needed to evaluate the state and render the button control appropriately.

**NOTE** *If creating an owner-drawn button control is so much work, why bother? The answer is simple: it allows you to develop a proprietary graphical look for your application. If you do this successfully, your application appears to be more sophisticated, slick, and powerful than a competitor's application. Microsoft recognizes this reality, and outfits business-centric applications like Access and Excel with finely tooled graphics—using controls they don't release to anyone else. Never underestimate the appeal of an attractive user interface on your users!*

## Reconsidering the Vector Drawing Program

Chapter 11 developed the basic framework for a control-based drawing program using the label control. The program worked well, and introduced a basic framework that could accommodate any type of control. The only problem is that the .NET framework doesn't include controls for common shapes like circles, triangles, and squares. Instead, the program "faked" a square by using a label control with a border.

Now that you've covered GDI+, there's a far better solution available, and it only takes a little bit more coding. The basic concept is to create an owner-drawn control that paints the appropriate shape. Substitute this control in the place of the bordered label. The drawing framework handles the dragging, resizing, and coloring automatically by setting properties like Location, Size, and Font.

There is a possible problem. If the user draws a circle, you want the circle shape to act like a circle for all mouse operations. In other words, the user shouldn't be able to click on a part of the control outside the circle and use that to move the control. Similarly, this "invisible" portion of the control shouldn't overwrite other controls on the drawing surface.

Figure 13-5 shows a drawing program with shapes that doesn't take this into account.

*Figure 13-5. A flawed drawing program*

## Solving the Bounding Problem

Luckily, .NET makes it easy to create a control that has a nonrectangular bounding area. In fact, you saw this technique in Chapter 5 with shaped forms. All that's required is to set the control's Region property, which defines a new clipping region.

Figure 13-6 shows a drawing program that uses the region property to define control borders. Note that this does have a side effect: the control cannot be as effectively antialiased (or blended with the background). As a result, the border appears more jagged.

This new drawing program supports rectangles, circles, and squares, but it could easily support any arbitrary or unusual shape. The program works by dynamically creating an instance of a custom shape control.

The shape control has the following features:

- It provides a ShapeType enumeration that defines the shapes it can represent. The programmer chooses a shape by setting the Shape property.

- The shape control uses a private _Path member variable that references a GraphicsPath object with the associated shape. Whenever the Shape property is modified, the control creates a new GraphicsPath, and adds the appropriate shape to it. It then sets the control's Region property, effectively setting its clipping bounds to match the shape.

- The painting logic is the easiest part. It simply uses the FillPath() method to draw the shape and the DrawPath() method to outline it.

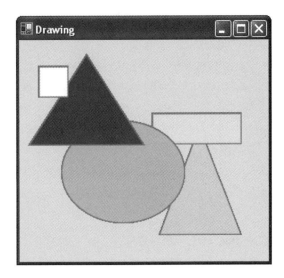

*Figure 13-6. A corrected drawing program*

Here's the complete Shape class code:

```
Public Class Shape
    Inherits System.Windows.Forms.UserControl

    ' The types of shapes supported by this control.
    Enum ShapeType
        Rectangle
        Ellipse
        Triangle
    End Enum

    Private _Shape As ShapeType = ShapeType.Rectangle
    Private _Path As GraphicsPath

    Public Property Shape() As ShapeType
        Get
            Return _Shape
        End Get
        Set(ByVal Value As ShapeType)
            _Shape = Value
            RefreshPath()
            Me.Invalidate()
        End Set
    End Property
```

```
' Create the corresponding GraphicsPath for the shape, and apply
' it to the control by setting the Region property.
Private Sub RefreshPath()
    _Path = New GraphicsPath()
    Select Case _Shape
        Case ShapeType.Rectangle
            _Path.AddRectangle(Me.ClientRectangle)
        Case ShapeType.Ellipse
            _Path.AddEllipse(Me.ClientRectangle)
        Case ShapeType.Triangle
            Dim pt1 As New Point(Me.Width \ 2,0)
            Dim pt2 As New Point(0,Me.Height)
            Dim pt3 As New Point(Me.Width,Me.Height)
            _Path.AddPolygon(New Point() {pt1, pt2, pt3})
    End Select
    Me.Region = New Region(_Path)
End Sub

Protected Overrides Sub OnResize(ByVal e As System.EventArgs)
    MyBase.OnResize(e)
    RefreshPath()
    Me.Invalidate()
End Sub

Protected Overrides Sub OnPaint( _
  ByVal e As System.Windows.Forms.PaintEventArgs)
    MyBase.OnPaint(e)
    e.Graphics.SmoothingMode = SmoothingMode.AntiAlias
    e.Graphics.FillPath(New SolidBrush(Me.BackColor), _Path)
    e.Graphics.DrawPath(New Pen(Me.ForeColor, 4), _Path)
End Sub

End Class
```

The drawing framework needs a slight modification: instead of creating a label control, it creates a Shape object and sets the Shape property depending on the user's menu selection.

```
Private Sub mnuNewShape_Click(ByVal sender As System.Object, _
  ByVal e As System.EventArgs) _
  Handles mnuRectangle.Click, mnuEllipse.Click, mnuTriangle.Click

    ' Create and configure the shape.
    Dim NewShape As New Shape()
    NewShape.Size = New Size(40, 40)
    NewShape.ForeColor = Color.Coral

    ' Configure the appropriate shape.
    If sender Is mnuRectangle Then
        NewShape.Shape = Shape.ShapeType.Rectangle
    ElseIf sender Is mnuEllipse Then
        NewShape.Shape = Shape.ShapeType.Ellipse
    ElseIf sender Is mnuTriangle Then
        NewShape.Shape = Shape.ShapeType.Triangle
    End If

    ' To determine where to place the shape, you need to convert the
    ' current screen-based mouse coordinates into relative form coordinates.
    NewShape.Location = Me.PointToClient(Me.MousePosition)

    ' Attach a context menu to the shape.
    NewShape.ContextMenu = mnuLabel

    ' Connect the shape to all its event handlers.
    AddHandler NewShape.MouseDown, AddressOf lbl_MouseDown
    AddHandler NewShape.MouseMove, AddressOf lbl_MouseMove
    AddHandler NewShape.MouseUp, AddressOf lbl_MouseUp

    ' Add the shape to the form.
    Me.Controls.Add(NewShape)

End Sub
```

With this minor modification, the drawing program now handles the owner-drawn controls seamlessly, supporting the same features for resizing, dragging, and changing the fill color.

One minor quirk appears with the ellipse shape. The drawing program only allows a shape to be resized using its bottom right corner. However, the ellipse's corners are clipped off to fit the circular region.

A simple workaround is to add the ability to resize the shape from any of its sides. The revised MouseMove event handler is shown as follows.

```
Private Sub lbl_MouseMove(ByVal sender As Object, _
  ByVal e As System.Windows.Forms.MouseEventArgs)

    ' Retrieve a reference to the active shape.
    Dim CurrentCtrl As Control
    CurrentCtrl = CType(sender, Control)

    If IsDragging = True Then
        ' Move the control.
        CurrentCtrl.Left = e.X + CurrentCtrl.Left - ClickOffsetX
        CurrentCtrl.Top = e.Y + CurrentCtrl.Top - ClickOffsetY

    ElseIf IsResizing = True Then
        ' Resize the control, according to the resize mode.
        If CurrentCtrl.Cursor Is Cursors.SizeNWSE Then
            CurrentCtrl.Width = e.X
            CurrentCtrl.Height = e.Y
        ElseIf CurrentCtrl.Cursor Is Cursors.SizeNS Then
            CurrentCtrl.Height = e.Y
        ElseIf CurrentCtrl.Cursor Is Cursors.SizeWE Then
            CurrentCtrl.Width = e.X
        End If

    Else
        ' Change the cursor if the mouse pointer is on one of the edges
        ' of the control.
        If (e.X + 5) > CurrentCtrl.Width And (e.Y + 5) > CurrentCtrl.Height Then
            CurrentCtrl.Cursor = Cursors.SizeNWSE
        ElseIf (e.X + 5) > CurrentCtrl.Width Then
            CurrentCtrl.Cursor = Cursors.SizeWE
        ElseIf (e.Y + 5) > CurrentCtrl.Height Then
            CurrentCtrl.Cursor = Cursors.SizeNS
        Else
            CurrentCtrl.Cursor = Cursors.Arrow
        End If
    End If
End Sub
```

> **NOTE** *Be sure to check out the DrawingShapes example with this chapter. With remarkably few lines of code, it implements a drawing program that lets you add, move, resize, and remove shapes. Using these principles, you could create something more practical for your organization, like a custom diagramming tool.*

## A Simple Graphing Control

The last control considered here is a simple bar chart. It's a good demonstration of how you can create a higher-level GDI+ control. Instead of representing a single shape or button, it renders a complete display according to the supplied data.

The basis of the chart is a BarItem class that stores information for a single bar. This information consists of a numerical value and a short title that can be displayed along with the bar.

```
Public Class BarItem
    Public ShortForm As String
    Public Value As Decimal

    Public Sub New(ByVal ShortForm As String, ByVal value As Decimal)
        Me.ShortForm = ShortForm
        Me.Value = value
    End Sub
End Class
```

The data for a bar chart is made up of a collection of BarItem objects. Thus, to support the control you can create a strongly typed collection that only accepts BarItem objects. You could use an ordinary ArrayList or Hashtable collection with the control, but you would not be able to prevent the user from adding invalid objects to the chart data.

```
Public Class BarItemCollection
    Inherits CollectionBase

    Public Sub Add(ByVal item As BarItem)
        Me.List.Add(item)
    End Sub
```

```vb
Public Sub Remove(ByVal index As Integer)
    ' Check to see if there is an item at the supplied index.
    If index > Count - 1 Or index < 0 Then
        Throw New System.IndexOutOfRangeException()
    Else
        List.RemoveAt(index)
    End If
End Sub


Public Property Item(ByVal index As Integer) As BarItem
    Get
        ' The appropriate item is retrieved from the List object and
        ' explicitly cast to the BarItem type.
        Return CType(List.Item(index), BarItem)
    End Get
    Set(ByVal Value As BarItem)
        List.Item(index) = Value
    End Set
End Property

End Class
```

The SimpleChart control provides a BarItemCollection through its Bars property. The client programmer must create and add the appropriate BarItem objects. A more sophisticated control might add dedicated UITypeEditors that allow BarItem objects to be created and added at design time.

```vb
Public Class SimpleChart
    Inherits System.Windows.Forms.UserControl

    Private _Bars As New BarItemCollection()

    Public Property Bars() As BarItemCollection
        Get
            Return _Bars
        End Get
        Set(ByVal Value As BarItemCollection)
            _Bars = Value
            RebuildChart()
        End Set
    End Property


    ' (Drawing logic omitted.)

End Class
```

The last ingredient is the drawing logic for the chart. This logic consists of two parts. The first part steps through the data and determines the maximum BarItem value. All other bar items are sized proportionally.

```
Private _BarWidth, _MaxValue As Integer

Public Sub RebuildChart()

    If Bars.Count = 0 Then Exit Sub

    ' Find out how much space a single bar can occupy.
    _BarWidth = Me.Width \ _Bars.Count

    ' Set the maximum value on the chart.
    _MaxValue = 0
    Dim Bar As BarItem
    For Each Bar In _Bars
        If Bar.Value > _MaxValue Then _MaxValue = Bar.Value
    Next

    Me.Invalidate()
End Sub
```

The RebuildChart() method is public, and the client must call it after adding the appropriate BarItem objects. Alternatively, you could add a BarChanged event to the BarItemCollection class, and rebuild the chart in the SimpleChart control whenever this event occurs. However, this approach could hamper performance, because the chart would be recalculated multiple times, as each individual bar is added.

The OnPaint() routine steps through the collection of bars, and draws each one onto the form with the appropriate proportional size. Each bar is created using two rectangles and an outline, for a nice shadowed effect. The BarItem.ShortForm text is also drawn onto each bar.

```
Protected Overrides Sub OnPaint(ByVal e As System.Windows.Forms.PaintEventArgs)
    MyBase.OnPaint(e)

    If _Bars.Count = 0 Then Exit Sub

    Dim X As Integer = 0
    Dim BaseLine As Integer = Me.Height
    Dim Bar As BarItem
```

```
        ' Draw each item.
        For Each Bar In _Bars
            Dim Height As Integer = CType(Bar.Value / _MaxValue * Me.Height, Integer)
            Dim Top As Integer = Me.Height - Height

            ' Draw bar (two rectangles are used for a shadowed effect),
            ' along with an outline.
            e.Graphics.FillRectangle(Brushes.LightBlue, X + 4, Top, _
                                    _BarWidth - 7, Height)
            e.Graphics.DrawRectangle(New Pen(Color.White, 4), X + 4, Top, _
                                    _BarWidth - 4, Height)
            e.Graphics.FillRectangle(Brushes.SteelBlue, X + 8, Top + 4, _
                                    _BarWidth - 9, Height - 5)

            ' Draw title.
            Dim TextFont As New Font("Tahoma", 8)
            e.Graphics.DrawString(Bar.ShortForm, TextFont, Brushes.White, _
                                X + 15, Top + 5)

            X += _BarWidth
        Next

        ' Draw the grid.
        e.Graphics.DrawLine(Pens.Black, 0, Me.Height - 1, Me.Width, Me.Height - 1)
        e.Graphics.DrawLine(Pens.Black, 0, 0, 0, Me.Height)

    End Sub
```

The code that follows creates a simple chart, which is displayed in Figure 13-7.

```
Private Sub Form1_Load(ByVal sender As System.Object, _
  ByVal e As System.EventArgs) Handles MyBase.Load

    SimpleChart1.Bars.Add(New BarItem("1999", 10))
    SimpleChart1.Bars.Add(New BarItem("2000", 20))
    SimpleChart1.Bars.Add(New BarItem("2001", 5))
    SimpleChart1.Bars.Add(New BarItem("2002", 27))
    SimpleChart1.RebuildChart()

End Sub
```

This is the same pattern you could follow to create any type of static control. In many ways, it's an easier task than creating a button or a user input control because it doesn't need to support user input or receive the focus, although it may require a significant amount of drawing code. For a faster refresh, you could apply the double-buffering techniques discussed earlier in this chapter.

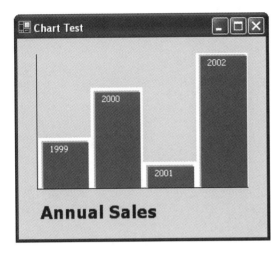

*Figure 13-7. A sample chart*

If you want to start tweaking the SimpleChart control, there are several interesting avenues. You might want to start by developing a better axis, allowing customizable bar captions, or creating a pie chart mode (the Graphics class also exposes a DrawPie() and FillPie() method). Look for SimpleChart project with the online samples for this chapter.

## The Last Word

GDI+ controls represent the fusion of two remarkable new features: the next-generation drawing framework GDI+, and .NET's simple and elegant class-based control development. The potential for owner drawn .NET controls is limitless, and major tool vendors have already begun developing .NET equivalents for common UI widgets like advanced scrollbars and image controls. Look for these on the Internet—some are even available to experiment with at no cost.

If you want to master control development, the best approach is to review as many code examples as possible. There's no limit to what you can accomplish with dedication and a little ingenuity, but owner-drawn controls can require as much sheer code as a basic sales ordering database application. Microsoft, on its MSDN home page, provides several control samples that range from quirky and useless to genuinely ground breaking.

The next chapter shifts the focus to a new topic: integrating Help into your .NET applications, and creating intelligent interfaces.

# CHAPTER 14

# Help and Application-Embedded Support

HELP: IS IT THE FINAL POLISH on a professional application or a time-consuming chore? It all depends on the audience, but most commercial applications need a support center where users can seek assistance when they become confused or disoriented. Without this basic aid, you (or your organization's technical support department) are sure to be buried under an avalanche of support calls.

In this chapter, you learn

- How to integrate Windows Help files into your applications. You look at launching Help manually, and using the context-sensitive HelpProvider.

- When to design your own Help, and how you can weave it into an application using an extensible database-based or XML-based framework.

- How to break down the limits of Help and design application-embedded support: user assistance that's integrated into the software it documents, instead of slapped on in a separate file as an afterthought. You explore some basic approaches like affordances and wizards (through visual inheritance), and a few advanced techniques like animated agents.

## The Case for Help

In recent years there has been a shift away from printed documentation. The occasional weighty manual (like the book you're holding now) is still required for learning advanced tools, but the average piece of office productivity or business software no longer assumes the user is willing to perform any additional reading. Instead, these programs are heavily dependent on natural, instinctive interfaces, and use online Help to patch the gaps and answer the occasional user question.

Online Help doesn't have to take the form of a second-rate user manual, however. The advantages of online Help are remarkable:

- **Increased control.** With a little effort, you can determine exactly what information users see when they click the F1 key. With a printed book, users might look for information using the index, table of contents, or even a third-party "…For Dummies" guide, and you have no way of knowing what they will find.

- **Rich media.** With online Help you can use as many pictures as you want, in any combination, and even include sounds, movies, and animated demonstrations.

- **Search tools and context-sensitivity.** Help systems can automate most of the drudgery associated with finding information. They can look for keywords with a full-text search (rather than relying on a human-compiled index), and programs can use context-sensitivity to make sure users see the appropriate topic immediately.

All help standards provide these advantages in one form or another. In the next section, you explore the Help landscape.

## Types of Help

Standardized Help has existed since the Windows platform was created, and even in the DOS world in little known tools like QuickHelp. Throughout the years (and versions of Windows), Help has continued to evolve, passing through several distinct stages, which are described in the next few sections.

### WinHelp

The WinHelp format used in Windows 3.0 still exists, and can be used in the most modern Windows application. Unfortunately, it looks irredeemably garish. Help files from different authors tended to look—and act—differently.

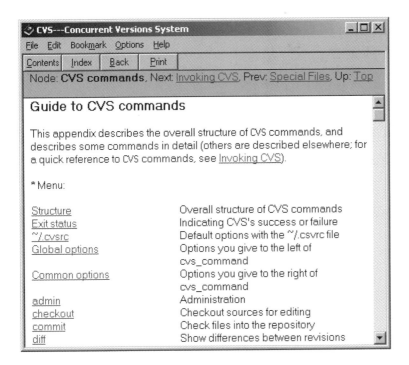

*Figure 14-1. WinHelp: a piece of living history*

## WinHelp 95

When Windows 95 was introduced, a new standard (often referred to as WinHelp 95) took over. WinHelp 95 files are familiar to almost any computer user, and they are still used in countless programs.

WinHelp 95 was a major improvement in the Help world. Whereas the original WinHelp forced developers to create their own contents page with hyperlinks, WinHelp 95 files use a separate contents file (with the extension .cnt) to define the standardized multilevel table of contents. WinHelp 95 really has two parts: the .cnt contents page (which also provides a standardized index and full-text search), and the .hlp help file that provides the actual topics. When a user double-clicks a topic, the table of contents disappears, and is replaced with the appropriate help window.

The standardized table of contents was both the most significant advance and the most obvious limitation of WinHelp 95. The obvious problem is that users often need to jump back and forth between the table of contents and the topic pages before they find the content they need. This process is tedious, and it feels complicated because there can be multiple windows scattered about the desktop.

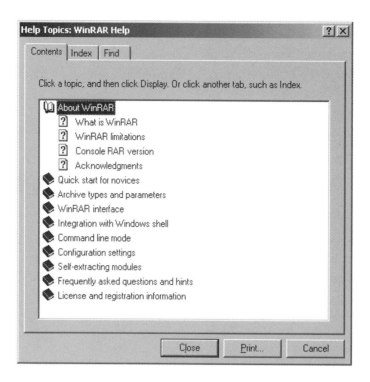

*Figure 14-2. WinHelp 95: a facelift*

## HTML Help

The next version of WinHelp was named HTML Help, because the source files were written in HTML markup instead of the RTF format. HTML Help debuted with Windows 98 and also shipped with Internet Explorer 4. A common source of confusion about HTML Help is the idea that it is somehow supposed to provide help over the web or browser-integrated help. While HTML Help depends on some components that are also used in Internet Explorer, it really has little to do with the Internet. Instead, HTML Help is an improvement to WinHelp that combines the table of contents and topic views in the same window (see Figure 14-3).

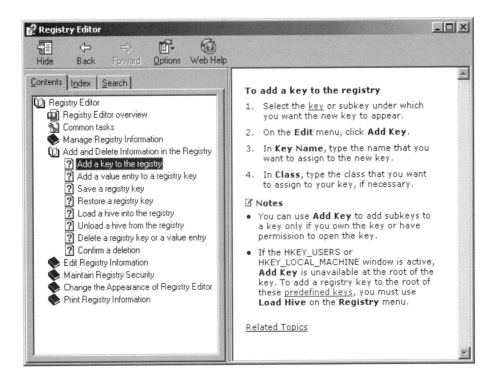

*Figure 14-3. HTML Help: the industrial revolution of help*

The new HTML Help view makes it dramatically easier to browse through a long, multilevel table of contents without losing your place. By dividing and subdividing information into its smallest bits, Help developers are able to put fairly lengthy, complex content in a help file. With HTML Help, developers also started to use DHTML and JavaScript text directly in their Help to create collapsible headings and other neat tricks. In some cases (for example, the Visual Studio 6 documentation and the SQL Server documentation), Microsoft refers to these help files as "books online." HTML Help files always use the .chm extension.

## MS Help 2

The next revolution to the Help world is tentatively titled MS Help 2, and it's the help engine used by Microsoft's MSDN help in Visual Studio .NET. The first Help 2 engine ships with Visual Studio .NET, but it isn't yet supported by most third-party tools, and there isn't a great deal of information about it (some basic information is available at `http://helpware.net`). Help 2 promises some long-awaited improvements to HTML help, like a redesigned user interface, and the ability to embed a help window in an application interface with minimum fuss. However, it also has its idiosyncrasies. For example, every Help 2 file must be registered with the Windows operating system. You can't simply copy the appropriate .HxS file to another computer.

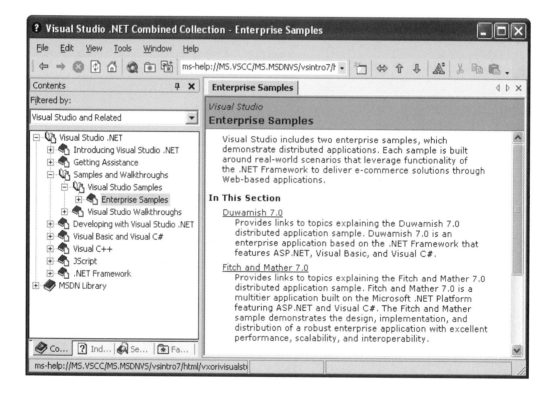

*Figure 14-4. Help 2: a new standard?*

> **NOTE** *One of the exciting features with MS Help 2 is that it can plug into the Visual Studio .NET Help collection. That means that tool vendors can distribute Help with their components that will pop into the Dynamic Help window in the Visual Studio .NET IDE when the component is being used.*

## Some Help Authoring Tools

Microsoft provides only rudimentary tools for compiling source files to create Help systems. To have the full range of tools for designing, linking, and configuring your Help, you will probably need to turn to a third-party design tool. Creating Help is beyond the scope of this book, but there are a few starting points:

- The "professional" Help design systems tend to ship with countless tools—and intimidating prices. Two leading examples are RoboHelp (http://www.ehelp.com) and ForeFront Help Center (http://www.componentone.com/ffhelp/ff.htm), although numerous other mutually incompatible design tools are available.

- Some Help systems are designed from the ground up with single-sourcing in mind, with varied degrees of success. Doc-to-Help (http://www.wextech.com) attempts to integrate printed documents in Microsoft Word with Help, and WebWorks Publisher (http://www.quadralay.com) works magic with FrameMaker files— at the cost of forcing you to learn and use a proprietary language.

- Numerous smaller-scale utilities assist with the compilation or some aspects of development (like creating a table of contents) but don't assume you'll use an HTML editor or other tool to write the actual content. An example of a program like this is FAR (http://www.helpware.net), which is unique in being one of the first third-party tools to introduce support for MS Help 2. You can also find many cheaper Help tools at shareware sites online.

# Classic Bad Help

Have you ever had this experience? You find an unusual option buried deep in an application, and it piques your curiosity. You hit F1, curious to find out what this option accomplishes. But your optimism dwindles when you read the description provided by the context-sensitive Help system: "To enable option X, click once on the option X check box. To disable option X, click the option X check box again to remove the check mark. Click OK to save your changes."

Clearly something is missing here. You want to know what option X does; the Help wants to explain, in oddly explicit detail, how to use a check box. The situation is ridiculous, as the function of option X is not at all obvious, but the way to use a check box is an instinctive part of every computer user's understanding. If you don't know how to use a check box, you probably wouldn't have guessed to press the F1 key for help.

This is a classic example of bad help. Some of the characteristics of bad Help include

- **It describes the user interface.** Users don't need to know how the interface works—they will often discover that by trial and error. They need to know what it does.

- **It's long.** Even HTML Help doesn't have the same bandwidth as a printed document, and endless scrolling is sure to frustrate users.

- **It uses visual clues.** Instructing the user to look at the "top left" or "middle right" may seem logical enough, but with the application running in another (potentially minimized) window, it can cause confusion.

- **It omits information.** Printed documents can afford to choose what they cover. However, Help documents are shipped with the software, and expected to provide a matching reference. Thus, you can't ignore any option or setting that's in the interface.

To understand good help, you need to recognize that most Help is designed to provide reference information. Help really shines compared to a printed book when it's able to use context sensitivity to automatically display a piece of information about a specific window or setting. This is the type of information that all users need occasionally while working with an application they mostly understand.

On the other hand, Help is relatively poor at providing tutorial-based learning, which explains tasks that incorporate many different parts. In this case, it's generally easier to use a printed book. Help that tries to provide descriptive task-based learning is generally frustrating for a number of reasons—users can't see the help window at the same time they look at the program window, the help window doesn't provide enough space for the long descriptions that are needed, and most users don't want to read a large amount of information from the computer screen anyway.

When creating Help, you should aim to divide it into discrete topics that describe individual windows, complete with all their details. This provides the most useful context-sensitive Help system.

> **TIP**  *Help can be used for tutorial-based learning. . .but not ordinary help. Instead, applications and games that teach users as they work need to incorporate custom solutions, which are generally referred to as application-embedded support. You look at this technology later in the chapter. Application-embedded support supplements the standardized reference-based Help systems; it doesn't replace them.*

## Basic Help with the HelpProvider

One easy way to use Help with a .NET application is by adding the HelpProvider control. This "invisible" control shows up in the component tray (Figure 14-5).

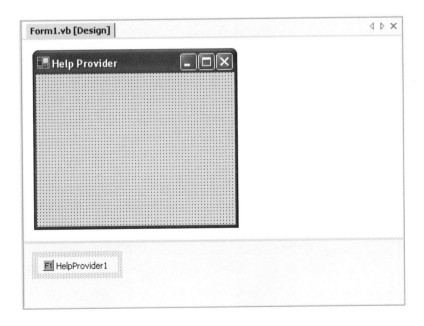

*Figure 14-5. The HelpProvider*

The HelpProvider uses a basic HelpNamespace property that sets the help source. This could be a path to an ordinary .hlp file, an HTML Help .chm file, or even a URL. To bind a control to this HelpProvider, you simply need to set the extended ShowHelp property to True. In other words, when you add a HelpProvider to a form, every control acquires a special property in the designer (with a name like ShowHelp on HelpProvider). Set this to True, and the help file is automatically launched if the user presses the F1 key while this control has focus.

You can also connect or disconnect help manually in code, using the HelpProvider.SetShowHelp() method. Just pass the control that you want to use as an argument.

```
Private Sub HelpTest_Load(ByVal sender As System.Object, _
  ByVal e As System.EventArgs) Handles MyBase.Load

    ' This turns on F1 help support for cmdAdd.
    hlp.SetShowHelp(cmdAdd, True)

    ' This disables it.
    hlp.SetShowHelp(cmdAdd, False)

End Sub
```

**NOTE** *There really isn't any difference between using the SetShowHelp() method at the extended ShowHelp property provided by the designer. With providers, Visual Studio .NET simply translates your selections into the appropriate method calls, and adds the code the form code. So when you set the ShowHelp property, you are still in fact using the SetShowHelp() method.*

You can also set the HelpKeyword and HelpNavigator properties in conjunction to configure which topic is shown when the Help is invoked. Table 14-1 outlines all the possible options you have with the HelpNavigator enumeration. Note that while HTML Help supports all these choices, the support in WinHelp and WinHelp 95 is notoriously poor.

*Table 14-1. Values for the HelpNavigator Enumeration*

| HelpNavigator | Description |
| --- | --- |
| TableOfContents | Shows the table of contents for the Help file. This is the most common option if you aren't linking to a specific topic. |
| Index | Shows the index for the Help file, if it exists. |
| KeywordIndex | Shows the index, and automatically highlights the first topic that matches the HelpKeyword property. For example, if HelpKeyword is "format" for this control, the most similar entry is highlighted in the index list. |
| Find | Shows the search page for the Help file, which allows the user to perform unguided text searches. This feature tends to provide poorer (and slower) results than the index or table of contents, and is thus avoided if possible. |
| Topic | The most useful option for context-sensitive help. If you choose this option, you can set the topic identifier as a HelpKeyword. For example, you could use the topic URL in an HTML Help file (like about.htm). When the Help is launched, this topic is browsed to and displayed automatically. |

For example, the following two lines of code define a context-sensitive link that binds a control to a specific topic in an HTML Help file.

```
' Specify a topic link.
hlp.SetHelpNavigator(ctrl, HelpNavigator.Topic)

' Identify the topic.
hlp.SetHelpKeyword(ctrl, "Welcome.html")
```

Note that the topic name is "Welcome.html." In this case, the example is using a .chm file, and the original HTML Help project included the topic in a source file named Welcome.html. Once the .chm file is created, this file no longer exists separately. Instead, like all topics, it is combined into the compiled help file. However, the file name can still be used as a help keyword to select the topic. Your other option (and your only option with the older WinHelp format) is to use context integers, which are numbers that uniquely identify each topic.

Alternatively, you don't need to use a Help file at all. Instead, you can display a pop-up window with a short message (formerly referred to as "What's This Help"). To do so, make sure that you do not set the HelpProvider.HelpNamespace property, which always takes precedence. Then, either set the HelpString on HelpProvider property at design-time, or use the SetHelpString method, as shown here:

```
hlp.SetHelpString(cmdAdd, "Choose another item from the catalog.")
hlp.SetHelpString(cmdDelete, "Delete the selected item from your order.")
```

The resulting pop-up message is shown in Figure 14-6.

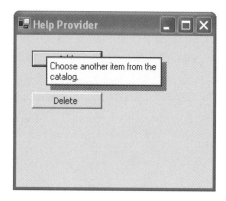

*Figure 14-6. What's This Help*

> **NOTE** *What's This Help was at one point considered a great new approach for creating help, because it doesn't force the user to look in another window. Instead, it integrates help directly in the interface. What's This Help never really caught on, for a number of reasons, including the fact that it only allows the display of limited, unformatted information (for example, you can't bold command names), and it forces the user to understand the rather complicated model of changing focus to the correct control, and then pressing F1.*

Note that when you set use the SetHelpString() or SetHelpKeyword() methods, you automatically enable help for the control. That means that you don't need to call the SetShowHelp() method, unless you want to explicitly disable help for the control.

## Control-Based and Form-Based Help

Control-by-control context-sensitivity is usually too much for an application. It's rare that a Help file is created with separate topics for every control in a window, and even if it were, most users simply pressing F1 as soon as they encounter a confusing setting. In other words, they don't explicitly tab to the setting they want to find out about to give it focus before invoking Help. For that reason, the control that is launching Help is quite possibly not the control that the user is seeking information about.

One easy way around this is to define an individual context-sensitive help topic for every form. For a settings dialog, this topic should contain a list of every option. Nicely designed Help might even use dynamic HTML to make this list collapsible (see, for example, Figure 14-7).

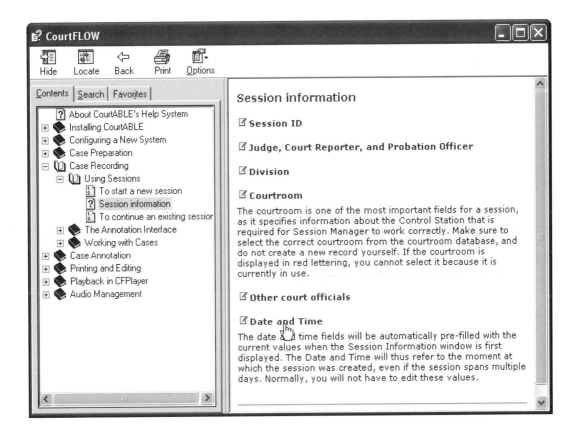

*Figure 14-7. Collapsible help for one window*

The only subtlety to understand with form-based Help is that when you enable Help for the form, you also enable Help for every control it contains. If the user presses F1 while the focus is on a control that is specifically configured with different Help settings, these settings take precedence. If, however, the current control has ShowHelp set to False, the request will be forwarded to the containing form, which launches its own Help. This process works analogously with all container controls, and it allows you to define Help that's as specific as you need, while still being able to fall back on a generic form-wide topic for controls that aren't specifically configured.

> **TIP** *The online samples for this chapter include a HelpTest project that shows a simple project with three windows. Each of three windows uses a different granularity of help: form-based, frame-based, and control-based. You can run this application with the included help file to get a better understanding of the options you have for linking context-sensitive help to an application.*

## Invoking Help Programmatically

The examples so far require the user to press the F1 key. This automated approach doesn't work as well if you want to provide your own buttons that allow the user to trigger help when needed. Sometimes, this sort of prominent reminder can reassure the user that help is nearby.

To trigger help programmatically, you need to use the shared ShowHelp() method of the Help class (found in the System.Windows.Forms namespace). The Help class works analogously to the HelpProvider—in fact, the HelpProvider uses the Help class behind the scenes when the user presses F1.

There are several overloaded versions of the ShowHelp() method. The simplest requires a help filename (or URL) and the control that is the parent for the help dialog (this second parameter is required for low-level Windows operating system reasons). Here's an example that shows the test.hlp file:

```
Help.ShowHelp(Me, "test.hlp")
```

Additionally, you can use a version of the ShowHelp() method that requires a HelpNavigator, one that requires a keyword, or one that requires both a keyword and a HelpNavigator. Here's an example that could be used for context-sensitive help:

```
Help.ShowHelp(Me, "test.hlp", HelpNavigator.Topic, "about.htm")
```

To save yourself some work when using this technique with the HelpProvider, you would probably retrieve these values from another control. For example, you might provide a button on your form that invokes the default form help:

```
Private Sub cmdHelp_Click(ByVal sender As System.Object, _
  ByVal e As System.EventArgs) Handles cmdHelp.Click

    Help.ShowHelp(Me, hlp.HelpNamespace, hlp.GetHelpNavigator(Me), _
                hlp.GetHelpKeyword(Me))

End Sub
```

Similarly, you might use a right-click context menu for a control that provides the control's default help:

```
Private Sub mnuHelp_Click(ByVal sender As System.Object, _
  ByVal e As System.EventArgs) Handles mnuHelp.Click

    Dim ctrl As Control = mnuLabel.SourceControl
    Help.ShowHelp(ctrl, hlp.HelpNamespace, hlp.GetHelpNavigator(ctrl), _
                hlp.GetHelpKeyword(ctrl))

End Sub
```

This menu event handler is written using the SourceControl property, which means it's generic enough to be used with any control. When the menu is clicked, it retrieves the control attached to the menu, and gets its assigned Help keyword.

## Help Without the HelpProvider

Now that you are this far, it's possible to unshackle yourself completely from the HelpProvider class. It works like this—handle the KeyDown event of every form that should display help, and check for the F1 key. If it is pressed, launch the appropriate help programmatically with the Help class.

There are two tricks to making this work. The first one is setting the form's KeyPreview property to True, which makes sure it will receive all key press events, regardless of what control has focus. The second sticky point is to make sure you create an event handler for the KeyDown event, not the KeyPress event, which doesn't react to the special F1 key.

The code itself is simple:

```
Private Sub Form1_KeyDown(ByVal sender As Object, _
  ByVal e As System.Windows.Forms.KeyEventArgs) Handles MyBase.KeyDown

    If e.KeyCode = Keys.F1 Then
        Help.ShowHelp(Me, "..\test.hlp")
    End If

End Sub
```

So now that you've seen how it can be done, why would you want to do it? There are actually a number of reasons that you might take this approach when using context-sensitive Help. You examine two of the most common in the next two sections.

## Using Database-Based Help

Help files, like any other external resource, change. You don't want to embed information like topic URLs all over your user interface, because they are difficult and time-consuming to update. Instead, you can use a basic form event handler that calls a method in a custom AppHelp class. It would look something like this:

```
Private Sub Form1_KeyDown(ByVal sender As Object, _
  ByVal e As System.Windows.Forms.KeyEventArgs) Handles MyBase.KeyDown

    If e.KeyCode = Keys.F1 Then
        Global.Help.ShowHelp(Me)
    End If

End Sub
```

The Global class simply provides the current AppHelp instance through a shared Help property:

```
Public Class Global
    Public Shared Help As AppHelp
End Class
```

The AppHelp.ShowHelp() method examines the submitted form, compares it with a list of forms in a database, and thus determines the appropriate context topic, which it launches. Note that for performance reasons, this list of form-topic mappings would be read once when the application starts, and stored in a member variable.

The AppHelp class is shown in the following example. The database code needed to retrieve the FormHelpMappings table has been omitted.

```
Public Class AppHelp
    Public FormHelpMappings As DataTable
    Public HelpFile As String

    Public Sub ShowHelp(HelpForm As Form)
        Dim Row As DataRow
        For Each Row In FormHelpMappings.Rows
            If HelpForm.Name = Row("FormName") Then
                ' A mactch was found. Launch the appropriate help topic.
                Help.ShowHelp(HelpForm, HelpFile, HelpNavigator.Topic, _
                            Row("Topic"))
                Exit Sub
            End If
        Next
    End Sub

End Class
```

## Using Task-Based Help

Another reason you might take control of the help process is to get around the limitations of form-based help. Form-specific help works well in a dialog-based application, but falters when you create a document-based or workspace-based program where users perform a number of different tasks from the same window. Rather than try to write the code needed to dynamically modify help keywords, you can use the AppHelp class to track the current user's task. When Help is invoked, you can use this information to determine what topic should be shown.

Here's the remodeled AppHelp class. Note that in this case, it doesn't decide what topic to show based on form name, but based on one of the preset task types. The logic that links tasks to topics is coded centrally in the AppHelp class (not in the user interface), and it could be moved into a database for even more control. An enumeration is used to ensure that the client code always sets a valid value.

```
Public Class AppHelp

    ' These are the types of tasks that have associated help topics.
    Enum Task
        CreatingReport
        CreatingReportWithWizard
        ManagingReportFiles
        ImportingReport
    End Enum

    Public HelpFile As String
    Public CurrentTask As Task

    ' Show help based on the current task.
    Public Sub ShowHelp(HelpForm As Form)
        Dim Topic As String
        Select Case CurrentTask
            Case Task.CreatingReport
                Topic = "Reports.htm"
            Case Task.CreatingReportWithWizard
                Topic = "Wizard.htm"
            Case Task.ManagingReportFiles
                Topic = "Reports.htm"
            Case Task.ImportingReport
                Topic = "Importing.htm"
        End Select

        Help.ShowHelp(HelpForm, HelpFile, HelpNavigator.Topic, Topic)
    End Sub

End Class
```

Now, the code simply needs to "remember" to set the task at the appropriate times.

```
Global.Help.CurrentTask = AppHelp.Task.CreatingReport
```

When help is invoked, the form doesn't need to determine what task is underway—the AppHelp class simply uses the most recent task setting.

```
Private Sub Form1_KeyDown(ByVal sender As Object, _
  ByVal e As System.Windows.Forms.KeyEventArgs) Handles MyBase.KeyDown


    If e.KeyCode = Keys.F1 Then
        Global.Help.ShowHelp(Me)
    End If

End Sub
```

This system could be made much more complex by using a task list or tracking multiple different types of context information in the AppHelp class, which is conceptually similar to how many advanced consumer applications (like office productivity software) work.


## Creating Your Own Help

Another advanced option you might want to pursue is creating your own Help from scratch, rather than relying on one of the formats I've described. This technique has significant drawbacks: namely, you surrender advanced features like text searching, hierarchical table of contents, and an index. However, it also has significant advantages, the most important being that you can easily integrate Help content into your application. With the current HTML Help system, it is almost impossible to embed and control a help window in your application. MS Help 2 promises some improvements, but the required tools have not yet appeared.

Creating your own Help generally follows two approaches:

- You store help as long strings in a database record. This generally works best when you are using your custom Help for error messages, a tip of the day feature, or some other simple content.

- You store links to an HTML file that is contained in the program directory (or a Help subdirectory). This allows you to easily create files using any HTML design tool, take advantage of linking, and even provide the Help externally (possibly through an Internet browser). Hosting an HTML window in your application is much easier than trying to integrate a help window.

These designs allow you to provide a design like the one shown in Figure 14-8. It provides a slide-out window that can be used to give a list of steps with information for the current task. The information itself is retrieved from a database and displayed in the application.

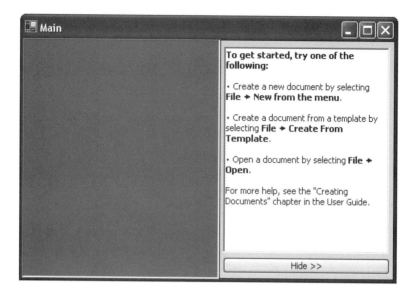

*Figure 14-8. Integrated custom Help*

You'll notice that this .NET example uses a RichTextBox control to display a formatted list of instructions. RichTextBox controls do not support linking, which makes them less useful for complex Help than a full HTML window. Unfortunately, the .NET framework does not provide a dedicated HTML control. Instead, you need to import the Internet Explorer ActiveX control, which will efficiently provide the same functionality (see Figure 14-9).

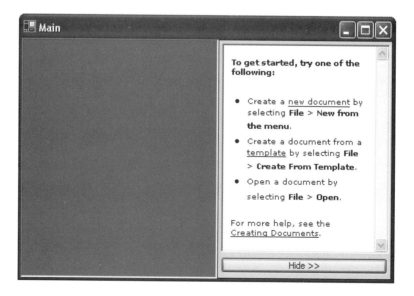

*Figure 14-9. Integrated custom HTML Help*

This design begins to enter a new topic: application-embedded support, which examines how help can be integrated into applications.

## Application-Embedded Support

One of the crucial shortcomings with the Help systems you have looked at is that they are all designed to provide fine-grained reference information about specific windows and controls. As I described earlier, help usually fails miserably when it tries to walk the user through a long, involved task. However, better help is possible. What's needed is a change to how help is designed and integrated in applications.

Application-embedded support represents that change. Quite simply, embedded help is user assistance that is a first class member of an application. It's designed as part of the software, not added to the software after it's complete. Embedded help provides far greater user assistance, but also requires far more development work.

Some examples of embedded help include

- **Process-oriented.** Some applications reserve a portion of their interface for continuous tip messages, or use a tiny information icon that a user can click for more information about the current task. This type of help trains users as they work, and is used to great effect in fairly complex computer games (like the popular hit The Sims). Wizards are another example of process-oriented help.

- **Stationary embedded.** This is the most common form of embedded help, and it refers to the content added to dialog boxes to explain options (affordances) and actual embedded help windows.

- **Agents.** This is one of the most advanced and time-consuming types of embedded help. It was pioneered largely by Microsoft in Microsoft Office (and later abandoned). Microsoft's attitude to agents is extremely schizophrenic— it provides tools aimed to make it easy for all developers to use this level of support, but it only occasionally devotes the intense coding time needed to integrate it into its flagship applications.

- **Bidirectional help.** To some, this is a holy grail of embedded help, but it's rarely achieved, and usually only in a primitive form. Essentially, one of the critical drawbacks with Help is that it's cut off from the applications in two ways. Not only does the user have to leave the application to read most Help files, but once the appropriate information is found in the Help file, the user has to perform the actual work. There's no way for the Help file to act on the user's behalf, and actually show the user how to do what is needed. Some Help files do provide rudimentary "Show Me" links that can prompt the application to display the appropriate window, but this communication is difficult and fragile. With bidirectional help, Help can perform the necessary task, once it determines what the user needs.

## Affordances

Affordances are the visual "clues" designed to demystify a complex application. For example, Windows uses brief descriptions to provide a little information about your computer's Internet settings, as shown in Figure 14-10.

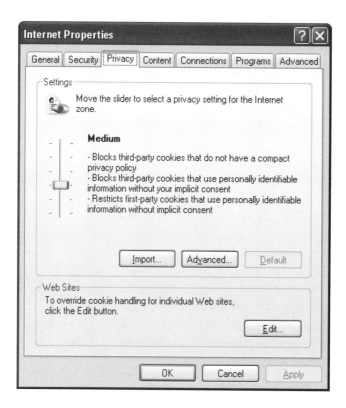

*Figure 14-10. A dialog with affordances*

Help and affordances represent a bit of a paradox. Nothing can clarify a confusing dialog box more than a couple of well-placed words or icons. On the other hand, users often automatically ignore descriptions, error messages, or anything else that requires reading. They either try to figure out the task on their own or, in the case of an error, repeat the task a few times and then give up.

Given this problem, what is the role of Help in an application? I refuse to believe that Help is useless, as I routinely see innovative games and web sites that have no problem guiding users through new and unusual interfaces with a few carefully integrated explanations. Unfortunately, the customary current stand-alone Help is designed to provide reference information. It's very poor at the task-based explanations that most beginning users require—in fact, in this case it's really little more than a limited electronic book.

## Integrating Help and user interface

Of course, integrating help content into the user interface is not a happy solution for the programmer. To fend off the cycle of endless recompiles and tweaking, you can try to read information dynamically from a database, but this approach usually fails because the content is not guaranteed to be the appropriate length and fit in an attractive way in the space provided. Windows controls and Forms have fixed bounds, and do not automatically resize to fit their contents unless you add the code to accommodate this behavior.

Generally, the most practical approach is to add a few words when needed in a dialog box, but to fall back on a secondary window embedded in the application for more extensive information. This window, which you explored in the previous section, is the perfect compromise—it doesn't force the user to leave the application, and it can easily accommodate HTML or RTF documents of various lengths and with embedded formatting. Microsoft is also beginning to standardize a variation of this approach in some of its latest releases.

## Agents

Agents are the animated characters that appear in applications to guide users through a task. The most infamous example of Agents is the (now defunct) Clippy character included with Microsoft Office. Most developers don't consider agents for their applications because of several factors:

- Agents require first-rate design work. An ugly agent is worse than no agent at all.

- Agents require tedious programming. Every action or tip the agent gives must be individually triggered by the application code. If not handled properly, this can lead to Help code that is tangled up with the application's core functionality.

- Agents are "silly," and appeal more for their novelty than for any actual assistance they provide.

These are legitimate concerns. However, in a consumer application, an agent can also act as an appealing and distinctive feature that attracts the user's attention. Agents also perform the remarkable trick of turning tedium into fun. Quite simply, users often enjoy using programs with agents.

Creating a program with agent support is not as difficult as most developers believe, because Microsoft provides some remarkable tools, and a set of four standard characters that can be freely distributed with your applications. To download the agent libraries, refer to http://msdn.microsoft.com/library/en-us/ msagent/userinterface_3y2a.asp. The Microsoft Agent Control is only available as a COM component, but it can be easily consumed in a .NET program by creating a runtime callable wrapper, a task Visual Studio .NET carries out automatically when you add the reference. Figure 14-11 shows the reference you must add for the Microsoft Agent control.

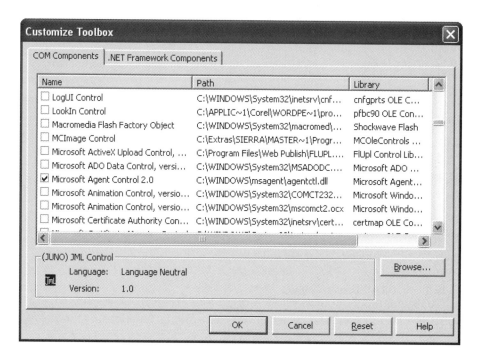

*Figure 14-11. The Microsoft Agent control*

The Microsoft Agent Control allows you to use Merlin, a genie, Peedy (a bird), or Robbie (a robot), or all of them at once. All components are complete with roto-scoped animations, can perform various actions as you direct them, can move about the screen, can think or "speak" text (either using a poor voice synthesizer that's included, or a .wav file you specify). When speaking with a voice file, the characters' mouths even move to synchronize closely with the words, creating a lifelike illusion. Best of all, Microsoft quietly gives these features away for free. You can purchase other Agent characters from third-party sites online, or create them independently, although the tools provided won't help you create lifelike animations on your own.

The online samples include an AgentTryout application that allows you to put an agent character through its paces, speaking and thinking the text you specify, moving about the screen, and performing various animations (see Figure 14-12).

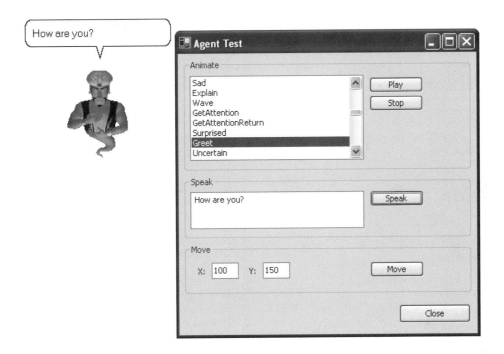

*Figure 14-12. The agent tryout application*

The AgentTryout interacts with any of the four agent characters through a special AgentController class, which encapsulates all the functionality for controlling movements, speech, and action. This class code can be reused in any application.

The AgentTryout interacts with any of the four agent characters through a special AgentController class, which encapsulates all the functionality for controlling movements, speech, and action. This class code can be reused in any application.

```vb
Public Class AgentController

    ' Agent variable.
    Private AgentChar As AgentObjects.IAgentCtlCharacterEx

    ' Name of the initialized character.
    Private CharacterName As String

    ' Balloon constants
    Const BalloonOn As Short = 1
    Const SizeToText As Short = 2
    Const AutoHide As Short = 4
    Const AutoPace As Short = 8

    Public Sub New(ByVal AgentHost As AxAgentObjects.AxAgent, _
                ByVal Character As String)

        AgentHost.Characters.Load(Character)
        AgentChar = AgentHost.Characters(Character)

        CharacterName = Character

        ' You could put your own options in this menu, if desired.
        AgentChar.AutoPopupMenu = False


        ' Set balloon style.
        AgentChar.Balloon.Style = AgentChar.Balloon.Style Or BalloonOn
        AgentChar.Balloon.Style = AgentChar.Balloon.Style Or SizeToText
        AgentChar.Balloon.Style = AgentChar.Balloon.Style Or AutoHide
        AgentChar.Balloon.Style = AgentChar.Balloon.Style And (Not AutoPace)

    End Sub

    Public Sub Dispose()
        If AgentChar.Visible = True Then
            AgentChar.StopAll()
            AgentChar.Hide()
        End If
    End Sub

    Public Sub Show()
        AgentChar.Show()
    End Sub
```

```
Public Sub Hide()
    AgentChar.Hide()
End Sub


Public Sub StopAll()
    AgentChar.StopAll()
End Sub


Public Sub Speak(ByVal Text As String)
    AgentChar.StopAll()
    AgentChar.Speak(Text, "")
End Sub


Public Sub Think(ByVal Text As String)
    AgentChar.StopAll()
    AgentChar.Think(Text)
End Sub


Public Sub Animate(ByVal Animation As String)
    AgentChar.StopAll()
    AgentChar.Play(Animation)
End Sub


Public Sub MoveTo(ByVal x As Single, ByVal y As Single)
    AgentChar.MoveTo(x, y)
End Sub


Public Sub GestureAt(ByVal x As Single, ByVal y As Single)
    AgentChar.GestureAt(x, y)
End Sub


' Tests if the agent is visible.
' If the agent is not visible it will be shown.
Private Function IsAgentVisible() As Boolean
    If AgentChar.Visible Then
        Return True
    Else
        AgentChar.Show()
        Return False
    End If
End Function
```

```
Public Function GetAnimations() As Array
    Dim List As New ArrayList()
    Dim AnimationName As String
    For Each AnimationName In AgentChar.AnimationNames
        List.Add(AnimationName)
    Next
    Return List.ToArray(GetType(String))
End Function
```

```
End Class
```

Using the AgentController class is easy. All you need to do is create an instance of the Microsoft Agent Control on your form, and then create a new instance of the AgentController class using the interop class. The AgentController wraps all the functionality you will need to use. All you need to do is call the appropriate method.

For example, the AgentTryout project uses the code below to create the Agent and fill a list control with a list of supported animations:

```
Private Controller As AgentController()

Private Sub Form1_Load(sender As Object, _
  e As System.EventArgs) Handles MyBase.Load
    ' Create the agent.
    Controller = New AgentController(AxAgent1, "Genie")

    ' List the supported animations.
    lstAnimations.DataSource = Controller.GetAnimations()

    ' Show the agent.
    Controller.Show()
End Sub
```

The animation is played with a single line of code in response to a button click:

```
Private Sub cmdPlay_Click(sender As System.Object, _
  e As System.EventArgs) Handles cmdPlay.Click
    Controller.Animate(lstAnimations.Text)
End Sub
```

Moving, thinking, and speaking (shown below) are similarly easy:

```
Private Sub cmdSpeak_Click(sender As System.Object, _
  e As System.EventArgs) Handles cmdSpeak.Click
    Controller.Speak(txtSpeak.Text)
End Sub
```

Even if you don't like the idea of animated characters, it's hard to complain about the agent control. Similar functionality from a third-party developer comes at quite a price.

> **NOTE** *To use the Agent control successfully, you need to use Microsoft's ActiveX control version, which is normally used only in web pages. The COM component version, which is described in the documentation for use with Visual Basic 6, will not work correctly in a .NET program. Luckily, both the ActiveX control and the COM component provide the same interface to interact with the agent character.*

## The Last Word

This chapter began with the built-in .NET framework support for Help, and then began to expand on it with integrated help and animated agents. In the process, the chapter delved into the old world of ActiveX components, demonstrating that COM is far from gone, even after the .NET revolution.

Help strategies and systems vary widely depending on the intended audience and the application design. In this chapter we toured the wide and diverse world of Help programming. None of the solutions examined here can be used in every scenario. Instead, it helps to keep some basic principles in mind:

- A help file should describe the purpose of various settings, not how to use common controls. No one needs an explanation about how to click a check box. Instead, users need to know why they should click the check box.

- The best affordances are descriptive labels, not instructions. No dialog box has the space or formatting power of a printed document.

- The best error is one that doesn't happen. It may take more effort in your code to disable or hide invalid options, but it prevents dozens of common mistakes in the input fields.

- Help must be context-sensitive. A confused user won't search through a Help file to find a relevant topic—a printed document is better at that.

- Perform usability tests. When writing a program, you design based on who you believe the audience is. At some point, you need to bring in some new users, and find out what their capabilities really are.

# Index

# Apress Titles

| ISBN | PRICE | AUTHOR | TITLE |
|------|-------|--------|-------|
| 1-893115-73-9 | $34.95 | Abbott | Voice Enabling Web Applications: VoiceXML and Beyond |
| 1-893115-01-1 | $39.95 | Appleman | Dan Appleman's Win32 API Puzzle Book and Tutorial for Visual Basic Programmers |
| 1-893115-23-2 | $29.95 | Appleman | How Computer Programming Works |
| 1-893115-97-6 | $39.95 | Appleman | Moving to VB .NET: Strategies, Concepts, and Code |
| 1-59059-023-6 | $39.95 | Baker | Adobe Acrobat 5: The Professional User's Guide |
| 1-59059-039-2 | $49.95 | Barnaby | Distributed .NET Programming |
| 1-893115-09-7 | $29.95 | Baum | Dave Baum's Definitive Guide to LEGO MINDSTORMS |
| 1-893115-84-4 | $29.95 | Baum, Gasperi, Hempel, and Villa | Extreme MINDSTORMS: An Advanced Guide to LEGO MINDSTORMS |
| 1-893115-82-8 | $59.95 | Ben-Gan/Moreau | Advanced Transact-SQL for SQL Server 2000 |
| 1-893115-91-7 | $39.95 | Birmingham/Perry | Software Development on a Leash |
| 1-893115-48-8 | $29.95 | Bischof | The .NET Languages: A Quick Translation Guide |
| 1-59059-041-4 | $49.95 | Bock | CIL Programming: Under the Hood of .NET |
| 1-893115-67-4 | $49.95 | Borge | Managing Enterprise Systems with the Windows Script Host |
| 1-59059-019-8 | $49.95 | Cagle | SVG Programming: The Graphical Web |
| 1-893115-28-3 | $44.95 | Challa/Laksberg | Essential Guide to Managed Extensions for C++ |
| 1-893115-39-9 | $44.95 | Chand | A Programmer's Guide to ADO.NET in C# |
| 1-893115-44-5 | $29.95 | Cook | Robot Building for Beginners |
| 1-893115-99-2 | $39.95 | Cornell/Morrison | Programming VB .NET: A Guide for Experienced Programmers |
| 1-893115-72-0 | $39.95 | Curtin | Developing Trust: Online Privacy and Security |
| 1-59059-014-7 | $44.95 | Drol | Object-Oriented Macromedia Flash MX |
| 1-59059-008-2 | $29.95 | Duncan | The Career Programmer: Guerilla Tactics for an Imperfect World |
| 1-893115-71-2 | $39.95 | Ferguson | Mobile .NET |
| 1-893115-90-9 | $49.95 | Finsel | The Handbook for Reluctant Database Administrators |
| 1-59059-024-4 | $49.95 | Fraser | Real World ASP.NET: Building a Content Management System |
| 1-893115-42-9 | $44.95 | Foo/Lee | XML Programming Using the Microsoft XML Parser |
| 1-893115-55-0 | $34.95 | Frenz | Visual Basic and Visual Basic .NET for Scientists and Engineers |
| 1-893115-85-2 | $34.95 | Gilmore | A Programmer's Introduction to PHP 4.0 |
| 1-893115-36-4 | $34.95 | Goodwill | Apache Jakarta-Tomcat |
| 1-893115-17-8 | $59.95 | Gross | A Programmer's Introduction to Windows DNA |
| 1-893115-62-3 | $39.95 | Gunnerson | A Programmer's Introduction to C#, Second Edition |
| 1-59059-009-0 | $49.95 | Harris/Macdonald | Moving to ASP.NET: Web Development with VB .NET |
| 1-893115-30-5 | $49.95 | Harkins/Reid | SQL: Access to SQL Server |
| 1-893115-10-0 | $34.95 | Holub | Taming Java Threads |
| 1-893115-04-6 | $34.95 | Hyman/Vaddadi | Mike and Phani's Essential C++ Techniques |
| 1-893115-96-8 | $59.95 | Jorelid | J2EE FrontEnd Technologies: A Programmer's Guide to Servlets, JavaServer Pages, and Enterprise JavaBeans |
| 1-893115-49-6 | $39.95 | Kilburn | Palm Programming in Basic |
| 1-893115-50-X | $34.95 | Knudsen | Wireless Java: Developing with Java 2, Micro Edition |
| 1-893115-79-8 | $49.95 | Kofler | Definitive Guide to Excel VBA |
| 1-893115-57-7 | $39.95 | Kofler | MySQL |
| 1-893115-87-9 | $39.95 | Kurata | Doing Web Development: Client-Side Techniques |

| ISBN | PRICE | AUTHOR | TITLE |
|------|-------|--------|-------|
| 1-893115-75-5 | $44.95 | Kurniawan | Internet Programming with VB |
| 1-893115-38-0 | $24.95 | Lafler | Power AOL: A Survival Guide |
| 1-893115-46-1 | $36.95 | Lathrop | Linux in Small Business: A Practical User's Guide |
| 1-893115-19-4 | $49.95 | Macdonald | Serious ADO: Universal Data Access with Visual Basic |
| 1-59059-044-9 | $49.95 | MacDonald | User Interfaces in VB .NET: Windows Forms and Custom Controls |
| 1-893115-06-2 | $39.95 | Marquis/Smith | A Visual Basic 6.0 Programmer's Toolkit |
| 1-893115-22-4 | $27.95 | McCarter | David McCarter's VB Tips and Techniques |
| 1-59059-021-X | $34.95 | Moore | Karl Moore's Visual Basic .NET: The Tutorials |
| 1-893115-76-3 | $49.95 | Morrison | C++ For VB Programmers |
| 1-59059-003-1 | $39.95 | Nakhimovsky/Meyers | XML Programming: Web Applications and Web Services with JSP and ASP |
| 1-893115-80-1 | $39.95 | Newmarch | A Programmer's Guide to Jini Technology |
| 1-893115-58-5 | $49.95 | Oellermann | Architecting Web Services |
| 1-59059-020-1 | $44.95 | Patzer | JSP Examples and Best Practices |
| 1-893115-81-X | $39.95 | Pike | SQL Server: Common Problems, Tested Solutions |
| 1-59059-017-1 | $34.95 | Rainwater | Herding Cats: A Primer for Programmers Who Lead Programmers |
| 1-59059-025-2 | $49.95 | Rammer | Advanced .NET Remoting |
| 1-893115-20-8 | $34.95 | Rischpater | Wireless Web Development |
| 1-893115-93-3 | $34.95 | Rischpater | Wireless Web Development with PHP and WAP |
| 1-893115-89-5 | $59.95 | Shemitz | Kylix: The Professional Developer's Guide and Reference |
| 1-893115-40-2 | $39.95 | Sill | The qmail Handbook |
| 1-893115-24-0 | $49.95 | Sinclair | From Access to SQL Server |
| 1-893115-94-1 | $29.95 | Spolsky | User Interface Design for Programmers |
| 1-893115-53-4 | $44.95 | Sweeney | Visual Basic for Testers |
| 1-59059-002-3 | $44.95 | Symmonds | Internationalization and Localization Using Microsoft .NET |
| 1-59059-010-4 | $54.95 | Thomsen | Database Programming with C# |
| 1-893115-29-1 | $44.95 | Thomsen | Database Programming with Visual Basic .NET |
| 1-893115-65-8 | $39.95 | Tiffany | Pocket PC Database Development with eMbedded Visual Basic |
| 1-893115-59-3 | $59.95 | Troelsen | C# and the .NET Platform |
| 1-59059-011-2 | $59.95 | Troelsen | COM and .NET Interoperability |
| 1-893115-26-7 | $59.95 | Troelsen | Visual Basic .NET and the .NET Platform |
| 1-893115-54-2 | $49.95 | Trueblood/Lovett | Data Mining and Statistical Analysis Using SQL |
| 1-893115-68-2 | $54.95 | Vaughn | ADO.NET and ADO Examples and Best Practices for VB Programmers, Second Edition |
| 1-59059-012-0 | $49.95 | Vaughn/Blackburn | ADO.NET Examples and Best Practices for C# Programmers |
| 1-893115-83-6 | $44.95 | Wells | Code Centric: T-SQL Programming with Stored Procedures and Triggers |
| 1-893115-95-X | $49.95 | Welschenbach | Cryptography in C and C++ |
| 1-893115-05-4 | $39.95 | Williamson | Writing Cross-Browser Dynamic HTML |
| 1-893115-78-X | $49.95 | Zukowski | Definitive Guide to Swing for Java 2, Second Edition |
| 1-893115-92-5 | $49.95 | Zukowski | Java Collections |
| 1-893115-98-4 | $54.95 | Zukowski | Learn Java with JBuilder 6 |

Available at bookstores nationwide or from Springer Verlag New York, Inc. at 1-800-777-4643; fax 1-212-533-3503. Contact us for more information at sales@apress.com.

# Apress Titles Publishing SOON!

| ISBN | AUTHOR | TITLE |
|------|--------|-------|
| 1-59059-022-8 | Alapati | Expert Oracle 9i Database Administration |
| 1-59059-053-8 | Bock/Stromquist/ Fischer/Smith | .NET Security |
| 1-59059-015-5 | Clark | An Introduction to Object Oriented Programming with Visual Basic .NET |
| 1-59059-000-7 | Cornell | Programming C# |
| 1-59059-056-2 | Cornell | Programming VB .NET, Second Edition |
| 1-59059-043-0 | Ezzio | Using and Understanding Java Data Objects |
| 1-59059-033-3 | Fraser | Managed C++ and .NET Development |
| 1-59059-038-4 | Gibbons | .NET Development for Java Programmers |
| 1-59059-030-9 | Habibi/Camerlengo/ Patterson | The Sun Certified Java Developer Exam with J2SE 1.4 |
| 1-59059-006-6 | Hetland | Instant Python with Ten Instant Projects |
| 1-59059-029-5 | Kampa/Bell | Unix Storage Management |
| 1-59059-049-X | Lakshman | Oracle 9i PL/SQL Application Development |
| 1-59059-045-7 | MacDonald | User Interfaces in C#: Windows Forms and Custom Controls |
| 1-893115-27-5 | Morrill | Tuning and Customizing a Linux System |
| 1-59059-050-3 | Pearce | Debugging VB .NET Development |
| 1-59059-028-7 | Rischpater | Wireless Web Development, Second Edition |
| 1-59059-026-0 | Smith | Writing Add-Ins for Visual Studio.NET |
| 1-893115-43-7 | Stephenson | Standard VB: An Enterprise Developer's Reference for VB 6 and VB .NET |
| 1-59059-035-X | Symmonds | GDI+ Programming in C# and VB .NET |
| 1-59059-032-5 | Thomsen | Database Programming with Visual Basic .NET, Second Edition |
| 1-59059-007-4 | Thomsen/Dunn | Building Web Services with VB .NET |
| 1-59059-042-2 | Thomsen/Hansen | Enterprise Development with Visual Studio .NET, UML and MSF |
| 1-59059-027-9 | Torkelson/Petersen/ Torkelson | Programming the Web with Visual Basic .NET |
| 1-59059-018-X | Tregar | Writing Perl Modules for CPAN |
| 1-59059-055-4 | Troelsen | C# and the .NET Platform, Second Edition |
| 1-59059-047-3 | Zukowski | Definitive Guide to Swing for Java 2, Third Edition |

Available at bookstores nationwide or from Springer Verlag New York, Inc. at 1-800-777-4643; fax 1-212-533-3503. Contact us for more information at sales@apress.com.

**Apress™**

# *books for professionals by professionals™*

## About Apress

Apress, located in Berkeley, CA, is a fast-growing, innovative publishing company devoted to meeting the needs of existing and potential programming professionals. Simply put, the "A" in Apress stands for *"The Author's Press™"* and its books have *"The Expert's Voice™."* Apress' unique approach to publishing grew out of conversations between its founders Gary Cornell and Dan Appleman, authors of numerous best-selling, highly regarded books for programming professionals. In 1998 they set out to create a publishing company that emphasized quality above all else. Gary and Dan's vision has resulted in the publication of over 50 titles by leading software professionals, all of which have *The Expert's Voice™.*

## Do You Have What It Takes to Write for Apress?

Apress is rapidly expanding its publishing program. If you can write and refuse to compromise on the quality of your work, if you believe in doing more than rehashing existing documentation, and if you're looking for opportunities and rewards that go far beyond those offered by traditional publishing houses, we want to hear from you!

Consider these innovations that we offer all of our authors:

- **Top royalties with *no* hidden switch statements**
  Authors typically only receive half of their normal royalty rate on foreign sales. In contrast, Apress' royalty rate remains the same for both foreign and domestic sales.

- **A mechanism for authors to obtain equity in Apress**
  Unlike the software industry, where stock options are essential to motivate and retain software professionals, the publishing industry has adhered to an outdated compensation model based on royalties alone. In the spirit of most software companies, Apress reserves a significant portion of its equity for authors.

- **Serious treatment of the technical review process**
  Each Apress book has a technical reviewing team whose remuneration depends in part on the success of the book since they too receive royalties.

Moreover, through a partnership with Springer-Verlag, New York, Inc., one of the world's major publishing houses, Apress has significant venture capital behind it. Thus, we have the resources to produce the highest quality books *and* market them aggressively.

If you fit the model of the Apress author who can write a book that gives the "professional what he or she needs to know™," then please contact one of our Editorial Directors, Gary Cornell (gary_cornell@apress.com), Dan Appleman (dan_appleman@apress.com), Peter Blackburn (peter_blackburn@apress.com), Jason Gilmore (jason_gilmore@apress.com), Karen Watterson (karen_watterson@apress.com), or John Zukowski (john_zukowski@apress.com) for more information.